Lecture Notes in Computer Science   7948

Commenced Publication in 1973
Founding and Former Series Editors:
Gerhard Goos, Juris Hartmanis, and Jan van Leeuwen

Gerhard W. Dueck   D. Michael Miller (Eds.)

Reversible Computation

5th International Conference, RC 2013
Victoria, BC, Canada, July 4-5, 2013
Proceedings

 Springer

Volume Editors

Gerhard W. Dueck
University of New Brunswick
Faculty of Computer Science
550 Windsor Street
Fredericton, NB E3B 5A3, Canada
E-mail: gdueck@unb.ca

D. Michael Miller
University of Victoria
Department of Computer Science
Victoria, BC V8W 2Y2, Canada
E-mail: mmiller@uvic.ca

ISSN 0302-9743   e-ISSN 1611-3349
ISBN 978-3-642-38985-6   e-ISBN 978-3-642-38986-3
DOI 10.1007/978-3-642-38986-3
Springer Heidelberg Dordrecht London New York

Library of Congress Control Number: 2013940507

CR Subject Classification (1998): B.6.1, F.3.1-2, F.1.1-2, J.2, F.2.2, D.2.11-13, D.4.7

LNCS Sublibrary: SL 2 – Programming and Software Engineering

© Springer-Verlag Berlin Heidelberg 2013

Typesetting: Camera-ready by author, data conversion by Scientific Publishing Services, Chennai, India

Printed on acid-free paper

Springer is part of Springer Science+Business Media (www.springer.com)

Preface

Reversible computing is a model of computing where the computational process is in some measure reversible, either in a logical or physical sense, and in certain areas, both. Reversible computation is of importance to a broad range of areas of computer science, engineering, mathematics, and physics including low-power circuit design, coding/decoding, program debugging, testing, databases, discrete event simulation, reversible algorithms, reversible specification formalisms, reversible programming languages, process algebras, and the modeling of biochemical systems. Furthermore, reversible logic provides a basis for describing and working with quantum computation and its applications as well as other emerging computational technologies.

RC 2013 was the fifth in a series of annual meetings designed to gather researchers for the dissemination and discussion of novel results and concepts in all aspects of reversible computation. The first four events were held in York, UK (2009), Bremen, Germany (2010), Ghent, Belgium (2011), and Copenhagen, Denmark (2012). RC 2013 was thus the first of the meetings to be held outside Europe. This volume comprises the proceedings for RC 2013.

The RC 2013 program included two invited presentations. The first presentation, by Barry C. Sanders, Director, Institute for Quantum Science & Technology, University of Calgary, Canada, addressed the challenges of "Efficiently Designing Quantum Circuits for Efficient Quantum Simulation." The full paper appears in these proceedings.

The invited presentation by Michele Mosca, Deputy Director Academic, Institute for Quantum Computing, University of Waterloo, Canada, addressed "Quantum Computing and the Synthesis and Optimization of Quantum Circuits." Mosca's presentation considered recent tremendous experimental advances in controlling quantum systems and the related impressive progress in the theory of fault-tolerant quantum error correction, which has greatly reduced the experimental 'thresholds' that would enable efficiently scalable quantum computing systems. As larger and larger quantum computers are built, there will be a greater need for automated methods for mapping high-level quantum algorithms into operations to be executed on physical devices. The efficient synthesis and optimization of quantum circuits is a critical step in this process. Mosca highlighted some recent advances using a range of mathematical tools.

The call for papers attracted 37 submissions by 90 authors from 14 countries. All contributed papers were reviewed by at least three members of the RC 2013 Program Committee or their designated subreviewers. Based on those reviews and extensive discussion by the Program Committee, 19 papers were selected for presentation at RC 2013 to make up sessions on physical implementation, arithmetic, programming and data structures, modeling, synthesis and optimization, as well as alternative technologies.

The list of Program Committee members is provided elsewhere in this volume. We take this opportunity to thank these 15 experts from across the international reversible computation community for their hard work and dedication to the quality of RC 2013. We also thank the 20 additional reviewers for their important contributions. It has been our great pleasure to serve as Program Co-chairs for RC 2013 and as editors for these proceedings.

Financial support for RC 2013 was provided by the Pacific Institute for the Mathematical Sciences and by the Department of Computer Science, Faculty of Engineering, and the Office of the Vice-President Research at the University of Victoria. We also acknowledge organizational support provided by Lisa Jungmann and Robert Wille, University of Bremen, and by Derek Church, Michelle Fuller, and Marleen Willems, University of Victoria.

To conclude, we offer our sincere appreciation to Anna Kramer and Elke Werner, Springer, Heidelberg, Germany, for their assistance and guidance in the preparation of these proceedings.

July 2013   Gerhard W. Dueck
                                                              D. Michael Miller

Organization

Program Committee Chairs

Gerhard W. Dueck University of New Brunswick, Canada
D. Michael Miller University of Victoria, Canada

Program Committee

Holger Bock Axelsen	University of Copenhagen, Denmark
Stéphane Burignat	University of Ghent, Belgium
Alexis De Vos	University of Ghent, Belgium
Simon Gay	University of Glasgow, UK
Markus Grassl	National University of Singapore
Jarkko Kari	University of Turku, Finland
Martin Kutrib	University of Giessen, Germany
Kazutaka Matsuda	University of Tokyo, Japan
Shin-Ichi Minato	Hokkaido University, Japan
Jacqueline Rice	University of Lethbridge, Canada
Irek Ulidowski	University of Leicester, UK
Janis Voigtländer	University of Bonn, Germany
Robert Wille	University of Bremen, Germany
Tetsuo Yokoyama	Nanzan University, Japan
Paolo Zuliani	Newcastle University, UK

Organizing Committee

Gerhard W. Dueck	University of New Brunswick, Canada
Lisa Jungmann	University of Bremen, Germany
D. Michael Miller	University of Victoria, Canada
Robert Wille	University of Bremen, Germany

Additional Reviewers

Nabila Abdessaied	Andreas Malcher
Mika Hirvensalo	Katja Meckel
Katsunobu Imai	Torben Æ. Mogensen
Sebastian Jakobi	Kenichi Morita
Oliver Keszöcze	Daniel Morrison

Noor Nayeem
Beatrice Palano
Tom Ridge
Zahra Sasanian
Eleonora Schönborn

Julia Seiter
Mathias Soeken
Krysta M. Svore
Himanshu Thapliyal
Michael Kirkedal Thomsen

Sponsors

RC 2013 was sponsored by the Pacific Institute for the Mathematical Sciences and by the Department of Computer Science, Faculty of Engineering, and the Office of the Vice-President Research at the University of Victoria.

Table of Contents

Invited Address

Physical Implementation

Arithmetic

Programming and Data Structures

Efficient Algorithms
for Universal Quantum Simulation

Barry C. Sanders*

Institute for Quantum Science and Technology, University of Calgary,
Calgary, Alberta T3A 0E1, Canada
http://www.iqst.ca/people/peoplepage.php?id=4

Abstract. A universal quantum simulator would enable efficient simulation of quantum dynamics by implementing quantum-simulation algorithms on a quantum computer. Specifically the quantum simulator would efficiently generate qubit-string states that closely approximate physical states obtained from a broad class of dynamical evolutions. I provide an overview of theoretical research into universal quantum simulators and the strategies for minimizing computational space and time costs. Applications to simulating many-body quantum simulation and solving linear equations are discussed

Keywords: Quantum Computing, Quantum Algorithms, Quantum Simulation.

1 Introduction

A quantum computer could allow some problems to be solved more efficiently, by enabling efficient execution of quantum algorithms, as compared to executing classical algorithms on a classical computer that are inferior for those problems [1]. The "classical computer" refers to a computer that is built strictly according to the principles of classical physics but more specifically is equivalent to a Turing machine [2]. The subtle issues of a quantized computer operating over real rather than binary fields are not discussed here [3]. The study of "quantum simulation" focuses on simulating properties and dynamics of quantum systems whether by classical or quantum computation, and the topic of "efficient algorithms for quantum simulation" focuses on quantum simulation problems that do not have efficient classical algorithms.

Let me clear about terminology employed here. By the term simulation, I mean that certain pre-specified properties of the quantum system are accurately predicted by the simulation but not necessarily all properties. Accuracy refers to each answer being no worse than some error tolerance ϵ. For example one might wish to know the mean momentum, the standard deviation of the momentum,

* This project has been supported by NSERC, CIFAR, AITF, USARO, MITACS and PIMS, and I acknowledge numerous valuable discussions with Nathan Wiebe about these concepts.

G.W. Dueck and D.M. Miller (Eds.): RC 2013, LNCS 7948, pp. 1–10, 2013.
© Springer-Verlag Berlin Heidelberg 2013

and average energy. The simulation is successful if these quantities are accurately predicted by the simulator even if other irrelevant quantities are poorly predicted. The term efficiency refers to the simulation yielding an accurate solution to the problem with a resource (e.g., run-time and space usage) cost that increases no faster than a polynomial function of the input bit string and of $1/\epsilon$.

Explicitly defining simulation is important because various notions of quantum simulation using quantum computers, either purpose-built or universal, with various terminology. The term "digital quantum simulator" is sometimes employed to refer to a programmable quantum simulator, and the term "analogue quantum simulator" refers to a quantum system designed to behave analogously to a the quantum system being studied [4], and usually these terms are employed when error correction is not assumed hence making these systems not scalable. Analogue quantum simulation is sometimes called "quantum emulation" [5]. Our term "universal quantum simulator" is in concordance with "digital quantum simulator" provided that the latter uses a fault tolerant architecture as we assume simulation on a scalable quantum computer.

Quantum simulation can deal with non-relativistic single-particle quantum mechanics described by Schrödinger's equation

$$i\frac{d}{dt}|\psi(t)\rangle = \hat{H}(t)|\psi(t)\rangle \tag{1}$$

with self-adjointness $\hat{H} = \hat{H}^\dagger$ implying unitary dynamics, but self-adjointness is not necessary. Alternatively simulation of relativistic quantum mechanics or many-body quantum dynamics [6] or quantum field theories [7] may be sought. For simplicity we focus on the easiest case of single-body dynamics (1) and thence to the many-body case.

After choosing the equation to be studied, the question then arises as to which problem is to be solved. Two possible problems include solving the state $|\psi(t)\rangle$ over some time domain or determining the spectrum of the Hamiltonian $\hat{H}$. Instead of finding the spectrum or some aspect of the spectrum such as the smallest or largest spectral gap, the problem could be about finding eigenvectors of $\hat{H}$ such as the ground state. For simulation purposes a natural question would be to estimate the expectation values of some observable

$$\langle\psi(t)|\hat{\mathcal{O}}|\psi(t)\rangle. \tag{2}$$

Some of the problems discussed here could be tractable on a classical computer hence making quantum algorithms uninteresting; other problems such as finding ground states could be intractable as well on a quantum computer [8].

2   Algorithms and Complexity for Quantum Simulation

For algorithmic quantum simulation we are interested in those problems that are intractable on a classical computer yet tractable on a quantum computer. We can rule out solving problems that are amenable to the usual classical methods such as the following [9]. One approach is to diagonalize the Hamiltonian directly, which is always possible in principle but, as the problem size is polylogarithmic in dimension and diagonalization is polynomially expensive with respect to dimension, the cost of diagonalization is thus superpolynomially expensive hence is not efficient in general.

Another approach to quantum simulation is to integrate the dynamical equation, for example Schrödinger's equation (1), directly. For example the Runge-Kutta technique is popular. Alternatively the dynamics can be tackled by constructing the evolution operator and using the Magnus, or Baker-Campbell-Hausdorff method, expansion. Product formulæ are valuable as a unitary evolution can be factorized into an approximate product of unitary evolutions. Product formulæ include the Forest-Ruth or symplectic integration, method, and the Trotter-Suzuki expansion is also valuable, especially for quantum simulation as we shall see.

Quantum Monte Carlo simulations include stochastic Green functions techniques and variational, diffusion or path-integral Monte-Carlo methods. Density matrix renormalization group techniques have become popular especially for one-dimensional many-body systems with slowly increasing entanglement with respect to the number of particles.

Perhaps the best insight into quantum simulation can be gained by studying Feynman's own words in his seminal 1982 paper on quantum computing based on a his keynote talk on the topic "Simulating Physics With Computers" [10]. Feynman asks,

> Can a quantum system be probabilistically simulated by a classical (probabilistic, I'd assume) universal computer? In other words, a computer which will give the same probabilities as the quantum system does. If you take the computer to be the classical kind I've described so far, (not the quantum kind described in the last section) and there're no changes in any laws, and there's no hocus-pocus, the answer is certainly, No! This is called the hidden-variable problem: it is impossible to represent the results of quantum mechanics with a classical universal device.

The concept of quantum simulation can be understood from the schematic in Fig. 1. The essence of this figure, which is fully explained in the caption, is that the quantum simulation necessarily approximates all information and quantum information into bit strings and qubit strings and delivers an approximation to the final state as a finite qubit string.

Let us now perform exegesis on Feynman's words to seek an understanding of what he meant. In order to understand his meaning, we delve into computer science notions of complexity, not something that Feynman himself used. Thus, we seek to interpret a statement more than three decades old through the lens of modern computational complexity theory.

To understand, we cast quantum simulation as a decision problem: the computational problem is constructed so that the answer can only be Yes or No. To assess whether the quantum simulation is efficient, the question is then how hard, i.e., how do the computational resources scale with problem size expressed

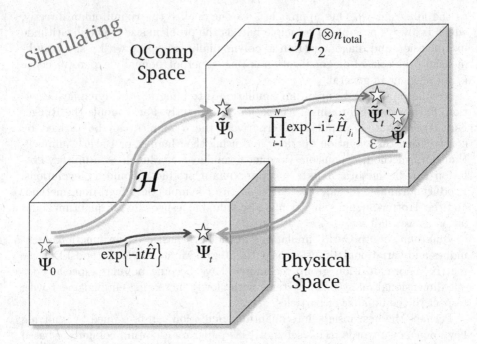

Fig. 1. Quantum simulation is depicted by showing evolution of a state Ψ_0 in a Hilbert space $\mathcal{H}$ for the Physical Space and the evolution of the state's approximation $\tilde{\Psi}_0$ in the n-qubit space $\mathcal{H}_2^n$ in the quantum computer, or QComp Space. In the physical world, the evolution is given by $\exp\{-it\hat{H}\}$ for $\hat{H}$ the system Hamilttonian and t the time of evolution. The resultant state is Ψ_t. In the quantum computer, all information is restricted to finite bit strings and all quantum information to finite qubit strings so even continuous time t is broken up into discrete intervals of duration t/r and the Hamiltonian matrix is approximated by $\tilde{\hat{H}}$. The resultant simulated state is $\tilde{\Psi}_t'$, which is different from the approximation of the true state $\tilde{\Psi}_t$ by less than a distance ϵ.

as the number of bits n required to specify the input state, in order to answer the question? Note that the resources to prove Yes or No can differ, which leads to complexity classes and their complements. We are especially interested in the time and space costs, which we denote as T and S, respectively.

Quantum simulation problems are no worse then EXP, which is the class of problems that can be solved with T and S increasing no more than an exponential function of n. That EXP is the worst case follows from using the Heisenberg matrix representation for the dynamics and seeing that the size of the register and the computational time for matrix operations leads to decision problems being in EXP.

Aaronson points out that Feynman (inadvertently) reduced the complexity of quantum mechanics to PSPACE; i.e., S increases no more than polynomially in n by introducing path integrals [11]. The class of decision problems solvable efficiently on a quantum computer is BQP, which refers to bounded-error quantum polynomial and is inside PSPACE. The aim of quantum simulation thus needs to focus on narrower problems than those in PSPACE. Feynman's words "give the same probabilities" hints at the correct approach. One should ask questions pertaining to expectation values of certain observables and accept answers that are probabilistically equivalent to the true probabilities for these observables in the physical world.

Feynman's comment, "classical kind ... the answer is certainly, No!" is more problematic. He suggests that the classical simulation is provably inferior to the quantum simulation because of "the hidden-variable problem: it is impossible to represent the results of quantum mechanics with a classical universal device". This question of provable superiority remains unresolved today, and the hidden-variable problem does not lead to its resolution. Feynman's idea that there is a strict separation between two computational complexity classes can be regarded as a hard one to settle by thinking about this problem along the lines of any reduction in the polynomial complexity hierarchy. Such problems are famously difficult.

Lloyd recognized in 1996 that the key to formalizing Feynman's claim lay in how to discrete the time evolution into discrete gate steps with a bound on the accumulated error due to time discretization [12]. Specifically Lloyd used the Trotter product formula

$$\mathrm{e}^{\mathrm{i}t(\hat{A}+\hat{B})} \rightarrow \lim_{n \to \infty} \left(\mathrm{e}^{\mathrm{i}t\hat{A}/n} \mathrm{e}^{\mathrm{i}t\hat{B}/n} \right)^n. \tag{3}$$

to approximate the evolution operator, with the Hamiltonian expressed as the sum $\sum_{j=1}^{m} \hat{H}_j$ as

$$\exp\left\{ -\mathrm{i}t \sum_{j=1}^{m} \hat{H}_j \right\} = \left(\prod_{i=1}^{N} \exp\left\{ -\mathrm{i}\frac{t}{r}\hat{H}_{j_i} \right\} \right)^r + \sum_{j>j'} \left[\hat{H}_j, \hat{H}_{j'} \right] \frac{t^2}{2r} + \mathrm{error}. \tag{4}$$

Lloyd proved that this simulation had a T and S costs that are only poly(n). This result can generalized to a time-dependent Hamiltonian and the errors tightened [9].

In 2003, Aharonov and Ta-Shma analyzed the general question of what Hamiltonian systems are efficiently simulatable [13]. Their work was motivated by strong claims about adiabatic quantum computing solving NP-Hard problems. They tackled the problem by considering which quantum states can be efficiently generated and cast the problem into the oracle setting: $\hat{H}$ is in a black-box, which is queried with an assigned cost per query. A key result of their work is their demonstration of equivalence between quantum state generation and statistical zero knowledge problems. Another important result is the Sparse Hamiltonian Lemma: If $\hat{H}$ acting on n qubits is d-sparse s.t. $d \in O(\text{poly}n)$ and the list of nonzero entries in each row is efficiently computable, then $\hat{H}$ is *simulatable* if $\|\hat{H}\| \leq \text{poly}n$.

We can use Childs's rules for simulatability [14] to augment the Sparse Hamiltonian Lemma. The system is simulatable if the Hamiltonian is a sum $\sum_i \hat{H}_j$

with each $\hat{H}_j$ acting on $O(1)$ qubits or is $\sqrt{-1}\times$ a commutator of two simulatable Hamiltonians or is efficiently convertible to a simulatable Hamiltonian by efficient unitary conjugation or is sparse and efficiently computable. The basic element for simulating Hamiltonian evolution is depicted in Fig. 2 for the case of a diagonal Hamiltonian. The circuit is easily generalized to one-sparse Hamiltonian generated evolution whether diagonal or not [15].

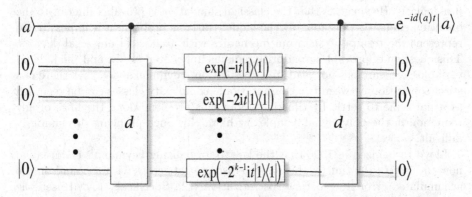

Fig. 2. Simulating evolution for diagonal $\hat{H}$ with $d(a) = \langle a|\hat{H}|a\rangle \in \{0,1\}^k$. The row numbers a of the Hamiltonian are written onto a string of qubits, and the string of qubits in the $|0\rangle$ state are ancillary. The depicted circuit circuit then effects the transformation $|a,0\rangle \mapsto |a,d(a)\rangle \mapsto e^{-itd(a)}|a,d(a)\rangle \mapsto e^{-itd(a)}|a,0\rangle = e^{-i\hat{H}t}|a,0\rangle$.

The quantum simulation circuit is designed to approximate the desired unitary evolution operator U by a sequence $\prod_{\nu=1}^{N} U_{j_\nu}$ where each U_{j_ν} is generated by one of m one-sparse Hamiltonians. Generalizing the Trotter formula using the Suzuki iteration method leads to a much more efficient way of performing this unitary factorization, i.e., to a product of unitary gates with the length of this sequence of unitary gates being $t^{1+o(1)}$ [16,17].

The Hamiltonian in the oracle is promised to be d-sparse with $d \in \text{poly}(n)$. This creates the algorithmic challenge of reducing the d-sparse Hamiltonian into a disjoint sum of one-sparse Hamiltonians. The decomposition is aided by first converting sparse Hamiltonians into graphs of low degree and then colouring the graph so that it is a disjoint union of degree-one graphs; hence the corresponding Hamiltonian is a direct sum of one-sparse Hamiltonians each corresponding to one colour of the graph [16,17].

The Hamiltonian is converted to a graph as follows. Let x label a row of the Hamiltonian matrix and y the column. As the Hamiltonian is d-sparse, there are at most d column numbers that hold nonzero elements for row x. We call these column entries $y_{1,...,d}$ in no particular order; i.e., the increasing sequence of indices $1,...,d$ does not imply increasing values of y_i. Now construct the graph by assigning each x a vertex so that there are now 2^n vertices but no edges yet.

For given x, we construct an edge to another vertex value x' if $x' = y_i$ such that y_i is one of the column indices where row x and column y_i has a nonzero

Hamiltonian matrix element. The weight of the edge is the value of that matrix element $\langle x|\hat{H}|y_i\rangle$. If we simplify $\hat{H}$ to having only real matrix entries and note that $\hat{H} = \hat{H}^\dagger$, then we can assign the Hamiltonian an undirected graph because $\langle x|\hat{H}|y_i\rangle = \langle y_i|\hat{H}|x\rangle$. The Hamiltonian is thus faithfully represented by a degree-d undirected graph. A superior colouring algorithm that yields a direct sum of one-sparse Hamiltonians can reduce T and S costs for the associated quantum query algorithm to determine the sequence of operations for evolution generated by a d-sparse Hamiltonian.

Table 1 provides a summary of some advances over the years in reducing T and S costs. In some cases one cost is reduced at the expense of the other. Although the efficiency of quantum simulation has been known for quite some time, quantum simulations could be the first practical application of quantum computing. Cost reductions reduce the waiting time for non-trivial quantum simulations to become a reality and hence are important.

Table 1. Key developments in reducing time T and space S costs for a quantum computer to simulate time-independent Hamiltonian generated evolution as a function of the number of qubits n representing the system, the sparseness d of the Hamiltonian, the allowed error ϵ, and the norm of the Hamiltonian $\|\hat{H}\|$. The authors are listed in the first column along with references and the year in the second column. The final row and column is given by • to show that the space cost is not explicitly known. The iterated logarithm $\log^*$ in the table is the number of successive iterations of the base-two logarithm function required to reduce the number to one or less.

Who	Year	T	S
Lloyd[12]	1996	$O(t^2)$	$O(n)$
AT[13]	2003	$O\left(n^9 d^4 \frac{t^2}{\epsilon}\right)$	$O(n)$
Childs[14]	2003	$O\left(n^2 d^{4+o(1)} \frac{t^{3/2}}{\sqrt{\epsilon}}\right)$	$O(n)$
BACS[16]	2007	$O\left(\log^* n d^{4+o(1)} \frac{t^{1+1/2k}}{\epsilon^{1/2k}}\right)$	$O(n\log^* n)$
CK[18]	2010	$O\left(\left[d^3 + d^2 \log^* n\right] \frac{t^{1+1/2k}}{\epsilon^{1/2k}}\right)$	$O(nd + n\log^* n)$
CB[19]	2010	$O\left(\|\hat{H}\|_{\max} d \frac{t}{\sqrt{\epsilon}}\right)$	•

3 Applications

Although quantum computing was founded on the principle of quantum simulation, other algorithms such as factorization have dominated the field for many years. The reason quantum simulation is back in full force can be understood from the prescient quote from a 1997 paper by Abrams and Lloyd[6]:

> But the problem of simulation — that is, the problem of modeling the full time evolution of an arbitrary quantum system — is less technologically demanding. While thousands of qubits and billions of quantum logic operations are needed to solve classical difficult factoring problems [16],

it would be possible to use a quantum computer with only a few tens of qubits and a few thousand operations to perform simulations that would be classical intractable [17].

Abrams and Lloyd specifically showed that the quantum simulator would efficiently simulate fermionic systems. Combined with other results on bosonic and anionic systems, the quantum simulator is thus known to be an efficient simulator of all types of many-body systems.

Various many-body systems are considered for experimental quantum simulation in order to learn properties about the system that are unreachable with classical simulations due to intractability. Let us assign X, Y and Z as the Pauli operators on a single qubit. The Hamiltonians for these many-body systems include the Ising Hamiltonian $J \sum_{\langle i,j \rangle} Z_i \otimes Z_j + B \sum_i X_i$, the XY Hamiltonian $J_x \sum_{\langle i,j \rangle} X_i \otimes X_j + J_y \sum_{\langle i,j \rangle} Y_i \otimes Y_j$, the Heisenberg Hamiltonian $J_x \sum_{\langle i,j \rangle} X_i \otimes X_j + J_y \sum_{\langle i,j \rangle} Y_i \otimes Y_j$ and the honeycomb Hamiltonian $J_x \sum_{x-\text{link}} X_i \otimes X_j - J_y \sum_{y-\text{link}} Y_i \otimes Y_j - J_z \sum_{x-\text{link}} Z_i \otimes Z_j$. Whereas earlier the algorithm for simulation is designed for the broadest class of simulatable Hamiltonians, if the Hamitlonian is known explicitly and is a sum of strictly local Hamiltonians, then there is a straightforward circuit-construction algorithm for unitary gates generated by a tensor product of Pauli operators [20].

Whereas quantum simulators are evidently useful for simulating quantum dynamics by design, they can be used more broadly, for example to solve giant sets of coupled linear equations [21]. This approach takes quantum simulators beyond applicability just to quantum systems, but we have to be careful about what we mean by "solve" as we had to be careful about what we meant by "solve" Schrödinger's equation earlier.

The problem to be solved by the quantum linear equation solver can be understood by the following statement.

> Given matrix A, vector $\boldsymbol{b}$, and matrix M, find a good approximation of $\boldsymbol{x}^{\mathrm{T}} M \boldsymbol{x}$ such that $A\boldsymbol{x} = \boldsymbol{b}$.

The strategy for using a quantum simulator to solve this problem is as follows. Begin by replacing $\boldsymbol{b}$ by the quantum state $|b\rangle = \sum_{i=1}^{N} b_i |i\rangle$ with $|i\rangle$ the computational basis.

The solution would be $|x\rangle = \hat{A}^{-1}|b\rangle$, but inverting $\hat{A}$ is hard so a method has to be found to circumvent this difficulty. The operator $\hat{A}$ has eigenvalues λ_j and eigenvectors $|u_j\rangle$ for $j = 1, \ldots, N$, and we express $|b\rangle = \sum_{j=1}^{N} \beta_j |u_j\rangle$ in the $\hat{A}$-eigenbasis. The concept is to recognize that

$$|x\rangle = \hat{A}^{-1}|b\rangle = \sum_{j=1}^{N} \frac{\beta_j}{\lambda_j} |u_j\rangle. \qquad (5)$$

This approach is achieved by using the phase-estimation approach, namely by taking $b\rangle$ with ancilla to obtain $\sum_{j=1}^{N} \beta_j |u_j\rangle |\lambda_j\rangle$. Then the non-unitary linear map $|\lambda_j\rangle \mapsto \lambda_j^{-1} |\lambda_j\rangle$ is constructed in a quantum circuit. Finally the circuit uncomputes $|\lambda_j\rangle$ to obtain the approximation $|x\rangle$.

4　Conclusions

This article provides an overview of algorithmic quantum simulation, approaches to implementing and improving these algorithms, and applications of quantum algorithms for quantum simulation. Theoretical research in this area is challenging because it draws in so many different techniques from such different areas, for example graph theory, operator algebra, and computational complexity. The field is exciting from a technological perspective because non-trivial problems could be solved with smaller quantum computers than for other planned applications of quantum computing such as to factorization.

References

1. DiVincenzo, D.P.: Quantum Computation. Science 270, 255–261 (1995)
2. Bernstein, E., Vazirani, U.: Quantum Complexity Theory. SIAM J. Comp. 26, 1411–1473 (1997)
3. Adcock, M.R.A., Høyer, P., Sanders, B.C.: Limitations on continuous variable quantum algorithms with Fourier transforms. New J. Phys. 11, 103035 (2009)
4. Buluta, I., Nori, F.: Quantum Simulators. Science 326, 108–111 (2009)
5. Neeley, M., Ansmann, M., Bialczak, R.C., Hofheinz, M., Lucero, E., O'Connell, A.D., Sank, D., Wang, H., Wenner, J., Cleland, A.N., Geller, M.R., Martinis, J.M.: Emulation of a Quantum Spin with a Superconducting Phase Qudit. Science 325, 722–725 (2009)
6. Abrams, D.S., Lloyd, S.: Simulation of Many-Body Fermi Systems on a Universal Quantum Computer. Phys. Rev. Lett. 79, 2586–2589 (1997)
7. Jordan, S.P., Lee, K.S.M., Preskill, J.: Quantum Algorithms for Quantum Field Theories. Science 336, 1130–1133 (2012)
8. Kempe, J., Kitaev, A., Regev, O.: The Complexity of the Local Hamiltonian Problem. SIAM J. Comput. 35, 1070–1097 (2006)
9. Wiebe, N., Berry, D.W., Høyer, P., Sanders, B.C.: Higher order decompositions of ordered operator exponentials. J. Phys. A: Math. Theor. 43, 065203 (2010)
10. Feynman, R.P.: Simulating physics with computers. Int. J. Theor. Phys. 21, 467–488 (1982)
11. Aaronson, S.: Quantum Computing since Democritus. Cambridge University Press, Cambridge (2013)
12. Lloyd, S.: Universal Quantum Simulators. Science 273, 1073–1078 (1996)
13. Aharonov, D., Ta-Shma, A.: Adiabatic Quantum State Generation and Statistical Zero Knowledge. In: Proc. 35th Annual ACM Symp. on Theory of Computing, pp. 20–29. ACM, New York (2003)
14. Childs, A.M.: Quantum information processing in continuous time. Ph.D. thesis, Massachusetts Institute of Technology (2004)
15. Childs, A.M., Cleve, R., Deotto, E., Farhi, E., Guttman, S., Spielman, D.A.: Exponential algorithmic speedup by quantum walk. In: Proc. 35th Annual ACM Symp. on Theory of Computing, pp. 59–68. ACM, New York (2003)
16. Berry, D.W., Ahokas, G., Cleve, R., Sanders, B.C.: Efficient quantum algorithms for simulating sparse Hamiltonians. Comm. Math. Phys. 270, 359–371 (2007)
17. Berry, D.W., Ahokas, G., Cleve, R., Sanders, B.C.: Quantum algorithms for Hamiltonian simulation. In: Chen, G., Kauffman, L., Lomonaco, S.J. (eds.) Mathematics of Quantum Computation and Quantum Technology, Ch. 4, pp. 89–110. Taylor & Francis, Oxford (2007)

18. Childs, A.M., Kothari, R.: Simulating sparse Hamiltonians with star decompositions. In: van Dam, W., Kendon, V.M., Severini, S. (eds.) TQC 2010. LNCS, vol. 6519, pp. 94–103. Springer, Heidelberg (2011)
19. Childs, A.M., Berry, D.W.: Black-box Hamiltonian simulation and unitary implementation 12, 29–62 (2012)
20. Raeisi, S., Wiebe, N., Sanders, B.C.: Quantum-Circuit Design for Efficient Simulations of Many-Body Quantum Dynamics. New J. Phys. 14, 103017 (2012)
21. Harrow, A.W., Hassidim, A., Lloyd, S.: Quantum Algorithm for Linear Systems of Equations. Phys. Rev. Lett. 103, 150502 (2009)

Reversible Delay-Insensitive Distributed Memory Modules

Daniel Morrison and Irek Ulidowski

Department of Computer Science, University of Leicester, England
{dm181,iu3}@mcs.le.ac.uk

Abstract. We introduce two eight-line one-bit memory modules which are useful in the modelling of distributed memory in asynchronous delay-insensitive circuits. Our modules are reversible and together with the Merge element are serial-universal. We show how they can be used to realise Morita's Rotary Element and other reversible modules thus showing their computation universality. We also propose three sets of modules that are universal for all modules.

1 Introduction

Delay-insensitive (DI) circuits are a category of asynchronous circuits which make no assumption about delays within elements or wires. As a type of asynchronous circuit, they have no global clock. It is shown in [11] that typical logical gates such as NAND and XOR are not Turing-complete when operated in a DI environment. Hence, DI circuits use different types of modules. These operate based upon the presence or absence of signals rather than the values of signals like typical gates. However, DI circuits of these modules are inefficient when implemented in CMOS due to a significant overhead. As the need for a replacement technology for CMOS arises DI circuits are seen as a possible future direction for the industry. Their implementation in several alternative technologies such as cellular automata ([7]) and RSFQ circuits ([18]) is considered a potential option.

Asynchronous circuits in general have numerous advantages ([3]), one of which is efficient energy usage. Without a global clock, only modules which are performing useful computation use power. Reversible circuit elements are also energy efficient ([1]) for different reasons as operations result in no loss of information, which correlates directly to energy usage. Combining these two properties is desirable.

Keller ([5]) initially characterised the conditions required for correct DI operation, and also gave various universal sets of primitives. Much subsequent work by Patra and Fussell ([17,16]) went into finding more efficient sets of universal primitives. In these cases, efficiency is measured as low *modularity* (the maximum number of input-output lines for modules in a set) and low *cardinality* (number of modules in a set).

Reversible elements were originally studied by Fredkin and Toffoli ([1]) and resulted in synchronous universal logic elements. More recently, research by Morita,

G.W. Dueck and D.M. Miller (Eds.): RC 2013, LNCS 7948, pp. 11–24, 2013.
© Springer-Verlag Berlin Heidelberg 2013

Lee, Peper and Adachi has been carried out into finding efficient (where efficiency is measured as the number of states of a module, and the cardinality and modularity of a set) universal sets of reversible DI modules with memory, such as Rotary Element (RE) ([13]), and Reading Toggle (RT) and Inverse Reading Toggle (IRT) ([10]). Morita et al. have enumerated the full set of possible 2-state elements with two, three and four pairs of input/output lines in [15]. How these various concepts relate to each other as well as to cellular automata has been discussed by Morita in [14].

We consider additionally another notion of efficiency. Namely, the number of *transitions* required (the processing of an input followed by the production of an output is considered a transition) in a circuit to produce its final output. Its importance relates to the fact that more transitions correspond to both higher power usage and longer processing time.

In this paper we introduce a new pair of DI modules based upon the idea of distributed memory. We then prove computation-universality of these modules, and show cases where their use substantially reduces the number of transitions compared with similar circuits using other reversible elements with memory such as RE and RT/IRT. This is demonstrated in both synchronous and asynchronous design styles. We conclude by proposing three new universal sets, each containing one of our memory modules.

2   Asynchronous Delay-Insensitive Networks

We formalise the concept of a delay-insensitive network by introducing the notion of both a *Sequential Machine* and a *Serial Module*, with formal definitions being adapted from [10]. A Sequential Machine is a 4-tuple $N = \{Q, \Sigma, \triangle, \delta\}$. Q is a non-empty finite set of states. Σ and $\triangle$ are non-empty finite sets of input and output symbols. δ is a partial transition function defined as $\delta : Q \times \Sigma \to Q \times \triangle$. Informally, it represents an input in a given state causing a transition to a new state whilst causing an output.

A Serial Module is an abstraction of a Sequential Machine and is a 3-tuple $M = (I, O, N)$ where N is defined as a Sequential Machine, and I and O are input and output lines in one-to-one correspondence with Σ and $\triangle$ in N respectively. Furthermore, we also define a *Reversible Sequential Machine* (as in [10]) identically to a Sequential Machine, with the exception that δ is bijective. A *Reversible Serial Module* ([10]) is defined analogously with N being an instance of a Reversible Sequential Machine rather than a Sequential Machine.

A *network* or *circuit* of modules is a collection of instances of modules, such that the output of a module is connected to at most one input of another module. Similarly an input of a module is connected to at most one output of another module. If an input or output is not connected, it is assumed that a signal will never occur on this line during execution of the network. Connections between modules are informally referred to as *wires*. A wire may also be a connection between a module and an arbitrary *environment* (an undefined network of modules), with the required behaviour of the surrounding environment being stated where appropriate. A connection to an environment is visually represented by the appropriate end of the wire left unconnected.

Operational restrictions on networks of these modules were formulated by Keller ([5]). To summarise, an input to the Sequential Machine of a module is represented by a "signal" on the corresponding line to the Sequential Module. When the input is processed by the corresponding machine, the signal is "absorbed" by the module and the line is then considered "empty". After processing the input, the Sequential Machine places a signal on the corresponding output line of the module, moves to the appropriate state, and then repeats the previous behaviour. No line may contain more than one signal at any given time. If a circuit operates correctly regardless of arbitrary delays in both wires and modules, it is known as *delay-insensitive*. As in [5], arbitration within modules between inputs is not embodied by default. In the case of Serial Modules, this requires that at most one input is active at any given time.

The behaviour of a module simulated by a network of other modules is referred to as a *realisation* or *decomposition* of a module. A set of modules is referred to as being *serial-universal* if any arbitrary Serial Module can be realised using only modules from the set. We also define the *modularity of a module* to be the total number of input/output lines. Similarly, we define the *modularity of a set* to be the largest modularity of all modules within the set.

We illustrate this concept by giving the definition of RE taken from [13] in a similar manner to the definitions of RT and IRT in [10]. A definition of RE in a similar style is also given in [15]. An RE is a 2-state, 4-input, 4-output Reversible Serial Module shown in Fig. 1. It is defined as $(\{n, s, w, e\}, \{n', s', w', e'\}, N_{\mathrm{RE}})$ where N_{RE} is a Reversible Sequential Machine $(\{V, H\}, \Sigma_{\mathrm{RE}}, \triangle_{\mathrm{RE}}, \delta_{\mathrm{RE}})$. Let $\mu : \{n, s, w, e\} \to \Sigma_{\mathrm{RE}}$ and $\nu : \{n', s', w', e'\} \to \triangle_{\mathrm{RE}}$ be the mappings between the module and sequential machine. The definition of δ_{RE} is given in Fig. 1. The inputs n, s, w and e represent, informally, the "north", "south", "west" and "east" directions of input respectively. The outputs are analogous. V and H represent "vertical" and "horizontal" respectively, and refer to the depiction of the state as a rotating bar. Instead of the full definition of each module that we consider, we shall use CCS-like notation ([12]) to specify its behaviour, similarly as trace notation and automata are used in [17] and [9] respectively. Each state of a module has a name, for RE these are V and H, and we give equations for each state that specify which outputs occur in response to which

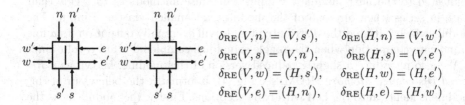

$$\delta_{\mathrm{RE}}(V, n) = (V, s'), \qquad \delta_{\mathrm{RE}}(H, n) = (V, w')$$
$$\delta_{\mathrm{RE}}(V, s) = (V, n'), \qquad \delta_{\mathrm{RE}}(H, s) = (V, e')$$
$$\delta_{\mathrm{RE}}(V, w) = (H, s'), \qquad \delta_{\mathrm{RE}}(H, w) = (H, e')$$
$$\delta_{\mathrm{RE}}(V, e) = (H, n'), \qquad \delta_{\mathrm{RE}}(H, e) = (H, w')$$

Fig. 1. RE and corresponding definition of δ_{RE}

inputs, and how this changes the state of the module. For example, RE in the V state is defined as $V = (n, \overline{s'}).V + (s, \overline{n'}).V + (w, \overline{s'}).H + (e, \overline{n'}).H$ where $(n, \overline{s'}).V$ means that the input n causes the output s' and a change to state V, and $+$ is the choice operator, which is used here to represent that RE in the V state has four different pairs of input/output behaviours. RE in H state is $H = (n, \overline{w'}).V + (s, \overline{e'}).V + (w, \overline{e'}).H + (e, \overline{w'}).H$.

In the following sections, we occasionally use a serial delay-insensitive Merge module (denoted by M), shown in Fig. 2.

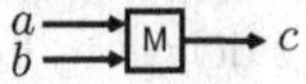

$$a \atop b \longrightarrow \boxed{M} \longrightarrow c \qquad\qquad M = (a, \overline{c}).M + (b, \overline{c}).M$$

Fig. 2. Merge element and behaviour specification

Concluding the section, we note a related work on DI process algebra in [2,4]. Reversible process calculus CCSK and its extension with the execution control operator in [19,20] can also be used to model our DI modules and circuits.

3   Distributed Memory Module

The *Distributed Memory* (DM) module is an 8-line, 4-state module with 1-bit memory, given in Fig. 3. In the following, states S_0 and S_1 are referred to as *steady states* and S_a and S_b as *processing states*. The module is composed of two systems of functionality, represented by the dashed line. The ports to the left are responsible for controlling the modification of the internal state, while the ports to the right are responsible for querying the state. In S_0, the module may be said to "hold" the value 0, and similarly for S_1 and the value 1. Informally, the behaviour of the module is described as follows. In a steady state, a query may occur via the lines q or p, which outputs the held value or its inverse respectively, via lines 0 or 1. An input via the r line causes an output via the s line, and the module moves to the other steady state. Alternatively, an input via c causes the module to output via s and move to a processing state (S_a or S_b depending on whether the steady state was S_0 or S_1 respectively). It remains in this state until an input via r, during which it will move to a new steady state (the complement of the previous steady state) and output a.

A circuit of these modules connected in a ring with each module's s output connected to the next module's r input will cause all modules to toggle their state in series when any one of the modules is signalled via the c input. The module which initiated the distributed toggle will eventually output on its a line to indicate completion when the toggle signal has completed a full revolution.

We also introduce a slightly reduced version of this module, known as a *Reduced Distributed Memory* (RDM, see Fig. 4). Informally, the behaviour of this module is identical to the DM with two exceptions. Firstly, the module lacks the 1 and c lines. Secondly, if q is signalled when in S_1, or p is signalled when in S_0, the module automatically enters the corresponding processing state.

$$S_0 = (q, \overline{0}).S_0 + (p, \overline{1}).S_0 + (r, \overline{s}).S_1 + (c, \overline{s}).S_a$$
$$S_a = (r, \overline{a}).S_1$$
$$S_1 = (q, \overline{1}).S_1 + (p, \overline{0}).S_1 + (r, \overline{s}).S_0 + (c, \overline{s}).S_b$$
$$S_b = (r, \overline{a}).S_0$$

Fig. 3. Distributed Memory module and behaviour specification

Proposition 1. RDM can be simulated by a single DM by connecting the DM's 1 line to its c line.

Both modules are to be operated in environments such that at most one input may occur at any given time, and are therefore Serial Modules. The previous state and input is always determined by the current state and the output, and hence both modules are reversible.

$$S_0 = (q, \overline{0}).S_0 + (p, \overline{s}).S_a + (r, \overline{s}).S_1$$
$$S_a = (r, \overline{a}).S_1$$
$$S_1 = (q, \overline{s}).S_b + (p, \overline{0}).S_1 + (r, \overline{s}).S_0$$
$$S_b = (r, \overline{a}).S_0$$

Fig. 4. Reduced Distributed Memory module and behaviour specification

In the diagrams that follow, we indicate a steady state of either S_0 or S_1 with a 0 or 1 in the centre of a module respectively. The use of a DM or RDM can be distinguished via the presence of eight or six lines respectively. We also rearrange the locations of ports in order to improve readability of diagrams.

Next, we illustrate the use of our module in the domain of irreversible DI networks, as shown in papers such as [5] and [17]. In Fig. 5 we give the definition of Select from [5]. We show in Fig. 6 how it can be decomposed into RDMs and Merges, and furthermore we illustrate the behaviour when undergoing the transition $(T, \overline{T_1}).S_1$.

Theorem 2. {M, DM} and {M, RDM} are serial-universal.

Proof. The universality of {M, RDM} follows from the universality of {M, Select} in [5] and the construction of Select using {M, RDM} in Fig. 6. It follows by Proposition 1 that {M, DM} is serial-universal.

We note that Select can be decomposed into 3 DMs. Furthermore, it is clear from Fig. 6 that the p input is unused. We can therefore introduce a third version of DM which is identical to RDM but does not contain a p input (we denote it $RDM \backslash p$). This module has only 5 lines.

Corollary 3. The set {M, RDM\p} is serial-universal and has cardinality 2 and modularity 5.

The set {M, RDM\p} is an improvement over existing serial-universal sets in [5] and [17]. {M, Select} in [5] has modularity 7. While the set {K, G, M} from [5] has modularity 5, it also has cardinality 3 .

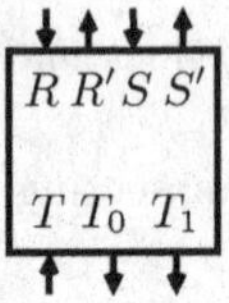

$$S_0 = (S, \overline{S'}).S_1 + (R, \overline{R'}).S_0 + (T, \overline{T_0}).S_0$$
$$S_1 = (S, \overline{S'}).S_1 + (R, \overline{R'}).S_0 + (T, \overline{T_1}).S_1$$

Fig. 5. Select module and behaviour specification

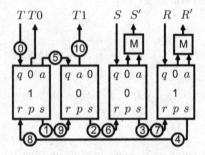

Fig. 6. Select using RDMs and Merges undergoing the transition $(T, \overline{T_1}).S_1$ in the state S_1. Each intermediate transition is represented by a circle on the appropriate wire. There may be more than one transition, thus more than one circle, on a wire, and the numbers in the circles indicate the order of the transitions. The final state is the same as the one depicted. The intermediate circuit states are not shown.

4   Reversible Modules

DM is particularly desirable in that (similarly to RE), it is its own functional inverse. This can be seen by running DM backwards and by changing output lines to input lines (and vice versa) as given by the pairs $(0, q), (1, p), (s, r)$ and (a, c). This is a particularly desirable property as it implies that the reverse behaviour of a circuit of DMs can be achieved without using different modules. However RDM, much like RT or IRT (Fig. 7), does not have this property.

4.1   Universality

We show computation-universality of both the DM and RDM via two methods. Firstly, we demonstrate the construction of RE using just RDMs (Fig. 8). This construction uses only four modules, an alternative to the approach using six

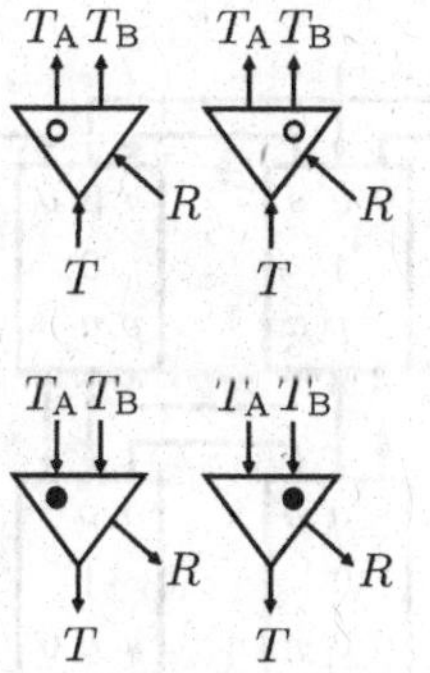

$$A = (R,\overline{T_A}).A + (T,\overline{T_A}).B$$
$$B = (R,\overline{T_B}).B + (T,\overline{T_B}).A$$

$$A = (T_A,\overline{R}).A + (T_B,\overline{T}).B$$
$$B = (T_B,\overline{R}).B + (T_A,\overline{T}).A$$

Fig. 7. Reading Toggle (top) and Inverse Reading Toggle (bottom)

Select modules as demonstrated in [6]. Furthermore, unlike in [6], this decomposition does not use Merge and is therefore fully reversible. We also contrast this approach with a decomposition using RT/IRT as demonstrated in [10]. Whilst our modules are more complex than RT/IRT, the resulting decomposition is much simpler and more intuitive. This decomposition in particular demonstrates the advantage that our module has in circuits which require multiple copies of a single memory value. The need for additional modules dedicated to controlling homogeneous updates is removed.

Theorem 4. DM and RDM are computation-universal.

Proof. Figure 8 demonstrates a construction of RE using only RDMs. The theorem follows from the universality of RE shown in [13]. Furthermore, DMs may be used in place of RDMs (Proposition 1), so DM is also universal.

We next demonstrate the construction of a synchronous Fredkin Gate (FG) to show the usefulness of our modules in the synchronous domain (Fig. 9) and we compare our construction with those that use REs in [15] and RT/IRTs in [8]. This construction is not delay-insensitive and delay elements are required in order to ensure correct operation. A triangle with a value x inside in Fig. 9 represents a *delay element* of x cycles: where a cycle is a single input-output transition. The circuit in Fig. 9 assumes that all inputs arrive simultaneously. The absence of a signal on a line represents a 0, and the presence of a signal represents a 1, as is standard in many synchronous systems and is identical to the approach shown in [8]. For comparison: our circuit uses 2 DMs, 5 delay elements and 8 cycles; [8] uses 12 RT/IRT pairs (24 modules total) and 12 delay elements, and [15] uses 8 REs, 9 delay elements and 20 cycles. Assuming that a delay does not count as a transition, our circuit uses a maximum of 10 transitions when $c = 1$, and a maximum of 2 transitions otherwise. [15] uses a maximum of 28 transitions if $c = 1$, and [8] uses considerably more.

To conclude the section, we show in Fig. 10 that RDMs can simulate a DM. Although this construction has a high transition cost, more efficient constructions exist for particular circuits. For example, Select can be realised with 3 DMs,

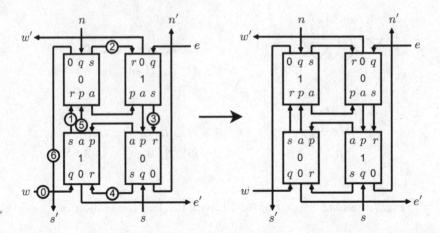

Fig. 8. Rotary Element using RDMs undergoing the transition $(w, \overline{s'}).H$. The left circuit shows the initial state of the circuit corresponding to the state V, as well as the series of transitions (represented by numbered circles on the appropriate wires) following a signal on w. The final state corresponding to H is shown on the right. The intermediate circuit states are not shown.

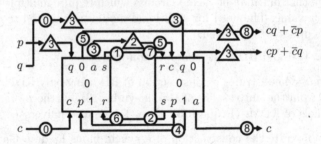

Fig. 9. Synchronous Fredkin Gate using DMs and delay elements. A triangle with a value x inside represents a delay element of x cycles: where a cycle is a single input-output transition. The diagram shows the series of transitions following simultaneous signals on q and c. This corresponds to $p = 0, q = 1, c = 1$. The final state is the same as the one depicted. The intermediate circuit states are not shown.

so if we used the construction from Fig. 10, we would need 15 RDMs. However, we see in Fig. 6 that we only need 4 RDMs.

Proposition 5. A DM may always be substituted for RDMs.

4.2   Constructing Other Reversible Modules

Three useful constructions of RT, IRT and Patra's Memory module (Mem) ([17], definition given in Fig. 11) are shown below in Fig. 12. In all cases a single module can be used. We now show a construction of a reversible Turing-tape module

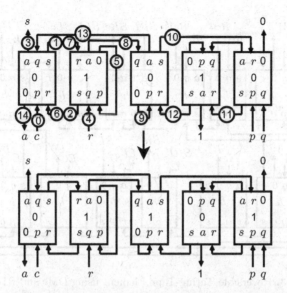

Fig. 10. DM using RDMs undergoing the transition $(c, \overline{s}).S_a$ in the state S_0, followed by the transition $(r, \overline{a}).S_1$ in the state S_a. The top circuit shows the initial state of the circuit corresponding to the state S_0, as well as the series of transitions (represented by numbered circles on the appropriate wires) following a signal on c, and eventually r. The final state corresponding to S_1 is shown on the bottom. The intermediate circuit states as well as the processing state S_a are not shown.

$$S_0 = (c, \overline{c'}).S_1 + (t, \overline{t_0}).S_0$$
$$S_1 = (c, \overline{c'}).S_0 + (t, \overline{t_1}).S_1$$

Fig. 11. Memory module and behaviour specification

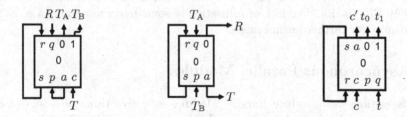

Fig. 12. (Left) RT in state A using RDM, (center) IRT in state A using DM and (right) Patra's Mem in state 0 using DM

taken from [13] (Fig. 13). A detailed operational description of its high-level behaviour is given in [13]. In summary, there exists an infinite series of tape modules in a linear array, with the leftmost module connected to the Turing

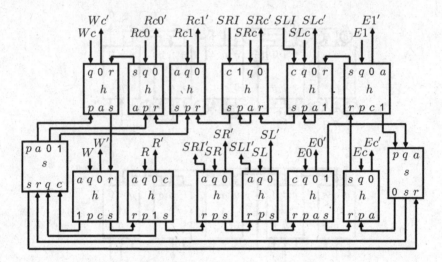

Fig. 13. Reversible Turing-Tape Element using DMs and RDMs

machine's control logic. The location of the tape's head is recorded by setting the tape module's h variable to 1. The value stored on the tape module is stored in the variable s. Whenever h is 0, the typical role of the module is to forward signals to its neighbour, where the signals will propagate until reaching the module whose value of h is 1, and a useful operation will be performed. We think that the use of DMs/RDMs for this construction demonstrates an advantage over the construction in [13], which uses REs. Due to the centralised storage of both h and s in the RE construction, trivial operations have a high transition cost. For example, when h is 0 and the module is to forward a signal from W to W', the RE construction requires 24 transitions. Due to the distributed nature of memory when using DMs/RDMs, h can be checked immediately, and this operation requires a single transition. Additionally, the construction demonstrated in Fig. 13 uses only 7 DMs and 7 RDMs, which is an improvement over the use of 19 REs in [13]. The lack of utilisation of some ports represents a possible opportunity for further optimisation.

5   Asynchronous Parallel Modules

In this section we introduce Parallel Modules and give three new sets of DI modules that are universal for all modules (or just universal for short).

A *Parallel Module* is defined as a 3-tuple $M = (I, O, N)$, where N is defined as a Sequential Machine, and I and O are input and output lines and $\mathcal{P}(I)$ and $\mathcal{P}(O)$ are in one-to-one correspondence with Σ and $\triangle$ in N respectively, where $\mathcal{P}(x)$ denotes the power-set of x. The behaviour is identical to that of a Serial

Module with the exception that a single input signal is not necessarily followed by a single output signal. Multiple input signals in combination (simultaneous or otherwise) cause a set of output signals. Unless otherwise stated, we also assume by default that there is no simultaneity between multiple valid sets of inputs (i.e. arbitration is not permitted, as in the previous sections). Partial inputs pend outside the module until a complete set has arrived, during which all are assimilated simultaneously. Outputs are produced simultaneously. This is a modification of the definition of Parallel Modules given by Keller ([5]), and is made here to reduce the number of states and simplify notation, but does not result in a loss of generality. A set of modules is referred to as being *universal for all modules* if any arbitrary Parallel Module can be realised using only modules from the set. We also use the terms *with-busy-waiting* and *without-busy-waiting* ([5]). A set is *without-busy-waiting universal* if any Parallel Module can be realised using only modules in the set such that a finite period of time after receiving an input it is guaranteed that no more transitions will occur until receiving another input. A set is *with-busy-waiting universal* if any arbitrary Parallel Module can be realised but the aforementioned condition cannot be guaranteed.

We use several standard modules such as Fork (F), Join (J) and 2×1 Join in the following results. They are defined in Fig. 14 and additional explanation can be found in [17]. We use an extended notation here where $a|b$ indicates the signals on a and b in any order, and we write, for example, $(a|b, \overline{c}|\overline{d}).X$ to mean the accepting of inputs on a and b (in any order), the production of outputs on c and d (in any order), and then a move to state X.

We also refer to Mutex and Sequencer (Fig. 15) from [17]. Sequencer is a special case in that multiple sets of valid inputs are permitted. If all three inputs are signalled, then only c and either r_0 or r_1 (arbitrarily selected) are assimilated, with the remaining input left pending until c is again signalled.

It is shown in [17] that the set {F, M, Mutex, 2×1 Join, Mem} is without-busy-waiting universal. We demonstrate a (reversible) construction of a 2×1 Join using {J, DM, RDM} in Fig. 16. Recall that Mem can be simulated with DM

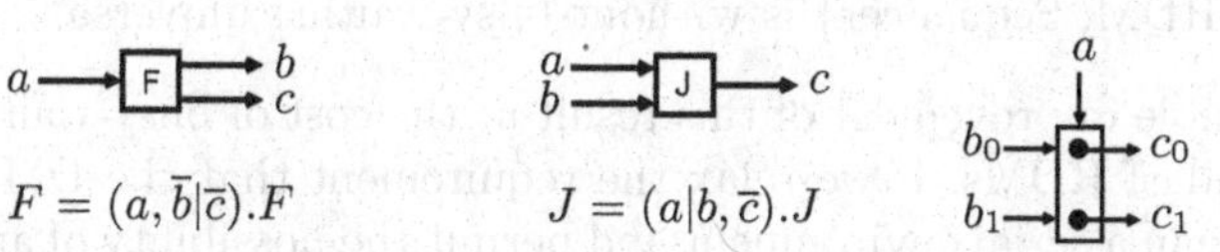

$$F = (a, \overline{b}|\overline{c}).F \qquad J = (a|b, \overline{c}).J$$

$$T = (a|b_0, \overline{c_0}).T$$
$$+ (a|b_1, \overline{c_1}).T$$

Fig. 14. Fork, Join and 2×1 Join modules

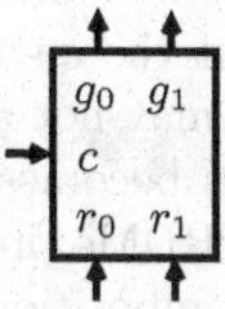

$$S = (c|r_0, \overline{g_0}).S + (c|r_1, \overline{g_1}).S$$

Fig. 15. Sequencer module and behaviour specification

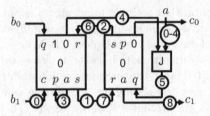

Fig. 16. 2x1 Join using Join, DM and RDM undergoing the transition $(a|b_1, \overline{c_1}).T$ in the state T. The series of transitions is represented by numbered circles on the appropriate wires. The circle with 0-4 indicates that the signal on a is pending during the transitions 0 to 4. The final state is the same as the one depicted. The intermediate circuit states are not shown.

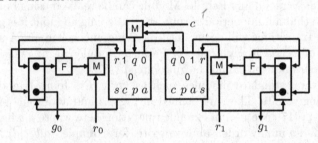

Fig. 17. With-busy-wait Sequencer using Merges, aDMs and 2x1 Joins

(Fig. 12), and DM can always be decomposed into RDM (Proposition 5). We obtain the following result:

Theorem 6. {F, M, Mutex, J, RDM} is without-busy-waiting universal.

It is also shown in [17] that the set {F, M, Select, Sequencer} is without-busy-waiting universal for all modules. Since Select can be decomposed into RDMs, we obtain the following result:

Theorem 7. {M, F, RDM, Sequencer} is without-busy-waiting universal.

There might be a possible improvement of this result at the cost of busy-waiting and using DMs instead of RDMs. If we relax the requirement that the DM be only allowed to operate in a serial environment and permit the possibility of arbitration, such that the module will process a single input at a time, causing others to pend until processed (similar to ATS in [17]), we can decompose the Sequencer into a series of *arbitrating-DMs* (denoted by aDM), 2x1 Joins (and hence, aDMs and Joins) and Merges (Fig. 17). This still requires that the environment does not provide invalid inputs at any point, and a situation may not arise such that an input pends until the module enters a state where it becomes invalid. Note that the lack of atomicity when decomposing DM into RDMs prevents the use of RDMs (as well as other simpler modules) in this decomposition.

Conjecture 8. {M, F, J, aDM} is with-busy-waiting universal.

6   Conclusion and Future Work

In this paper we have introduced a new pair of reversible DI modules based upon the idea of distributed memory. We have proven these elements' computation-universality, and shown cases where their use reduces the number of transitions compared with similar circuits using other reversible elements with memory such as RE and RT/IRT. Their use has been demonstrated in both the synchronous and asynchronous domains. We have also proposed three sets of DI modules, each containing one of our memory modules, and we have shown them to be universal.

The use of the proposed memory modules in the modelling of circuits for distributed computing algorithms (e.g. Leader election) remains unexplored, and provides an interesting direction for further research. Low-level binary operations such as arithmetic operations are also a possible future area of study.

Acknowledgements. We thank the referees of Reversible Computation 2013 for their comments and suggestions. The second author acknowledges partial support from the JSPS Invitation Fellowship grant S13054.

References

1. Fredkin, E.F., Toffoli, T.: Conservative logic. International Journal of Theoretical Physics 21(3/4), 219–253 (1982)
2. Josephs, M.B., Furey, D.: Delay-insensitive interface specification and synthesis. In: Proceedings of DATE 2000, pp. 169–173. IEEE Computer Society (2000)
3. Josephs, M.B., Nowick, S.M.: Scanning the technology: Applications of asynchronous circuits. Proceedings of the IEEE, 223–233 (1999)
4. Josephs, M.B., Udding, J.T.: An overview of D-I algebra. In: Proceedings of HICSS 1993, pp. 329–338. IEEE Computer Society (1993)
5. Keller, R.M.: Towards a theory of universal speed-independent modules. IEEE Transactions on Computers 23(1), 21–33 (1974)
6. Lee, J., Adachi, S., Peper, F., Mashiko, S.: Delay-insensitive computation in asynchronous cellular automata. Journal of Computer and System Sciences 70(2), 201–220 (2005)
7. Lee, J., Adachi, S., Peper, F., Morita, K.: Embedding universal delay-insensitive circuits in asynchronous cellular spaces. Fundamenta Informaticae 58(3-4), 295–320 (2003)
8. Lee, J., Huang, X., Zhu, Q.-S.: Decomposing Fredkin Gate into simple reversible elements with memory. Journal of Digital Content Technology and its Applications 4(5), 153–158 (2010)
9. Lee, J., Peper, F., Adachi, S., Morita, K.: Universal delay-insensitive circuits with bidirectional and buffering lines. IEEE Transactions on Computers, 1034–1046 (2004)
10. Lee, J., Peper, F., Adachi, S., Morita, K.: An asynchronous cellular automaton implementing 2-State 2-Input 2-output reversed-twin reversible elements. In: Umeo, H., Morishita, S., Nishinari, K., Komatsuzaki, T., Bandini, S. (eds.) ACRI 2008. LNCS, vol. 5191, pp. 67–76. Springer, Heidelberg (2008)

11. Martin, A.J.: The limitations to delay-insensitivity in asynchronous circuits. In: Proceedings of AUSCRIPT 1990, pp. 263–278. MIT Press (1990)
12. Milner, R.: A Calculus of Communicating Systems. Prentice Hall (1980)
13. Morita, K.: A simple universal logic element and cellular automata for reversible computing. In: Margenstern, M., Rogozhin, Y. (eds.) MCU 2001. LNCS, vol. 2055, pp. 102–113. Springer, Heidelberg (2001)
14. Morita, K.: Reversible computing systems, logic circuits, and cellular automata. In: Proceedings of ICNC, pp. 1–8 (2012)
15. Morita, K., Ogiro, T., Tanaka, K., Kato, H.: Classification and universality of reversible logic elements with one-bit memory. In: Margenstern, M. (ed.) MCU 2004. LNCS, vol. 3354, pp. 245–256. Springer, Heidelberg (2005)
16. Patra, P., Fussell, D.S.: Building-blocks for designing DI circuits. Technical report, University of Texas at Austin (1993)
17. Patra, P., Fussell, D.S.: Efficient building blocks for delay insensitive circuits. In: Proceedings of Async 1994, pp. 196–205. Society Press (1994)
18. Patra, P., Fussell, D.S.: Efficient delay-insensitive RSFQ circuits. In: Proceedings of ICCD 1996, pp. 413–418. IEEE Computer Society (1996)
19. Phillips, I.C.C., Ulidowski, I.: Reversing algebraic process calculi. Journal of Logic and Algebraic Programming 73(1-2), 70–96 (2007)
20. Phillips, I.C.C., Ulidowski, I., Yuen, S.: A reversible process calculus and the modelling of the ERK signalling pathway. In: Glück, R., Yokoyama, T. (eds.) RC 2012. LNCS, vol. 7581, pp. 218–232. Springer, Heidelberg (2013)

Energy Recovery and Logical Reversibility in Adiabatic CMOS Multiplier

Ismo Hänninen, Hao Lu, Craig S. Lent, and Gregory L. Snider

University of Notre Dame,
Center for Nano Science and Technology, Notre Dame, IN 46556, USA
{ismo.hanninen,hlu1,lent,snider.7}@nd.edu

Abstract. Overcoming the IC power challenge requires signal energy recovery, which can be achieved utilizing adiabatic charging principles and logically reversible computing in the circuit design. This paper demonstrates the energy-efficiency of a Bennett-clocked adiabatic CMOS multiplier via a simulation model. The design is analyzed on the logic gate level to determine an estimate for the number of irreversible bit erasures occurring in a combinatorial implementation, showing considerable potential for minimizing the logical information loss.

Keywords: Multipliers, computer arithmetic, adiabatic charging, reversible logic.

1   Introduction

Reversible logic is a strict requirement for quantum computing, however, overcoming the power challenge of the traditional digital integrated circuits potentially benefits from the associated energy recovery enabled by the reversible computation principles. Standard Complementary Metal Oxide Semiconductor (CMOS) technology does not recover signal energy, which leads to considerable energy waste and heat dissipation, limiting the attainable device densities and operating frequencies, and thereby, also the available computing power. While the technology scales down, expected to follow the predictions of the International Roadmap for Semiconductors (ITRS), the loss of signal energy and limiting the related heat become all the more important factors for circuit design. [1]

Adiabatically charged logic recovers part of the signal energy, and if the circuits are slowed down, asymptotically nearly all of the energy can be recovered. The cost of asymptotically adiabatic logic is usually high in circuit area, complexity, or timing. Either reversible logic gates or timing-based logical reversibility is required [2].

Computer arithmetic is a field where the energy-efficiency of the implementations restricts the available performance, measured for example as operations per Watt. In addition to the requirements of high-performance computing, the battery life of portable and embedded systems has become one of the most important technology drivers. Therefore, an especially interesting area of reversible computation is the design of computer arithmetic, including the multiplier unit presented in this paper.

G.W. Dueck and D.M. Miller (Eds.): RC 2013, LNCS 7948, pp. 25–35, 2013.
© Springer-Verlag Berlin Heidelberg 2013

This paper demonstrates a reversible multiplier unit, which is based on CMOS transistors but driven with adiabatic power-clocks. Full logical reversibility is achieved via concatenated Bennett-type clocking approach, avoiding costs in logic complexity while placing all the overhead in the timing and the clock generation. Based on HSPICE simulation model, the design successfully recovers the signal energy and surpasses comparable static CMOS unit in the low-frequency regime up to tens of MHz. The design has been also fabricated with a 2 μm technology, while measurements are in progress.

Part of the paper concentrates on the logical reversibility of multiplication and the specific multiplier design. Previous work indicates that the theoretical binary multiplication should be achievable with a linear number of bit erasures vs. operand word length, at the very least. The existing implementations including the design proposed here are not optimized on the logic level for minimization of erasures, which is demonstrated with the estimated information loss in the static CMOS multiplier variant.

This paper is organized as follows: Sec. 2 outlines the procedures of adiabatic driving and the requirement of logical reversibility, while Sec. 3 describes the prototyped multiplier design. Design analysis is presented in Sec. 4 and the degrees of reversibility discussed in Sec. 5. The conclusion follows in Sec. 6.

2   Signal Energy Recovery

The energy-efficiency of any integrated circuit technology is closely related to the method of signal representation and the associated signal energy, which has to overcome the thermal noise floor by a significant margin [1]. In standard static CMOS, every switching event leads potentially to the dissipation of all the signal energy related to a certain circuit node. Most of this loss can be avoided by utilizing adiabatic charging principles, which can be fully implemented only by logically reversible circuits.

2.1   Adiabatic Charging

The energy dissipation in standard circuits occurs when electrical currents are driven through transistors with a finite on-resistance and resistive signal lines. The resistive losses are proportional to the voltage difference for example between the terminals of a transistor device, which gives rise to the approach of limiting this voltage difference and avoiding abrupt currents. For example, a static CMOS inverter gate in Fig. 1(a) represents information by the output node voltage, and dissipates all of the signal energy during the operation. During a switching event, either the pull-up or pull-down network loses

$$E_{CMOS} = \frac{1}{2}CV_{DD}^2 , \tag{1}$$

where C is the output node capacitance including the wiring and next gate input, and V_{DD} is the operating voltage. This energy is practically all the signal energy.

This circuit can be modified to recover signal energy by utilizing ramped power-clock signals instead of static operating voltage and ground. An example of such energy-recovering 1n1p-logic [3] inverter is shown if Fig. 1(b) with the corresponding dual clock waveforms in Fig. 1(c), which can input energy into the circuit and recover it back to the clock. The adiabatic energy loss is

$$E_{\text{adiabatic}} - RC^2 V_{\text{DD}}^{\,2} / t_{\text{ramp}} , \qquad (2)$$

where t_{ramp} is the time duration of the ramp. The pipelining of this type of asymptotically adiabatic logic is challenging due to the need to utilize reversible gates or include garbage signals. For an introduction into a classification of adiabatic circuit families the reader is referred to [2], which describes also quasi-adiabatic approaches enabling simply pipelining but losing some part of the signal energy.

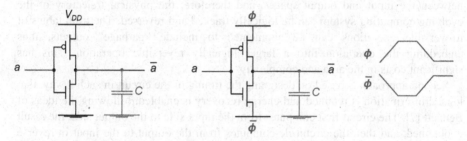

Fig. 1. CMOS inverter. (a) Standard static CMOS implementation, (b) adiabatic 1n1p CMOS implementation, and (c) dual-rail power-clock.

2.2   Reversible Logic and Operations

Recovering the signal energy to the desired extent is possible using asymptotically adiabatic logic, where the energy is transferred inside the circuit avoiding any abrupt discharge of a high potential to ground. However, based on current experience, designing such circuits imply that the logic operations utilized have to be reversible in nature.

The logical reversibility is connected to the physical reversibility of the system, that is, the physical, thermodynamically described state of the system has to mirror to some degree the computation that is performed. Fifty years ago, Rolf Landauer proposed this connection in [4], and recently in 2012, the Landauer's Principle was confirmed with a generic one-bit memory experiment recently reported in [5]. A bit erasure at the room temperature has an inevitable energy cost of about 0.003 aJ, which usually has to be dissipated as heat into the environment. This part of the signal energy cannot be adiabatically recovered, unless we incorporate logical reversibility into the circuit.

However, in the traditional circuits the bit erasure energy is insignificant compared to the other losses. For example, the end-of-the-roadmap CMOS will dissipate about three orders of magnitude higher energy per switching event [1]. Losses in the emerging technologies like quantum-dot cellular automata (QCA) [6] are also various, but not counting the information loss, all of them are like friction in nature: they can be made as small as desired by switching more slowly, while the energy-per-bit-erasure is unaffected by the speed. Therefore, it is necessary to design the system to utilize adiabatic charging for the logic or clock signal, in addition to achieving some degree of logical reversibility. From the circuit design perspective, reversible logic and adiabatic operation are desirable, but they incur various costs. An erasure-aware circuit involves tradeoffs between performance, timing, circuit area, and power, balancing the effects of the erasures and adiabatic operation. There are two approaches to achieve logical reversibility.

First approach is based on using logically reversible gates like the Toffoli or Fredkin gates. The truth table of this type of gates contains only one-to-one mappings between the input and output spaces, and therefore, the physical trajectory of the evolving computing system can be logically tracked and reversed. The truth tables of irreversible operations can be augmented to include "garbage" outputs, thus embedding the operation into a larger logically reversible operation. This has significant costs in the area and complexity.

Second approach is based on designing the timing of the circuit in such a way, that logical information is retained and energy recovery is enabled, following the ideas of Bennett [7]. The circuit first computes from the input side to the output side, the result is obtained, and then the circuit de-computes from the output to the input in reverse order. This can be efficiently implemented by Bennett-clocking technique [8], which is feasible for both CMOS circuits and many emerging technologies. The reversibility is retained by holding the predecessor parts of the circuits steady while successor stages compute, then relaxing after the whole computation has been finished. This is illustrated for a three-block design in Fig. 2, including the dual-rail power-clock signals necessary for 1n1p asymptotically adiabatic logic [3] we utilized in the presented multiplier.

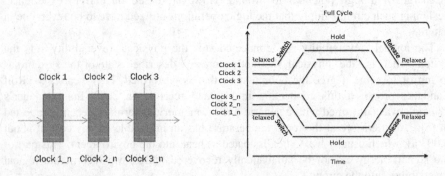

Fig. 2. Reversible Bennett-clocking. (**a**) Consequent logic blocks, (**b**) power-clock waveforms, vertically offset for clarity.

3   Combinatorial Multiplier

The designed 4-bit multiplier unit is based on a standard combinatorial structure laid out manually using CMOS transistors on a 2 µm technology node. The significant modifications are related to the static operating voltage and ground networks, which have been replaced with dynamic power-clock signals. These lines can be controlled to provide either static potentials for irreversible operation or ramped potentials for reversible Bennett-clocking. While the circuit has been fabricated on silicon, the measurements are currently work-in-progress, and we report only the simulation results.

Both modes of operation have been simulated in Synopsys HSPICE 2012, using a level 3 MOSFET model with parameters extracted from the devices made at the University of Notre Dame. The n-type transistors have a W/L ratio of 6 µm / 2µm with a threshold voltage of 0.7V, while the p-type transistors have a W/L ratio of 12 µm / 2 µm with a threshold voltage of -0.5V. The gate oxide thickness is 20nm.

3.1   Logical Structure and Implementation

The combinatorial structure of the standard multiplier unit is inherently logically irreversible, composing of standard CMOS logic gates and not utilizing any registers [9]. The unit takes as input two 4-bit words A = (A3, A2, A1, A0) and B = (B3, B2, B1, B0) and produces the 8-bit output word F = (F7,…, F0). The unsigned binary multiplication is defined if Fig. 3(a), while the grouping used for the addition of the summands AiBj in the implementation is depicted in Fig. 3(b), utilizing a Wallace tree arrangement for the addition of the slices of three-bit groups and a final two-operand carry-lookahead adder. The structure is shown in Fig. 4, consisting of 11 logic levels.

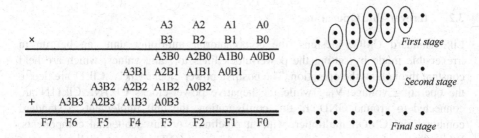

Fig. 3. (a) 4-bit binary multiplication, and (b) grouping the summands AiBj and combining them with a Wallace adder tree and a final carry lookahead adder

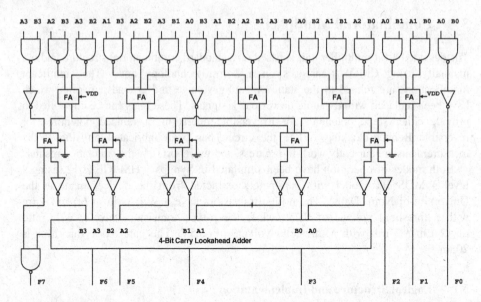

Fig. 4. Combinatorial multiplier based on Wallace tree summation and a final stage carry lookahead adder. The full adder (FA) units are used as half or full adders, depending on the location.

The design was laid out manually using a 2 μm CMOS technology, resulting in the fabricated layout shown in Fig.5. Instead of static operating voltage lines V_{DD} and ground lines GND, we connected individual positive power-clocks Clk1...Clk11 to the pull-up side of the logic gates and negative power-clocks Clk1N...Clk11N to the pull-down side, effectively forming a programmable 11-stage pipeline. The control of the timing can be used to select irreversible or reversible operating mode.

3.2   Irreversible Operation

Like standard CMOS designs, the combinatorial multiplier unit can be run in irreversible mode by setting the power-clock lines to static values, which are held constant throughout the operation. The positive power-clocks Clk1...Clk11 are tied to the operating voltage V_{DD}, while the negative power-clocks Clk1N...Clk11N are connected to ground GND. In this configuration, the unit implements a standard combinatorial CMOS multiplier, without pipelining or any sequential components. While the power-clocks virtually implement V_{DD} and GND and are trivially simple to control, this mode of operation loses the logic signal energy exactly like traditional irreversible CMOS logic.

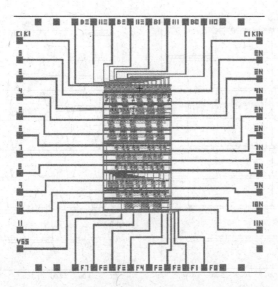

Fig. 5. Multiplier unit layout in 2 μm CMOS. The contact pads for inputs A0…A3 and B0…B3 are interleaved at the top, the outputs F0…F7 at the bottom, positive power-clocks Clk1…Clk11 on the left, and negative power-clocks Clk1N…Clk11N on the right.

3.3   Reversible Bennett-Clocked Operation

The multiplier unit can be configured into fully reversible mode by utilizing the 11 dual-rail power-clock signals with the ramp-up and ramp-down timing defined by the requirements of Bennett-clocking, conceptually defined in Fig. 2. This forms an 11-stage 1n1p-type asymptotically adiabatic logic circuit [3], where the computing part takes 11 steps and un-computing part 11 steps, while the unit is performing only one multiplication operation. The design shown in Fig. 5 contains all the logic needed for computing and un-computing, shared under the Bennett-clocking scheme. Slowing down the operating frequency, asymptotically all of the signal energy can be recovered, even while we retain the simple CMOS logic complexity and area costs. However, the unit is not capable of pipelining, and the generation of the complicated power-clock signals is challenging.

4   Design Analysis

The design analysis is based on the layout and HSPICE simulation model, with part of the simulation waveforms is shown in Fig. 6. Power consumption is the main optimization goal in this design, but we consider also the standard cost metrics of complexity, circuit area, and performance in short. The logic complexity and area of the proposed multiplier core is practically equal to a static CMOS counterpart, if the circuitry required for generating the power-clocks is not considered. Determining this cost is ongoing work.

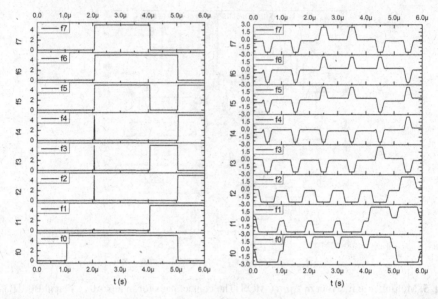

Fig. 6. Part of simulation output waveforms. (a) Irreversible operation with two signal levels and a voltage swing of 0—5 V. (b) Reversible operation with three signal levels and a voltage swing of −2.5—2.5 V. Only the outputs F0...F7 are shown.

The highest result throughput is dependent on the operating frequency, but it should be noted that the irreversible combinatorial multiplier is limited by the longest signal path across the whole unit, while the reversible Bennett-clocked multiplier is divided into 11 stages, which each has an internal delay similar to a corresponding standard pipeline stage. The frequency limits for the multipliers are not equal, but generally, a small stage can be switched faster that the whole unit, while on the other hand, the adiabatic energy recovery is less with higher frequencies.

Power consumption of the multiplier was determined by averaging the results of HSPICE simulations in the range from 10 kHz to 1 GHz, shown in Fig. 7 as Watts vs. operating frequency. Irreversible mode has nearly two orders of magnitude higher power than the reversible from the slow end up to 1 MHz, while the modes get closer together from 20 or 30 MHz upwards, depending on the circuit parasitics. The irreversible multiplier is less affected by the parasitics than the reversible version, where the parasitic components clearly must be carefully controlled.

The designed layout is based on 2 μm CMOS, which is not ideal for the reversible multiplier. Based on preliminary work, moving to a 20 nm technology would raise the operating frequency by two orders magnitude, while the reversible design would surpass the irreversible up to a frequency of several GHz.

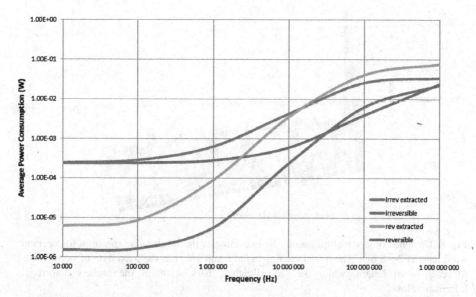

Fig. 7. Simulated average power consumption, irreversible vs. reversible operation. Including the paracitics extracted from the layout has adverse effects on both modes of operation, but more pronounced on the reversible operation.

5   Degree of Logical Reversibility

The Bennett-clocked multiplier is asymptotically adiabatic and recovers potentially nearly all of the signal energy, but with the cost of timing complexity. The combinatorial design itself is irreversible CMOS logic, which without the clocking approach both loses signal energy due to the static voltage operating principle and the bit erasures. In static CMOS, the energy loss due to losing logical information is insignificant compared to the total signal energy loss, however, adiabatic logic families and emerging technologies will benefit from avoiding the bit erasures in multiplication.

The amount of logical information loss in the standard irreversible multiplier can be estimated in a gate-level analysis, which gives a bound for the number of Landauer bit erasures. While the inverter gates are logically reversible, even though a static CMOS implementation wastes all the signal energy, the other logic gates used in the design, NANDs and NORs, can be coarsely approximated to lose up to two bits of information each. With around 140 of these gates, we can expect 280 bit erasures per multiplication operation in this 4-bit structure. With growing word length, the complexity and the number of potential erasures scale according to a square-law.

Previous work on the theoretical binary multiplication operation indicates, that although the multiplication result value spectrum in Fig. 8 has a very complicated structure, it is possible to encode the logical relationship between the inputs and outputs uniquely with additional bits. The amount of extra bits scales linearly with the operand word length, and the theoretical minimum for full 4-bit multiplication is 5

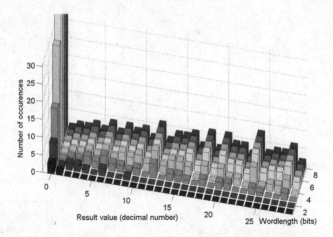

Fig. 8. Unsigned binary multiplication, the beginning of the result value spectrum for operand word lengths 2—8 bits. The trivial multiplication result zero has the maximum of occurrences for each word length, while the second-highest bars represent the highest non-trivial information loss.

erasures [10]. Therefore, multiplication should be amenable to modifications increasing the conservation of information and also the signal energy, even without Bennett-clocking. Currently, the authors are not aware of this type of developments having been published.

6   Conclusion

Signal energy recovery enables high-efficiency computing, but has significant costs in circuit area, complexity, or timing. In this work, a configurable multiplier unit was designed and comparisons between irreversible and Bennett-clocked asymptotically adiabatic reversible mode conducted. With the simulated and prototyped 2 μm technology, the reversible operation was more efficient into the tens of MHz region. Based on expected scaling, the true benefits of adiabatic energy recovery will become significant using more state-of-the-art 20 nm technology node. There the adiabatic operation would be orders of magnitude better up to GHz region.

The multiplier unit presented was not optimized for inherent logical reversibility, and therefore, Bennett-clocking is the only way to enable energy recovery. However, when examined on pure combinatorial logic level, it turns out that this kind of standard structure discards two orders of magnitude more information than the theoretical minimum of binary multiplication operation. This suggests that there is considerable potential to increase the degree of reversibility in the multiplier implementations without using the full Bennett embedding.

Currently, the analysis methods for the reversibility of circuit structures require development, as does the theoretical understanding of the connection between logical and physical reversibility. This area of research will likely become more and more important as the CMOS technology transitions to the limits of predicted physical scaling and beyond-CMOS technologies emerge. With transistor-less technologies utilizing charge-mode logic, the Landauer's Principle and bit erasures will be significant design factors.

References

1. International Technology Roadmap for Semiconductors ITRS report (2009), http://www.itrs.net/Links/2009ITRS/Home2009.htm
2. Starosel'skii, V.I.: Adiabatic Logic Circuits: A Review. Russian Microelectronics 31(1), 37–58 (2002)
3. Valiev, K.A., Starosel'skii, V.I.: A Model and Properties of a Thermodynamically Reversible Logic Gate. Russian Microelectronics 29(2), 83–98 (2000)
4. Landauer, R.: Irreversibility and heat generation in the computing process. IBM J. Res. Dev. 5, 183–191 (1961)
5. Berut, A., Arakelyan, A., Petrosyan, A., Ciliberto, S., Dillenschneider, R., Lutz, E.: Experimental verification of Landauer's principle linking information and thermodynamics. Nature 483, 187–189 (2012)
6. Lent, C., Tougaw, P.: A device architecture for computing with quantum dots. Proc. IEEE 85(4), 541–557 (1997)
7. Bennett, C.: Logical reversibility of computation. IBM J. Res. Dev. 17, 525–532 (1973)
8. Lent, S., Liu, M., Lu, Y.: Bennett clocking of quantum-dot cellular automata and the limits to binary logic scaling. Nanotechnology 17, 4240–4251 (2006)
9. Koren, I.: Computer Arithmetic Algorithms, 2nd edn. A. K. Peters, Ltd., Natick (2002)
10. Hänninen, I., Takala, J., Lent, C.: Irreversible bit erasures in binary multipliers. In: Proc. IEEE Int. Symp. Circuits Syst., Rio de Janeiro, Brazil, May 15-18, pp. 2369–2372 (2011)

Comparing CMOS-Based and NEMS-Based Adiabatic Logic Circuits

Samer Houri, Alexandre Valentian, and Hervé Fanet

DACLE, CEA-LETI, Minatec Campus, 17 rue des Martyrs, Grenoble France
{Samer.Houri,Alexandre.Valentian,Herve.Fanet}@cea.fr

Abstract. In this paper, a detailed comparison between the expected performance of CMOS-based and nanoelectromechanical systems (NEMS) based adiabatic logic circuits is presented. The modeling of the NEMS devices is done using a 1-dimensional reduced order model (1d ROM) of the electromechanical switches. This model will give an honest analytical depiction of the NEMS-based adiabatic circuits. The performance of NEMS-based circuits compares favorably with that of CMOS-based circuits. To the best knowledge of the authors, this is the first reported detailed comparison between NEMS and CMOS devices for adiabatic circuits.

Keywords: Adiabatic Circuits, Nanoelectromechanical systems, NEMS Switches.

1 Introduction

Along with the need to embed electronic systems into the surrounding environment, such as autonomous sensors, processors and communication nodes, comes the need for ever lower power consumption per operation in logic circuits. In order to accommodate the requirement of ultra low power consumption, a variety of approaches are being explored: these include device level improvements, e.g. the use of fully depleted SOI substrates [1], multigate devices like finFETs [2], semiconductor nanowires [3] and materials like III-V semiconductors [4] and Carbon nanotubes (CNT) [5]. In parallel, circuit- and architecture-level solutions are also being pursued in order to push down the power consumption of logic circuits. Along with classical circuit-level solutions, such as subthreshold circuits [5] and core parallelism [5], more fundamentally different, i.e. non-mainstream, approaches to low power logic and computing circuits are possible, of special interest amongst these are: adiabatic logic circuits [6], reversible computation [7]-[8], and quantum computation [9].

This work explores the combination of two such concepts in logic circuits. On the one hand, adiabatic logic circuits, i.e. logic circuits that make use of the adiabatic charging-discharging principle in order to minimize resistive losses during circuit operation; on the other hand, the use of nanoelectromechanical systems (NEMS) relays as a replacement for CMOS switching elements.

The NEMS-based adiabatic circuit combination is an especially appealing one, since NEMS switches practically do not duffer from leakage current and therefore no

G.W. Dueck and D.M. Miller (Eds.): RC 2013, LNCS 7948, pp. 36–45, 2013.

static losses, which is a major limiting factor in the performance of CMOS-based adiabatic circuits. On the other hand, the use of adiabatic charging offsets the losses due to the relatively high voltages usually required to operate NEMS devices. Although the results presented in this work are for adiabatic logic circuits, they may be expanded to include reversible logic design, since reversible computation needs to rely on adiabatic logic blocks.

By using the simplest logic circuit model, this paper starts by giving the expected energy dissipation of CMOS-based switching elements, after which the performance of NEMS-based adiabatic circuits is discussed. The analysis of energy dissipation will be explicitly derived based on a 1-dimensional reduced order electromechanical model (1d ROM) of the NEMS switches functioning in the non-pull-in regime. Finally a comparison between the performance of CMOS-based and NEMS-based adiabatic circuits will be made.

2   Dissipation in CMOS-Based Adiabatic Logic

In this work, the dissipation calculation will be based on the simplified circuit model shown in Fig. 1. This model considers a simple RC circuit as the load, denoted by R_S for series resistance, and C_L for the load capacitance (which in case of non-reversible architecture is due to fan-out interconnect) respectively. In both the CMOS as well as the NEMS models the series resistance R_S will be considered to be dominated by the switching element itself, while the load capacitance is dominated by the interconnect load capacitance C_L; as well as having a variable capacitance component C_S in the case of NEMS switches, this variable capacitance represents the change in the NEMS device capacitance upon commutation. An expression of the variable capacitance will be derived in the subsequent section based on the ROM model. Energy dissipation will be considered for a four phase power clock, each segment having a period T as shown schematically in Fig. 1.

In the following, a detailed description of the dissipation in CMOS-based adiabatic circuits is done; the sources of dissipation can be attributed to either adiabatic or non-adiabatic residues. While it is possible to reduce the adiabatic residues by increasing the adiabatic gain factor, the non-adiabatic losses are independent of the adiabatic charging-discharging parameters and depends only on the device parameters and the power clock signal.

The energy dissipated in a complete charge-discharge clock cycle is given by the following equation:

$$E_{Total} = E_{adia} + E_{non\text{-}adia} \tag{1}$$

where E_{total}, E_{adia}, and $E_{non\text{-}adia}$, are respectively the total energy dissipation, the energy dissipated due to adiabatic losses, and the energy dissipated through non-adiabatic processes.

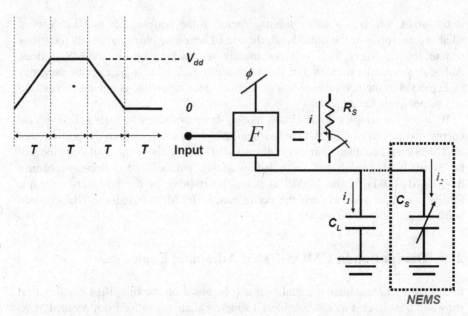

Fig. 1. Schematic representation of an equivalent logic circuit showing the four phase power clock with equal length segments, F represent the block's logic function, R_S is the series resistance dominated by the switch resistance, C_L represents the load capacitance that is mainly due to the output interconnect capacitance, and C_S represents the NEMS switch variable capacitance. The current provided by the power clock is labeled i, the current going into the static interconnect capacitance (C_L) is labeled i_1, and that going into the variable capacitance of the NEMS switch (C_S) is labeled i_2.

In the case of CMOS circuits, the above expression may be re-expressed as:

$$E_{Total} = 2\xi\left(\frac{R_S C_L}{T}\right)C_L V_{dd}^2 + \frac{1}{2}C_L V_{th,p}^2 + V_{dd}\overline{I_{leak}}T \qquad (2)$$

where ξ is a factor representing the efficiency of the adiabatic charging process: it takes the values of $\xi = 1$ for a ramped voltage power clock like the one shown in Fig. 1; R_S and C_L take the meanings defined previously, and V_{dd} is the supply voltage of the hold phase of the power clock as shown in Fig. 1.

In equation (2), the first term represents the adiabatic residues [9-10] of a charge-discharge cycle, this term is considered to be accurate for $\left(\frac{R_S C_L}{T}\right) > 10$. The second term in the above expression represents the energy dissipation due to the sudden voltage drop that is due to the threshold voltage of p-type MOSFET ($V_{th,p}$) in a partially adiabatic CMOS circuit [10-11]. Finally, the last term represents the power dissipation due to leakage current, i.e. the passive power dissipation, where in the above expression $\overline{I_{leak}}$ represents the average leakage current over a clock phase period.

While equation (1) is a generic expression that applies to both NEMS-based and CMOS-based circuits, equation (2) is CMOS specific. It is worth noting that the MOSFET device capacitance also changes depending on the applied voltage, however, that is usually a second order term that is dropped from energy dissipation calculations. Therefore, the variable capacitance in Fig. 1 is only applicable in the case of NEMS devices.

The leakage current encountered in a CMOS-based adiabatic circuit is herein derived for the linearly ramped four phase power clock shown in Fig. 1.

The leakage current will be calculated for the generic logic circuit shown in Fig. 2: although the exact circuit design may vary depending on the logic used [11], the values derived herein may be considered as a good approximation for most CMOS-based adiabatic logic circuits.

Fig. 2 shows an adiabatic circuit having an arbitrary logic function F: once the input is in its hold phase the synchronized power clock ϕ will start its 4-phase period. During the time the power clock is applied, either the logic block or its complement will be passing, and therefore either the output or the inverted output will follow the clock voltage. This means that for any arbitrary logic block, the same leakage current will be experienced on one of the two latch nMOS transistors as shown in Fig. 2.

Knowing that the main leakage current component in a MOSFET is due to the sub-threshold leakage, the leakage current is therefore given by the following expression:

$$I_{leakage} = I_0 \left(1 - \exp\left(\frac{-V_{DS}}{Vt} \right) \right) \tag{3}$$

where $I_{leakage}$ is the leakage current, I_0 is a function of the transistor's size, V_t is the thermal voltage $V_t = \dfrac{kT}{q}$, where k is the Boltzmann constant, T is the temperature in Kelvin, and q is the electron charge ($V_t = 25$ mV for room temperature), and V_{DS} is the source-drain voltage which is assumed to perfectly follow the power clock.

Taking the four phases of the power clock shown in Fig. 1 into account, the leakage energy term expressed in equation (2) may be re-expressed: by replacing the leakage current with equation (3) and the voltage by that corresponding to each clock phase as follows:

$$E_{leakage} = \int_0^T V_{dd} I_0 \left(1 - \exp\left(\frac{-t V_{dd}}{TV_t} \right) \right) \frac{t}{T} dt + \int_T^{2T} V_{DD} I_0 \left(1 - \exp\left(\frac{-V_{dd}}{V_t} \right) \right) dt$$

$$+ \int_{2T}^{3T} V_{dd} I_0 \left(1 - \exp\left(\frac{-V_{dd}\left(1 - \dfrac{t}{T}\right)}{TV_t} \right) \right) \left(3 - \frac{t}{T} \right) dt \tag{4}$$

where in equation (4), all values take their previously defined meaning: the first, second and third integrals correspond to the rising phase, the hold phase, and the decreasing phase of the power clock respectively.

By making the approximation $exp(-V_{dd}/V_t) \sim 0$, it is possible to obtain the following simple expression for leakage dissipation:

$$E_{leakage} = 2I_0 V_{dd} T \tag{5}$$

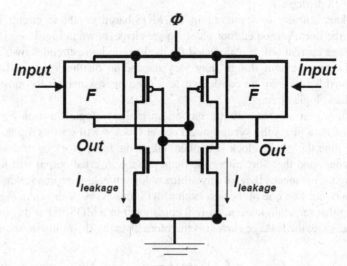

Fig. 2. Schematic representation of a CMOS implementation of a logic function F, also identifying the leakage current. This architecture is known as the PFAL architecture, however, the obtained results apply as a first order approximation to other architectures as well.

3   Dissipation in NEMS-Based Adiabatic Logic Circuits

The interest in NEMS relays as switching elements for logic circuit operation has increased significantly in recent years due to their highly appealing property of zero leakage current (see [12] for a comprehensive review).

3.1   NEMS Switches Reduced Order Model

Although NEMS switches of varying design, dimensions, and materials have been constructed and demonstrated, this paper relies on a 1-dimesional generic model that may be applied to all devices equally in order to obtain a generic formulation of the energy efficiency and performance of NEMS-based adiabatic logic circuits.

A typical 3-terminal electrostatic NEMS switch is schematically shown in Fig. 3(a): an electrostatic force is created between the gate electrode (G) and the suspended structure when a bias voltage is applied brings the structure, which is connected to the source (S), into contact with the drain electrode (D). The drain electrode is assumed to play no role in the electrostatic actuation of the structure. The equivalent 1-dimensional reduced order model is shown schematically in Fig. 3(b), where the structure is modeled as a simple parallel plate capacitor with a varying gap. If the ratio of air gap (d) to actuation gap (g) is $\dfrac{d}{g} > \dfrac{1}{3}$, an instability known as pull-in takes place. The pull-in results in a hysteretic effect as shown for an ideal I-V plot in Fig. 3(c), in which case the voltage at which pull-in takes place known as the pull-in voltage (V_{pi}), is larger than the voltage at which the structure breaks contact known as the pull-out voltage V_{po}. In case that the contact is established before the onset of pull-in, i.e. $\dfrac{d}{g} \leq \dfrac{1}{3}$, the ideal I-V relationship takes the form shown in Fig. 3(d).

The underlying assumptions made in this work are as follows: first, the mechanical commutation (τ) time is longer than the electric time constant of the circuit, i.e. $\tau \gg R_S C_L$ which is a very reasonable assumption. Therefore the voltage on the

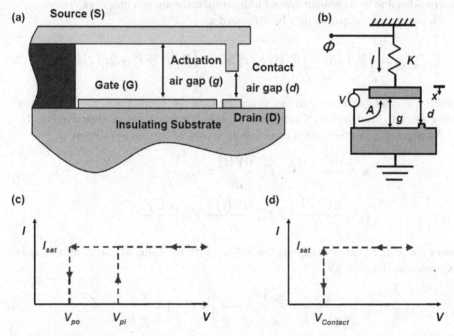

Fig. 3. Schematic representation of a nanoelectromechanical electrostatic relay switch (a) showing the source (S), drain (D), and gate (G). Also visible are the actuation and contact gaps. The reduced order model of the NEMS structure is shown in (b), A represents the equivalent parallel plate capacitor area, x shows the direction of displacement of the structure, V and I represent the applied actuation voltage and the source-to-drain current respectively, and ϕ represents the power clock signal. The contact air gap plays no role in electrostatic actuation. Schematic representations of typical I-V plots in NEM switches are shown for the case of pull-in (c) and non-pull-in (d) devices, where I_{sat} represents the saturation current of the device.

device gate follows the clock phase without any delay. Furthermore, for proper circuit operation it is necessary to have $T \geq \tau$. Finally, the analysis performed herein is applicable to NEMS relays operating in the non-pull-in regime, i.e. the regime shown in Fig. 3(d).

3.2   Dissipation Calculation in NEMS-Based Adiabatic Circuits

The power dissipated in a NEMS relay-based adiabatic logic circuit may be expressed as follows:

$$E_{Total} = E_{Electrical} + E_{Mechanical} \tag{6}$$

where E_T, $E_{Electrical}$ and $E_{Mechanical}$ are the total energy dissipation, the energy dissipated through electrical resistance, and the energy dissipated through mechanical damping respectively.

While the mechanical energy dissipation may depend on the ramp period T, it remains a small component compared to the electrical loss components, as such it will be considered to be a constant second order residue throughout this work.

The electrical dissipation may be expressed as:

$$E_{Electrical} = \int_0^T R_S i^2 dt = \int_0^T R_S \left(i_1 + i_2\right)^2 dt = \int_0^T R_S \left(i_1^2 + i_2^2 + 2 i_1 i_2\right) dt \tag{7}$$

where i, i_1, and i_2 are the currents going through the series resistance R_S, the load capacitance C_L, and device (NEMS) capacitance C_S respectively, as shown in Fig. 1.

An expression for the current in each branch may be derived as follows:

$$i_1 = \frac{dC_L V(t)}{dt} = C_L \frac{dV(t)}{dt} = C_L \frac{V_{dd}}{T} \tag{8.a}$$

$$i_2 = \frac{dC_S V(t)}{dt} = C_S \frac{dV(t)}{dt} + V(t)\frac{dC_S}{dt} \tag{8.b}$$

From the reduced order model shown in Fig. 3(b), the value of capacitance may be expressed as (for x << g):

$$C_S = \frac{\varepsilon_0 A}{(g - x)} \approx \frac{\varepsilon_0 A}{g}\left(1 + \frac{x}{g}\right) = C_0\left(1 + \frac{x}{g}\right) \tag{9}$$

where C_0 is the NEMS switch capacitance when no gate voltage is applied.

Knowing that the equilibrium between electrostatic and restoring elastic forces in the reduced order model gives the following voltage-displacement relationship [13]:

$$\frac{x}{g}\left(1-\frac{x}{g}\right)^2 = \alpha V^2 \Rightarrow \frac{x}{g} \approx \alpha V^2$$

$$\textit{and}$$

$$\alpha = \frac{\varepsilon_0 A}{2Kg^3} \,\&\, x < \frac{g}{3}$$

(10)

where K is the equivalent spring constant of the movable mechanical structure.

The resulting equations in (9) and (10) rely on approximations that are valid for small x, i.e. $x < g$; these approximations result in reduced accuracy in modeling the device, however, in doing so they also provide simple analytical expressions of the power dissipation.

By combining equations (6) through (10) and replacing expressions (9) and (10) in (8), an approximate analytical expression for power dissipation per complete four phase clock cycle is obtained, given by (for $\xi = 1$):

$$E_{Total} = \frac{2R_S V_{dd}^2}{T}\left[C_L^2 + C_0^2\left(1+2\frac{x}{g}\right) + 2C_0 C_L\left(1+\frac{x}{g}\right)\right] + E_{Mechanical}$$

(11)

$$\text{for } x \le \frac{g}{3} \,\&\, V_{dd} \le V_{pi}$$

Two significant differences between equations (2) and (11) are to be noticed. First in (11), there is no term that is directly dependent on T, as is the case with the leakage current in (2), which means that, as the voltage ramp period is increased, the dissipated energy will asymptotically tend to a lower limit without increasing again. Furthermore, in (2) the dissipation term that depends on the threshold voltage is considerably larger than the mechanical dissipation term found in NEMS-based circuits, compared to their respective adiabatic power dissipation.

For comparison, the energy dissipation per clock cycle given by equations (2) and (11) is plotted in arbitrary units in Fig. 4. The lower limits given by the constant dissipation terms, i.e. mechanical energy dissipation and threshold-dependent terms in equations (11) and (2) respectively, are shown indicated by dashed lines. While CMOS-based circuits show a V-shaped energy-frequency dissipation, the dissipation in NEMS-based circuits asymptotically tends to a lower limit given by the mechanical energy dissipation $E_{Mechanical}$. Note that the NEMS-based circuits are not able to run beyond their mechanical commutation frequency, hence the sudden stop in the plot corresponding to NEMS.

A factor of merit (FOM) chosen as the energy dissipation-period product, i.e. $E_{Total}*T$, is also plotted in Fig. 4, in arbitrary units, for both CMOS-based and NEMS-based circuits.

The graphs plotted in Fig. 4 help understand the behavior of both CMOS and NEMS-based adiabatic logic circuits: they do show that NEMS-based circuits are considerably more efficient in the low frequency regime compared to their CMOS-based counterparts and that, when operating near their optimum performance, they tend to dissipate significantly lower amounts of energy compared to the optimum afforded by CMOS devices. This could be expected to come at the expense of slower running circuits, since NEMS switches have yet to show a reliable high frequency switching behavior.

The characterization of the contact resistance in a NEMS switch is currently under experimental investigation. These experimentally obtained parameters will help build more accurate models of NEMS switches and obtain a better comparison with CMOS-based circuits.

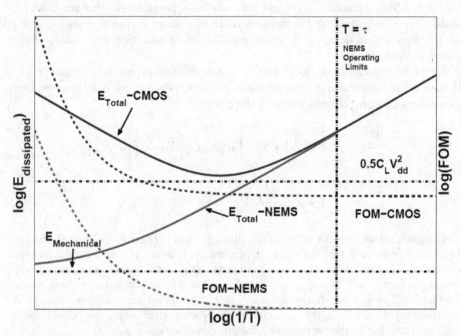

Fig. 4. Plots showing the total energy dissipation (solid lines) and the FOM (dashed lines) for CMOS (blue color) and NEMS based (red color) adiabatic logic circuits. NEMS energy dissipation shows an asymptotic lower limit at low frequencies, given by the mechanical energy dissipated per switching operation, while CMOS energy dissipation shows a clear optimum resulting from the leakage current. The FOM shows that for both devices, once a certain value is attained, the FOM tends to an asymptotic value. The plots for NEMS-based circuits stop abruptly at $T = \tau$, which is usually lower than CMOS device operating frequencies.

4   Conclusions

Based on a simplified reduced order model, the energy performance of adiabatic logic circuits that use NEMS switching elements instead of CMOS switching elements is derived. The derivation presented in this work is specific to NEMS switches operating in the non-pull-in regime; beyond that, the derivation is universal in the sense that it is applicable to most switch designs, once the lumped parameters used in this work are replaced with their respective real device parameters.

In addition a simple analytical expression for the leakage dissipation in CMOS-based adiabatic logic circuits is also derived. It is found that the NEMS-based circuits offer the distinctive advantage of zero static losses, and therefore the possibility of operating the circuit at low frequencies without any energy dissipation penalties. Furthermore, the lowest permissible energy dissipation in a NEMS-based adiabatic logic circuit is given by the mechanical dissipation term which is expected to be orders of magnitude lower than the one afforded by CMOS-based circuits.

References

1. Collinge, J.P.: Silicon-on- Insulator Technology: Materials to VLSI. Kluwer (1988)
2. Hisamoto, D., Lee, W.C., Kedzierski, J., Takeuchi, H., Asano, K., Kuo, C., Anderson, E., King, T.J., Bokor, J., Hu, C.M.: FinFET-A Self-Aligned Double-Gate MOSFET Scalable to 20 nm. IEEE Transactions on Electron Devices 47, 2320–2325 (2000)
3. Singh, N., Agarwal, A., Bera, L.K., Liow, T.Y., Yang, R., Rustagi, S.C., Tung, C.H., Kumar, R., Lo, G.Q., Balasubramanian, N., Kwong, D.L.: A dual-strained CMOS structure through simultaneous formation of relaxed and compressive strained-SiGe-on-insulator. IEEE Electron Device Letters 27, 350–353 (2006)
4. Chau, R., Datta, S., Majumder, A.: Opportunities and challenges of III-V nanoelectronics for future high-speed, low-power applications. In: IEEE Compound Semiconductor Integrated Circuit Symposium, Palm Springs (2005)
5. Javey, A., Guo, J., Wang, Q., Lundstrom, M., Dai, H.: Ballistic carbon nanotube field-effect transistors. Nature 424, 654–657 (2003)
6. Koller, J.G., Athas, W.C.: Adiabatic switching, low energey computing, and the physics of storing and erasing information. In: Proceedings Workshop on Physics and Computation, pp. 267–270 (1992)
7. Bennett, C.H.: Logical reversibility of computation. IBM Journal of Research and Development 17, 525–532 (1973)
8. De Vos, A.: Reversible Computing: Fundamentals, Quantum Computing, and Applications. Wiley-VCH (2010)
9. Benioff, P.: The Computer as a Physical System: A Microscopic Quantum-Mechanical Hamiltonian Model of Computers as Represented by Turing Machines. Journal of Statistical Physics 22, 563–591 (1980)
10. Athas, W.C., Svensson, L.: Reversible logic issues in adiabatic CMOS. In: Workshop on Physics and Computation Proceedings, pp. 111–118 (1994)
11. Teichmann, P.: Adiabatic Logic: Future Trend and System Level Perspective. Springer, Dordrecht (2012)
12. Loh, O., Espinosa, H.D.: Nanoelectromechanical contact switches. Nature Nanotechnology 7, 283–295 (2012)
13. Nathanson, H.C.: The Resonant Gate Transistor. IEEE Transactions on Electron Devices 14, 117–133 (1967)

Strength of the Reversible, Garbage-Free $2^k \pm 1$ Multiplier

Eva Rotenberg[1], James Cranch[2],
Michael Kirkedal Thomsen[1], and Holger Bock Axelsen[1]

[1] DIKU, Dept. of Computer Science, University of Copenhagen, Denmark
{roden,shapper,funkstar}@diku.dk
[2] Dept. of Computer Science, University of Sheffield, United Kingdom
jdc41@cam.ac.uk

Abstract. Recently, a reversible garbage-free $2^k \pm 1$ constant-multiplier circuit was presented by Axelsen and Thomsen. This was the first construction of a garbage-free, reversible circuit for multiplication with non-trivial constants. At the time, the strength, that is, the range of constants obtainable by cascading these circuits, was unknown.

In this paper, we show that there exist infinitely many constants we cannot multiply by using cascades of $2^k \pm 1$-multipliers; in fact, there exist infinitely many primes we cannot multiply by. Using these results, we further provide an algorithm for determining whether one can multiply by a given constant using a cascade of $2^k \pm 1$-multipliers, and for generating the minimal cascade of $2^k \pm 1$-multipliers for an obtainable constant, giving a complete characterization of the problem. A table of minimal cascades for multiplying by small constants is provided for convenience.

Keywords: Number theory, constant multiplication, reversible circuit design, Mersenne numbers.

1 Introduction

Ever since reversible logic circuits were introduced by Fredkin and Toffoli [4, 8] construction of circuits for arithmetic operations have received much attention. However, the requirement that reversible circuits should not produce any garbage makes design of reversible arithmetic operations much harder. Today, most of the efficient garbage-free circuit designs are implementations of addition[1] [2, 3, 7, 9, 10].

Lately however, there has been some work on garbage-free, reversible constant multipliers [1, 5]. To the best of our knowledge, the first non-trivial garbage-free constant multiplier (*i.e.*, where the constant is different from a power of 2) was the $2^k \pm 1$-multiplier designed by Axelsen and Thomsen [1]. In that paper it was observed that the combination of bit-shifts with the $2^k \pm 1$ multiplier gives us a method for reversible multiplication by any number which can be written as a

---

[1] Because the circuits are reversible a good design of an addition circuit also implies a good design of a subtraction circuit.

G.W. Dueck and D.M. Miller (Eds.): RC 2013, LNCS 7948, pp. 46–57, 2013.
© Springer-Verlag Berlin Heidelberg 2013

product of 2^{k_0} and $2^{k_i} \pm 1$'s, but also any integer that can be represented as a fraction of such products; for division we can use the inverse circuit, since the circuits are both reversible and garbage-free. For instance, one can multiply by the constant 21 by cascading the constant multipliers for 7 and 3. One can also multiply by 11 by cascading the inverse of the multiplier for 3 after the multiplier for 33. But, still, the precise range of constants was unknown.

In this paper, we observe that the obtainable constants are those which lie in the subgroup of the rational numbers generated by the Mersenne numbers $2^n - 1$, $n \in \mathbb{N}$. This allows us to use number theory to explore the range effectively. We use *Zsigmondy's Theorem* to construct a method for showing if a number is unobtainable and then use *Lifting the Exponent* to show that infinitely many unobtainable numbers exist. We also show that representations (corresponding to circuit choices for multiplier cascades) are unique up to some refactoring of 63; a special case which stems from Zsigmondy's Theorem.

First, in Section 2, we show that there exist infinitely many numbers x for which one cannot find a cascade of $2^k \pm 1$ multipliers that multiply by x. Furthermore, we prove that infinitely many primes are unobtainable. In Section 3, we raise the question of the length of multiplier cascades, or equivalently, the representation length of a number. It turns out that given a representation of a number, it is very easy to transform it into a minimal representation or to determine that it was already minimal. We provide an algorithm for determining whether a constant is obtainable, and, in positive cases, providing a representation for that given number. One can then go on to use the minimalisation algorithm to obtain the minimal cascade which multiplies by the given constant. In Appendix A, we provide a table of odd constants up to 201 and their (minimal) representations and lengths, if available, with unobtainability explicitly marked.

2   Why 23 and Infinitely Many Other Primes Are Out of Range

We ask ourselves: For which $n \in \mathbb{N}$ can we multiply reversibly by n, only by cascading $2^k \pm 1$-multipliers and ordinary bit-shifts?

Cascading constant multiplier circuits corresponds to multiplication of the constants, and cascading the inverse corresponds to division. In this section we show that even if we allow the cascades to grow to unbounded lengths, there are still constants they cannot multiply by.

We want to investigate the numbers that can be written as a fraction of products of numbers of the form 2^k or $2^k \pm 1$. In order to do this, we define the reachable subset $\mathbb{M} \subseteq \mathbb{N}$ of as the smallest subset of natural numbers satisfying

$$
\begin{aligned}
\mathbb{M} = \;&\{2^n \mid n \in \mathbb{N}_0\} &&\text{(bit-shifts)} \\
\cup\;&\{2^n \pm 1 \mid n \in \mathbb{N}\} &&(2^n \pm 1 \text{ multipliers}) \\
\cup\;&\{ab \mid a, b \in \mathbb{M}\} &&\text{(Cascade of the } \cdot a\text{- and } \cdot b\text{-multipliers)} \\
\cup\;&\{b \mid a, ab \in \mathbb{M}\}. &&\text{(Cascade with the } \cdot a\text{-multiplier inverted)}
\end{aligned}
$$

Since $\mathbb{M}$ is closed with respect to multiplication, we are interested in which prime numbers belong to $\mathbb{M}$.

2.1   Connection to the Mersenne Numbers

Notice that the numbers in $\mathbb{M}$ include the well-known set of Mersenne numbers.

Definition 1. *A Mersenne number is a number of the form* $2^n - 1$, $n \in \mathbb{N}$.

We can use this to describe the class $\mathbb{M}$ in a different and more algebraic way. We can, namely, exclude numbers of the form $2^k + 1$ from our generating set and still get the same set of numbers.

Definition 2. *Define the* Mersennary rationals *as the subgroup* G_M *of the multiplicative group of rationals* $\mathbb{Q}^*$ *generated by* 2 *and* $\{2^n - 1 \mid n \in \mathbb{N}\}$, *i.e., generated by* 2 *and the Mersenne numbers.*

Note 1. $G_M \cap \mathbb{N} = \mathbb{M}$.

Proof. Because $2^n + 1 = \frac{(2^n+1)\cdot(2^n-1)}{2^n-1} = \frac{2^{2n}-1}{2^n-1}$, $\mathbb{M}$ is clearly a subset of G_M by the definition of $\mathbb{M}$. Conversely, if a natural number $b \in G_M$ then b can by definition be written in the form $\frac{ab}{a}$ where $a, ab \in \mathbb{M}$, and thus $b \in \mathbb{M}$. $\square$

Definition 3. *We call the numbers in* $\mathbb{M}$ Mersennary numbers. *The primes in* $\mathbb{M}$ *will be called* Mersennary primes.

The question of whether all natural numbers belong to $\mathbb{M}$ can now be restated as follows: Are all numbers Mersennary? The answer to this is "no", but this leads to other questions: Are infinitely many primes non-Mersennary? Unfortunately, "yes", so then: Can a computer effectively tell me if a number is Mersennary? "Yes", fortunately, it can and we will later show the algorithm for this.

When a number is Mersennary, it means we can write it as a product of elements of the form $2^n - 1$ and a single power of 2. Such a choice of elements we call a *representation* of the number.

Definition 4. *A* Mersennary representation *of a number* m, *is an integer sequence* $\{z_n\}_{n \in \mathbb{N}_0}$, $z_n \in \mathbb{Z}$ *with only finitely many non-zero elements, and* $z_1 = 0$, *such that*

$$m = 2^{z_0} \prod_{n \in \mathbb{N}} (2^n - 1)^{z_n}, z_n \in \mathbb{Z}.$$

In a slight abuse of nomenclature we shall often refer to the right hand side of this equation as the representation π, rather than the sequence.

For example, a representation of 75 is $z_2 = -1, z_4 = 2$ (and all other $z_i = 0$), as $75 = (15^2)/3$. A representation of m need not be unique, since $63 = 7 \cdot 3^2$ (and thus has two representations). As we shall see later, however, this particular identity is the only source of non-uniqueness of representations. We therefore say that a representation is *63-free* if $z_6 = 0$, *i.e.*, if 63 does not appear in the representation, and the 63-free representation *is* unique, cf. Theorem 5.

2.2   Why 23 Is a Problematic Number

Here we prove that (infinitely many) non-Mersennary numbers do exist. We do this by exhibiting a sound heuristic for determining that a prime is non-Mersennary, and apply it to some small numbers, the smallest non-Mersennary of which is 23.

First, we define the *width* of an odd number, which becomes handy later when dealing with Mersennary numbers.

Definition 5. *The* width *of an odd number n is the multiplicative order of 2 modulo n, i.e, the order of $[2]$ in $(\mathbb{Z}/n)^*$;*

$$w(n) = |[2]_n|.$$

For example, $w(3) = 2$, $w(7) = 3$, $w(5) = 4$, etc. The width is well-defined because 2 is coprime to any odd number by definition, so $[2] \in (\mathbb{Z}/n)^*$. Note that the width of n is at most $n - 1$.

We use the width to define the following central theorem, which we shall prove below in this section.

Theorem 1. *If two primes $p \neq q$ have the same width W, then neither p nor q are Mersennary.*

This theorem is important as a tool for falsifying the hypothesis that a given number is Mersennary. We can use it as a basis for the following heuristic.

Algorithm 1. *For falsification of the hypothesis that a given prime number p is Mersennary. (Sound heuristic.)*

- *Calculate the width $w(p)$ of p.*
- *Factorise $2^{w(p)} - 1$.*
- *Calculate the width of each factor $(\neq p)$ of $2^{w(p)} - 1$. If any of these widths equals $w(p)$, then p is not Mersennary.*

Example 1. $w(23) = 11$, $2^{11} - 1 = 23 \cdot 89$, $w(89) = 11$, so 23 is not Mersennary.

Although this algorithm may be incomplete, as we have only shown one direction to hold, we shall show a complete solution in Section 3.1. The key to showing our result is the following theorem.

Theorem 2 (Zsigmondy's Theorem[2] [11]). *Given $n \neq 6$ there exists at least one prime dividing $2^n - 1$ that does not divide $2^k - 1$ for any $k < n$.*

In other words, each Mersenne number introduces at least one *new* prime; new in the sense that it does not divide any smaller Mersenne number.

Note 2. $2^W - 1$ is the least Mersenne number divisible by n iff n has width W.

---

[2] The theorem as stated here is actually a special case of Zsigmondy's theorem, and is sometimes referred to as *Bang's theorem*.

Proof. Assume n divides $2^W - 1$. Then we can write that as $2^W - 1 = n \cdot m$ for some $m \in \mathbb{N}$. But this holds if and only if $[2^W - 1]_n \equiv 0$ or equivalently $[2^W]_n \equiv 1$. Now, 2 modulo n has order W if W is the smallest number satisfying the equation $[2^W]_n \equiv 1$, so by definition n has width $w(n) = W$.   □

The next step is to note that the factors in a representation of a Mersennary number cannot be arbitrarily large.

Lemma 1. *If a prime p is Mersennary, then $2^{w(p)} - 1$ is the largest Mersenne number in the (63-free) representation of p.*

Proof. Let $\prod_{i \in \mathbb{N}}(2^i - 1)^{z_i}$ be a representation of p, and assume that $2^k - 1$ is the largest factor with non-zero exponent. By Zsigmondy's Theorem, $2^k - 1$ introduces a new prime p_k which does not divide any smaller $2^s - 1$, $s < k$, so $w(p_k) = k$. But then $p_k^{z_k}$ must divide our original p, which means $p_k = p$ and $z_k = 1$, and so $w(p) = k$.   □

In other words, we can write p as $(2^{w(p)} - 1) \cdot \prod_{i < w(p)}(2^i - 1)^{z_i}$, $z_i \in \mathbb{Z}$.
    This now makes it easy to prove the earlier theorem: *If two primes $p \neq q$ have the same width W, then neither p nor q is Mersennary.*

Proof (Theorem 1). Assume for the purpose of contradiction that we have a (63-free) Mersennary representation π for p. It follows from Lemma 1 above that π has $2^W - 1$ as its highest factor:

$$p = (2^W - 1) \cdot \prod_{i < W}(2^i - 1)^{z_i}, z_i \in \mathbb{Z}.$$

But since q does not divide any smaller $2^k - 1$, $k < W$, and since q *does* divide $2^W - 1$, we have now shown q divides p, a contradiction.   □

Example 2. 47 and 178481 are not Mersennary; both have width 23.

Example 3. 29 and 113 are not Mersennary; both have width 28.

Example 4. 37 and 109 are not Mersennary; both have width 36.

Note 3. The product of a Mersennary number with a non-Mersennary number is non-Mersennary.

Otherwise, one could divide the representation of the product with the representation of the Mersennary number, obtaining a representation of the assumed non-Mersennary number. One the other hand, the product of two non-Mersennary numbers can be Mersennary, *e.g.* $23 \cdot 89 = 2047$.

Note 4. There exist infinitely many non-Mersennary numbers.

For instance, the sequence $\{2^i \cdot 23\}_{i \in \mathbb{N}}$ consists of non-Mersennary numbers, as does $\{(2^i - 1) \cdot 23\}_{i \in \mathbb{N}}$. The non-Mersennary numbers below 50 are: $23, 29, 37, 46,$ and 47.

2.3 There Are Infinitely Many Non-mersennary Primes

Every composite Mersenne number with prime exponent, *i.e.*, a composite number of the form $2^p - 1$ where p is prime, gives us a new non-Mersennary prime.[3] However, it is unknown whether infinitely many such Mersenne numbers exist. Luckily, we can still prove that infinitely many non-Mersennary prime numbers exist, by the following useful definition and lemma.[4]

Definition 6. *For a prime p and a number n, let $v_p(n)$ denote the greatest power in which p divides n.*

For example, $v_3(18) = 2$, as 3^2 divides 18, and no higher power of 3 divides 18.

Lemma 2 (Lifting the Exponent). *Assume p is an odd prime that divides $a - b$ and assume p does not divide a or b, then*

$$v_p(a^n - b^n) = v_p(a - b) + v_p(n).$$

We are here only interested in the special case where $a = 2^k$ and $b = 1$:

If p divides $2^k - 1$; then $v_p(2^{k \cdot n} - 1) = v_p(2^k - 1) + v_p(n)$.

This entails $v_{23}(2^{11 \cdot 23^{j-1}} - 1) = v_{23}(2^{11} - 1) + v_{23}(23^{j-1}) = j$. Therefore, $|[2]_{23^j}|$ divides $11 \cdot 23^{j-1}$. However, no proper divisor d of $11 \cdot 23^{j-1}$ will work as the order of $[2]_{23^j}$, as a simple analysis shows that $v_{23}(2^d - 1) < j$, which contradicts that $[2^d - 1]_{23^j} \equiv 0$. In other words, we know the exact width of 23^j, namely $w(23^j) = 11 \cdot 23^{j-1}$.

Note 5. If some prime $f \neq 23$ is a factor of $2^{11 \cdot 23^i} - 1$, then, given $j > i$, f divides $2^{11 \cdot 23^j} - 1$ as many times as it divides $2^{11 \cdot 23^i} - 1$. This clearly holds, as

$$\begin{aligned}
v_f(2^{w(23^j)} - 1) = v_f(2^{11 \cdot 23^{j-1}} - 1) &= v_f((2^{11 \cdot 23^{i-1}})^{23^{j-i}} - 1) \\
&= v_f(2^{11 \cdot 23^{i-1}} - 1) + v_f(23^{j-i}) = v_f(2^{w(23^i)} - 1),
\end{aligned}$$

since f does not divide 23^x for any $x \geq 1$ when $f \neq 23$.

This also holds for the other prime factor 89 of $2^{11} - 1$, since 89 does not divide 23^x for any $x \geq 1$.

Theorem 3. *There are infinitely many non-Mersennary primes.*

Proof. We will prove this by showing that each $s_j = 2^{w(23^j)} - 1$ introduces a new prime, which is not Mersennary. We proceed by case analysis on j.

First case, $j = 1$. We have $s_1 = 2^{11} - 1$, which introduces the prime 89, which is not Mersennary.

---

[3] If $2^p - 1$ is composite with p prime, then its prime factors have width p, and are thus not Mersennary.

[4] This is a well-known result. See [6] for an expository note.

Second case, $j > 1$. According to Note 5, any factor $\neq 23$ of any s_i divides s_{j-1} exactly as many times as s_j. Thus, s_j/s_{j-1} leaves us with the product of 23 and some natural number $n \in \mathbb{N}$, where n is coprime to any s_i with $i < j$. Now, recall that a product of a non-Mersennary number with a Mersennary number must again be non-Mersennary (Note 3). Since s_j and s_{j-1} are both Mersennary, $s_j/s_{j-1} \in \mathbb{N}$ is Mersennary. Therefore, since $23 \cdot n$ is Mersennary and 23 is non-Mersennary, n must also be non-Mersennary, and, thus, contains a non-Mersennary prime that is not a factor of s_i for any $i < j$.   □

2.4   Wieferich Primes Are Also Non-mersennary

Definition 7. *A* Wieferich prime *is a prime p such that p^2 divides $2^{p-1} - 1$.*

Two such primes are currently known: 1093 and 3511.

To prove Wieferich primes are never Mersennary we need a small lemma:

Lemma 3. *For a prime $p > 2$, the (multiplicative) order of $[2]$ in $(\mathbb{Z}/p^2)^*$ is either the order of $[2]$ in $(\mathbb{Z}/p)^*$, or p times that.*

Proof. Let d be the order of 2 modulo p. Then $(2^d)^p$ is congruent to 1 modulo p^2. But then, either $[2^d]$ was already congruent to $[1]$, or it was an element of order p. Since d divides $p - 1$, and thus is coprime to p, this means that $[2]$ has order d or $d \cdot p$.   □

Theorem 4. *Any Wieferich prime p is non-Mersennary.*

Proof. Since p^2 divides $2^{p-1} - 1$, the order of $[2]$ in $(\mathbb{Z}/p^2)^*$ divides $p - 1$. Since this is less than p, Lemma 3 gives us that the order of 2 must be the same both modulo p and modulo p^2.

Now, let k be the order of 2 modulo p. If p is Mersennary, then it has a (63-free) Mersennary representation $(2^k - 1)\prod_{i<k}(2^i - 1)^{z_i}$, where p divides only the $2^k - 1$ term (by Lemma 1). In particular, p then divides $2^{k} - 1$ exactly with exponent 1. But p^2 also has order k, and so divides $2^k - 1$ as well, which is a contradiction, so p cannot be Mersennary.   □

3   Representations and Representation Lengths

So far, we have mainly considered which numbers are in the subset of constants $\mathbb{M} \subseteq \mathbb{N}$ reachable by cascading some number of $2^k \pm 1$-multipliers. But the size and precise number of $2^k \pm 1$-multiplier circuits needed in order to multiply by a given constant is also interesting. We have shown that we do not need $2^k - 1$ multipliers with k larger than the width of the constant, but how long cascades (how many multipliers) can we need?

Example 5. We can write 19 as $2^9 + 1$ divided by $9 \cdot 3$. In other words, we need to cascade 3 of the $2^k \pm 1$-multipliers in order to multiply by 19. Can we determine if a better solution exists, and what it might be?

When we talk about representation lengths, it makes a difference which forms of constants we allow to occur as elements (*i.e.*, as individual multipliers in the cascade); even though they form the same subset of the reachable constants in total. Let us distinguish between a *Mersennary representation* consisting of elements 2, $\{2^n - 1 \mid n \in \mathbb{N}\}$ and a *plus/minus representation* consisting of elements $\{2^x \mid x \in \mathbb{N}\} \cup \{2^n \pm 1 \mid n \in \mathbb{N}\}$.

A Mersennary representation $2^{z_0} \prod_{n \in \mathbb{N}} (2^n - 1)^{z_n}$ is said to be of *length* $\sum_{n \in \mathbb{N}} |z_n|$, the sum of the absolute values of the exponents. Note that the z_0 is not counted towards the length, as bit shifts are trivial. Similarly, a plus/minus representation defined by $2^{z_0} \prod_{n \in \mathbb{N}} (2^n - 1)^{z_n} (2^n + 1)^{y_n}$ is said to be of length $\sum_{n \in \mathbb{N}} (|z_n| + |y_n|)$.

Example 6. The length of the Mersennary representation of 75 is 3, as 75 was represented as $15^2/3$ having exponents $z_2 = -1$ and $z_4 = 2$, giving the sum $|2| + |-1| = 3$. A plus/minus representation of 75 is $5 \cdot 15$, which has length 2.

Theorem 5. *The 63-free Mersennary representation of a Mersennary number is uniquely defined.*

Proof. Let $\pi_1 = \{a_i\}_{i \in \mathbb{N}_0}$ and $\pi_2 = \{b_i\}_{i \in \mathbb{N}_0}$ be distinct 63-free Mersennary representations of Mersennary numbers a and b.

Let $2^k - 1$ be the the *widest* factor on which these representations differ. That is, $a_k \neq b_k$, and for all $j > k$, $a_j = b_j$. Now, $(2^k - 1)$ has a prime divisor p which does not divide any narrower factors, according to Zsigmondy's Theorem. p may divide some factors wider than $(2^k - 1)$, but all such factors have the same exponents in π_1 and π_2. Thus, p must appear with the *same* exponent x in the prime factorisations of both $a/(2^k - 1)^{a_k}$ and $b/(2^k - 1)^{b_k}$. (Recall that the prime factorisation of a rational number is well-defined and unique.) But p must at the same time appear with *different* exponents in the prime factorisation of $(2^k - 1)^{a_k}$ and $(2^k - 1)^{b_k}$ since $a_k \neq b_k$. This means that a and b have different prime factorisations, and so must be distinct. □

This also shows that the identity $63 = 3^2 \cdot 7$ is the only source of ambiguity in Mersennary representations.

Corollary 1. *For any two Mersennary representations π_1 and π_2 of a Mersennary number, $\pi_1 = \pi_2 \cdot (\frac{63}{3^2 \cdot 7})^z$ for some $z \in \mathbb{Z}$.*[5]

Given a number n, let x be the largest number such that 63^x divides n. Then a representation of n has minimal length *if* the exponent of 63 in the representation is x. This makes it very easy to minimize a Mersennary representation.

Algorithm 2. *Algorithm for transforming a given Mersennary representation to an equivalent minimal representation.*

- *Substitute all occurences of $3 \cdot 3 \cdot 7$ by 63.*

---

[5] Formally, if $\pi_1 = \{a_i\}_{i \in \mathbb{N}_0}$ and $\pi_2 = \{b_i\}_{i \in \mathbb{N}_0}$ both represent the same Mersennary number, then there exists $z \in \mathbb{Z}$, such $a_2 = b_2 - 2z, a_3 = b_3 - z$ and $a_6 = b_3 + z$.

Our next question is: How do we substitute a Mersennary representation for a plus/minus representation of a given number? First, let us observe the following corollary to the uniqueness theorem (Theorem 5).

Theorem 6. $2^k + 1$ *has a unique Mersennary representation (up to the refactoring of 63) of the form*

$$2^k + 1 = \frac{2^{2k} - 1}{2^k - 1}$$

With the obvious exception of $2^3 + 1$ which is also equal to $(2^2 - 1) \cdot (2^2 - 1)$; the exception in Zsigmondy's Theorem, $63 = 7 \cdot 3 \cdot 3$.

Proof. This follows from Theorem 5.   □

This provides us with a way to translate a minimal Mersennary representation to a plus/minus representation which corresponds to a minimal cascade of $2^k \pm 1$-multipliers.

Algorithm 3. *Given a minimal Mersennary representation $2^{z_0} \prod_{i \in \mathbb{N}} (2^i - 1)^{z_i}$ of n, a minimal plus/minus representation of n can be obtained as follows:*

- *Substitute each fraction of the form $\frac{2^{2k}-1}{2^k-1}$ by $2^k + 1$.*
- *Substitute $3^{\pm 2n}$ by $9^{\pm n}$.*
- *Substitute $\frac{2^{12}-1}{3 \cdot 7}$ by $65 \cdot 3$.*
- *Substitute $\frac{2^{12}-1}{7 \cdot 15^2}$ by $\frac{65}{5^2}$.*
- *Substitute $3 \cdot 7 \cdot 15$ by $63 \cdot 5$, and $\frac{2^{12}-1}{63}$ by 65.*

The first point is a general case, while the last are special cases that relate to 63 or its factors. One may also make substitutions such as $\frac{2^{4k}-1}{2^k-1}$ by $(2^{2k}+1) \cdot (2^k+1)$ to minimize the number of gates and the delay in the final cascade.

Example 7. A minimal Mersennary representation of the number 5 is $\frac{2^4-1}{2^2-1}$ which we recognise as being on the form $\frac{2^{2k}-1}{2^k-1}$ for $k = 2$. We substitute for $2^k + 1 = 2^2 + 1$ and achieve a representation length of 1 as expected.

Corollary 2. *Numbers with arbitrarily long minimal representations exist.*

Proof. As example we take the sequence $\{31^j\}_{j \in \mathbb{N}}$, and we show that 31^j has representation length j. Note that $(2^5 - 1)^j$ is a Mersennary representation of 31^j. By Theorem 5 this is also a minimal Mersennary representation of 31^j. Since no fractions occur this Mersennary representation is also the minimal plus/minus representation of 31^j.   □

The sequence $\{5^j\}_{j \in \mathbb{N}}$ would do as well, with a detour of a Mersennary representation length twice the plus/minus representation length.

3.1 Determining the Representation of a Given Number

The largest factor in the Mersennary representation of any Mersennary number n is upper bounded by the width of (the odd component of) n. In fact, as we saw in Lemma 1, the largest factor is completely determined by the widest prime in n's prime factorisation.

This allows us to provide an algorithm which determines whether a number is Mersennary and, if it is, returns a Mersennary representation of that number.

Algorithm 4. *Given a number n_0, we calculate a Mersennary representation π of n_0 (if any exists) as follows:*

1. *Set $n := n_0$ and $\pi := []$.*
2. *Calculate the prime factorisation of n, and the width of each factor.*
3. *If $n = 2^{x_0}$, then update the representation $\pi := 2^{x_0} :: \pi$ and return π.*
4. *One (or more) of the prime factors will have the largest width: pick one such, p, which appears with exponent x and width W.*
5. *Calculate the exponent y with which p appears in the factorisation of $2^W - 1$.*
6. *If $x \bmod y \neq 0$, n_0 cannot be Mersennary. Return "n_0 is not Mersennary."*
7. *Set $n := n/(2^W - 1)^{x/y}$, and update the representation $\pi := (2^W - 1)^{x/y} :: \pi$.*
8. *Update the prime factorisation of n (using the factorisation of $2^W - 1$).*
9. *If n still has prime factors of width W, then n_0 cannot be Mersennary. Return "n_0 is not Mersennary."*
10. *Otherwise goto step three.*

The algorithm terminates, because there are only finitely many primes in a representation of a given number, and these primes have (possibly fewer) finitely many widths. Steps three to ten are maximally repeated once per width.

The correctness of the algorithm follow from the results in Section 2: If the widest prime in a number has width W, we need to divide by $2^W - 1$ to get rid of that prime. If that does not work because of a mismatch between the power of the prime in the factorisation of the number and the power of the prime in the factorisation of $2^W - 1$ (as with Wieferich primes) then the number, n, cannot be Mersennary. If dividing by $2^W - 1$ enough times to get rid of one prime of width W does not get rid of all the primes of width W, then the number n cannot be Mersennary. Finally, since we in all steps divide by a Mersennary number, if we at any point have a non-Mersennary n, the original n_0 must be non-Mersennary (as we saw in Note 3).

4   Conclusion and Future Work

In this paper we have provided an algorithm (Algorithm 4) for determining whether one can multiply by a given number by cascading $2^k \pm 1$ multipliers, and, if affirmative, which provides some cascade which multiplies by that constant. We have also given algorithms (Algorithms 2 and 3) for turning any cascade into the minimal equivalent cascade of $2^k \pm 1$ multipliers. All in all, one can get from constant to minimal cascade using the algorithms provided in this paper.

As for theoretical results, we have proven that the range of $2^k \pm 1$ multipliers does not include all numbers, not even all small numbers, and, in fact, that infinitely many primes are out of reach. This provides an argument for creating and studying new constant multiplier designs.

Another use of the algorithm for determining minimal cascades can be to compare the $2^k \pm 1$ multiplier cascades to the multiplier circuit design for arbitrary constants presented in [5]. This could be a first step to general algorithm that, for a given constant, could give the smallest multiplier approach. Finally, a design for $2^k \pm 2^l \pm 1$ constant multipliers was also presented in [1]. It is clear that this multiplier family has a larger range than the $2^k \pm 1$ multipliers (*e.g.* $23 = 2^4 + 2^3 - 1$), but it is currently unknown exactly how large the range is.

Acknowledgements. The authors thank the anonymous referees for useful corrections. Michael Kirkedal Thomsen and Holger Bock Axelsen also thank the *Danish Council for Strategic Research* for partially supporting this work through the *MicroPower* research project (http://topps.diku.dk/micropower).

References

1. Axelsen, H.B., Thomsen, M.K.: Garbage-free reversible integer multiplication with constants of the form $2^k \pm 2^l \pm 1$. In: Glück, R., Yokoyama, T. (eds.) RC 2012. LNCS, vol. 7581, pp. 171–182. Springer, Heidelberg (2013)
2. Cuccaro, S.A., Draper, T.G., Kutin, S.A., Moulton, D.P.: A New Quantum Ripple-carry Addition Circuit arXiv:quant-ph/0410184 (2005)
3. Draper, T.G., Kutin, S.A., Rains, E.M., Svore, K.M.: A Logarithmic-Depth Quantum Carry-Lookahead Adder arXiv:quant-ph/0406142 (2008)
4. Fredkin, E., Toffoli, T.: Conservative Logic. International Journal of Theoretical Physics 21(3-4), 219–253 (1982)
5. Mogensen, T.Æ.: Garbage-Free Reversible Constant Multipliers for Arbitrary Integers. In: Dueck, G.W., Miller, D.M. (eds.) RC 2013. LNCS, vol. 7948, pp. 70–83. Springer, Heidelberg (2013)
6. Parvardi, A.H.: Lifting The Exponent, LTE (2011), http://www.artofproblemsolving.com/Resources/Papers/LTE.pdf
7. Thomsen, M.K., Axelsen, H.B.: Parallelization of Reversible Ripple-carry Adders. Parallel Processing Letters 19(1), 205–222 (2009)
8. Toffoli, T.: Reversible Computing. In: de Bakker, J.W., van Leeuwen, J. (eds.) ICALP 1980. LNCS, vol. 85, pp. 632–644. Springer, Heidelberg (1980)
9. Van Rentergem, Y., De Vos, A.: Optimal Design of a Reversible Full Adder. International Journal of Unconventional Computing 1(4), 339–355 (2005)
10. Vedral, V., Barenco, A., Ekert, A.: Quantum Networks for Elementary Arithmetic Operations. Physical Review A 54(1), 147–153 (1996)
11. Zsigmondy, K.: Zur Theorie der Potenzreste. Monatshefte für Mathematik und Physik 3(1), 265–284 (1892)

A   Plus/Minus Representations Up to 201

This appendix provides a table of plus/minus representation lengths and minimal representations for the odd numbers up to 201.

The table contains the number, its length, and a description. If the number is Mersennary, its minimal plus/minus representation is provided. If the number is non-Mersennary, the description contains either a prime of same width or a decomposition of the number into a product of a Mersennary and a non-Mersennary number, $m \cdot n, m \in M, n \notin M$, cf. Note 3.

The big prime of the same width as 197 is split on two lines for space reasons.

Num	Len	Descr.
3	1	3
5	1	5
7	1	7
9	1	9
11	2	$33 \cdot 3^{-1}$
13	2	$65 \cdot 5^{-1}$
15	1	15
17	1	17
19	3	$513 \cdot 9^{-1} \cdot 3^{-1}$
21	2	$3 \cdot 7$
23	NA	89
25	2	5^2
27	2	$3 \cdot 9$
29	NA	113
31	1	31
33	1	33
35	2	$5 \cdot 7$
37	NA	1417
39	3	$65 \cdot 5^{-1} \cdot 3$
41	3	$1025 \cdot 5^{-2}$
43	2	$129 \cdot 3^{-1}$
45	2	$5 \cdot 9$
47	NA	178481
49	2	7^2
51	2	$3 \cdot 17$
53	NA	157
55	3	$33 \cdot 3^{-1} \cdot 5$
57	2	$513 \cdot 9^{-1}$
59	NA	3033169
61	NA	1321
63	1	63
65	1	65
67	NA	20857
69	NA	$3 \cdot 23$
71	NA	122921
73	2	$511 \cdot 7^{-1}$
75	2	$5 \cdot 15$
77	3	$33 \cdot 3^{-1} \cdot 7$
79	NA	121369
81	2	9^2
83	NA	8831418697
85	2	$5 \cdot 17$
87	NA	$3 \cdot 29$
89	NA	23
91	3	$65 \cdot 5^{-1} \cdot 7$
93	2	$3 \cdot 31$
95	4	$513 \cdot 9^{-1} \cdot 3^{-1} \cdot 5$
97	NA	673
99	2	$3 \cdot 33$
101	NA	8101
103	NA	2143
105	2	$7 \cdot 15$
107	NA	28059810762433
109	NA	37
111	NA	$3 \cdot 37$
113	NA	29
115	NA	$5 \cdot 23$
117	3	$65 \cdot 5^{-1} \cdot 9$
119	2	$7 \cdot 17$
121	3	$33^2 \cdot 9^{-1}$
123	4	$1025 \cdot 5^{-2} \cdot 3$
125	3	5^3
127	1	127
129	1	129
131	NA	409891
133	4	$513 \cdot 9^{-1} \cdot 3^{-1} \cdot 7$
135	2	$9 \cdot 15$
137	NA	26317
139	NA	168749965921
141	NA	$3 \cdot 47$
143	3	$33 \cdot 65 \cdot 15^{-1}$
145	NA	$5 \cdot 29$
147	3	$3 \cdot 7^2$
149	NA	593
151	3	$(2^{15} - 1) \cdot 31^{-1} \cdot 7^{-1}$
153	2	$9 \cdot 17$
155	2	$5 \cdot 31$
157	NA	53
159	NA	$3 \cdot 53$
161	NA	$7 \cdot 23$
163	NA	135433
165	2	$5 \cdot 33$
167	NA	57912614113275649087721
169	4	$65^2 \cdot 5^{-2}$
171	2	$513 \cdot 3^{-1}$
173	NA	101653
175	3	$5^2 \cdot 7$
177	NA	$3 \cdot 59$
179	NA	62020897
181	NA	54001
183	NA	$3 \cdot 61$
185	NA	$5 \cdot 37$
187	3	$33 \cdot 3^{-1} \cdot 17$
189	2	$3 \cdot 63$
191	NA	420778751
193	NA	22253377
195	2	$3 \cdot 65$
197	NA	26828803997912886929710867041891989490486893845712448833
199	NA	153649
201	NA	$3 \cdot 67$

Constant-Factor Optimization of Quantum Adders on 2D Quantum Architectures

Mehdi Saeedi, Alireza Shafaei, and Massoud Pedram

Department of Electrical Engineering, University of Southern California,
Los Angeles, CA 90089-2562
{msaeedi,shafaeib,pedram}@usc.edu

Abstract. Quantum arithmetic circuits have practical applications in various quantum algorithms. In this paper, we address quantum addition on 2-dimensional nearest-neighbor architectures based on the work presented by Choi and Van Meter (JETC 2012). To this end, we propose new circuit structures for some basic blocks in the adder, and reduce communication overhead by adding concurrency to consecutive blocks and also by parallel execution of expensive Toffoli gates. The proposed optimizations reduce total depth from $140\sqrt{n} + k_1$ to $92\sqrt{n} + k_2$ for constants k_1, k_2 and affect the computation fidelity considerably.

Keywords: Quantum Adders, 2D Quantum Architectures, Nearest Neighbor Interaction.

1 Introduction

Quantum algorithms are often described in the quantum circuit model of computation, where for a quantum circuit with n qubits, any pairs of qubits can interact. However, current advances in physical quantum technologies can only allow qubit interactions in one-, two-, or three-dimensional spaces. Restricting interactions to only linear dimension results in $O(n)$ overhead. On the other hand, working with 2D (or 3D) quantum architectures where each qubit can interact with 4 (or 6) neighboring qubits provides more flexibility.

For a given quantum circuit C one can construct an interaction graph $G_C = (V_C, E_C)$, the nodes of which represent qubits in C with edges between them when a gate in C involves the related qubits. Additionally, the architecture (or fabric) of a quantum computing system can be described by a simple connected graph $G_Q = (V_Q, E_Q)$ where vertices V_Q represent qubits and edges E_Q represent adjacent qubit pairs that gates can be applied on [1]. Accordingly, the problem of mapping a quantum circuit C with arbitrary interactions between qubits onto a quantum architecture with limited interaction distance can be mapped to the problem of embedding graph G_C into graph G_Q.

In general, the graph embedding problem is NP-hard. However, optimal embedding methods with polynomial time complexities for several classes of graphs have been proposed [2]. In [3], the concept of *dilation* in graph embedding has

G.W. Dueck and D.M. Miller (Eds.): RC 2013, LNCS 7948, pp. 58–69, 2013.
© Springer-Verlag Berlin Heidelberg 2013

been applied to find a depth lower bound for a quantum circuit after embedding. In this case, dilation is defined as the maximum distance between adjacent nodes of the graph after embedding. Working with proven properties of log-depth binary trees and considering the fact that log-depth quantum addition circuits exist, Choi and Van Meter [3] showed that the depth lower bound of the exact quantum addition circuit on a k-dimensional quantum architecture is $\Omega(\sqrt[k]{n})$. In [4], the authors examined the minimum overhead in depth for emulating a circuit C by a circuit C' subject to the constraints imposed by the interaction constraints and showed that this overhead is $O(n)$ for 1D, $O(\sqrt{n})$ for 2D, $O(\log^2 n)$ or $O(\log n)$ (depending on the approach) for hypercube.

Exploring an efficient realization of a given quantum algorithm or quantum circuit for a restricted architecture has been followed by a number of researchers during the recent years. Physical implementations of the quantum Fourier transform (QFT) [5, 6], Shor's factorization algorithm [7–9], quantum error correction [10], and general reversible circuits [11] for 1D/2D architectures have been explored in the past. Worst-case synthesis cost of a general/Boolean unitary matrix under the 1D restriction has been discussed in [12–15]. In [16–18] heuristic methods for converting an arbitrary quantum circuit to its equivalent circuit on 1D architectures have been proposed.

Quantum adder and its modular version have applications in different quantum algorithms including Shor's factoring algorithm. In [19], a quantum adder with $\Theta(\sqrt{n})$ depth on 2D quantum architectures was proposed which has $140\sqrt{n}-72$ depth, in terms of one- and two-qubit quantum gates. Asymptotically, the depth of the proposed adder is optimal. However, constant-factor optimization is possible and in fact desirable. Besides the effect of reducing circuit size/depth on physical realization, any additional gate in the circuit longest path can reduce circuit fidelity to some extent. Based on the analysis done in [20] for fault-tolerant error correction with a concatenated 7-qubit CSS code [21], nearest-neighbour communication overhead results in 175x reduction in error threshold. Improving error threshold is costly and may include using a more sophisticated quantum control protocol to have gates with higher fidelities or applying a more robust error correction code. Therefore, reducing unnecessary communication overhead for a useful quantum computation is vital. Because of the effect of addition on e.g., modular multiplication and modular exponentiation circuits [9, 22, 23], reducing communication overhead for quantum adder by circuit optimization — the focus of this work — is of particular interest.

In this paper, we show how $140\sqrt{n}+$const depth in [19] can be further improved to $92\sqrt{n}+$const. For this purpose, we reconsider the basic blocks in the suggested quantum adder and introduce some constant-factor optimizations in communication overhead in different stages. To physically implement a given circuit, one needs to decompose all gates into primitive one- and two-qubit gates. To decompose a 3-qubit Toffoli ($\mathcal{T}$) gate, we use Clifford+T gates which are universal and have fault-tolerant (FT) implementation [21]. Fig. 1 shows the decomposition of the Toffoli gate into one- and two-qubit gates. To consider depth, we report circuit depth in terms of single-qubit, CNOT ($\mathcal{C}$) and SWAP ($\mathcal{S}$) gates.

The rest of this paper is organized as follows. In Section 2, the method in [19] is discussed. We introduce the reduction techniques in Section 3. The result of the proposed reductions is analyzed in Section 4 and Section 5. We finally conclude the paper in Section 6.

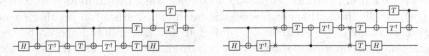

Fig. 1. Decomposition of the Toffoli gate into one-qubit and six CNOT gates [24] and the implementation with adjacent qubits

2   Quantum Addition on 2D Architectures

In this section, we describe the circuit structure in [19] for quantum addition on 2D architectures. For an n-qubit quantum circuit, the method in [19] arranges the qubits in $\sqrt{n} \times \sqrt{n}$ arrays where each qubit can interact with its four neighboring qubits with no additional cost. Additionally, the circuit was divided into 3 phases which are executed sequentially. In the first phase, ripple-carry addition is performed on the first column, and carry-lookahead addition is performed on the other $\sqrt{n} - 1$ columns. In the second phase, carry propagation is performed between columns, and finally in phase 3 carry generation and summation are performed.

In the first phase, after using a half-adder and $\sqrt{n} - 1$ full-adders output carries $c_2, \cdots c_{\sqrt{n}+1}$ will be available. It is done in $32\sqrt{n} - 17$ unit-time steps in [19]. The carry-lookahead addition in other columns produces

$$g_{k\sqrt{n}+j} = a_{k\sqrt{n}+j} \cdot b_{k\sqrt{n}+j} \tag{1}$$

$$p_{k\sqrt{n}+j} = a_{k\sqrt{n}+j} \oplus b_{k\sqrt{n}+j} \tag{2}$$

for $1 \leq k \leq \sqrt{n} - 1$ and $1 \leq j \leq \sqrt{n}$. After computing g_i and p_i values in all columns in parallel, $G[i,j]$ and $P[i,j]$ are computed in serial based on (3) and (4) for $1 \leq k \leq \sqrt{n} - 1$, and $2 \leq j \leq \sqrt{n}$ where $G[k\sqrt{n}+1, k\sqrt{n}+1] = g_{k\sqrt{n}+1}$ and $P[k\sqrt{n}+1, k\sqrt{n}+1] = p_{k\sqrt{n}+1}$. This part takes $34\sqrt{n} - 19$ time steps in [19]. Accordingly, the first phase in [19] results in $34\sqrt{n} - 19$ time steps.

$$G[k\sqrt{n}+1, k\sqrt{n}+j] = g_{k\sqrt{n}+j} \oplus p_{k\sqrt{n}+j} \cdot G[k\sqrt{n}+1, k\sqrt{n}+j-1] \tag{3}$$

$$P[k\sqrt{n}+1, k\sqrt{n}+j] = p_{k\sqrt{n}+j} \cdot P[k\sqrt{n}+1, k\sqrt{n}+j-1] \tag{4}$$

In the second phase, column-level carries are computed as shown in (5) for $1 \leq k \leq \sqrt{n} - 1$ in $18\sqrt{n} - 18$ time steps.

$$c_{(k+1)\sqrt{n}+1} = G[k\sqrt{n}+1, (k+1)\sqrt{n}] \oplus c_{k\sqrt{n}+1} \cdot P[k\sqrt{n}+1, (k+1)\sqrt{n}] \tag{5}$$

Table 1. Basic blocks in 2D adder [19] and their depths in terms of unit-cost gates. The last term (i.e., 3) in total depth represents 2 NOTs and one CNOT gate used to construct the final output in [19].

Name	#steps: gate sequence	Circuit
H, T, CNOT (C), SWAP ($\mathcal{S}$)	1	
Toffoli ($\mathcal{T}$(a,b,0))	14: 2 $\mathcal{S}$+ 12 1-qubit	H(0)C(b,0)T†(0)$\mathcal{S}$(b,0)C(a,b)T(b)C(0,b) T†(b)C(a,b)$\mathcal{S}$(b,0)T(b)T†(0)C(a,b)H(0) T(a)T†(b)C(a,b)
Half-adder(a,b,0)	15: 1 $\mathcal{T}$+ 1 $\mathcal{C}$	$\mathcal{T}$(a,b,0)$\mathcal{T}$(a,b)
Full-adder(c,a,b,0)	32: 2 $\mathcal{T}$+ 2 $\mathcal{C}$+ 2 $\mathcal{S}$	$\mathcal{T}$(a,b,0)$\mathcal{T}$(a,b)$\mathcal{S}$(c,a)$\mathcal{T}$(a,b,0)$\mathcal{T}$(a,b)$\mathcal{S}$(c,a)
g,p(a,b,0)	15: 1 $\mathcal{T}$+ 1 $\mathcal{C}$	$\mathcal{T}$(a,b,0)$\mathcal{T}$(a,b)
G,P(P,G,a,p,g,0)	34: 2 $\mathcal{T}$+ 6 $\mathcal{S}$	$\mathcal{S}$(G,a)$\mathcal{S}$(P,G)T(a,p,g)$\mathcal{S}$(G,a)$\mathcal{S}$(g,0)T(a,p,g) $\mathcal{S}$(G,a)$\mathcal{S}$(P,G)$\mathcal{S}$(G,a)
Column_carry(P,G,C)	18: 1 $\mathcal{T}$+ 4 $\mathcal{S}$	$\mathcal{S}$(P,G)$\mathcal{T}$(C,G,P)$\mathcal{S}$(G,C)$\mathcal{S}$(P,G)$\mathcal{S}$(G,C)
Carry(P,G,a,p,C)	18: 1 $\mathcal{T}$+ 4 $\mathcal{S}$	$\mathcal{S}$(P,G)$\mathcal{S}$(p,C)$\mathcal{S}$(a,p)$\mathcal{T}$(a,G,P)$\mathcal{S}$(G,a)$\mathcal{S}$(P,G)
Carry1(p,g,c)	16: 1 $\mathcal{T}$+ 2 $\mathcal{S}$	$\mathcal{S}$(g,c)$\mathcal{T}$(p,g,c)$\mathcal{S}$(p,g)
SUM(c,P,a,p)	5 : 1 $\mathcal{C}$+ 4 $\mathcal{S}$	$\mathcal{S}$(c,P)$\mathcal{S}$(P,a)$\mathcal{T}$(a,p)$\mathcal{S}$(P,a)$\mathcal{S}$(c,P)
SUM1(c,a,p)	3 : 1 $\mathcal{C}$+ 2 $\mathcal{S}$	$\mathcal{S}$(c,a)$\mathcal{T}$(a,p)$\mathcal{S}$(c,a)
SUM2(p,c)	1 : 1 $\mathcal{C}$	$\mathcal{T}$(c,p)
phase 1	$34\sqrt{n} - 19$: g,p + $(\sqrt{n} - 1)$G,P	
phase 2	$18\sqrt{n} - 18$: $(\sqrt{n} - 1)$ Column_carry	
phase 3	$18\sqrt{n} + 1$: $(\sqrt{n} - 1)$ Carry + Carry1 + SUM1	
clearing ancillae	$70\sqrt{n} - 39$: phase 1 + phase 2 + phase 3 - SUM1	
total depth	$140\sqrt{n} - 72$: phase 1 + phase 2 + phase 3 + clearing ancillae + 3	

In phase 3 output carries are calculated sequentially as (6) for $1 \leq k \leq \sqrt{n} - 1$ and $j = \sqrt{n} - 1, ..., 1$.

$$c_{k\sqrt{n}+j+1} = G[k\sqrt{n} + 1, k\sqrt{n} + j] \oplus c_{k\sqrt{n}+1} \cdot P[k\sqrt{n} + 1, k\sqrt{n} + j] \qquad (6)$$

Finally, addition outputs are calculated as shown in (7) for $1 \leq k \leq \sqrt{n} - 1$ and $1 \leq j \leq \sqrt{n}$. Altogether, operations in phase 3 can be performed in $18\sqrt{n} + 1$ time steps.

$$s_{k\sqrt{n}+j} = a_{k\sqrt{n}+j} \oplus b_{k\sqrt{n}+j} \oplus c_{k\sqrt{n}+j} \qquad (7)$$

Considering the three subcircuits for phase 1, phase 2, and phase 3 in sequence leads to $70\sqrt{n} - 36$ time steps in [19]. Applying the inverse circuit to clear ancillae leads to $140\sqrt{n} - 72$ time steps for the complete adder.

Based on the equations (1)-(7), Table 1 reports circuit depth in different blocks. In this table, we used the same notation in [19] for circuit blocks — g,p to compute g_i, p_i values in (1) and (2); G,P to compute $G[i,j]$ and $P[i,j]$ values in (3) and (4); Column_carry to compute column-level carries in (5); Carry & Carry1 to compute carries in (6); and SUM, SUM1 & SUM2 to compute final outputs in (7).

3   The Proposed 2D Adder

In this section, we revise the basic blocks in [19] and introduce additional parallelism in various parts to reduce circuit depth. Basically, the proposed optimizations are based on (1) new circuit structures for CARRY and SUM basic blocks

(2) reducing communication overhead in Column_carry, (3) parallel execution of expensive Toffoli gates in G,P blocks as well as in Full-adders, and (4) reducing interaction overhead by adding concurrency to consecutive blocks.

3.1   New Circuits

Working with the same circuit structures in [19] for Half-adder, g,p, and G,P blocks as reported in Table 1, we define several new structures for the other blocks.

- **Full-adder**: The first $\mathcal{T}$ and $\mathcal{C}$ gates in the Full-adder blocks in [19] can be executed in parallel with the gates in the Half-adder circuit. This saves one $\mathcal{T}$ and one $\mathcal{C}$ for all $\sqrt{n} - 1$ Full-adders.
- **Column_Carry**: Fig. 4 shows the new structure of Column_Carry block. In this circuit, $c[k\sqrt{n}+1]$ is from the previous column (e.g., c_4 in Fig. 2). After the computation, the new carry, e.g., c_7, is moved down, to be used by the next Column_Carry block. The previous carry, e.g., c_4 is placed near to the Carry module. This new structure saves 1 SWAP gate.
- **Carry**: Fig. 5 shows the new structure for Carry block. Since $c[k\sqrt{n}+1]$ is required to compute all carries in different rows, $c[k\sqrt{n}+1]$ is moved up in this figure. On the other hand, the generated carry is required to compute sum values, and hence is moved down. This new circuit uses 5 SWAP gates (vs. 4 in [19]).
- **SUM**: Applying the proposed circuit for Carry results in adjacent $c[k\sqrt{n}+j+1]$ and $p[k\sqrt{n}+j+1]$ values (see Fig. 5). Based on (7) sum outputs can be computed by a single CNOT gate. This saves 4 SWAP gates in [19]. In order to construct s_i values on b_i qubits, one needs to add one SWAP gate $\mathcal{S}(p[k\sqrt{n}+1], c[k\sqrt{n}+1])$. However, this SWAP gate can be removed because of an identical SWAP gate in the Carry circuit. Accordingly, we define another circuit block Carry1 with excluding the SWAP on $c[k\sqrt{n}+1]$ and $P[k\sqrt{n}+1][k\sqrt{n}+j]$ (for $j=1$) qubits. We do not need to use SUM1 and SUM2 blocks in the proposed 2D adder structure.

3.2   Reducing Communication Overhead

To use adjacent gates in the 2D quantum adder, we use a set of SWAP gates inside each circuit block. The added SWAP gates are used for communication between those gates required for the computation. In other words, the added SWAP gates are not required for the computation, and should be reduced as much as possible. Independent optimization of different blocks can reduce communication overhead inside each subcircuit, but has no view about the neighboring subcircuits. In this section, we consider consecutive circuit blocks to reduce communication overhead further. Note that the optimizations given in this section are based on the new circuit blocks given in Section 3.1.

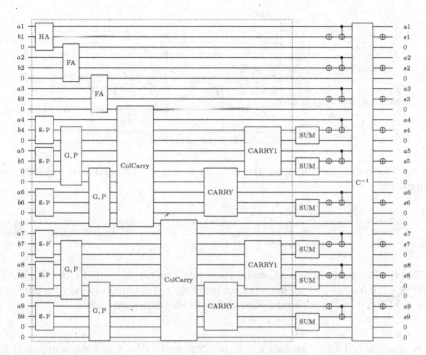

Fig. 2. The revised block diagram of a 2D 9-bit adder in [19] based on the blocks used in this paper. The critical path in this circuit is g,p--→G,P--→ColCarry--→ColCarry--→CARRY--→CARRY1--→SUM. The C^{-1} block is the reverse of the circuit shown in the dashed box. This reverse circuit with the NOTs and CNOTs shown are applied to clear ancillae in [19]. Except for ColCarry (Column_carry), the number of inputs and outputs for other modules are the same as the ones shown in this figure. In Column_carry, the number of inputs/outputs is 3 — i.e., the first line and the last two lines are actual inputs and outputs. Note that these three lines are neighbor in the 2D layout. The qubit placement for this 2D grid and their values during the computation (up to clearing ancillae) are given in Fig. 3.

- **G,P ⇒ Carry:** Reconsider (3), (4), and (6) and note that the result of Column_carry in (5), i.e., $c[k\sqrt{n}+1]$, is constructed on the last qubit in the Carry block (see Fig. 4 and Fig. 5). Fig. 6 shows the blocks in sequence. To simplify the circuit, note that the last three SWAP gates in G,P can be moved to right. Next, the resulting circuit can be reconstructed as shown in Fig. 6(b). Accordingly, three SWAP gates in each G,P block can be saved. Fig. 7 shows the new circuits for Carry and Carry1. Note that some of G,P blocks are directly connected to the Carry (or Carry1) blocks without any interaction with Column_carry blocks. For such cases, we can apply the same mechanism.
- **G,P ⇒ G,P:** Each G,P block constructs two outputs based on (4) and (3) where $G[k\sqrt{n}+1, k\sqrt{n}+j]$ depends on $G[k\sqrt{n}+1, k\sqrt{n}+j-1]$ and $P[k\sqrt{n}+1, k\sqrt{n}+j]$ depends on $P[k\sqrt{n}+1, k\sqrt{n}+j-1]$. Since $G[k\sqrt{n}+1, k\sqrt{n}+j]$

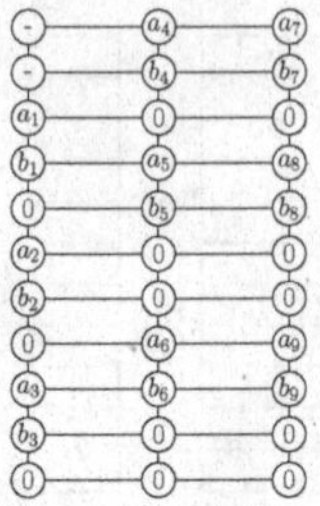

-	a_4	a_7
-	b_4, p_4, s_4	b_7, p_7, s_7
a_1	$0, g_4, c_4$	$0, g_7, c_7$
b_1, s_1	a_5	a_8
$0, c_2$	b_5, p_5, s_5	b_8, p_8, s_8
a_2	$0, g_5, P[4,5], c_4, c_5$	$0, g_8, P[7,8], c_7, c_8$
b_2, s_2	$0, G[4,5], P[4,5]$	$0, G[7,8], P[7,8]$
$0, c_3$	a_6	a_9
a_3	b_6, p_6, s_6	b_9, p_9, s_9
b_3, s_3	$0, g_6, P[4,6], c_4, c_6$	$0, g_9, P[7,9], c_7, c_9$
$0, c_4$	$0, G[4,6], c_7$	$0, G[7,9], c_{10}$

Fig. 3. The qubit placement for the 2D grid in Fig. 2 and their values during the computation

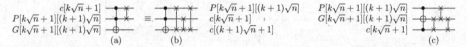

Fig. 4. (a) Circuit structure for Column_carry based on (5). Note that $c[(k-1)\sqrt{n}+1]$ and $P[(k-1)\sqrt{n}+1][k\sqrt{n}]$ are not adjacent (see Fig. 2). (b) Circuit in (a) with adjacent gates. (c) Circuit in (b) with relabelled qubits to show adjacent qubits.

is constructed first, we can use it to construct $G[k\sqrt{n}+1, k\sqrt{n}+j+1]$ in parallel to construction of $P[k\sqrt{n}+1, k\sqrt{n}+j-1]$. This can save one Toffoli and one SWAP. Fig. 8 shows the result of this optimization.

4   Depth Analysis

In this section, we analyze the circuit depth of a 2D n-bit quantum adder based on the circuit structures proposed for each block.

- **Phase 1 — Half-adder+Full-adder:** We can execute Half-adder and the first two gates ($\mathcal{T}+\mathcal{C}$) in all Full-adders in parallel. This results in $1\mathcal{T}+1\mathcal{C}+(\sqrt{n}-1)(2\mathcal{S}+1\mathcal{C}+1\mathcal{T})$ time steps.
- **Phase 1 — g,p+G,P:** Each g,p block includes one Toffoli gate and one CNOT gate. Except for the first G,P block, the other $\sqrt{n}-2$ G,P blocks include 3 SWAPs and 1 Toffoli. The first G,P block includes two Toffoli and two SWAP gates. Circuit depth can be calculated as $(1\mathcal{T}+1\mathcal{C})+(2\mathcal{T}+2\mathcal{S})+(\sqrt{n}-2)(3\mathcal{S}+1\mathcal{T})$.

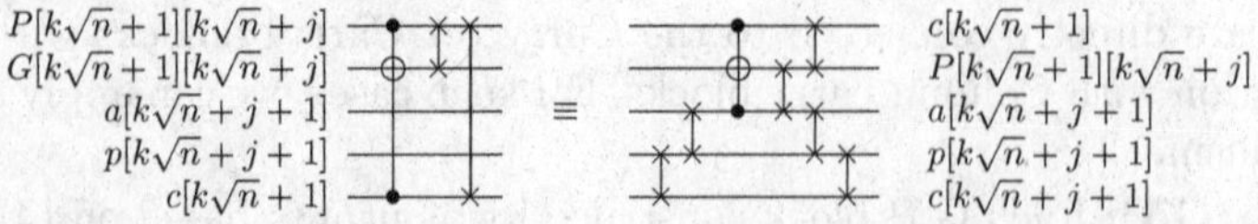

Fig. 5. Circuit structure for Carry based on (6). Inputs $a[k\sqrt{n}+j+1]$ and $p[k\sqrt{n}+j+1]$ are not used in the computation.

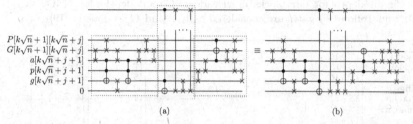

$P[k\sqrt{n}+1][k\sqrt{n}+j]$
$G[k\sqrt{n}+1][k\sqrt{n}+j]$
$a[k\sqrt{n}+j+1]$
$p[k\sqrt{n}+j+1]$
$g[k\sqrt{n}+j+1]$
0

(a)   (b)

Fig. 6. (a) G,P, Column_carry, and Carry blocks in cascade. The three rightmost SWAP gates in G,P can be merged with gates in the Carry block to construct a new circuit shown in (b).

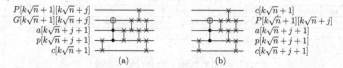

$P[k\sqrt{n}+1][k\sqrt{n}+j]$
$G[k\sqrt{n}+1][k\sqrt{n}+j]$
$a[k\sqrt{n}+j+1]$
$p[k\sqrt{n}+j+1]$
$c[k\sqrt{n}+1]$
(a)   (b)
$c[k\sqrt{n}+1]$
$P[k\sqrt{n}+1][k\sqrt{n}+j]$
$a[k\sqrt{n}+j+1]$
$p[k\sqrt{n}+j+1]$
$c[k\sqrt{n}+j+1]$

Fig. 7. New circuit structures for Carry (a) and Carry1 (b) based on the optimization shown in Fig 7. Note that the first SWAP gate can be executed in parallel with gates in the previous block (see Fig. 7).

- **Phase 2 — Column_carry:** There are $\sqrt{n}-1$ Column_carry blocks in cascade. This results in $\sqrt{n}-1(1\mathcal{T}+3\mathcal{S})$ time steps.
- **Phase 3 — Carry + SUM:** There are $\sqrt{n}-2$ Carry blocks followed by one Carry1 block and one SUM block. Therefore, circuit depth is $(\sqrt{n}-2)(1\mathcal{T}+4\mathcal{S})+(3\mathcal{S}+1\mathcal{T})+1\mathcal{C}$.

Table 2 reports circuit depth for each component and the total depth in the proposed 2D quantum adder. As can be seen in this table, circuit depth is improved by a factor of $\frac{26}{35}$ (i.e., %24).

In [25], a new circuit for Peres with depth=5C+3 has been proposed (Fig. 10(a)). After inserting one CNOT (to have Toffoli) and two SWAP gates to have adjacent gates, one can use the new circuit with depth=6C+2$\mathcal{S}$+4 in order to further optimize the proposed 2D adder. Note that in [25], a circuit structure for Toffoli gate with depth=6C+2 has been proposed too, Fig. 9. However, working

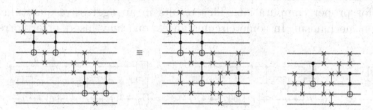

Fig. 8. Construction of $G[k\sqrt{n}+1,k\sqrt{n}+j+1]$ can be done in parallel to construction of $P[k\sqrt{n}+1,k\sqrt{n}+j-1]$ in two consecutive G,P blocks. The right circuit shows the new circuit structure for G,P (except for the first G,P block).

Table 2. Circuit depth for our blocks in 2D adder. Circuit depths for CNOT ($\mathcal{C}$), SWAP ($\mathcal{S}$), and Toffoli ($\mathcal{T}$) gates are considered as 1, 1, and 14 as done in [19].

Block	Circuit	Ours	[19]
Half-adder	$1\mathcal{T}+1\mathcal{C}$	15	15
Full-adder	$2\mathcal{S}+1\mathcal{C}+1\mathcal{T}$	17	32
g,p	$1\mathcal{T}+1\mathcal{C}$	15	15
G,P (first)	$2\mathcal{T}+2\mathcal{S}$	30	34
G,P (others)	$3\mathcal{S}+1\mathcal{T}$	17	34
Column_carry	$1\mathcal{T}+3\mathcal{S}$	17	18
Carry	$1\mathcal{T}+4\mathcal{S}$	18	18
Carry1	$3\mathcal{S}+1\mathcal{T}$	17	18
SUM	$1\mathcal{C}$	1	5
Phase1-1	$1\mathcal{T}+1\mathcal{C}+(\sqrt{n}-1)(2\mathcal{S}+1\mathcal{C}+1\mathcal{T})$	$17\sqrt{n}-2$	$32\sqrt{n}-17$
Phase1-2	$(1\mathcal{T}+1\mathcal{C})+(2(\mathcal{T}+2\mathcal{S})+(\sqrt{n}-2)(3\mathcal{S}+1\mathcal{T})$	$17\sqrt{n}+11$	$34\sqrt{n}-19$
Phase2	$(\sqrt{n}-1)(1\mathcal{T}+3\mathcal{S})$	$17\sqrt{n}-17$	$18\sqrt{n}-18$
Phase3	$(\sqrt{n}-2)(1\mathcal{T}+4\mathcal{S})+(3\mathcal{S}+1\mathcal{T})+1\mathcal{C}$	$18\sqrt{n}-18$	$18\sqrt{n}+1$
clearing ancillae	Phase1-2+Phase2+Phase3-SUM	$52\sqrt{n}-24$	$70\sqrt{n}-39$
2D Adder	Phase1-2+Phase2+Phase3+clearing ancillae+3	$104\sqrt{n}-46$	$140\sqrt{n}-72$

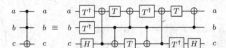

Fig. 9. Toffoli decomposition with depth 6C+2 [25]

with Peres gate results in a more compact circuit in terms of the number of SWAP gates. Following this path results in depth=$92\sqrt{n}$+const for the proposed 2D quantum adder. Table 3 compares circuit depth based on different costs for Toffoli and SWAP gates.

5   Error Correction

To protect quantum information from errors due to e.g., noise or decoherence, quantum error correction (QEC) should be used in any large-scale quantum computation. In the recent years, various models for QEC have been proposed [21]. A common technique, known as concatenated quantum code, is to encode a logical qubit into the state of several physical qubits (e.g., 7 in Steane code and 9 in Bacon-Shor code [21], both for one level of concatenation).

Let assume each unitary operation should be followed by quantum error correction for proper computation. This results in an aggressive quantum error correction mechanism. In some circumstances, one may insert error correction

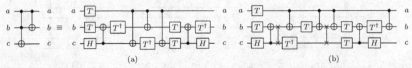

Fig. 10.   (a) Peres decompositions with depth 5C+3 [25], (b) Toffoli with adjacent gates based on Peres decomposition (depth=6C+2$\mathcal{S}$+4)

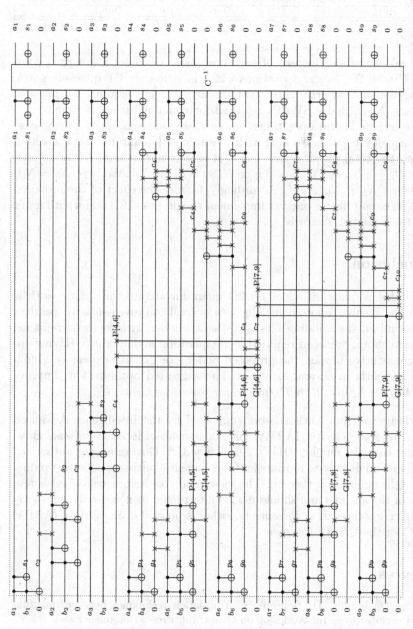

Fig. 11. A 9-bit adder based on the proposed blocks. Carry, $G_{i,j}$, p_i, and g_i values are shown in this figure. The C^{-1} block is the reverse of the circuit shown in the dashed box applied with the NOTs and CNOTs shown to clear ancillae. All gates use adjacent gates in the 2D layout. For qubit locations see the table in Fig. 3.

Table 3. Circuit depth for the proposed adder and the one in [19] considering different costs for Toffoli and SWAP gates

$\mathcal{T}$-depth=14,$\mathcal{S}$-depth=1		$\mathcal{T}$-depth=14,$\mathcal{S}$-depth=3		$\mathcal{T}$-depth=12,$\mathcal{S}$-depth=3		$\mathcal{T}$-depth=12,$\mathcal{S}$-depth=1	
Ours	[19]	Ours	[19]	Ours	[19]	Ours	[19]
$104\sqrt{n}$	$140\sqrt{n}$	$144\sqrt{n}$	$176\sqrt{n}$	$132\sqrt{n}$	$160\sqrt{n}$	$92\sqrt{n}$	$124\sqrt{n}$

after several operations, instead of each operation. Consider a quantum computation U with N_U logical operations which include only FT quantum gates. Moreover, assume that error correction for each FT gate requires N_E physical instructions. N_E includes SWAPs required for communication. Normally, N_E differs for various logical operations; however, we can consider the worst-case value among all FT gates. Working with concatenated quantum error correction techniques, the total physical gate count at concatenation level L can be estimated as $N_L = N_{L-1} + N_{L-1} \times N_E$ or $N_L \approx N_{L-1} \times N_E$. We have $N_0 = N_U$, and therefore, $N_L = N_U(N_E)^L$. Accordingly, besides the effect of the proposed approach on circuit depth, one can implement the proposed 2D adder with fewer gates — the reduction factor is $\frac{24}{35}$.

6   Conclusion

We considered a quantum adder on 2D quantum architectures. Our work is based on the results reported in [19] with several improvements. In particular, we optimized the building blocks of the 2D adder with focus on reducing the communication overhead required in 2D quantum architectures. Having optimized consecutive blocks, the proposed adder can execute expensive Toffoli gates concurrently in several locations. The suggested optimizations improve depth=$140\sqrt{n} + k_1$ in [19] to $92\sqrt{n} + k_2$ for constants k_1 and k_2.

Acknowledgements. Authors were supported by the Intelligence Advanced Research Projects Activity (IARPA) via Department of Interior National Business Center contract number D11PC20165. The U.S. Government is authorized to reproduce and distribute reprints for Governmental purposes notwithstanding any copyright annotation thereon. The views and conclusions contained herein are those of the authors and should not be interpreted as necessarily representing the official policies or endorsements, either expressed or implied, of IARPA, DoI/NBC, or the U.S. Government.

References

1. Cheung, D., Maslov, D., Severini, S.: Translation techniques between quantum circuit architectures. In: Workshop on Quant. Inf. Proc. (December 2007)
2. Díaz, J., Petit, J., Serna, M.J.: A survey of graph layout problems. ACM Comput. Surv. 34(3), 313–356 (2002)
3. Choi, B.-S., Van Meter, R.: On the effect of quantum interaction distance on quantum addition circuits. J. Emerg. Technol. Comput. Syst. 7(3), 11(1-17) (2011)

4. Beals, R., et al.: Efficient distributed quantum computing arXiv:1207.2307v2 (2012)
5. Takahashi, Y., Kunihiro, N., Ohta, K.: The quantum Fourier transform on a linear nearest neighbor architecture. Quant. Inf. Comput. 7, 383–391 (2007)
6. Maslov, D.: Linear depth stabilizer and quantum Fourier transformation circuits with no auxiliary qubits in finite neighbor quantum architectures. Phys. Rev. A 76 (2007)
7. Fowler, A.G., Devitt, S.J., Hollenberg, L.: Implementation of Shor's algorithm on a linear nearest neighbour qubit array. Quant. Inf. Comput. 4, 237–245 (2004)
8. Kutin, S.A.: Shor's algorithm on a nearest-neighbor machine. In: Asian Conf. on Quant. Inf. Sci. (2007)
9. Pham, P., Svore, K.M.: A 2D nearest-neighbor quantum architecture for factoring arXiv:1207.6655 (2012)
10. Fowler, A.G., Hill, C.D., Hollenberg, L.C.L.: Quantum error correction on linear nearest neighbor qubit arrays. Phys. Rev. A 69, 042314.1–042314.4 (2004)
11. Arabzadeh, M., Saheb Zamani, M., Sedighi, M., Saeedi, M.: Depth-optimized reversible circuit synthesis. Quant. Inf. Proc. 12(4), 1677–1699 (2013)
12. Möttönen, M., Vartiainen, J.J.: Decompositions of general quantum gates. In: Trends in Quant. Comput. Research, Ch. 7. NOVA Publishers, New York (2006)
13. Shende, V.V., Bullock, S.S., Markov, I.L.: Synthesis of quantum-logic circuits. IEEE Trans. CAD 25(6), 1000–1010 (2006)
14. Saeedi, M., Arabzadeh, M., Saheb Zamani, M., Sedighi, M.: Block-based quantum-logic synthesis. Quant. Inf. Comput. 11(3-4), 0262–0277 (2011)
15. Saeedi, M., Saheb Zamani, M., Sedighi, M., Sasanian, Z.: Reversible circuit synthesis using a cycle-based approach. J. Emerg. Technol. Comput. 6(4), 13(1–26) (2010)
16. Saeedi, M., Wille, R., Drechsler, R.: Synthesis of quantum circuits for linear nearest neighbor architectures. Quant. Inf. Proc. 10(3), 355–377 (2011)
17. Hirata, Y., Nakanishi, M., Yamashita, S., Nakashima, Y.: An efficient conversion of quantum circuits to a linear nearest neighbor architecture. Quant. Inf. Comput. 11(1-2), 0142–0166 (2011)
18. Shafaei, A., Saeedi, M., Pedram, M.: Optimization of quantum circuits for interaction distance in linear nearest neighbor architectures. In: Design Autom. Conf. (2013)
19. Choi, B.-S., Van Meter, R.: A $\sqrt{n}$-depth quantum adder on the 2D NTC quantum computer architecture. J. Emerg. Technol. Comput. Syst. 8(3), 24(1-22) (2012)
20. Szkopek, T., et al.: Threshold error penalty for fault-tolerant quantum computation with nearest neighbor communication. IEEE Trans. Nano. 5(1), 42–49 (2006)
21. Nielsen, M., Chuang, I.: Quantum Computation and Quantum Information. Cambridge Univ. Press (2000)
22. Markov, I.L., Saeedi, M.: Constant-optimized quantum circuits for modular multiplication and exponentiation. Quant. Info. Comput. 12(5-6), 361–394 (2012)
23. Markov, I.L., Saeedi, M.: Faster quantum number factoring via circuit synthesis. Phys. Rev. A 87, 012310 (2013)
24. Shende, V.V., Markov, I.L.: On the CNOT-cost of TOFFOLI gates. Quant. Inf. Comput. 9(5-6), 461–486 (2009)
25. Amy, M., Maslov, D., Mosca, M., Rötteler, M.: A meet-in-the-middle algorithm for fast synthesis of depth-optimal quantum circuits. IEEE Trans. CAD arXiv:1206.0758v3 (2013)

Garbage-Free Reversible Constant Multipliers
for Arbitrary Integers

Torben Ægidius Mogensen

DIKU, University of Copenhagen
Universitetsparken 5, DK-2100 Copenhagen O, Denmark
torbenm@diku.dk

Abstract. We present a method for constructing reversible circuitry for multi-plying integers by arbitrary integer constants. The method is based on Mealy machines and gives circuits whose size are (in the worst case) linear in the size of the constant. This makes the method unsuitable for large constants, but gives quite compact circuits for small constants. The circuits use no garbage or ancillary lines.

1 Introduction

In [2], de Vos presents reversible circuitry for integer linear transformations. In one of the instances, multiplication of a number by 5 is needed, and in order to achieve this, de Vos copied the number, shifted and added. The shifted copy of the number became part of the output as *garbage bits*, which is undesirable. To remedy this [1] modified a ripple-carry adder so it can perform multiplications by constants of the form $2^n \pm 1$ (using multiplication by 5 as an example) without producing garbage. The method is not easily generalised to other numbers except by using a pipeline of several such multipliers (and their inverses). For example, multiplication by 19 can be done by multiplying by 513 and dividing by 9 and 3 (all of which are of the form $2^n \pm 1$). This doesn't generalise to all odd numbers. For example, 23 can not be written as a fraction where the enumerator and denominator are both product of numbers of the form $2^n \pm 1$. To handle more constants, the authors extended their method to also handle constants of the form $2^n \pm 2^m \pm 1$ by modifying a three-input adder. While this extension increases the number of possible constant multipliers, it is not clear that all constants are within reach of their method.

We propose a way of making compact multipliers for arbitrary integer multipliers by simulating state machines, specifically Mealy machines. This leads to very compact multipliers garbage-free for small constants. Additionally, these circuits use no garbage or ancillary lines.

2 Mealy Machines

A Mealy machine [5,7] is a finite-state automaton where each state transition both reads and writes a symbol. Huffman [4] studied reversible (loss-less) Mealy machines, i.e, Mealy machines where the transition relation is reversible: Knowing the current state

G.W. Dueck and D.M. Miller (Eds.): RC 2013, LNCS 7948, pp. 70–83, 2013.
© Springer-Verlag Berlin Heidelberg 2013

and the previous output bit is enough to find the previous state and the previous input bit. As an example, the reversible Mealy machine in Figure 1 reads the bits of a binary number in little-endian order and outputs the number multiplied by 5 as a binary number in little-endian form – assuming there are at least two leading zeros in the input number, so the final state is state 0. As an example, the input sequence 10100 (representing 5 in little-endian notation) gives the sequence of transitions $0 \rightarrow_1^1 2 \rightarrow_0^0 1 \rightarrow_0^1 3 \rightarrow_1^0 1 \rightarrow_1^0 0$ which produces the output sequence 10011, which is little-endian for 25.[1]

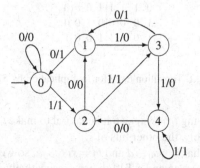

Fig. 1. Mealy machine for multiplication by 5

The state in the Mealy machine represents a carry with a value between 0 and 4, so given state s and input bit a, the next state is $t = (s + 5a)/2$ and the output bit is $b = (s + 5a)\%2$, where / and % are integer division and remainder operators. This, obviously, generalises to arbitrary multiplication factors yielding an n-state machine for multiplication by n. For odd factors, this is the minimal number of states. Even factors can be decomposed into an odd factor and a power of two, the latter of which is just a bit shift. So we will look only at odd factors.

The Mealy machine is reversible: Knowing the constant multiplier k, the state t and the output bit b uniquely determines the previous state s and the input bit a: We have $2t + b = s + k \cdot a$, $a, b \in \{0, 1\}$ and $s, t \in \{0, \dots k-1\}$. So if $2t + b \geq k$, $a = 1$ and $s = 2t + b - k$, and if $2t + b < k$, $a = 0$ and $s = 2t + b$.

3   Representing the Mealy Machine in Reversible Logic

We will use $\lceil \log_2 k \rceil$ bits to represent the k states of the Mealy machine. This leaves some bit combinations unused. We don't care about the transitions for these as long as the full transition table is reversible. So we need to find reversible circuits that coincide with the Mealy-machine transition table for states 0 to $k-1$. The remaining states will have transitions that follow from the choice of circuit that represents the desired state transition function on states 0 to $k-1$.

Using three bits s_2, s_1 and s_0 for the states in the Mealy machine in Figure 1 and a as the input bit, the next state represented by t_2, t_1 and t_0 and the output bit b is determined using the transition table shown in Figure 2.

---

[1] In the transitions, the input bits are shown as superscripts and the output bits as subscripts.

s_2	s_1	s_0	a	t_2	t_1	t_0	b
0	0	0	0	0	0	0	0
0	0	0	1	0	1	0	1
0	0	1	0	0	0	0	1
0	0	1	1	0	1	1	0
0	1	0	0	0	0	1	0
0	1	0	1	0	1	1	1
0	1	1	0	0	0	1	1
0	1	1	1	1	0	0	0
1	0	0	0	0	1	0	0
1	0	0	1	1	0	0	1

Fig. 2. Transition table for multiplication by 5

If $a = 0$, $t \doteq s/2$ (implying $t_i = s_{i+1}$), so it is natural to make t_i a modification of s_{i+1} controlled by a and, possibly, the other bits of s.

It is fairly easy to see that $b = s_0 \oplus a$ and $t_0 = s_1 \oplus s_0 a$, so we can make these using a Feynman (controlled not) gate and a Toffoli gate, respectively. We can combine these into a single Peres gate.[2]

t_1 is a bit harder, but it can be obtained as $s_2 \oplus a \oplus (s_1 s_0 a)$, so we need one Feynman gate and a 4-input Toffoli gate.

We don't have any s_3 to use as basis for t_2. We could use a constant-0 wire controlled by the other inputs, but that would make a a garbage output and require an ancillary wire. So, instead, we make t_2 a modification of a. We can see that $t_1 = 1 \Leftrightarrow t_2 \neq a$ except when $t_1 = 1$ and $b = t_0 = 0$, which gives us $t_2 = a \oplus t_1 \oplus t_1 \overline{t_0} b$, so we can do this with two Toffoli gates (one of which has mixed inputs). In total, we have:

$$b = s_0 \oplus a$$
$$t_0 = s_1 \oplus s_0 a$$
$$t_1 = s_2 \oplus a \oplus s_1 s_0 a$$
$$t_2 = a \oplus t_1 \oplus t_1 \overline{t_0} b$$

The entire circuit for the transition function is shown in Figure 3 and the expanded transition table in Figure 4.[3]

Note that, since the state is a carry value between 0 and 4, the circuit can calculate $5x + y$, where y is a value between 0 and 4. If using the circuit in reverse for dividing by 5, the state gives the division remainder.

---

[2] A Peres gate is a combination of a Toffoli gate and a Feynman gate that has a lower quantum cost than a Toffoli gate.

[3] The three unused states (below the line) in the transition table form a three-state Mealy automaton. When starting in state 7, this is the Mealy automation for multiplication by 3 except that the output bit b is negated.

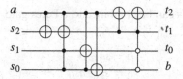

Fig. 3. Transition circuit for multiplication by 5

s_2	s_1	s_0	a	t_2	t_1	t_0	b
0	0	0	0	0	0	0	0
0	0	0	1	0	1	0	1
0	0	1	0	0	0	0	1
0	0	1	1	0	1	1	0
0	1	0	0	0	0	1	0
0	1	0	1	0	1	1	1
0	1	1	0	0	0	1	1
0	1	1	1	1	0	0	0
1	0	0	0	0	1	0	0
1	0	0	1	1	0	0	1
1	0	1	0	1	1	0	1
1	0	1	1	1	0	1	0
1	1	0	0	1	1	1	0
1	1	0	1	1	0	1	1
1	1	1	0	1	1	1	1
1	1	1	1	1	1	0	0

Fig. 4. Expanded transition table for multiplication by 5

4 More Examples

A multiplier by 3 needs two state bits s_0 and s_1 and from the calculations in Section 5, we get

$$b = s_0 \oplus a$$
$$t_0 = s_1 \oplus a\overline{s_0}$$
$$t_1 = a \oplus bt_0$$

which gives the circuit

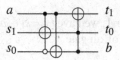

Note that the two first gates can be combined to a Peres gate. Multiplication by 7 uses the formulas

$$b = s_0 \oplus a$$
$$t_0 = s_1 \oplus a\overline{s_0}$$
$$t_1 = s_2 \oplus a\overline{s_0 s_1}$$
$$t_2 = a \oplus bt_0 t_1$$

which are implemented by

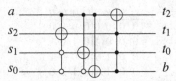

As we shall see in Section 5.3, the similarity between these two multipliers is a general form for multipliers by $2^n - 1$.

5   Generalising to Arbitrary Odd Multipliers

We will use the same idea as above for arbitrary odd multipliers k: The state number s is a carry value from 0 to $k - 1$ represented as a binary number $s_j \ldots s_0$, where $j = \lfloor \log_2(k) \rfloor$. The input bit is a, the output bit is b and the new state t is represented as $t_j \ldots t_0$. Similarly, we write k as a binary number $k_j \ldots k_0$. Since we are interested in odd multipliers only, $k_0 = 1$.

Using the carry value (division remainder) as state number, we get a simple formula for the next state and the output bit: $t = (s + ak)/2$ and $b = (s + ak)\%2$, respectively. Since $k_0 = 1$, the latter can be simplified to $b = s_0 \oplus a$, as we also saw in example circuits above. Given that $t = (s + ak)/2$, we have that $t_i = (s + ak)/2^{i+1}\%2$.

We start by looking at the last few bits of t:

$$\begin{aligned}
t_0 &= t\%2 \\
&= (s + ak)/2\%2 \\
&= (s\%4 + ak\%4)/2\%2 \\
&= (s_0 + 2s_1 + ak_0 + 2ak_1)/2\%2 \\
&= (s_0 + 2s_1 + a + 2ak_1)/2\%2 \\
&= ((s_0 + a)/2 + s_1 + ak_1))\%2 \\
&= (s_0 a + s_1 + ak_1))\%2 \\
&= (s_1 + a(s_0 + k_1))\%2 \\
&= s_1 \oplus a(s_0 \oplus k_1)
\end{aligned}$$

So, dependent on whether k_1 is 0 or 1, we have $t_0 = s_1 \oplus as_0$ or $t_0 = s_1 \oplus a\overline{s_0}$, so in both cases it can be implemented by a Toffoli gate.

Moving in to the next bit (when $k > 3$), we get

$$
\begin{aligned}
t_1 &= (t/2)\%2 \\
&= (s+ak)/4\%2 \\
&= (s\%8+ak\%8)/4\%2 \\
&= (s_0+2s_1+4s_2+ak_0+2ak_1+4ak_2)/4\%2 \\
&= (s_0+2s_1+4s_2+u+2ak_1+4ak_2)/4\%2 \\
&= ((s_0+2s_1+a+2ak_1)/4+s_2+ak_2)\%2
\end{aligned}
$$

We special case on the values of k_1 and k_2:

$$
\begin{aligned}
k_1 = k_2 = 0: \quad t_1 &= ((s_0+2s_1+a)/4+s_2)\%2 \\
&= (s_0 s_1 a+s_2)\%2 \\
&= s_2 \oplus s_0 s_1 a
\end{aligned}
$$

$$
\begin{aligned}
k_1 = 0,\ k_2 = 1: \quad t_1 &= ((s_0+2s_1+a)/4+s_2+a)\%2 \\
&= (s_0 s_1 a+s_2+a)\%2 \\
&= s_2 \oplus a \oplus s_0 s_1 a
\end{aligned}
$$

$$
\begin{aligned}
k_1 = 1,\ k_2 = 0: \quad t_1 &= ((s_0+2s_1+3a)/4+s_2)\%2 \\
&= (a(s_0 \vee s_1)+s_2)\%2 \\
&= s_2 \oplus a(\neg \overline{s_0 s_1}) \\
&= s_2 \oplus a \oplus a\overline{s_0 s_1}
\end{aligned}
$$

$$
\begin{aligned}
k_1 = k_2 = 1: \quad t_1 &= ((s_0+2s_1+3a)/4+s_2+a)\%2 \\
&= (a(s_0 \vee s_1)+s_2+a)\%2 \\
&= s_2 \oplus a \oplus a(\neg \overline{s_0 s_1}) \\
&= s_2 \oplus a\overline{s_0 s_1}
\end{aligned}
$$

In some of the above reductions, we have used the equality $xy = x \oplus x\bar{y}$. We will use this again on several occasions below. The general case is

$$
\begin{aligned}
t_i &= (s+ak)/2^{i+1}\%2 \\
&= ((s\%2^{i+1}+a(k\%2^{i+1}))/2^{i+1}+s/2^{i+1}+a(k/2^{i+1}))\%2 \\
&= s_{i+1} \oplus ak_{i+1} \oplus (s\%2^{i+1}+a(k\%2^{i+1}))/2^{i+1}\%2
\end{aligned}
$$

We note that the contents of the outer parentheses is greater than or equal to 2^{i+1} if and only if $a = 1$ and $s\%2^{i+1}+k\%2^{i+1} \geq 2^{i+1}$. So we can rewrite to

$$
\begin{aligned}
t_i &= s_{i+1} \oplus ak_{i+1} \oplus a(s\%2^{i+1}+k\%2^{i+1} \geq 2^{i+1}) \\
&= s_{i+1} \oplus ak_{i+1} \oplus a(s\%2^{i+1} \geq 2^{i+1}-k\%2^{i+1})
\end{aligned}
$$

We use C_k^i as a shorthand for $2^{i+1}-k\%2^{i+1}$. We see that, if $k_{i+1} = 0$, we can reduce $s_{i+1} \oplus ak_{i+1} \oplus a(s\%2^{i+1} \geq C_k^i)$ to $s_{i+1} \oplus a(s\%2^{i+1} \geq C_k^i)$. If $k_{i+1} = 1$, we instead get $s_{i+1} \oplus a \oplus a(s\%2^{i+1} \geq C_k^i) = s_{i+1} \oplus a(s\%2^{i+1} < C_k^i)$.

In both cases, the inequality can be expressed as a logical formula of the bits in $s\%2^{i+1}$, i.e, the last $i+1$ bits of s. This logical formula can be written in disjunctive normal form, so we get $t_i = s_{i+1} \oplus a(V_1 \vee \cdots \vee V_m)$, where each disjunct V is a conjunction of the variables $s_1 \cdots s_0$, some of which may be negated. All disjuncts specify exactly one bit patterns of the word $s_1 \cdots s_0$, so only one of the disjuncts can be true. Hence, we can rewrite the formula to $t_i = s_{i+1} \oplus aV_1 \oplus \cdots \oplus aV_m$. We can reduce this using the following rules:

$$
\begin{aligned}
xy \oplus x\bar{y} &= x & &\text{resolution} \\
x \oplus x\bar{y} &= xy & &\text{negation} \\
xy\bar{z} \oplus x\bar{y}z &= xy \oplus xz & &\text{cross}
\end{aligned}
$$

The cross rule does not reduce the number of gates, but it does reduce their size. Optimal reduction is computationally hard, as the choice of which pairs to reduce can affect later reductions. The reduced formula can be implemented as a sequence of mixed-input Toffoli gates.

For the last output bit, we have

$$
\begin{aligned}
t_j &= (s+ak)/2^{j+1} \% 2 \\
&= s+ak > 2^{j+1} \\
&= a \wedge s+k > 2^{j+1} \\
&= a \wedge s > 2^{j+1} - k \\
&= a \oplus a(s \leq 2^{j+1} - k) \\
&= a \oplus (b \oplus s_0)(s \leq 2^{j+1} - k) \\
&= a \oplus b(s \leq 2^{j+1} - k) \oplus s_0(s \leq 2^{j+1} - k)
\end{aligned}
$$

Rewriting this way avoids garbage, as we have b as a modification of s_0, t_i as a modification of s_{i+1} when $i < j$ and t_j as a modification of a. So all inputs are consumed when producing the outputs, and no ancillary or garbage lines are needed.

To get a linear layout of the circuit, we prefer to use b and $t_0 \ldots t_{j-1}$ instead of $s_0 \ldots s_j$ when computing t_j. There is no simple general formula, but we can use the same trick as above: List all combinations of positive and negative b and $t_0 \ldots t_{j-1}$ that give $t_j \neq a$ and write this as a disjunctive normal form. Essentially, we generate the truth table for $t_j \oplus a$ as a function of b and $t_0 \ldots t_{j-1}$, rewrite this into a logical formula in disjunctive normal form and reduce it using the resolution and negation rules.

5.1 Example: Multiplication by 23

As shown in [6], no sequence of multipliers and dividers by constants of the form $2^n \pm 1$ (like those shown in [1]) can multiply by 23. Hence, 23 is an interesting case for our construction. $23 = 10111_2$, so $k_0 = k_1 = k_2 = k_4 = 1$ and $k_3 = 0$. As shown above, this gives

$$
\begin{aligned}
b &= s_0 \oplus a \\
t_0 &= s_1 \oplus a\bar{s_0} \\
t_1 &= s_2 \oplus a\bar{s_0}\bar{s_1} \\
t_2 &= s_3 \oplus a(s\%8 \geq 8 - 23\%8) \\
&= s_3 \oplus a(s\%8 \geq 1) \\
&= s_3 \oplus a(s_0 \vee s_1 \vee s_2) \\
&= s_3 \oplus a \oplus a\bar{s_0}\bar{s_1}\bar{s_2}
\end{aligned}
$$

$$t_3 = s_4 \oplus a \oplus a(s\%16 \geq 16 - 23\%16)$$
$$= s_4 \oplus a \oplus a(s\%16 \geq 9)$$
$$= s_4 \oplus a \oplus as_3(s\%8 \geq 1)$$
$$= s_4 \oplus a \oplus as_3(s_0 \vee s_1 \vee s_2)$$
$$= s_4 \oplus a \oplus as_3 \oplus as_3\overline{s_0}\overline{s_1}\overline{s_2}$$

By inspection of the truth table, we see that $t_4 \neq a$ for the following values:

t_3	t_2	t_1	t_0	b
1	0	1	1	1
1	1	0	0	0
1	1	0	0	1
1	1	0	1	0
1	1	0	1	1
1	1	1	0	0
1	1	1	0	1
1	1	1	1	0
1	1	1	1	1

With resolution, the last eight rows can be combined to $t_3 = t_2 = 1$. So the reduced formula is $t_4 = a \oplus t_3t_2 \oplus t_3\overline{t_2}t_1t_0b$, where the last term represents the first line in the table. The entire circuit for multiplication by 23 is shown below.

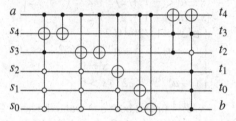

5.2 Size of Circuits

For any t_i, the disjunctive normal form can have $O(2^i)$ disjuncts, so the circuits can be quite large: A constant k uses $\lceil \log_2(k) \rceil$ state bits, so the upper bound is

$$\sum_{i=0}^{\lceil \log_2(k) \rceil - 1} 2^i = 2^{\lceil \log_2(k) \rceil} - 1$$

This bound is not tight, and in most cases the circuit is much smaller. For example, the formula above gives 31 as a bound for the number of gates for implementing multiplication by 23, but, as shown above, we need only 9 Toffoli gates (two of which can be combined to a Peres gate). We can tighten the estimate a bit by the following observation: If a formula in disjunctive normal form for i variables has more than 2^{i-1} disjuncts, two of these must differ in only one variable, so they can be combined using the resolution rule. Hence, we can lower the upper bound on the size of formulas by a factor of 2.

There are, also, some special cases of k that give much smaller formulas and circuits. We review these below.

5.3 Multiplying by $k = 2^n - 1$

If $k = 2^n - 1$, we note that $j = n - 1$. We have $t = (s + a(2^n - 1))/2 = (s + a2^n - a)/2$.
This gives

$$
\begin{aligned}
t_j = t_{n-1} &= t/2^{n-1}\%2 \\
&= (s + a2^n - a)/2/2^{n-1}\%2 \\
&= (s + a2^n - a)/2^n\%2 \\
&= \begin{cases} 0 & , s = 0 \\ ((s-a)/2^n + a)\%2 & , s > 0 \end{cases} \\
&= \begin{cases} 0 , s = 0 \\ a , s > 0 \end{cases} \\
&= a \oplus (a = 1 \wedge s = 0) \\
&= a \oplus (b = 1 \wedge t = k/2) \\
&= a \oplus (b = 1 \wedge t = 2^{n-1} - 1) \\
&= a \oplus b t_0 \cdots t_{n-2} \overline{t_{n-1}} \\
&= a \oplus b t_0 \cdots t_{n-2}
\end{aligned}
$$

The last step is valid because state $2^n - 1$ is not used, so t_{n-1} can not be 1 when all the other bits of t are 1. For $i < n - 1$, we get

$$
\begin{aligned}
t_i &= t/2^i\%2 \\
&= (s + a(2^n - 1))/2/2^i\%2 \\
&= (s + a(2^n - 1))/2^{i+1}\%2 \\
&= \begin{cases} a(2^n - 1)/2^{i+1}\%2 & , \ s = 0 \\ ((s-a)/2^{i+1} + a2^{n-i-1})\%2 , & \ s > 0 \end{cases} \\
&= \begin{cases} a & , \ s = 0 \\ (s-a)/2^{i+1}\%2 , & \ s > 0 \end{cases}
\end{aligned}
$$

We note that $(s-a)/2^{i+1} = s/2^{i+1}$ unless both $a = 1$ and the last $i + 1$ bits of s are all 0. If this is the case, the two values differ by 1. So $(s-a)/2^{i+1}\%2 = s/2^{i+1}\%2 \oplus a\overline{s_0 \cdot s_i} = s_{i+1} \oplus a\overline{s_0 \cdot s_i}$. Since this also applies to the $s = 0$ case, we get $t_i = s_{i+1} \oplus a\overline{s_0 \cdot s_i}$ when $i < n - 1$. This is a single Toffoli gate.

So, if $k = 2^n - 1$, only $n + 1$ gates are required for the multiplier circuit (per bit of the number that is multiplied by k), and this can be reduced to n gates if the gates for b and t_0 are combined to a Peres gate.

5.4 Multiplying by $k = 2^n + 1$

If $k = 2^n + 1$, we note that $j = n$, so $t = (s + a2^n + a)/2 = (s + a)/2 + a2^{n-1}$.

We first look at the two high bits (t_n and t_{n-1}) together. These represent $t/2^{n-1} = ((s+a)/2 + a2^{n-1})/2^{n-1} = (s+a)/2^n + a$. This can have values 0, 1 and 2, or 00, 01 and 10 in binary. We note that the two bits are different unless they both are 0, so we can write

$$
\begin{aligned}
t_n &= t_{n-1} \oplus \neg((s+a)/2^n + a = 0) \\
&= t_{n-1} \oplus \neg(a = 0 \wedge s < 2^n) \\
&= t_{n-1} \oplus (a = 1 \vee s = 2^n) \\
&= t_{n-1} \oplus a \oplus (a = 0 \wedge s = 2^n)
\end{aligned}
$$

If $a = 0$ and $s = 2^n$, we have $b = 0$ and $t = 2^{n-1}$ (and vice versa). So we continue

$$
\begin{aligned}
t_n &= t_{n-1} \oplus a \oplus (a = 0 \wedge s = 2^n) \\
&= a \oplus t_{n-1} \oplus (b = 0 \wedge t = 2^{n-1}) \\
&= a \oplus t_{n-1} \oplus \overline{t_n t_{n-1} t_{n-2} \cdots t_0 b} \\
&= a \oplus t_{n-1} \oplus t_{n-1} t_{n-2} \cdots t_0 b
\end{aligned}
$$

The last step is valid because $t_n = 0$ is implied by $t_{n-1} = 1$, as both can not be 1 at the same time. This gives us t_n as a modification of a by a Feynman and a Toffoli gate.

For the other bits of t, we have that $a = 1$ gives $t_i = ((s + 1)/2 + 2^{n-1})/2^i \% 2$.

If $i = n-1$, this is $((s+1)/2 + 2^{n-1})/2^{n-1} \% 2 = ((s+1)/2^n + 1) \% 2 = \neg(((s+1)/2^n) \% 2)$. We note that $(s+1)/2^n = 0$ except when $s = 2^n$ or $s = 2^n - 1$, so when $a = 1$, $t_{n-1} = \neg(s_n \vee (s_0 \cdots s_{n-1})) = \neg(s_n \oplus (s_0 \cdots s_{n-1})) = s_n \oplus 1 \oplus (s_0 \cdots s_{n-1})$. The first equality holds because s_n and $(s_0 \cdots s_{n-1})$ can not be true at the same time. Combining the cases for $a = 0$ and $a = 1$, we get $t_{n-1} = s_n \oplus a \oplus a(s_0 \cdots s_{n-1})$.

If $i < n-1$ and $a = 1$, $t_i = ((s+1)/2 + 2^{n-1})/2^i \% 2 = ((s+1)/2^{i+1} + 2^{n-i-1}) \% 2 = (s+1)/2^{i+1} \% 2$ (because $n-i-1 > 0$). We note that $(s+1)/2^{i+1} = s/2^{i+1}$ except when the $i+1$ least bits of s are 1. So we have $(s+1)/2^{i+1} \% 2 = s/2^{i+1} \% 2 \oplus (s \% 2^i = 2^i - 1) = s_{i+1} \oplus (s_0 \cdots s_i)$. Combining with the case for $a = 0$, we get $t_i = s_{i+1} \oplus a(s_0 \cdots s_i)$.

So for b and the first $n - 1$ state bits, we need one gate and the last two state bits need 2 gates each. The total number of gates is, hence, $n + 4$. We can reduce this by one by combining the gates for b and t_0 to a Peres gate, so the total is $n + 3$.

6   Completing the Circuit

The circuits we have shown above are bit slices that can be combined to form by-k multipliers for any number of bits. The bit slices all take $j + 1 = \lfloor \log_2(k) \rfloor + 1$ state bits as part of the input and produces the same number of state bits as part of the output.

A multiplier having an n-bit number x as input needs $n + j + 1$ output bits to represent the output $k \cdot n$. But the last $j + 1$ bits are exactly the output state bits from the last bit slice. Furthermore, if the initial state bits are different from 0, the number these represent is added to the result. Conversely, if the multiplier is used in reverse for division, these state bits will hold the division remainder.

In general, if an n-bit multiplier by k has initial state S input A, output B and final state T, the relation is

$$
S + A \cdot k = B + 2^n T
$$

Where A and B are n-bit numbers and S and T are $(j+1)$-bit numbers. We number the bits (least significant to most significant) in S as $s_0 \cdots s_j$, in A as $a_0 \cdots a_{n-1}$ and in B as $b_0 \cdots b_{n-1}$. Since B and T together form an $(n+j+1)$-bit number $B + 2^n T$, we can number the bits in T as $b_n \cdots b_{n+j}$. This gives the following diagram for a full n-bit multiplier by k:

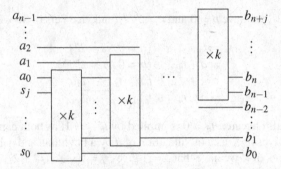

Where each box labelled "$\times k$" is a multiplier bit-slice.

For multipliers of the form $K = 2^m k$, where k is odd, multiplication by K can be done by a bit-shift by m and multiplication by k. It is still possible to add an arbitrary value r below K to the result by letting the low m bits of r be the low m bits of the result and letting the remaining bits of r form the input state s, using the equality $2^m kA + r = 2^m(kA + r/2^m) + r\%2^m$. For example, $24A + 13 = 8(3A + 1) + 5$, so multiplication by 24 and adding 13 is done by multiplying by 3 and adding 1, and then concatenating the result with the three bits in the value 5. Essentially, the least significant m bits of r are passed unchanged through the circuit forming the least significant m bit of the product, and the remaining bits of r are used as the initial state in a by-k multiplier, the result of which is used as the remaining bits of the product. Again, we can use the circuit in reverse and get division with remainder r.

6.1 Specialising to the Initial State

If the initial state S is a constant (such as 0), it is possible to specialise the first few bit-slices to this constant, which produces smaller circuits for these bit-slices. On the downside, division (using the circuit in reverse) will only be correct if the remainder is equal to the constant initial state (usually 0).

We will illustrate specialisation by an example: The by-5 multiplier. We had in Section 3 that the transition formulas for the by-5 multiplier (with added bit-slice subscript m) are

$$b_m = s_{0m} \oplus a_m$$
$$t_{0m} = s_{1m} \oplus s_{0m}a_m$$
$$t_{1m} = s_{2m} \oplus a_m \oplus s_{1m}s_{0m}a_m$$
$$t_{2m} = a_m \oplus t_{1m} \oplus t_{1m}t_{0m}b_m$$

Note that $s_{i(m+1)} = t_{im}$, as the output state of one bit-slice becomes the input state of the next. If $s_{00} = s_{10} = s_{20} = 0$, the formulas above reduce to

$$b_0 = 0 \oplus a_0 = a_0 \qquad\qquad b_1 = t_{00} \oplus a_1 = 0 \oplus a_1 = a_1$$
$$t_{00} = 0 \oplus 0a_0 = 0 \qquad\qquad t_{01} = t_{10} \oplus t_{00}a_1 = a_0 \oplus 0a_1 = a_0$$
$$t_{10} = 0 \oplus a_0 \oplus 00a_0 = a_0 \qquad t_{11} = t_{20} \oplus a_1 \oplus t_{10}t_{00}a_1 = 0 \oplus a_1 \oplus a_0 0a_1 = a_1$$
$$t_{20} = a_0 \oplus a_0 \oplus a_0 1\overline{a_0} = 0 \qquad t_{21} = a_1 \oplus t_{11} \oplus t_{11}\overline{t_{01}b_1} = a_1 \oplus a_1 \oplus a_1\overline{a_0 a_1} = 0$$

Nothing is gained by specialising the next bit-slice, though. The circuit for the first two bit-slices is shown below.

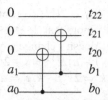

Without specialisation, these two bit-slices would have used a total of 12 gates (10 if Peres gates are used), so specialisation to the initial state can yield a significantly smaller circuits, though only for the first few bit-slices.

7 Unused States

For multiplication by k, we use $j+1$ state bits where $j = \lfloor \log_2(k) \rfloor$, so there are $2^{j+1} - k$ unused states. Starting in one of the unused states will (because of reversibility) also give a new state in the otherwise unused set of states, so the unused states also form a reversible Mealy machine. We noted in Section 3 that the three unused states for the by-5 multiplier forms a modified by-3 multiplier circuit: When starting in state 7, the output is the bit-wise negation of the input multiplied by 3.

But can we say anything in general about the automaton formed by the unused states in a by-k multiplier?

There are several possible ways to generate output for the unused states that retain reversibility, but we will assume that no extra gates are added to modify the behaviour of the unused states. For example, we will assume that $b = s_0 \oplus a$, though it would be possible to modify it to, say, $b = s_0 \oplus a \oplus s_j s_{j-1}$ (if $s_j s_{j-1}$ is never true in the normal states) without changing the behaviour of the normal states. Basically, this amounts to using the simplest possible circuits for the normal states.

As noted, the formula for b is $b = s_0 \oplus a$ and the formula for t_i, where $i < j$ is $t_i = s_{i+1} \oplus X_i$, where X_i depends only on a and $s_0 \cdots s_i$. Adding or subtracting 2^i to s flips s_i and, as a consequence, t_{i-1} (or b, if $i = 0$). But adding a multiple of 2^{i+1} to s does not change b nor $t_0 \cdots t_{i-1}$. We also note that, due to reversibility, unused states transition to unused states, so bit j of the target state (t_j) is always 1.

So we can find the transitions for an unused state by subtracting 2^j from the state number and apply the rules above to the resulting t. We can treat $t_0 \cdots t_{j-2}$ and b as a whole: For $s < k$, s transitions to $t = (s+ak)/2$ and $b = (s+ak)\%2$. So $2t + b = s + ak$ and, hence, $t_0 \cdots t_{j-2}$ and b combine to form $(s+ak)\%2^j$. Since $(s+ak)\%2^j$ is unaffected by adding 2^j to s, a state $s \geq k$ transitions to $(s-2^j+ak)\%2^j = (s+ak)\%2^j$, so $t_0 \cdots t_{j-2}$ and b are unchanged by adding 2^j to s. The following bit, t_{j-1}, is flipped by adding 2^j to s, so while a state $s < k$ makes $t_0 \cdots t_{j-1}$ and b be the bits of $(s+ak)\%2^{j+1}$, $s \geq k$ makes the same result bits be the bits of $(s - 2^j + ak)\%2^{j+1} \oplus 2^j$ (where $\oplus$ is bit-wise XOR). We note that taking the division remainder modulo 2^{j+1} will clear the top bit (if set), but we noted that the unused states all have this bit set, so in total we map a state $s \geq k$ to $((s-2^j+ak)|2^{j+1}) \oplus 2^j$, where $|$ is bit-wise OR. We can try to reduce this:

$$((s-2^j+ak)|2^{j+1}) \oplus 2^j$$
$$= ((s-2^j+ak) \oplus 2^j)|2^{j+1}$$
$$= (s+ak)|2^{j+1}$$

The latter step is true because $2^j < s < 2^{j+1}$, so subtracting 2^j from s just clears s_j, which is set again by the XOR. We note that $2^j < k < 2^{j+1}$, so $2^{j+1} < s+k < 2^{j+2}$. So, if $a = 1$, OR'ing 2^{j+1} to $s+ak$ doesn't change anything, but if $a = 0$, it adds 2^{j+1}. Hence, we can rewrite to $s+ak+(1-a)2^{j+1} = s+2^{j+1} - a(2^{j+1} - k)$.

If we define $s' = 2^{j+1} - 1 - s$, $k' = 2^{j+1} - k$, $t' = 2^{j+2} - 1 - t$ and $t = (s'+ak')/2$, we have

$$s + 2^{j+1} - a(2^{j+1} - k)$$
$$= (2^{j+1} - 1 - s + s') + s + 2^{j+1} - ak'$$
$$= 2^{j+2} - 1 - (s' + ak')$$

Taking the division remainder by 2 of this, we get $(2^{j+2} - 1 - (s' + ak'))\%2 = (s' + ak')\%2 \oplus 1$.

Dividing $2^{j+2} - 1 - (s' + ak')$ by two, we get $(2^{j+2} - 1 - (s' + ak'))/2 = (2^{j+2} - (s' + ak' + 1))/2 = 2^{j+1} - (s' + ak' + 1 + 1)/2 = 2^{j+1} - 1 - (s' + ak')/2 = 2^{j+1} - 1 - t = t'$.

We have used that, with integer division, $2x \geq y$ implies $(2x - y)/2 = x - (y + 1)/2$. This is easily seen by verifying the cases $y = 2n$ and $y = 2n + 1$ separately.

Put together, we have that the output bit is the negation of the result bit of multiplication by k', and that by using the mapping $s' = 2^{j+1} - 1 - s$ (which is bit-wise negation of s as a $(j+1)$-bit number) on both input and output states, we get state transitions for multiplication by k'. Hence, the behaviour we observed for the by-5 multiplier is true for arbitrary by-k multipliers constructed as above.

8   Conclusion and Related Work

We have shown a construction based on Mealy machines for reversible circuits for multiplication by arbitrary constants. We can multiply by constants of the form $2^n - 1$ using n gates per bit of the multiplicand and by constants of the form $2^n + 1$ using $n + 3$ gates per bit of the multiplicand. An upper bound for the number of gates needed for multiplication by an arbitrary constant k is $2k$ gates per bit of the multiplicand. The multiplier can without extra cost add a value less than k to the product. When the circuit used in reverse, this value is the division remainder. When used with an addend or remainder, the circuit produces no garbage bits and uses no ancillary lines.

If the initial state is constant, it is possible to specialise the first few bit-slice circuits to these constant state bits, which reduces the size of these bit-slices.

The multipliers presented by Axelsen and Thomsen in [1] use seven gates per bit to multiply by any constant of the form $2^n \pm 1$, so our approach is superior to theirs only for small numbers of this form, especially since we use many-input Toffoli gates where their gates have few inputs. We estimate that our approach wins for constants of the form $2^n - 1$ when $n < 6$ and for constants of the form $2^n + 1$ when $n < 4$, which is really only for multiplication by 5, since $3 = 2^1 + 1$ is better handled as $2^2 - 1$ and $9 = 2^3 + 1$ by using two by-3 multipliers in sequence.

But where our approach really wins is with multipliers for constants that are not of the form $2^n \pm 1$. Axelsen and Thomsen can build multipliers for some constants not of this form by chaining together a number of multipliers and dividers (inverse multipliers) for numbers of the form $2^n \pm 1$, but this doesn't work for all numbers. For example, multiplication by 23 can not be done in this way [6].

Axelsen and Thomsen extended their method to handle more constants by modifying a three-input adder, so they can handle constants of the form $2^n \pm 2^m \pm 1$, which includes $23 = 2^4 + 2^3 - 1$. This construction, however, is less efficient than the by-23 multiplier shown in Section 5.1, as it for each bit of the multiplicand uses 23 gates and four ancillary lines compared to 9 gates and no ancillary lines in our construction. Additionally, it is not known whether all constant multipliers can be constructed by stringing together multipliers and divisors for constants of the forms $2^n \pm 2^m \pm 1$ and $2^n \pm 1$, nor (when a multiplier can be constructed) is there a known upper bound on the number and size of circuits that need to be chained to do so.

Additionally, the multipliers presented here can, when used in reverse to do division, compute both the fraction and the division remainder, where the multipliers shown in [1], when used in reverse, can only divide numbers that divide evenly by k.

A problem with our approach, though, is that it uses gates with many inputs, which is costly. For example, the by-23 multiplier uses two six-input Toffoli gates and one five-input Toffoli gate, which are more expensive than three-input Toffoli gates. Using pass-transistor CMOS logic [3], an n-input Toffoli gate uses $4(n-1)$ pass transistors, so a six-input gate is (slightly) more than twice as expensive as a three-input gate.

In our current design, each state bit (except the last) is calculated independently of the other state bits. It might be possible to avoid large gates by exploiting dependencies between these calculations. Future work should address this issue.

References

1. Axelsen, H.B., Thomsen, M.K.: Garbage-free integer multiplication by constants. In: Glück, R., Yokoyama, T. (eds.) Reversible Computation. LNCS, vol. 7581, pp. 171–182 (2012)
2. Burignat, S., Vermeirsch, K., De Vos, A., Thomsen, M.K.: Garbageless reversible implementation of integer linear transformations. In: Glück, R., Yokoyama, T. (eds.) RC 2012. LNCS, vol. 7581, pp. 160–170. Springer, Heidelberg (2013)
3. De Vos, A.: Reversible Computing. Wiley, Chichester (2010)
4. Huffman, D.A.: Canonical forms for information-lossless finite-state logical machines. IRE Transactions on Information Theory 5(5), 41–59 (1959)
5. Mealy, G.H.: A method for synthesizing sequential circuits. Bell System Technical Journal 34(5), 1045–1079 (1955)
6. Rotenberg, E., Cranch, J., Thomsen, M.K., Axelsen, H.B.: Strength of the reversible, garbage-free $2^k \pm 1$ multiplier. In: Reversible Computation 2013 (2013)
7. Wikipedia. Mealy machine (2012), http://en.wikipedia.org/wiki/Mealy_machine

Identities in Modular Arithmetic
from Reversible Coherence Operations

Peter M. Hines

University of York

Abstract. This paper investigates some issues arising in categorical models of reversible logic and computation. Our claim is that the structural (coherence) isomorphisms of these categorical models, although generally overlooked, have decidedly non-trivial computational content. The theory of categorical coherence is based around reversible structural operations (canonical isomorphisms) that allow for transformations between related, but distinct, mathematical structures. A number of *coherence theorems* are commonly used to treat these transformations as though they are identity maps, from which point onwards they play no part in computational models. We simply wish to point out that doing so overlooks some significant computational content.

We give a single example (taken from an uncountably infinite set of similar examples, and based on structures used in models of reversible logic and computation) of a category whose structural isomorphisms manipulate modulo classes of natural numbers. We demonstrate that the coherence properties that usually allow us to ignore these structural isomorphisms in fact correspond to countably infinite families of non-trivial identities in modular arithmetic. Further, proving the correctness of these equalities without recourse to the theory of categorical coherence appears to be a hard task.

1 Introduction

1.1 Historical Background

In [6], J.-Y. Girard introduced *Linear Logic*, a striking new decomposition of classical logic. By contrast to previous approaches to logic, it was based around the twin related principles of *reversibility* and *resource-sensitivity*. Although the structural operations of copying and contraction (i.e. deletion against a copy) were not completely abandoned (as in sub-structural logics [22]), they were severely restricted. Via the Curry-Howard isomorphism [23] (also known as the 'proofs-as-programs' correspondence) linear logic also has a close connection with reversible and resource-sensitive versions of computing systems such as lambda calculus and combinatory logic [2].

The computational interpretation was pushed further in the *Geometry of Interaction* program [9], giving related models of linear logic [7,8] (see also [4]).

G.W. Dueck and D.M. Miller (Eds.): RC 2013, LNCS 7948, pp. 84–95, 2013.
© Springer-Verlag Berlin Heidelberg 2013

Although these models were degenerate in the logical sense (they identified conjunction with disjunction, and existential quantification with universal quantification) their computational content remained, as demonstrated by a series of practical computational interpretations in [8]. (As shown later [12], the dynamical part of the Geometry of Interaction system was implemented using precisely the same tools required to model reversible (space-bounded) Turing machines).

A significant challenge for logicians at this point was to give categorical models of both Linear Logic and the (related but distinct) Geometry of Interaction system, following the close correspondence between logics / type systems, and closed categories pioneered by [17]. For the purposes of this paper, we concentrate on the more computationally oriented Geometry of Interaction.

Several authors [1,10,15] noted that the dynamical, or computational, part of the Geometry of Interaction system was a form of *compact closure* [16] arising from categorical constructions [15,1] on the category of partial reversible functions. As pointed out in [10,11,2] (and implicit in [7]), the Geometry of Interaction is an essentially untyped (in the sense of λ-calculus) reversible computational system — this is a consequence of the requirements of reversibility and resource-sensitivity. Any categorical interpretation must take this into account.

1.2   The Purpose of This Paper

The purpose of this paper is simply to point out some previously overlooked, decidedly non-trivial, computational content that arises in these models (in fact, familiarity with the logical models and computational systems listed above is not a requirement for understanding this paper – but does help place the theory firmly within its historical context). The computational content comes, not from the dynamics of the GoI system (i.e. compact closure in categories of partial reversible functions), but simply from the fact that the system in question is untyped. Categorically, a model of an untyped system is a category with precisely one object (i.e. a monoid). Thus the GoI system is modelled within a monoid of partial reversible functions.

In categorical logic / categorical models of computation, it is standard to ignore completely a class of structural isomorphisms known as *coherence isomorphisms*. There is a formal justification for doing so — any category with non-trivial structural isomorphisms is equivalent (in a very precise sense) to one with trivial structural isomorphisms [21].

However, there is a subtlety that is often overlooked; the process of constructing this equivalent category with trivial structural isomorphisms involves modifying the collection of objects of the category (& hence, by the correspondence between categories and logics pioneered in [17], modifying the type system). An appendix to [14] (see also [13]) makes clear what this means for untyped systems; the 'equivalent' version with trivial structural isomorphisms has a countably infinite class of objects, and thus is no longer type-free.

As type-freeness is such an essential component of the GoI system, we are thus forced to deal with these structural isomorphisms – this paper studies a set of such isomorphisms that arise implicitly in [7]. We demonstrate that, although the category itself has only one object, modulo classes of integers play the same rôle as objects in this untyped setting. Thus, the structural isomorphisms correspond to (highly non-trivial) identities in modular arithmetic. Further, the classic theory of coherence that usually allows us to ignore structural isomorphisms completely in this case allows us to derive infinite sets of identities in modular arithmetic, essentially for free.

1.3   Categorical Identities Up to Isomorphism

In category theory, especially the theory of monoidal categories, *coherence isomorphisms* are reversible structural operations that transform objects of categories (frequently, concrete mathematical structures) into isomorphic objects that differ only by a simple structural equivalence.

The canonical example, of course, is *associativity*, where for foundational reasons one must replace the strict identity $X \otimes (Y \otimes Z) = (X \otimes Y) \otimes Z$ by a pair of mututally inverse isomorphisms

$$X \otimes (Y \otimes Z) \xrightarrow[\tau_{X,Y,Z}^{-1}]{\tau_{X,Y,Z}} (X \otimes Y) \otimes Z$$

These natural isomorphisms are required to satisfy a family of *coherence conditions* that ensure that any such re-bracketing is both reversible and confluent.

The distinction between a strict structural property (based on equality) and one that holds up to isomorphism is subtle, and a variety of coherence theorems [21] tell us that for all practical purposes, we may ignore this subtlety, and treat properties such as associativity as though they are strict. However, a passing comment in the appendix of [14] (expanded upon in a talk given by the author at Dagstuhl Seminar 12352, 'Information Flow and its Applications' [3]) observes that in various settings, these structural isomorphisms are concrete reversible arithmetic operations and the very coherence theorems used to ignore them have non-trivial computational content.

This paper expands upon these observations via a simple representative example. We give an untyped (i.e. single-object) unitless monoidal category whose structural isomorphisms are based on modular arithmetic, and then describe the significant computational advantage that the theory of categorical coherence provides in decisions procedures for equality of such reversible operations. In particular, we demonstrate that categorical diagrams based on k distinct nodes correspond to arithmetic identities over equivalence classes of the form $\{2^k.\mathbb{N} + x\}_{x=0\ldots2^k-1}$. Despite this, the coherence theorem for associativity provides, for free, a large (countably infinite) class of arithmetic identities over such modular clases that are guaranteed to be correct. At least to the author, these identities are not readily apparent simply from their algebraic description.

1.4 MacLane's Coherence Theorem for Associativity, and Untyped Monoidal Categories

MacLane's coherence theorem for associativity is commonly, although incorrectly, described as stating that 'all diagrams built from coherence isomorphisms commute'. This is a correct characterisation of the more technical result in some, but certainly not all, cases (in particular simple calculations will demonstrate that it does not hold the for constructions of this paper). The distinction becomes important when the objects of the category do not satisfy a 'freeness' condition with respect to the monoidal tensor, leading to what [21] refers to as *undesirable identifications between objects*. Thus, when the class of objects is not only a set, but is *finite*, the informal characterisation above can never coincide with the formal statement of the theorem.

This paper presents a rather extreme example of this: we exhibit a small (unitless) symmetric monoidal category with exactly one object N satisfying the equality[1] $N \otimes N = N$, as in the example of J. Isbell used by MacLane to motivate the notion of coherence up to isomorphism [21] p. 160.

This 'untyped' monoidal category is an example of a general construction introduced in [10,11] – see also [14,13]. As demonstrated in an Appendix to [14], there are uncountably many such untyped monoidal categories based on functions on $\mathbb{N}$ (in 1:1 correspondence with the interior points of the Cantor set, excluding a subset of measure zero), of which the one we present is merely the simplest.

We then describe which canonical diagrams of this category are predicted to commute by MacLane's coherence theorem for associativity, and demonstrate that these are non-obvious identities in modular arithmetic.

2   An Untyped Monoidal Category

We first give some simple arithmetic constructions on $\mathbb{N}$, based on arithmetic modulo 2^k, for $k \in \mathbb{N}$, with a close connection to the theory of symmetric monoidal categories [21]:

Definition 1. *Let us denote the monoid of bijections on the natural numbers by $\mathcal{J}$, and treat this as a single-object category. We define $\tau, \sigma \in \mathcal{J} = \mathcal{J}(\mathbb{N}, \mathbb{N})$ as follows:*

$$\tau(n) = \begin{cases} 2n & n \ (mod \ 2) = 0, \\ n+1 & n \ (mod \ 4) = 1, \\ \frac{n-1}{2} & n \ (mod \ 4) = 3. \end{cases}$$

$$\sigma(n) = \begin{cases} n+1 & n \ even, \\ n-1 & n \ odd. \end{cases}$$

---

[1] Note that this is strict equality, rather than isomorphism. For category-theorists worried about foundational questions related to a notion of equality between objects, we emphasise that this is a *small* category. Although $N \otimes (N \otimes N) = (N \otimes N) \otimes N$, this equality of objects does not imply that the corresponding associativity isomorphism is a strict identity.

We also give an operation that, given two bijections on $\mathbb{N}$, returns another bijection. Given arbitrary $f, g \in \mathcal{J}$, we define

$$(f \star g)(n) = \begin{cases} 2.f\left(\frac{n}{2}\right) & n \text{ even,} \\ 2.g\left(\frac{n-1}{2}\right) + 1 & n \text{ odd.} \end{cases}$$

The following properties of the above bijections and operations will be established via basic modular arithmetic. These properties are, as will be apparent, closely related to the structural properties and coherence conditions of symmetric monoidal categories:

Proposition 1. *Let* $(\_\star\_), \sigma, \tau$ *be as in Definition 1 above. Then for all* $f, g, h \in \mathcal{J}$, *the following properties hold:*

1. **Identities** $id \star id = id$
2. **Interchange** $(h \star k)(f \star g) = (hf \star kg)$
3. **Natural associativity** $\tau(f \star (g \star h)) = ((f \star g) \star h)\tau$
4. **Natural symmetry** $\sigma(g \star f) = (f \star g)\sigma$
5. **Pentagon** $\tau^2 = (\tau \star id)\tau(id \star \tau)$
6. **Hexagon** $\tau\sigma\tau = (\sigma \star id)\tau(id \star \sigma)$

Proof

1. By definition, $(id \star id)(n) = \begin{cases} 2\left(\frac{n}{2}\right) = n & n \text{ even,} \\ 2\left(\frac{n-1}{2}\right) + 1 = n & n \text{ odd.} \end{cases}$

2. Similarly, $(h \star k)(f \star g)(n) = \begin{cases} (h \star k)\left(2f\left(\frac{n}{2}\right)\right) & n \text{ even,} \\ (h \star k)\left(2g\left(\frac{n-1}{2}\right) + 1\right) & n \text{ odd.} \end{cases}$

Now observe that $2f\left(\frac{n}{2}\right)$ is always even, for arbitrary choice of $f \in \mathbf{Bij}(\mathbb{N}, \mathbb{N})$ and even $n \in \mathbb{N}$. Similarly, $2g\left(\frac{n-1}{2}\right) + 1$ is always odd, for arbitrary choice of $g \in \mathbf{Bij}(\mathbb{N}, \mathbb{N})$ and odd $n \in \mathbb{N}$. Thus

$$(h \star k)\left((f \star g)(n)\right) = \begin{cases} 2h\left(\frac{2f\left(\frac{n}{2}\right)}{2}\right) & n \text{ even,} \\ 2k\left(\frac{\left(2g\left(\frac{n-1}{2}\right)+1\right)-1}{2}\right) + 1 & n \text{ odd.} \end{cases}$$

Simplifying this expression,

$$(h \star k)(f \star g)(n) = (hf \star kg)(n) = \begin{cases} 2hf\left(\frac{n}{2}\right) & n \text{ even,} \\ 2kg\left(\frac{n-1}{2}\right) + 1 & n \text{ odd.} \end{cases}$$

3. We first establish explicit formulæ for $f \star (g \star h)$ and $(f \star g) \star h$. By definition,

$$(f \star (g \star h))(n) = \begin{cases} 2f\left(\frac{n}{2}\right) & n \text{ even,} \\ (g \star h)\left(\frac{n-1}{2}\right) + 1 & n \text{ odd.} \end{cases}$$

Unwinding the definition of $(g \star h)$,

$$(g \star h)\left(\frac{n-1}{2}\right) = \begin{cases} 2g\left(\frac{n-1}{4}\right) & \frac{n-1}{2} \text{ even,} \\ 2h\left(\frac{\left(\frac{n-1}{2}\right)-1}{2}\right) + 1 & \frac{n-1}{2} \text{ odd.} \end{cases}$$

Thus

$$(f \star (g \star h))(n) = \begin{cases} 2f\left(\frac{n}{2}\right) & n \ (mod\ 2) = 0, \\ 2g\left(\frac{n-1}{4}\right) + 1 & n \ (mod\ 4) = 1, \\ 2h\left(\frac{n-3}{4}\right) + 3 & n \ (mod\ 4) = 3. \end{cases}$$

Using similar reasoning,

$$((f \star g) \star h)(n) = \begin{cases} 4f\left(\frac{n}{4}\right) & n \ (mod\ 4) = 0 \\ 4g\left(\frac{n-2}{4}\right) + 2 & n \ (mod\ 4) = 2 \\ 2h\left(\frac{n-1}{2}\right) + 1 & n \ (mod\ 2) = 1 \end{cases}$$

From the explicit description of τ,

$$\tau(f \star (g \star h)) = \begin{cases} 4f\left(\frac{n}{2}\right) & n \ (mod\ 2) = 0 \\ 4g\left(\frac{n-1}{4}\right) + 2 & n \ (mod\ 4) = 1 \\ 2h\left(\frac{n-3}{4}\right) + 1 & n \ (mod\ 4) = 3 \end{cases}$$

and an almost identical calculation will verify that $((f \star g) \star h)\tau$ is given by the same formula.

4. Direct calculation gives that

$$\sigma(g \star f)(n) = (f \star g)\sigma(n) = \begin{cases} 2f\left(\frac{n}{2}\right) + 1 & n \ (mod\ 2) = 0 \\ 2g\left(\frac{n-1}{2}\right) & n \ (mod\ 2) = 1 \end{cases}$$

5. We first describe the individual parts of the Pentagon equation:

$$(id \star \tau)(n) = \begin{cases} n & n \ (mod\ 2) = 0 \\ 2n-1 & n \ (mod\ 4) = 1 \\ n+2 & n \ (mod\ 8) = 3 \\ \frac{n-1}{2} & n \ (mod\ 8) = 7 \end{cases}$$

Similarly,

$$(\tau \star id)(n) = \begin{cases} 2n & n \ (mod\ 4) = 0 \\ n+2 & n \ (mod\ 8) = 2 \\ \frac{n+1}{2} & n \ (mod\ 8) = 6 \\ n & n \ (mod\ 2) = 1 \end{cases}$$

Composing, on a case-by-case basis, gives

$$\tau^2(n) = (\tau \star id)\tau(id \star \tau)(n) = \begin{cases} 4n & n \ (mod\ 2) = 0 \\ n+2 & n \ (mod\ 4) = 1 \\ \frac{n+1}{2} & n \ (mod\ 8) = 3 \\ \frac{n-3}{4} & n \ (mod\ 8) = 7 \end{cases}$$

6. For the hexagon equation, direct calculations (that by this stage, we are happy to leave as an exercise) demonstrate that

$$\tau\sigma\tau(n) = (\sigma \star id)\tau(id \star \sigma)(n) = \begin{cases} 2n+2 & n \ (mod \ 2) \ = \ 0 \\ \frac{n+1}{2} & n \ (mod \ 4) \ = \ 1 \\ n-3 & n \ (mod \ 4) \ = \ 3 \end{cases}$$

Remark 1. $\mathcal{J}$ is a monoid — a one-object, or single-typed, category. Despite this, the above calculations demonstrate how the rôle of distinct objects in the theory of symmetric monoidal categories is instead played by certain subsets of $\mathbb{N}$ — the congruence classes of the form $\{2^k.\mathbb{N} + x\}_{x=0\ldots2^k-1}$.

As demonstrated in Proposition 1 above, $(\mathcal{J}, \star, \tau, \sigma)$ has all the structure of a symmetric monoidal category, except for the existence of a unit object. We axiomatise such situations as follows:

Definition 2. *Let $\mathcal{C}$ be a category. We say that $\mathcal{C}$ is **semi-monoidal** when it satisfies all the properties for a monoidal category except for the requirement of a unit object — i.e. there exists a **tensor** $(\ \square\ ) : \mathcal{C} \times \mathcal{C} \to \mathcal{C}$ together with a natural object-indexed family of **associativity isomorphisms** $\{\tau_{A,B,C} : A\square(B\square C) \to (A\square B)\square C\}_{A,B,C \in Ob(\mathcal{C})}$ satisfying MacLane's pentagon condition*

$$(\tau_{A,B,C}\square 1_D)\tau_{A,B\square C,D}(1_A\square\tau_{B,C,D}) \ = \ \tau_{A\square B,C,D}\tau_{A,B,C\square D}$$

*When there also exists a natural object-indexed natural family of **symmetry isomorphisms** $\{\sigma_{X,Y} : X\square Y \to Y\square X\}_{X,Y \in Ob(\mathcal{C})}$ satisfying MacLane's hexagon condition*

$$\tau_{A,B,C}\sigma_{A\square B,C}\tau_{A,B,C} \ = \ (\sigma_{A,C}\square 1_B)\tau_{A,C,B}(1_A\square\sigma_{B,C})$$

*we say that $(\mathcal{C}, \square, \tau, \sigma)$ is a **symmetric semi-monoidal category**.*

*A functor $\Gamma : \mathcal{C} \to \mathcal{D}$ between two semi-monoidal categories $(\mathcal{C}, \square_{\mathcal{C}})$ and $(\mathcal{D}, \square_{\mathcal{D}})$ is called (strictly) **semi-monoidal** when $\Gamma(f\square_{\mathcal{C}}g) = \Gamma(f)\square_{\mathcal{D}}\Gamma(g)$. All monoidal categories are semi-monoidal, but not vice versa; the relationship is precisely analogous to that between monoids and semigroups. When a semi-monoidal category does not contain a unit object, we call it **unitless monoidal**.*

*When a semi-monoidal category has only one object, we call it **untyped monoidal**, or simply **untyped**.*

Theorem 1. *The structure $(\mathcal{J}, \_\star\_, \tau, \sigma)$, as given in Definition 1 is an untyped symmetric monoidal category.*

Proof. This follows from Proposition 1 above.

Remark 2. As observed in [14], we may construct similar structures based on congruence classes of the form $\{p^k\mathbb{N} + x\}_{x=0\ldots p^k-1}$, for arbitrary $p \geq 2 \in \mathbb{N}$, and in general the untyped symmetric monoidal structures on the monoid of bijections on the natural numbers are in 1:1 correspondence with the interior points of the Cantor set (and thus are uncountably infinite). We also refer to [10,18] for many examples of these, given in terms of algebraic representations of inverse semigroups. As observed in the introduction, these are heavily used in models of reversible computation and logic.

2.1   Coherence in Unitless Monoidal Categories

When working with semi-monoidal categories, it would be exceedingly useful to be able to rely on MacLane's coherence theorems, for both associativity and (when appropriate) symmetry. A natural worry, therefore, is whether there is some exceedingly subtle interaction between the existence of a unit object, and the monoidal tensor, that means these theorems are not applicable in the absence of a unit object.

Readers familiar with the proof of MacLane's coherence theorem for associativity will recall that associativity and the units conditions are treated individually, and so this is unlikely to be the case. A conclusive argument is provided by an Appendix to [13], where the obvious procedure for adjoining a (strict) unit object to a semi-monoidal category is described, and proved to be adjoint to the equally obvious forgetful functor. Thus, a semi-monoidal category may be transformed into a monoidal category with no side-effects.

Despite this, there is a subtlety about *untyped* monoidal categories that is worth observing. In [21], MacLane gives an argument, due to J. Isbell, for considering associativity up to canonical isomorphism, rather than up to strict identity. This argument was based on a denumerable object D in the skeletal category of sets satisfying $D \otimes D = D$, and a proof that strict associativity at this object would force a collapse to a triviality (i.e. the unit object for this category). Isbell's argument was phrased in terms of a single category with categorical products — an appendix to [14] argues that this is the case in arbitrary untyped monoidal categories, and a full coherence result is given in [13].

2.2   Coherence in the Untyped Monoidal Category $(\mathcal{J}, \star)$

In Section 1, we have seen that canonical isomorphisms for the untyped monoidal category $(\mathcal{J}, \star)$ are simply arithmetic expressions, built using modular arithmetic. Thus, it is possible (albeit frequently tedious and complex – see also Section 3) to verify whether or not a diagram commutes by direct calculation. Fortunately, we are also able to use MacLane's coherence theorem for associativity to derive — from basic categorical principles — a large class of diagrams that are guaranteed to commute, and thus a large class of number-theoretic identities that are guaranteed to be true.

However, we are not able to use the common simplification of the associativity theorem — valid in a wide range of settings — that states *all canonical diagrams commute*. Since all arrows of $\mathcal{J}$ have the same source and target, this would imply that all arrows built recursively from the set $\{\tau, (\_\star\_), (\ )^{-1}\}$ are equal, and this is clearly not the case! Instead, we must use the full statement of MacLane's theorem, in order to give a large class of diagrams that are guaranteed to commute.

The coherence theorem for associativity is based on the free monogenic monoidal category. As we are interested in the unitless case, we work with this category, with the unit removed. Readers unhappy with this are invited to adjoin a unit object to $\mathcal{J}$, apply the coherence theorem for associativity, and then remove the unit object.

Definition 3. *We define* $(\mathcal{W}, \square)$*, the* **free monogenic semi-monoidal cat-egory***, to be precisely MacLane's free monogenic monoidal category [21], with the unit object removed. An explicit description follows:,*

- *(Objects) These are non-empty binary trees over a single variable symbol* x*. Thus,* $x \in Ob(\mathcal{W})$*, and, for all* $a, b \in Ob(\mathcal{W})$*, the formal string* $a\square b \in Ob(\mathcal{W})$*.*
- *(Arrows) Given* $w \in Ob(\mathcal{W})$*, the* **rank** *of* w *is the number of occurrences of the symbol* x *within the string* w*, so* $rank(x) = 1$*, and* $rank(w) \geq 1$ *for arbitrary* $w \in Ob(\mathcal{W})$*. There then exists a unique arrow between any two objects* a, b *of the same rank, which we denote* $(b \leftarrow a) \in \mathcal{W}(a, b)$*.*
- *(Composition) The composite of two unique arrows is simply the unique arrow with the appropriate source / target. Thus,* $(c \leftarrow b)(b \leftarrow a) = (c \leftarrow a)$*.*
- *(Tensor) On objects, the tensor of* a *and* b *is the formal string* $a\square b$*. The definition on arrows must then be* $(b, a)\square(v, u) = (b\square v, a\square u)$*.*
- *(Associativity isomorphisms) The canonical isomorphism from* $a\square(b\square c)$ *to* $(a\square b)\square c$ *is the unique arrow between these two objects.*

The arrows between objects of rank n *correspond to the rebracketings of binary trees with* n *leaves, in the obvious way.*

There is then a natural semi-monoidal functor, $Sub : (\mathcal{W}, \square) \to (\mathcal{J}, \star)$, the (unitless version of the) *Substitution functor* of [21] p. 162. Expanding out the abstract definition gives the following characterisation of this functor:

- $Sub(w) = \mathbb{N}$, for all $w \in Ob(\mathcal{W})$.
- $Sub(w \leftarrow w) = id_{\mathbb{N}}$
- $Sub(a\square v \leftarrow a\square u) = id_{\mathbb{N}} \star Sub(v \leftarrow u)$
- $Sub(v\square a \leftarrow u\square a) = Sub(v \leftarrow u) \star id_{\mathbb{N}}$
- $Sub(a\square b)\square c \leftarrow a\square(b\square c) = \tau$.

MacLane's theorem states that $Sub(\mathcal{W}, \square) \to (\mathcal{J}, \star)$ is indeed a (semi-) monoidal functor, and thus any diagram over $(\mathcal{J}, \star)$ that is the image of a diagram over $(\mathcal{W}, \square)$ under this functor is guaranteed to commute. This simple result gives a countably infinite set of diagrams that are guaranteed to commute (and thus a corresponding set of arithmetic identities that are guaranteed to hold). For example, in $(\mathcal{J}, \star, \tau)$, the following diagram commutes:

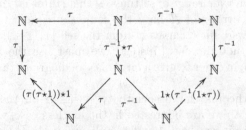

To prove that this commutes, simply note that it is the image of the following diagram over $(\mathcal{W}, \square)$

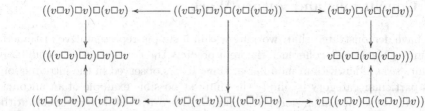

(We do not label the arrows of this diagram, since they are uniquely determined by their source and target. They may, of course, simply be thought of as re-bracketings of binary trees of rank 6).

3 Number-Theoretic Identities via Coherence

We have shown that MacLane's coherence theorem provides a countably infinite set of categorical diagrams that may be guaranteed to commute; however, the basic building blocks of these diagrams are the modular arithmetic operations of Definition 1 — thus the coherence theorem predicts identities within modular arithmetic. It is of course possible to verify that such diagrams, such as the above diagram, commute, using modular arithmetic and a case-by-case analysis, as in Section 1. However, to prove the following identities

$$\tau^2 = ((\tau(\tau \star 1)) \star 1)\tau(\tau^{-1} \star \tau) \ \text{ and } \ \tau^{-2} = (1 \star (\tau^{-1}(1 \star \tau^{-1})))\tau^{-1}(\tau^{-1} \star \tau)$$

as expressed by this diagram, would involve working with a case-by-case analysis of modulo classes of the form $\{n \ (mod \ 32) = k\}_{k=0\ldots31}$. The unfortunate referee assigned the task of verifying the calculations of Proposition 1 will agree that this is a task to be avoided, if at all possible.

In general, a canonical diagram with N nodes may be the image of a diagram in $(\mathcal{W}, \square)$ containing trees of depth N. An arithmetic check of the validity of this diagram may therefore require a case-by-case analysis that includes modulo classes $\{\mathbb{N} + x \ (mod \ K)\}_{x=0\ldots K}$, where $0 \leq K < 2^N$. Clearly this is unfeasible, even for moderately large N. However, when a diagram is indeed the image of a diagram in $(\mathcal{W}, \square)$ the coherence theorem for associativity allows us to assert equality between all paths within the diagram that have the same source and target — and thus the correctness of the (somewhat complicated) corresponding arithmetic identities.

Checking that an arbitrary diagram is within the image of this functor (and thus commutes) may be seen intuitively to be a much simpler task. In Section 4 below, we suggest that this task is in fact *linear*, instead of *exponential*.

Remark 3. As well as the modular arithmetic identities predicted by the coherence theorem for associativity, it may be observed that $(\mathcal{J}, \star)$ is a *symmetric* untyped monoidal category, and thus the theory of coherence of symmetry will predict an additional countably infinite set of identities. This is indeed correct, and coherence for other categorical properties (e.g. the distributivity of $\times$ over $\uplus$) also provide further sets of arithmetic identities. The study of these is work in progress.

4   Conclusions and Future Work

We have demonstrated that, working within a simple representative arithmetic example, MacLane's coherence theorem predicts the correctness of a countably infinite set of identities in modular arithmetic. As observed in the introduction, this particular category is simply the simplest possible example of an uncountably infinite set of similar untyped monoidal categories based on reversible arithmetic functions of the natural numbers. Thus, there appears to be considerable scope for deriving arithmetic and number-theoretic identities from categorical first principles.

Of equal interest – both in the category we give, or in any similar category — is whether we can go in the opposite direction; given a canonical diagram expressing some identities of modular arithmetic, is there a partial or complete decision procedure that will tell us whether it is the image of some diagram under MacLane's substitution functor (and thus whether the arithmetic identities expressed are correct)? We conjecture that not only is this the case, but that the complexity of this decision procedure is linear in the number of edges of the diagram (this conjecture is based on an algorithm presented by the author at the conference [3], based on Robinson's unification algorithm [5]).

We also expect to find further applications in a number of other fields. In particular, constructions similar to those of this paper were used in an algebraic setting to give full concrete representations of Thompson's V and F groups [19,20]. Thus, any results or decision procedures for the abstract categorical theory can reasonably be expected to find applications to the theory of these groups.

References

1. Abramsky, S.: Retracing some paths in process algebra. In: Sassone, V., Montanari, U. (eds.) CONCUR 1996. LNCS, vol. 1119, Springer, Heidelberg (1996)
2. Abramsky, S., Haghverdi, E., Scott, P.: Geometry of interaction and linear combinatory algebras. Mathematical Structures in Computer Science 12(5) (2002)
3. Abramsky, S., Krivine, J., Mislove, M.W.: Information Flow and Its Applications (Dagstuhl Seminar 12352). Dagstuhl Reports 2(8), 99–112 (2013)
4. Danos, V., Regnier, L.: Local and asynchronous beta reduction. In: Proceedings of the Eighth Annual IEEE Symp. on Logic in Computer Science (1993)
5. Gallier, J.: Logic for Computer Science. J. Wiley & sons (1987)
6. Girard, J.-Y.: Linear logic. Theoretical Computer Science 50, 1–102 (1987)
7. Girard, J.-Y.: Geometry of interaction 1. In: Proceedings Logic Colloquium 1988. North-Holland, pp. 221–260 (1989)
8. Girard, J.-Y.: Geometry of interaction ii. In: Martin-Löf, P., Mints, G. (eds.) COLOG 1988. LNCS, vol. 417, Springer, Heidelberg (1990)
9. Girard, J.-Y.: Toward a geometry of interaction. Contemporary Mathematics 92, 69–108 (1989)
10. Hines, P.: The algebra of self-similarity and its applications. PhD thesis, University of Wales, Bangor (1997)

11. Hines, P.: The categorical theory of self-similarity. Theory and Applications of Categories 6, 33–46 (1999)
12. Hines, P.: A categorical framework for finite state machines. Mathematical Structures in Computer Science 13, 451–480 (2003)
13. Hines, P.: Coherence in hilbert's hotel. Draft: available from arxiv:CT or peter.hines@york.ac.uk on request. arXiv:[math.CT]1304.5954 (2013)
14. Hines, P.: Types and forgetfulness in categorical linguistics and quantum mechanics. In: Sadrzadeh, M., Heunen, C. (eds.) Categorical Information Flow in Physics and Linguistics, pp. 215–248. Oxford University Press (2013)
15. Joyal, A., Street, R., Verity, D.: Traced monoidal categories. Mathematical Proceedings of the Cambridge Philosophical Society, 425–446 (1996)
16. Kelly, M., Laplaza, M.: Coherence for compact closed categories. Journal of Pure and Applied Algebra 19, 193–213 (1980)
17. Lambek, J., Scott, P.: Introduction to Higher Order Categorical Logic. Cambridge University Press (1986)
18. Lawson, M.V.: Inverse semigroups: the theory of partial symmetries. World Scientific, Singapore (1998)
19. Lawson, M.V.: Representations of the thompson group f via representations of the polycyclic monoid on two generators (2004)
20. Lawson, M.V.: Orthogonal completions of the polycyclic monoids. Communications in Algebra 35(5) (2007)
21. MacLane, S.: Categories for the working mathematician, 2nd edn. Springer, New York (1998)
22. Paoli, F.: Substructural Logics: A Primer. Kluwer (2002)
23. Sørensen, M., Urzyczyn, P.: Lectures on the Curry-Howard Isomorphism. Studies in Logic and the Foundations of Mathematics, vol. 149. Elsevier Science (1998)

Reversible Representation and Manipulation of Constructor Terms in the Heap

Holger Bock Axelsen and Robert Glück

DIKU, Department of Computer Science, University of Copenhagen
{funkstar,glueck}@diku.dk

Abstract. We currently have limited understanding of how complex data (*e.g.* algebraic data types) can be represented and manipulated in reversible machine code, in particular without generating garbage. In this paper we present methods for representing and manipulating binary trees (constructor terms) in the heap of a reversible machine. We also give methods for enforcing the so-called *first-match policy* for a simplified version of the recent reversible functional language RFUN by Yokoyama *et al.*, and simple methods to support let-calls via stack environments.

Keywords: Data structures, memory management, reversible programming.

1 Introduction

Reversible programming languages are scarce, and there are even fewer such languages with native support for complex data structures, to the frustration of reversible programmers everywhere. Recent developments may change this, however. The reversible *functional* programming language described in [16] (henceforth referred to as RFUN) has environments where variables bind to constructor terms. Another recent example is Π^o [9,10] with its rich type system. Thus, there is some hope that reversible programming may become easier in the future.

Now, reversible programming languages are usually considered in isolation, without regard for their place in the reversible programming stack, ignoring issues such as compilation. Also, these new languages handle very different types of data from those otherwise considered in reversible computation—usually bit values in circuits, or the flat strings used in reversible automata models. Furthermore, there is little to no understanding of how structured data can be represented and manipulated in low-level reversible machine code. One exception is the manipulation of (static size) arrays for Janus [1], but to the best of our knowledge more advanced data types have not yet been implemented. It is therefore basically unknown how one can manipulate complex structured data reversibly at the implementation level.

Besides the fundamental problem itself, this is a troubling hole in our knowledge for the following reason: there may be significant hidden costs associated with using complex data structures in reversible languages, *e.g.* unacceptable

G.W. Dueck and D.M. Miller (Eds.): RC 2013, LNCS 7948, pp. 96–109, 2013.
© Springer-Verlag Berlin Heidelberg 2013

slowdown or space consumption, when compared to their irreversible counterparts.[1] This is especially critical if we desire garbage-free implementations (and we generally do).

The main questions we are facing are as follows. First, how do we represent structured heap data in a reversible machine? Second, how do we manipulate such data reversibly, without generating garbage? Third, what are the costs of these methods?

Here, we present garbage-free methods for representing (Sect. 3) and manipulating (Sect. 4) constructor terms in the heap of a reversible machine. We use a simplified version of the RFUN language [16] to describe which (injective) high-level transformations on tree-structured data we wish to perform (Sect. 2), and PISA as the reversible assembler language [3,7,13]. We also provide a method for implementing RFUN's *first-match policy* (inherited in the simplified language), and outline an implementation of function calls. We discuss the methods further in Sect. 5 and conclude in Sect. 6.

2   RFUN for Tree-Structured Data

For concrete presentation purposes and to describe the high-level manipulation of tree-structured data a simplified version of the RFUN language is used in this paper. In this language, constructors build tree-structured data. Values consist of a constructor and its arguments, which again are constructor values. Values are thus recursively defined by constructor c and arguments v_i: $v ::= c(v_1, \ldots, v_n)$ where $n \geq 0$ and each constructor has a fixed arity.

As an example, the function *mirror* that recursively swaps the subtrees of a given binary tree can be written as follows. Here the nodes of the binary tree are formed by the binary constructor *Cons*, where each of its two arguments is again a subtree, and the nullary constructor *Nil* that represents the leaves.

$$\begin{aligned}
\textit{mirror } t \triangleq \textbf{ case } t \textbf{ of} \\
\textit{Cons}(a,b) \rightarrow \textbf{let } c = \textit{mirror } a \textbf{ in} \\
\textbf{let } d = \textit{mirror } b \textbf{ in } \textit{Cons}(d,c) \\
\textit{Nil} \quad\quad \rightarrow \textit{Nil}
\end{aligned}$$

Case-expressions deconstruct values into their arguments by pattern matching, such as the value of t in the example above, which is either a node with two subtrees (a,b) or a leaf of the tree. Constructor terms on the right-hand side of a case-expression, such as $Cons(d,c)$ or Nil, build new values.

The well-known language LISP was the first to be built on high-level abstract data formed by a single binary constructor (*Cons*) and a set of nullary constructors (atoms) [12]. The fundamental problem of representing and manipulating tree-structured data can even be further reduced by considering only the two constructors (*Cons*, *Nil*), and we shall follow this approach in this paper. The same simplified structures have also turned out to be quite useful in

---

[1] For example, statement x += e requires reversible simulation of expression e.

Grammar: Syntax domains:

q ::= d^* (program) $q \in$ Programs
d ::= $f\ x^* \triangleq e$ (definition) $d \in$ Definitions
e ::= l (left-expression) $f \in$ Functions
　 | **let** $x = f\ x^*$ **in** e (let-expression) $l \in$ Left-expressions
　 | **case** x **of** $\{c_i(x^*) \to e_i\}_{i=1}^m$ (case-expression) $e \in$ Expressions
l ::= x (variable) $x \in$ Variables
　 | $c(l_1, \ldots, l_n)$ (constructor) $c \in$ Constructors
c ::= Nil | $Cons$

Fig. 1. Syntax for simple RFUN for binary trees ($n \in \{0, 2\}, m \in \{1, 2\}$)

computability and complexity theory [11]. In fact, these two constructors are sufficient, even though not convenient for practical programming, to represent all tree-structured data. They can be generalized at the expense of additional mechanisms. For example, an (infinite) set of nullary constructors instead of just a single one (Nil), is a fairly trivial extension, with only little extra cost to our implementation. However, in order to focus on the essence of the problem of reversibly manipulating tree-structured data we restrict our attention to data built from these two constructors.

The simplified version of the first-order functional language (Fig. 1) that we use in this paper inherits its key features from RFUN including a new symmetric first-match policy and linearity of variable usage. It is tailored to ensure reversibility and is a modified version of a language that was originally defined for reversibility [16].

A *program* q is a sequence of function definitions. A *function definition* d consists of a function name f, variables x^* and an expression e. An expression e is a left-, let- or case-expression. A *left-expression* l can contain variables and constructor terms. We call $c_i(x^*) \to e_i$ the i-th *branch* of a case-expression.

Linearity. We consider only well-formed programs in the following sense: each variable in patterns appears at most once, and each variable is bound before its use and is used *linearly* in each branch. This is essential to a reversible language to avoid discarding values. Also, there is not implicit duplication of values (*e.g.* by using a variable twice in a branch). The duplication and comparison of values has to be programmed explicitly in our simplified language (a more convenient and explicit duplication/equality operator $\lfloor . \rfloor$ can be provided as in RFUN).

Symmetric first-match. The semantics of case-expressions is symmetric by requiring that the first-matching branch is the *same* at the entry *and* exit of a branch. This is essential for reversibility. Consider the following general case-expression.

$$
\begin{aligned}
\textbf{case } x \textbf{ of} \\
l_1 &\to \cdots \textbf{ in } l_1' \\
&\cdots \\
l_i &\to \cdots \textbf{ in } l_j' \\
&\cdots \\
l_n &\to \cdots \textbf{ in } l_m'
\end{aligned}
\tag{1}
$$

The value of x is matched in turn against the pattern of each branch $(l_1, l_2, \ldots)$ until the first successful match at some l_i. In each branch, the execution may ultimately reach one of several leaves, if there are nested case-expressions. After evaluating the right-hand side of the matching branch, and ending up at, say, the j-th leaf l'_j, then the return value must *not* match any of the preceding leaf left-expressions $(l'_1, \ldots, l'_{j-1})$. (Note that in general $i \le j$ and $n \le m$.) This *symmetric first-match policy* ensures that evaluation of branching function bodies is forward and backward deterministic.

The full language [16] allows more programming conveniences including *multiple nested patterns* in case-expressions, which can be expressed in our simplified language by nested case-expressions, and *rlet-expressions* which invoke the inverse of functions, which need to be written explicit in our language. These reversible programming features are not relevant for the tree-data manipulation problem studied in this paper.

3   Heap Data Structure Representation

In this section we describe the (static) heap structure we shall use, *i.e.*, how the heap concretely will represent an environment, in between manipulations.

Our heap structure is primarily motivated by the fact that RFUN uses (ground) constructor terms for its variable bindings. A natural reading is to view a constructor term as a tree with each constructor represented by a node, and its entries as child nodes, which makes for a straightforward representation via *pointer trees*. In general this allows many different concrete representation in machine memory of the abstract same constructor term.

Conceptually, the heap consists of *constructor cells* of fixed size (or, *cons cells* as in LISP). Specifically, we deal with two constructors in simplified RFUN, namely *Cons* and *Nil*, and our cons cells are three words long: this allows a cons cell to accommodate a constructor name (in the *constructor field*), and if necessary, pointers to two child nodes in the *children* (or *left* and *right*) fields.[2]

The heap structure is as follows. Constructor terms (pointer trees) live in the heap data area of memory. The *environment* contains pointers to the roots of these trees. The edge of the heap is given by the *heap pointer*. As is usual, we shall diagrammatically show the heap as growing downward. Below the heap pointer is an area of (zero-cleared) *free space*, into which the heap can grow, if necessary. The heap need not be densely populated, and can thus contain free cons cells. Such free cells are linked together in a (finite) *free list*, so that we may reuse them for constructing other trees. The *free list pointer* points to the head of the free list, and is null if the free list is empty. For technical reasons to be explained in Sect. 4.1, we place the following restriction on the free list, to be maintained as an invariant: the last element of the free list may *not* be the cons cell immediately above the heap pointer. Figure 2 shows an example heap representation.

---

[2] Three words are not necessarily the most compact representation for the binary trees of the simplified RFUN, but allows us to generalize it to other constructors later.

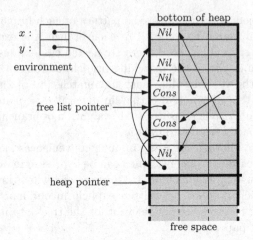

Fig. 2. Heap representing the environment $\{x \mapsto Nil, y \mapsto Cons(Nil, Cons(Nil, Nil)\}$. Gray memory cells are empty (zero-cleared).

Note that each cons cell in our heap example has reference count exactly one, *i.e.*, the heap is linear. This is not accidental, as RFUN uses variables linearly, so if we enforce that environments may only bind distinct variables to *separate* pointer trees, we can *guarantee* that the heap is linear. This is advantageous, in that we can then alter heap data representations directly (*update-in-place*). Our heap data is *mutable*, in contrast to conventional functional language implementations, where heap data is usually immutable. In a linear heap with mutable data the problem of garbage collection (in the conventional sense) becomes easy, as noted by Baker [5]. In fact, the combination of mutable data, linearity and reversibility actually means that garbage collection will be automatically performed simply by maintaining the heap structure across updates.

Using mutable data is not without drawbacks. In particular, the duplication operator $\lfloor . \rfloor$ from the general RFUN (omitted from our simplified version here) would be less efficient to implement directly, than if heap data were immutable. Duplication of immutable data merely requires copying a pointer to the data structure (breaking linearity), whereas if the heap data is mutable, an explicit traversal of the data structure appears necessary (again, noted by Baker [4]).

Although the static heap structure in Figure 2 appears fairly conventional, it thus has a number of differences from implementations used in irreversible functional languages, including LISP.

4   Heap Data Manipulation

In this section we explain our methods for construction and deconstruction of a tree at run-time, while maintaining the overall heap structure described above. The methods provide implementations of left-expressions as return values, and pattern matching in case-expressions (including the first-match policy), in our simplified language. We also describe how the stack may be used to handle environments, which implements let-calls.

4.1 Data Construction

Here, a left-expression is a constructor term over $Cons\backslash 2$, $Nil\backslash 0$ and named variables (Sect. 2). A left-expression is allowed to be a *nested* constructor term, so the top-level constructor may contain entries other than variables, *e.g.* the left-expression $Cons(Cons(x, Nil), y))$. If so, then the compiler can generate all the necessary construction code inductively over the constructor term. This means that the construction can be assumed to happen in straight-line code (or possibly as a sequence of calls to subroutines) that build *Nil* and *Cons* nodes. In particular, we can assume that the entries of a given *Cons* node have already been built as heap data, and are available as bindings in the environment.

We now describe how such nodes can be built in assembler code on a reversible register machine [3, 7, 13].

Building a Nil. Building a leaf node for a *Nil* in the heap is conceptually easy. We first get a pointer to a free cell, from either the free list or by growing the heap (how get_free() is implemented is described below). This gives us a pointer to a cons cell (say, in temporary register r_{cell}) with all fields zero-cleared. We then write the constant *Nil* (in some encoding) in the constructor field of the cell. Since *Nil* is a nullary constructor, nothing should be written in the (empty) children fields. Then, we simply return the cell pointer.[3]

In reversible assembly this can be done as follows.

```
< r_cell ← get_free() >    ; subroutine call
XORI r_t Nil               ; Nil is a constant
EXCH r_t M(r_cell)         ; write Nil in the constructor field
< return r_cell >
```

Note that the temporary register r_t is *zero-cleared* after the EXCH instruction: the constructor field of the new cons cell is initially zero and EXCH exchanges the contents of the register and the memory location. In this sense the reversible instruction set actually helps in maintaining linearity. For example, if a pointer is to be copied, this must be done *explicitly*.

Building a Cons. The method for building a binary node $Cons(a, b)$ is only slightly more involved. We first allocate a free cell for the node, and write *Cons* in the constructor field. The pointers to heap data a and b for the child nodes are supplied by the environment (*e.g.* in registers r_a and r_b). Now, by the linearity of RFUN and our linear heap structure, we know that this particular construction is the only use of either pointer. Thus, even though we have mutable data, we can place these pointers in the left and right child fields of the new *Cons* node, without destroying the consistency of the heap.

---

[3] Here, 'returning' can mean both as an RFUN return value, or as an intermediate value when building a nested constructor term.

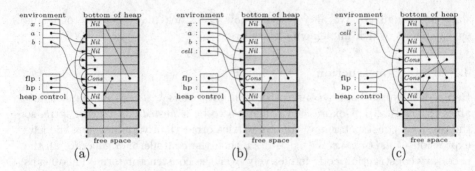

Fig. 3. How the heap changes while building a *Cons* node, corresponding to evaluating the left-expression $Cons(a,b)$ in the environment $\{x \mapsto Nil, a \mapsto Nil, b \mapsto Cons(Nil, Nil)\}$. (a) shows an initial heap representation. (b) shows the heap after allocating a free cons cell. We then write *Cons* in the constructor field, and move a and b from the environment into the children fields, resulting in the (c) heap representation.

Figure 3 shows how to build a *Cons* node. The method can be implemented with the following assembler code.

```
< r_cell ← get_free() >    ; subroutine call
XORI r_t Cons              ; Cons is a constant
EXCH r_t M(r_cell)         ; write Cons in the constructor field
ADDI r_cell 1              ;
EXCH r_a M(r_cell)         ; move pointer to a to the 'left' field
ADDI r_cell 1              ;
EXCH r_b M(r_cell)         ; move pointer to b to the 'right' field
SUBI r_cell 2              ; realign cell pointer
< return r_cell >
```

Note how similar this code is to how one would build the node irreversibly (even using immutable data) in a conventional implementation. This correspondence is made possible exactly because of the reversible heap design.

Using the *free list*. Now we consider the problem of how to retrieve a free cons cell. Naïvely, one might expect a simple implementation as follows.

```
EXCH r_cell M(r_flp)
SWAP r_cell r_flp
```

The r_{flp} register points to a memory location, which in turn contains a pointer to the tail of the free list. The EXCH instruction moves this tail pointer from the memory location $M(r_{flp})$ to register r_{cell}. By swapping[4] the tail pointer in r_{cell}

---

[4] Although SWAP would seem to be a natural instruction in a reversible architecture, neither PISA nor BobISA contain an instruction to swap the contents of two registers. However, it is easy to simulate reversibly, *e.g.* using the 'xor trick'.

with the head pointer in r_{flp}, we get the desired operation—effectively popping the head of the free list to r_{cell}.

However, this is only guaranteed to work if the free list is infinite, and it is not.[5] There are in fact *two* places where the free cell can come from: 1) the free list, or 2) by growing the heap (if the free list is empty). These two situations are handled differently, which means there is a *split* in control flow in the subroutine get_free(). Because the implementation language is reversible, an orthogonalizing condition is necessary to *join* the control flow again. This requires an important reversible programming trick [14].

Recall from Sect. 3 that the free list is empty if the free list pointer is null. If the free list is non-empty after popping a cons cell, then we obviously did not grow the stack. However, this is not quite enough to orthogonalize the following two situations.

- get_free() pops the *last* element off the free list.
- get_free() 'pops' an element off an empty free list, and grows the heap by one cons cell.

In both cases the free list will be empty after the allocation, so more than a zero check of the free list pointer is necessary. We resolve this by requiring that the *last* element of the free list must *never* be the cons cell at the top of the heap. This invariant is strong enough to provide us with an orthogonalizing condition to join the control flow: we grew the heap only if the free list is empty *and* the allocated pointer (r_{cell}) points to the top of the heap. Interestingly, this is remarkably similar to the solution of a related problem [14], namely, how to reversibly simulate an infinite stack with a finite one in a Turing-machine interpreter.

The body of the final get_free() subroutine is as follows.

```
if (r_flp == 0)              ; subroutine body get_free()
then                         ; grow heap:
   XOR  r_cell r_hp          ; cell := hp
   ADDI r_hp 3               ; hp++ (3 is the size of a cons cell)
else                         ; pop free list:
   EXCH r_cell M(r_flp)      ; cell ⇔ M(flp)
   SWAP r_cell r_flp         ; cell ⇔ flp
fi (r_flp == 0) && (r_cell == r_hp- 3)
```

The above gives pseudocode for the control flow in the style of Janus [14]. The *if-then-else-fi* reversible control flow statement works almost as a traditional *if-then-else*, except that is also has a joining assertion (the expression following the fi). This assertion must be true if control comes from the *then*-branch, and false otherwise, to guarantee reversibility. See [1] for garbage-free methods for translating this to PISA.

---

[5] This could be approximated by initializing all the heap space as a single free list — indeed, Baker assumes this structure for his pointer machine [5].

As a final remark, we mention the following compiler optimization: if another cons cell has been *deconstructed* immediately prior to the construction, then the interaction with the free list can be factored out. In RFUN code opportunities for this optimization can be applied in case-expressions when a pattern match with a constructor is followed by a left-expression with a top-level constructor (*e.g.* **case** x **of** $Cons(a, b) \to Cons(b, a)$).

4.2   Data Deconstruction

Deconstruction of tree-structured data in the heap is necessary in *pattern matching* of case-expressions, to direct control flow in the program. In our version of RFUN, case-expressions only contain flat patterns, so no nested constructors are allowed, and only the top-level constructor is matched.

Pattern Matching Constructors. To a great extent, pattern matching is 'merely' the inverse of the construction of values. As an example, consider the following case-expression with two branches.

$$\textbf{case } x \textbf{ of } \ Nil \qquad \to Cons(Nil, Nil)$$
$$Cons(a, b) \to \textbf{let } c = f \ a \textbf{ in } Cons(c, b)$$

Here, in the second branch, the *Cons* cell is deconstructed as follows: Pull the constructor field and child node pointers into temporary registers, and zero-clear the constructor field. Place the cons cell on the free list, and add the two children to the environment (a, b). This is exactly the inverse of the method for *constructing* a *Cons* cell, and it is safe to implement like this for the same reasons construction is safe: evaluating this case-expression removes x from the environment by linearity, and adds a, b to the environment in the e_2 branch.

When freeing the empty cons cell we have to maintain the free list *invariant*. Again, this is simply the inverse procedure used to allocate free cells, and can invoked by, say, a reverse subroutine call, or inlined with program inversion. The effect is exactly as desired: if the top cell of the heap is freed and the free list is empty, then shrink the heap. This maintains the invariant.

In fact, the key semantic difference to consider is that construction of a left-expression is *statically* determined by the program code, but deconstruction in pattern matching *dynamically* decides control flow. In turn, left-expressions can be implemented as straight-line code, but pattern matching requires *branching*.

Pattern matching can be implemented in reversible assembler as code with the following control structure.

```
if (constructor_field == Nil)
then
  deconstructNil()
  < code for branch e₁ >
else
  deconstructCons()
  < code for branch e₂ >
fi match(result, Cons(Nil, Nil))
```

Now, the forward branching condition is merely the constructor field value. Based on this we either deconstruct a *Nil* or a *Cons*, and evaluate the corresponding branch expression.[6] Although it might not be immediately obvious from a high-level RFUN function, it is very clear in the low-level implementation that control flow through the branches of a function body needs to be joined again. Eventually, all control flow through a function must arrive at a single return point regardless of which branch in a case-expression was taken. In RFUN, the branches of a function are orthogonalized by the first-match policy to ensure reversibility and thereby avoid information destruction, as described in Sect. 2.

Implementing the *first-match* Policy. The first-match policy makes RFUN programming significantly easier than the original pairwise orthogonalization of branches [8], and is even more important in that it resolves the control flow confluence of the branches of a function body, as we saw above. In a reversible implementation, we *must* orthogonalize the branches somehow, and the first-match policy is the key to making the implementation not just reversible, but also *garbage-free*. Here we propose a solution using pattern matching.

The first-match policy states that the value returned by the left-expression l_i in the leaf of a branch must not match any preceding leaf left-expression l_j ($j < i$). Thus, before returning from l_i, its value is *pattern matched* against all the preceding left-expressions, and it is a run-time error if it matches any of them. Thus, we have the run-time *assertion* that the return value does not unify with any of the preceding left-expressions. If we have two branches with two left-expressions in the leaves (l_1, l_2), as in the example above, the joining condition is a pattern match of the concrete return value of the evaluation of the function body, v, with the first left-expression l_1 (in our example, $Cons(Nil, Nil)$).

We have not yet described how pattern matching with left-expressions that include nested constructors may be performed. This is not difficult: we can simulate a one-branch case-expression with a left-expression for its pattern, by deconstructing the left-expression sequentially into nested case-expressions (of the same kind). For example,

$$\textbf{case } a \textbf{ of } Cons(Cons(x, Nil), y) \rightarrow e$$

can be simulated without using nested patterns by

$$\textbf{case } a \textbf{ of } \begin{array}{ll} Cons(t_1, y) \rightarrow \textbf{case } t_1 \textbf{ of} \\ \quad Cons(x, t_2) \rightarrow \textbf{case } t_2 \textbf{ of} \\ \quad Nil \quad\quad\quad \rightarrow e \end{array}$$

where t_1 and t_2 are fresh variables.

Of course, the *matching* operation used to implement the first-match policy is non-destructive, so we shall have to restore the return value. Thus it is not quite a pattern match in the same sense as in the RFUN language. Also, rather than

---

[6] If the case-expression has only one branch, then it acts as an assertion on the shape of its argument, and the missing branch should abnormally halt the computation.

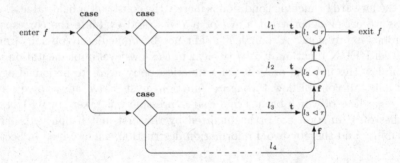

Fig. 4. Control flow for the reversible implementation of the first-match policy for a example function f with nested case-expressions. Here, there are four leaf let-expressions $(l_1, \ldots, l_4)$. The actual return value r is matched (denoted by $l \lhd r$) in turn against the corresponding left-expressions. The circle in the flow diagram denotes an assertion [15] that must be true when coming from an ingoing edge marked **t**, and false if the ingoing edge is marked **f**.

an abnormal halt, a failure merely returns **false**, as the matching is used as a conditional expression. Neither of these modifications will give rise to difficulties in implementation, however.

In general, we can now join all the branches of a function body as follows. Assuming the leaves are $\{l_1, \ldots, l_n\}$, we first join the n-th and $(n-1)$-th branch by matching the return value with l_{n-1}. Join the resulting merged branch with the $(n-2)$-th branch by matching the return value with l_{n-2}, and so forth until all branches are merged. Thus, the return value from the i-th branch will be matched against l_i (which will trivially succeed) and then matched against $l_{i-1}, \ldots, l_1$ as required (all of which should fail). Fig. 4 shows the control flow involved for an example with four leaves. This method provides a garbage-free implementation of the first-match policy if the joins (using the matchings as conditionals) are performed in the garbage-free manner of [1].

We remark that it is not unexpected that the first-match policy is not free to implement reversibly, nor is it surprising that the cost increases with the number of branches: this is inherent in the design of a reversible language which requires determinism in both computation directions. An optimizing compiler using static analysis can probably in many cases factor the constructor matching for the first-match policy into more efficient code. Such static program analyses are left for future work on optimizing compilers for reversible languages.

4.3   Call Stack Interaction

We here explain how function calls can be implemented by using the call stack for environments. Although this does not involve direct manipulation of the heap, this is needed for *let-calls*, which is the last major component of RFUN we need to implement. Fortunately, the linearity of RFUN allows us to sidestep most of the issues associated with parameter passing in reversible languages, *cf.* [14].

In particular, for the *caller* a let-call will always have the effect of *removing* the argument variables from the environment, replacing them with the single fresh variable for the result.[7] This allows us to use a fairly simple calling convention for RFUN functions, in combination with an existing method for parameterless procedure calls.[8]

For the *call sequence*, the caller pushes its complete environment onto the call stack (with the *non-argument* variables first, and the argument variables on top) and calls the callee. The *prologue* of the callee then extracts the arguments into its own local variables, and stores the return offset on the stack. Evaluation of the callee function body completely consumes these local variables, leaving only (a pointer to) the return value in, say, a designated *result register*. For the callee *epilogue*, the callee returns to the caller using the return offset on the stack (which is automatically removed in the return). The callee then restores the non-argument variables of its environment from the stack, and moves the result (pointer) to the fresh return variable into the environment as well, and proceeds with evaluating the rest of its function body. In particular, no garbage is generated using this calling convention.

This completes our description of the reversible heap.

5   Heap Data Properties

We here discuss further interesting properties of the heap representation.

When a program returns an output value, in fact, a link to the root of the result tree represented in the heap is returned. The free list maintained behind the scene, and not interesting to the user, will point to a list of unused cons cells and the heap pointer to an unclaimed memory region. If we start out with an empty free list, the final free list may grow as large as the largest intermediate data structure produced during program execution. Can we then get rid of the free list? Yes, by using the Bennett trick [2, 6], with the reasonable assumption that the input value is explicitly given in the program.

Clearly an abstract constructor value can be represented in many different concrete ways in the heap. However, the concrete linking of the cons cells in the heap does not matter to program execution. Two different internal representations of the same constructor value will yield two different internal representations of the same output value. This is good news because it means that for *inverse* execution of a program, we need not recreate the exact same free list by which the original output was accompanied. Any consistent heap representation of the same abstract tree data will do, including one with an empty free list.

---

[7] The full RFUN language allows conveniences such as left-expressions as arguments of function calls, and implicit pattern matching by a return left-expression. This can be supported as syntactic sugar for the simplified language, as described above for the first-match policy.

[8] Such subroutine calls are implemented in reversible assembly in [7]; see also [1,3,13].

Given these properties, one might question whether our heap representation is too liberal. Now, the free list is useful in that it can always be used to store heap data, and thus it does not seem reasonable to the authors to consider the free list *in toto* to be garbage data. On the other hand, there appears to be a way to keep the free list small during execution, by using *canonical heap forms* for constructor terms: we can adopt a heap representation format with one-to-one correspondence between the abstract and concrete data. However, we expect there to be non-trivial tradeoffs involved: if this canonical representation is to be maintained *continually*, it could require deep copying of *all* data on the heap for *every* manipulation. Further investigation is warranted.

6   Conclusion

In this paper we propose the design of a heap structure for tree-structured data for a reversible low-level machine, and provide methods for reversibly manipulating the structures in the heap. We give a simple high-level reversible functional language in which to describe functions that work on tree data, based on RFUN [16], and show how to implement its non-trivial features using these methods. In particular, we note that the implementation does not generate garbage data, and that "any consistent heap will do" for the methods to work. The methods presented here implement all major elements of RFUN for manipulating data: pattern matching (deconstruction), left-expressions (construction), let-calls (call stack interaction), and the first-match policy.

The extension of the methods to the full RFUN language remains for future work. However, arbitrary tree-structured data can be represented by binary trees and the generalization of *Nil* to a set of nullary constructors (atoms) is straightforward. Thus, the simplified RFUN (or a variant thereof) might be used as an intermediate language for the translation of RFUN. Recall that binary *Cons*-structures are the main data structures available in many programming languages used for non-trivial symbol manipulation, such as LISP. A more space-efficient representation may include n-ary constructor cells at the expense of a more involved mechanism for handling the free-list with cells of different sizes. Other possibilities to explore are an extension of RFUN with iterators over data structures (such as *map* and *fold*) and the implementation of the methods presented above in a complete compiler to a reversible register machine [3,7,13].

Acknowledgements. The authors thank the *Danish Council for Strategic Research* for (partial) support of this work through the *MicroPower* project.[9]

References

1. Axelsen, H.B.: Clean translation of an imperative reversible programming language. In: Knoop, J. (ed.) CC 2011. LNCS, vol. 6601, pp. 144–163. Springer, Heidelberg (2011)

---

[9] http://topps.diku.dk/micropower

2. Axelsen, H.B., Glück, R.: What do reversible programs compute? In: Hofmann, M. (ed.) FOSSACS 2011. LNCS, vol. 6604, pp. 42–56. Springer, Heidelberg (2011)
3. Axelsen, H.B., Glück, R., Yokoyama, T.: Reversible machine code and its abstract processor architecture. In: Diekert, V., Volkov, M.V., Voronkov, A. (eds.) CSR 2007. LNCS, vol. 4649, pp. 56–69. Springer, Heidelberg (2007)
4. Baker, H.G.: Lively linear Lisp – 'Look Ma, no garbage!'. ACM Sigplan Notices 27(9), 89–98 (1992)
5. Baker, H.G.: NREVERSAL of fortune – the thermodynamics of garbage collection. In: Bekkers, Y., Cohen, J. (eds.) IWMM-GIAE 1992. LNCS, vol. 637, pp. 507–524. Springer, Heidelberg (1992)
6. Bennett, C.H.: Logical reversibility of computation. IBM Journal of Research and Development 17(6), 525–532 (1973)
7. Frank, M.P.: Reversibility for Efficient Computing. Ph.D. thesis, EECS Dept., Massachusetts Institute of Technology (1999)
8. Glück, R., Kawabe, M.: A program inverter for a functional language with equality and constructors. In: Ohori, A. (ed.) APLAS 2003. LNCS, vol. 2895, pp. 246–264. Springer, Heidelberg (2003)
9. James, R.P., Sabry, A.: Information effects. In: POPL 2012, pp. 73–84. ACM (2012)
10. James, R.P., Sabry, A.: Isomorphic interpreters from logically reversible abstract machines. In: Glück, R., Yokoyama, T. (eds.) RC 2012. LNCS, vol. 7581, pp. 57–71. Springer, Heidelberg (2013)
11. Jones, N.D.: Computability and Complexity: From a Programming Language Perspective. MIT Press, Cambridge (1997)
12. McCarthy, J.: Recursive functions of symbolic expressions. Communications of the ACM 3(4), 184–195 (1960)
13. Thomsen, M.K., Axelsen, H.B., Glück, R.: A reversible processor architecture and its reversible logic design. In: De Vos, A., Wille, R. (eds.) RC 2011. LNCS, vol. 7165, pp. 30–42. Springer, Heidelberg (2012)
14. Yokoyama, T., Axelsen, H.B., Glück, R.: Principles of a reversible programming language. In: Proceedings of Computing Frontiers, pp. 43–54. ACM (2008)
15. Yokoyama, T., Axelsen, H.B., Glück, R.: Reversible flowchart languages and the structured reversible program theorem. In: Aceto, L., Damgård, I., Goldberg, L.A., Halldórsson, M.M., Ingólfsdóttir, A., Walukiewicz, I. (eds.) ICALP 2008, Part II. LNCS, vol. 5126, pp. 258–270. Springer, Heidelberg (2008)
16. Yokoyama, T., Axelsen, H.B., Glück, R.: Towards a reversible functional language. In: De Vos, A., Wille, R. (eds.) RC 2011. LNCS, vol. 7165, pp. 14–29. Springer, Heidelberg (2012)

An Introduction
to Quantum Programming in Quipper

Alexander S. Green[1],[*], Peter LeFanu Lumsdaine[2],[*],[**], Neil J. Ross[1],[*],[**],
Peter Selinger[1],[*],[**], and Benoît Valiron[3],[*]

[1] Dalhousie University, Halifax, NS, Canada
{agreen,selinger}@mathstat.dal.ca, Neil.JR.Ross@Dal.Ca
[2] Institute of Advanced Studies, Princeton, NJ, U.S.A.
p.l.lumsdaine@gmail.com
[3] University of Pennsylvania, Philadelphia, PA, U.S.A.
benoit.valiron@monoidal.net

Abstract. Quipper is a recently developed programming language for expressing quantum computations. This paper gives a brief tutorial introduction to the language, through a demonstration of how to make use of some of its key features. We illustrate many of Quipper's language features by developing a few well known examples of Quantum computation, including quantum teleportation, the quantum Fourier transform, and a quantum circuit for addition.

Keywords: Quantum Computation, Programming Languages, Quipper.

1 Introduction

1.1 Overview

Quipper [10] is an embedded functional programming language for quantum computation. It has been developed as part of IARPA's QCS project [13]. The stated goal of the QCS project is to *"accurately estimate and reduce the computational resources required to implement quantum algorithms on a realistic quantum computer"*, with an emphasis on using techniques that have been developed in the realms of computer science.

In this paper, we will look at how Quipper can be used to implement existing quantum algorithms, through a close look at some of the language features that

---

[*] This research was supported by the Intelligence Advanced Research Projects Activity (IARPA) via Department of Interior National Business Center contract number D12PC00527. The U.S. Government is authorized to reproduce and distribute reprints for Governmental purposes notwithstanding any copyright annotation thereon. Disclaimer: The views and conclusions contained herein are those of the authors and should not be interpreted as necessarily representing the official policies or endorsements, either expressed or implied, of IARPA, DoI/NBC, or the U.S. Government.

[**] This research was supported by NSERC.

G.W. Dueck and D.M. Miller (Eds.): RC 2013, LNCS 7948, pp. 110–124, 2013.
© Springer-Verlag Berlin Heidelberg 2013

have been added specifically for this task. Quipper's development was guided by the goal of implementing seven non-trivial quantum algorithms from the literature [3,5,11,12,14,17,18]. These algorithms were chosen by the QCS project, and provided to us in modified form. They cover a broad spectrum of techniques used in quantum computation. Each algorithm introduced its own challenges that helped guide the language features that are now available in Quipper.

We will use simple examples to try to demonstrate the use of Quipper, and to give insights into the types of problems that the various language features are useful for. We will consider three main stand-alone examples:

- Quantum teleportation will guide us through: Quipper's underlying circuit model, Quipper's primitive operations, quantum data-types, generic functions, comments, and labels.
- The quantum Fourier transform and quantum addition will help us look at: recursion, circuit-level operators, boxed circuits, and simulation.
- We will end by looking at Quipper's features that can be used to implement quantum oracles, including: automatic generation of circuits from classical code, synthesis of reversible circuits, and circuit transformations.

We will also have a brief look at how Quipper can be used to estimate the computational resources required by the algorithms that have been implemented.

In another recent paper [10], we have described in more detail the rationale behind the various design choices that went into Quipper, including a high-level overview of, and justification for, its language features. We also gave more background on general issues affecting quantum programming languages, and on the implementation of the language itself. By contrast, the aim of this present paper is to give a tutorial introduction to Quipper from a programmer's perspective, using examples that have been chosen to guide readers through some of Quipper's main features.

1.2   Quipper as an Embedded Language

Quipper has been implemented as an embedded language, using Haskell as the host language. Therefore, Quipper can be seen as a collection of data types, combinators, and a library of functions within Haskell, together with an *idiom*, i.e., a preferred style of writing embedded programs. In this paper, we present Quipper as if it were a language in its own right, i.e., without presupposing any knowledge of Haskell.

While the embedded language approach has many advantages (see [6, Sec. 1.3] for a general discussion), there are also certain potential pitfalls that programmers should be aware of. One of these is the temptation to "escape to the host language", i.e., to write general Haskell programs rather than following Quipper's intended idiom. This can break intended abstractions, and make the programs less portable in case of implementation changes. Another drawback of the embedded language approach is that compilation errors are often difficult to decipher, because the compiler presents them in terms of concepts of the host language, rather than the embedded language. Finally, while Haskell is a good fit for Quipper in many respects, it does lack two features that would be useful for a quantum programming language: *linear types* and *dependent types*. We must therefore live with checking certain well-formedness properties of programs at run-time, although they could in principle be checked by the type-checker in a dedicated language.

1.3   Quipper's Underlying Circuit Model

Quipper uses an extended circuit model of quantum computation. We allow for both quantum and classical wires and operations within a circuit. Quantum operations can be controlled by a classical wire, but not vice versa. A quantum wire can be explicitly measured, thus creating a classical wire. Quipper's circuit model also incorporates explicitly scoped ancilla wires, allowing for an ancilla to only come into scope for the part of the circuit in which it is used. This is achieved by allowing explicit qubit initialization and termination within a circuit.

Using a circuit model leads to three distinct phases of execution: compile time, circuit generation time, and circuit execution time. This, in turn, gives rise to an extra distinction among inputs. Inputs whose value is known at circuit generation time will be called *parameters*; whereas inputs whose value is only known at circuit execution time will be called *inputs*. To keep this distinction explicit, Quipper introduces three basic types for bits and qubits. We use the type `Bool` for a boolean parameter that is known at circuit generation time, the type `Bit` for a classical boolean input to a circuit, and the type `Qubit` for a quantum input to a circuit. A parameter of type `Bool` can easily be converted to an input of type `Bit`, but not vice versa. Also, because measurements can only occur at circuit runtime, the outcome of a measurement is a `Bit`, not a `Bool`.

2   Quipper by Example

2.1   Quantum Teleportation

Quipper's Primitive Operations. Although Quipper can be regarded as a language for describing quantum circuits, when actually developing computations within Quipper it is often preferable to think in terms of gates being applied in real time to qubits (or bits) that are held in variables. This procedural paradigm is the foundation for developing quantum computations in Quipper, on top of which more powerful higher-order operators are built.

Computations in Quipper take the form of functions. The following example shows how we can write a simple quantum function in Quipper.

```
plus_minus :: Bool -> Circ Qubit
plus_minus b = do
    q <- qinit b
    r <- hadamard q
    return r
```

The first line corresponds to the *type* of the function. We see that the input to the function is a boolean parameter. The output type of the function is `Circ Qubit`. The `Circ` part of the type is actually a type operator, and is used to state that the function being defined can have a physical side effect when it is evaluated (Haskell programmers will recognize this as a *monad*). The `Qubit` part of the output type tells us that the function returns a qubit. The body of the function usually starts with the keyword `do`, followed by a block of quantum operations to be evaluated in the given order. The body of the `plus_minus` function uses three operations. The `qinit` operator initializes a new qubit, in the state corresponding to b. Here, `False` corresponds to $|0\rangle$ and `True` corresponds to $|1\rangle$. The notation tells us that this newly created qubit is stored in the variable q. The operator `hadamard` applies the Hadamard gate to the qubit q, storing the updated qubit in the variable r. The last line returns the qubit r as the output of the whole function. In summary, this function introduces a newly initialized qubit in either of the states $|+\rangle$ or $|-\rangle$ depending on a boolean parameter. We also note that variables in the function body are used *linearly*: each qubit is written exactly once and read exactly once. This restriction is imposed by the laws of quantum physics. In Quipper's syntax, however, it would have been permitted to use the same name for the two variables q and r, and we will often do so in future examples.

Circuit Generation. After defining a quantum function in Quipper, there are various things we can do with it. The most basic of these is to evaluate the function to generate a circuit. When Quipper evaluates a circuit producing function, the circuit is produced lazily, on-the-fly. This is useful for defining very large circuits, whereby the whole circuit doesn't need to be stored in memory. Moreover, circuits can also be *consumed* lazily, for example by a transformation (see p. 122), or by passing instructions sequentially to an (actual or simulated) quantum computer (see p. 121).

A useful operation provided by Quipper is a circuit printing function that enables the circuits produced by Quipper to be exported in various formats. For example, to produce a PDF document from the circuit defined by the above `plus_minus` function, we can use the built-in Quipper operator `print_simple`. Note that parameters, but not inputs, must be specified at circuit generation time. Here, we set the parameter b to `False`.

```
print_plus_minus :: IO ()
print_plus_minus = print_simple PDF (plus_minus False)
```

The circuit diagrams used throughout the rest of this paper have been created directly from the given code examples. The next example illustrates how to control a quantum gate. This function inputs a qubit and returns a pair of qubits. The `qnot` operation applies a not-gate to the qubit b. Moreover, the infix operator `'controlled'` causes this operation to be controlled by the qubit a. The overall effect of the function `share` is to take a qubit in the state $\alpha|0\rangle + \beta|1\rangle$ and entangle it with a newly initialized qubit to create the state $\alpha|00\rangle + \beta|11\rangle$.

```
share :: Qubit -> Circ (Qubit, Qubit)
share a = do
  b <- qinit False
  b <- qnot b 'controlled' a
  return (a,b)
```

Previously defined quantum functions can be used as building blocks in other quantum functions. In fact, they can be used in exactly the same way as Quipper's built-in operators. In the next example, we use our previously defined functions, plus_minus and share, to produce a pair of qubits in the Bell state $\frac{1}{\sqrt{2}}(|00\rangle + |11\rangle)$.

```
bell00 :: Circ (Qubit, Qubit)
bell00 = do
  a <- plus_minus False
  (a,b) <- share a
  return (a,b)
```

A Teleportation Circuit. Let us now consider quantum teleportation (see [15] for an introduction). This involves two parties Alice and Bob. Alice's goal is to teleport a qubit q to Bob. Alice and Bob must each have access to a single qubit from an entangled Bell pair (a, b), which we can produce with the above bell00 function. We can think of Alice's role in terms of a function that inputs the two qubits q and a. The output of the function will be a pair of classical bits, produced by Alice by applying some unitary gates and then measuring both qubits.

```
alice :: Qubit -> Qubit -> Circ (Bit,Bit)
alice q a = do
  a <- qnot a 'controlled' q
  q <- hadamard q
  (x,y) <- measure (q,a)
  return (x,y)
```

Note that the function measure has been applied to a pair of qubits. In Quipper's syntax, this is simply an abbreviation for measuring both qubits in the pair. This abbreviated syntax is possible because the Quipper operator measure is a *generic* operator: it can be applied to any data structure containing qubits, and returns a corresponding data structure containing bits. Another example of a generic Quipper operator is cdiscard, which can be applied to any data structure containing classical bits. It is used in Bob's part of the teleportation protocol:

```
bob :: Qubit -> (Bit,Bit) -> Circ Qubit
bob b (x,y) = do
  b <- gate_X b 'controlled' y
  b <- gate_Z b 'controlled' x
  cdiscard (x,y)
  return b
```

The following function ties all the pieces of the teleportation example together. We can see that a Bell state is created, which is then used by Alice, along with the input qubit, to create a pair of classical bits. These are passed to Bob along with his qubit from the Bell state. The generated circuit diagram shows that Quipper joined together the various steps as expected.

```
teleport :: Qubit -> Circ Qubit
teleport q = do
    (a,b) <- bell00
    (x,y) <- alice q a
    b <- bob b (x,y)
    return b
```

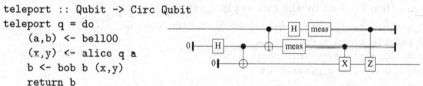

Quantum Data Types and Generic Functions. *Quantum data types* are types that are built up from Qubit by means of data constructors, such as tuples and lists. For example, (Qubit,[Qubit]) is the type whose elements are pairs of a qubit and a (variable but finite length) list of qubits. Every quantum data type, such as $qa = $ (Qubit,[Qubit]), has an associated *classical data type*, such as $ca = $ (Bit,[Bit]), and *boolean data type*, such as $ba = $ (Bool,[Bool]). We say that qa, ca, and ba have the same *shape*, but different *leaf types*. A Quipper function is called *generic* if it can act on data types of any shape.

We have already seen several examples of generic built-in Quipper functions, namely measure, cdiscard, and print_simple. However, what makes generic functions particularly useful in Quipper is the fact that it is easy to create new *user-defined* generic functions. We will now illustrate this feature by defining a generic version of the teleportation circuit.

In Quipper, the keyword QShape is used to declare that three types qa, ca, and ba are the quantum, classical, and boolean version of some data type. To define a generic version of the plus_minus function, we replace Bool and Qubit in its type by such a pair of related ba and qa:

```
plus_minus_generic :: (QShape ba qa ca) => ba -> Circ qa
plus_minus_generic a = do
    qs <- qinit a
    qs <- mapUnary hadamard qs
    return qs
```

We note that the qinit function is already generic. The operator mapUnary maps a function of type Qubit $\to$ Circ Qubit over every qubit in a quantum data structure. To extend the share function, we use the function qc_false which generates a boolean data structure of the correct shape, with every boolean set to False. The mapBinary function is similar to mapUnary, but maps a function of the type Qubit $\to$ Qubit $\to$ Circ (Qubit,Qubit) over every corresponding pair of qubits from two quantum data structures of the same shape. We also use the built-in controlled_not operation.

```
share_generic :: (QShape a qa ca) => qa -> Circ (qa, qa)
share_generic qa = do
    qb <- qinit (qc_false qa)
    (qb, qa) <- mapBinary controlled_not qb qa
    return (qa, qb)
```

Updating the bell00 function requires a little more thought, as we now need to explicitly know the shape of the data being teleported in order to generate enough Bell pairs. This is achieved by adding a shape argument to the function, which can then be used by the call to plus_minus_generic.

```
bell00_generic :: (QShape a qa ca) => a -> Circ (qa, qa)
bell00_generic shape = do
    qa <- plus_minus_generic shape
    (qa, qb) <- share_generic qa
    return (qa, qb)
```

The changes to Alice's function are very similar to those we have seen already.

```
alice_generic :: (QShape a qa ca) => qa -> qa -> Circ (ca,ca)
alice_generic q a = do
    (a, q) <- mapBinary controlled_not a q
    q <- mapUnary hadamard q
    (x,y) <- measure (q,a)
    return (x,y)
```

For Bob's function, we need a way of mapping classically controlled X- and Z-rotations over the input bits and qubits. The function mapBinary_c is similar to mapBinary, except that it expects a function of type Qubit $\rightarrow$ Bit $\rightarrow$ Circ (Qubit, Bit). Also, whereas the controlled_not function is a built-in operator, the classically controlled X and Z rotations are not. We use a where clause to define a generic controlled_gate function locally.

```
bob_generic :: (QShape a qa ca) => qa -> (ca,ca) -> Circ qa
bob_generic b (x,y) = do
    (b, y) <- mapBinary_c (controlled_gate gate_X) b y
    (b, x) <- mapBinary_c (controlled_gate gate_Z) b x
    cdiscard (x,y)
    return b
  where
    controlled_gate gate b x = do
      gate b 'controlled' x
      return (b,x)
```

The various parts of the generic teleportation function can now be tied together.

```
teleport_generic :: (QData qa) => qa -> Circ qa
teleport_generic q = do
    (a,b) <- bell00_generic (qc_false q)
    (x,y) <- alice_generic q a
    b <- bob_generic b (x,y)
    return b
```

Note that a generic Quipper function defines a *family* of circuits, one for each data type. To be able to print specific members of this family, we must replace the print_simple operator by the more general print_generic. The difference is that print_generic takes additional arguments to determine which instance of the circuit family to print. We show examples for teleporting a pair of qubits, and a list of three qubits:

```
print_generic PDF teleport_generic (qubit, qubit)
```

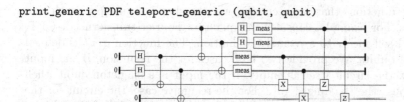

```
print_generic PDF teleport_generic [qubit,qubit,qubit]
```

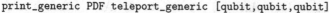
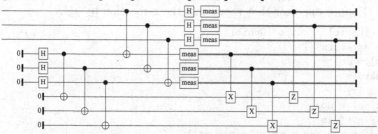

Comments and Labels. When reading very large circuits, it is sometimes hard to keep track of what each part of the circuit is doing, or which wires certain variables correspond to. As a convenience to the programmer, Quipper offers a way of adding comments and labels to a circuit:

```
teleport_generic_labeled :: (QData qa) => qa -> Circ qa
teleport_generic_labeled q = do
    comment_with_label "ENTER: bell00" q "q"
    (a,b) <- bell00_generic (qc_false q)
    comment_with_label "ENTER: alice" (a,b) ("a","b")
    (x,y) <- alice_generic q a
    comment_with_label "ENTER: bob" (x,y) ("x","y")
    b <- bob_generic b (x,y)
    return b
```

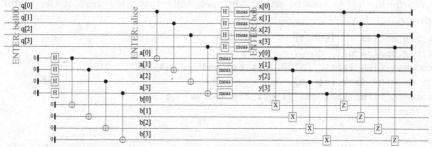

2.2 The Quantum Fourier Transform and Quantum Addition

Recursion. In Quipper it is possible to write circuit producing functions that are recursive over any parameters known at circuit generation time. Notably, we can write functions that are recursive over the shape of an input, such as a list of qubits. For example, consider the quantum Fourier transform, or QFT, which lends itself nicely to a recursive definition. The function qft' is defined over a list of qubits. We provide two base cases for the recursion. If the input list is empty, the circuit itself is empty. If the input is a singleton qubit, then the QFT is just the Hadamard gate. For the recursive case, the circuit for the QFT for $n + 1$ qubits consists of the circuit for the n qubit QFT, followed by a set of rotations over all $n + 1$ qubits. This set of rotations can also be defined in terms of a recursive function, which we call rotations. Also, rGate m is a built-in Quipper operator that represents the z-rotation by $\frac{2\pi i}{2^m}$.

```
qft' :: [Qubit] -> Circ [Qubit]
qft' [] = return []
qft' [x] = do
  hadamard x
  return [x]
qft' (x:xs) = do
  xs' <- qft' xs
  xs'' <- rotations x xs' (length xs')
  x' <- hadamard x
  return (x':xs'')
 where
  rotations :: Qubit -> [Qubit] -> Int -> Circ [Qubit]
  rotations _ [] _ = return []
  rotations c (q:qs) n = do
    qs' <- rotations c qs n
    let m = ((n + 1) - length qs)
    q' <- rGate m q 'controlled' c
    return (q':qs')
```

The function qft' expects its list of input qubits in little-endian order, but returns the output in big-endian order. Because this is confusing, we wrap it in another function qft_big_endian, which simply reverses the order of the input qubits. In Quipper, this is done not by swapping wires in a circuit, but by reordering *references* to wires; Quipper will attach the rest of the circuit appropriately.

```
qft_big_endian :: [Qubit] -> Circ [Qubit]
qft_big_endian qs = do
  comment_with_label "ENTER: qft_big_endian" qs "qs"
  qs <- qft' (reverse qs)
  comment_with_label "EXIT: qft_big_endian" qs "qs"
  return qs
```

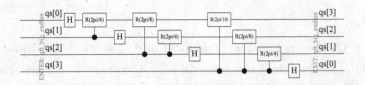

Circuit-Level Operations. Most operators we have seen so far work at the level of gates, i.e., their effect is to append gates one by one to a circuit under construction. Quipper also has the idiom of circuit-level operations, which are operations that can be applied to circuits as a whole. One example is the printing of circuits, but there are also circuit-level operations that can be used while constructing circuits. These often take a circuit generating function as input, and produce a new circuit generating function as an output, which can then be used just like any other circuit generating function. A useful example is the operator `reverse_generic_endo`, which reverses a whole circuit. The following function computes the inverse of the QFT.

```
inverse_qft_big_endian :: [Qubit] -> Circ [Qubit]
inverse_qft_big_endian = reverse_generic_endo qft_big_endian
```

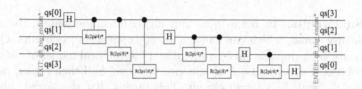

A Quantum Adder. As an application of the QFT, we look at a quantum circuit that performs addition [7], without the use of ancilla qubits. The circuit uses a QFT as a basis change. The inverse QFT is then applied at the end to change back to the computational basis. The part of the circuit that performs the actual addition, between the two uses of the QFT, once again lends itself to a recursive definition.

```
qft_adder :: [Qubit] -> [Qubit] -> Circ ()
qft_adder _ [] = return ()
qft_adder as (b:bs) = do
  qft_adder' as b 1
  qft_adder (tail as) bs
where
    qft_adder' :: [Qubit] -> Qubit -> Int -> Circ [Qubit]
    qft_adder' [] _ _ = return []
    qft_adder' (a:as) b n = do
      b <- rGate n b 'controlled' a
      qft_adder' as b (n+1)
```

The pattern of applying an initial computation, followed by some operation, followed by the inverse of the initial computation, is quite common in quantum computation. For this reason, Quipper provides a circuit-level operator `with_computed`, which automatically takes care of applying the inverse computation at the end. We use this here to complete the quantum addition circuit, using the QFT as the initial computation to be inverted at the end.

```
qft_add_in_place :: [Qubit] -> [Qubit] -> Circ ([Qubit], [Qubit])
qft_add_in_place a b = do
  label (a,b) ("a","b")
  with_computed (qft_big_endian b) $ \b' -> do
    qft_adder a (reverse b')
  label (a,b) ("a","b")
  return (a,b)
```

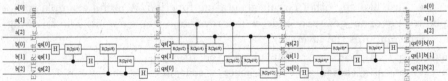

Boxed Subcircuits. In many quantum algorithms, the same subcircuit is reused multiple times, which can cause a lot of duplication in circuits. Quipper helps alleviate such duplication by providing a hierarchical model of circuits, in the form of boxed subcircuits. A circuit can be *boxed*, and then reused multiple times as a subcircuit in a larger circuit. This means that the boxed subcircuit only needs to be generated once, and then a call to the boxed subcircuit is placed in the main circuit, whenever the subcircuit would appear. Quipper also permits an iteration count to be attached to a boxed subcircuit call.

A subcircuit can be boxed by using the `box` operator, which takes as its arguments a name and a function to be boxed. Here, we replicate the previous example, but with the QFT boxed.

```
qft_add_in_place_boxed :: [Qubit] -> [Qubit] -> Circ ([Qubit], [Qubit])
qft_add_in_place_boxed a b = do
  label (a,b) ("a","b")
  with_computed (box "QFT" qft_big_endian b) $ \b' -> do
    qft_adder a (reverse b')
  label (a,b) ("a","b")
  return (a,b)
```

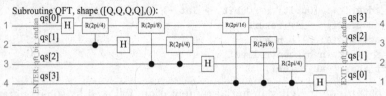

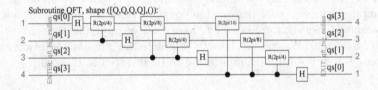

Simulation of Circuits. Unlike many quantum programming languages in the literature, Quipper was not designed as a front-end language for a quantum simulator; rather, it was designed to control an actual (future) quantum computer. Therefore, non-physical operations are not provided in Quipper. Nevertheless, during development and testing (and in the absence of an actual quantum computer), it is useful to be able to run simulations. Quipper provides three different simulators, which can be used depending on which gates are used within a circuit.

- Classical simulation - efficiently simulates classical circuits.
- Stabilizer simulation - efficiently simulates Clifford group circuits [1].
- Quantum simulation - simulates any circuit (with exponential overhead).

The simulators are generic: they take any circuit producing function and convert it into a function acting on the boolean counterparts to the quantum data types used in the circuit. Both the stabilizer simulator, and the quantum simulator are probabilistic.

2.3   Quantum Circuits from Classical Functions

Generating Circuits from Classical Code. A notable feature of Quipper is the ability to automatically generate reversible circuits from ordinary functional programs. This is achieved by inserting the Quipper keyword `build_circuit` right before the classical function definition. This causes Quipper to define a new circuit generating function, with the same name as the given classical function, preceded by `template_`, where any `Bool` arguments in the type are changed to `Qubit`. We found that this language feature is useful when defining many of the oracles that appear in quantum algorithms, as they are often of a classical nature, but need to be applied to a quantum register. We have used this feature, for example, to implement a quantum library for real fixed-point arithmetic. The following example shows a single-bit full adder. A quantum function named `template_adder` will be automatically generated.

```
build_circuit
adder :: (Bool,Bool,Bool) -> (Bool,Bool)
adder (a,b,carry_in) = (s,carry_out)
 where
  s = bool_xor (bool_xor a b) carry_in
  carry_out = (a && b) || (a && carry_in) || (b && carry_in)
```

The helper function `unpack` is used to tidy up the type of any circuit produced using the `build_circuit` keyword, by removing some unnecessary occurrences of the `Circ` operator.

```
adder_circ :: (Qubit,Qubit,Qubit)
   -> Circ (Qubit,Qubit)
adder_circ = unpack template_adder
```

The `build_circuit` feature is implemented using a Haskell extension known as *Template Haskell*; this gives programs access to their own syntax tree in parsed form. Because of this generality, essentially arbitrary Haskell functions can be used with the `build_circuit` keyword. However, the programmer must supply quantum templates for any library functions that are used, unless they are among the standard templates already predefined by Quipper.

Synthesis of Reversible Circuits. The circuit produced by `adder_circ` is not a self-contained reversible circuit, as the automatic transformation introduces ancilla qubits that may be left in an indeterminate state, possibly entangled with the outputs. The Quipper operator `classical_to_reversible` turns a circuit $f :: a \rightarrow$ Circ b into a reversible circuit $f' :: (a, b) \rightarrow$ Circ (a, b), ensuring that any ancillas are suitably un-computed and terminated, provided that f uses only reversible primitives.

```
adder_reversible :: ((Qubit,Qubit,Qubit),(Qubit,Qubit))
   -> Circ ((Qubit,Qubit,Qubit),(Qubit,Qubit))
adder_reversible = classical_to_reversible adder_circ
```

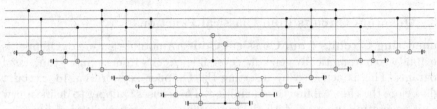

Circuit Transformations. Quipper provides a means for transforming circuits, on-the-fly, at circuit generation time. This allows for transformations such as gate decompositions, or adding certain types of error-correcting codes. Quipper provides some pre-defined transformers, as well as an extensible framework for user-defined transformers. Example transformers include the simulators, as well as a transformer to decompose circuits to only binary gates, or binary gates plus the Toffoli gate. In the following example, we apply the binary gate decomposition transformer to the adder circuit.

```
adder_circ_b :: (Qubit,Qubit,Qubit) -> Circ (Qubit,Qubit)
adder_circ_b = decompose_generic Binary adder_circ
```

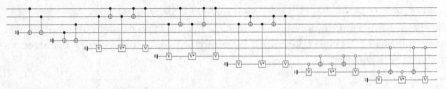

3   Final Remarks

3.1   Scalability and Resource Estimation

As we have seen, there are various things that Quipper can do with a generated circuit. However, when defining large circuits, it isn't always feasible to generate the circuit in its entirety. Quipper provides a mechanism by which one can count the resources associated with a circuit (e.g., number of gates, number of qubits, number of ancillas). Combining this feature with boxed subcircuits, we have been able to do resource estimation for some very large circuits. For example, our Quipper implementation of the triangle finding algorithm [14] produces a circuit containing over 30 trillion gates, which can be counted in under two minutes on a 1.2GHz laptop.

3.2   Prior Art

There have been a number of quantum programming languages introduced in the literature (see [8]). Among the languages that have actually been implemented are Ömer's QCL [16], a C-style language optimized for quantum simulation; the Quantum IO Monad [2], which is a quantum programming language also embedded in Haskell; and Giles's LQPL [9], a functional quantum programming language with linear types. However, most of the languages that can be found in the literature are not shown to be scalable to large problem sizes.

The problem of generating circuit descriptions from functional programs has also been studied outside of the realm of quantum computing; see, e.g., [4,6].

3.3   Conclusion

Quipper has many language features, and only a selection of them have been discussed in this introductory paper. The Quipper distribution also includes some libraries of commonly used quantum functions. For example, we provide an extensive library of arithmetic functions, both for integer arithmetic and fixed-point real arithmetic; and functions for random access to a quantum register using a quantum index. Although Quipper is still in active development, we feel that the current stable release is a full-featured and scalable language. Many of the improvements that we are hoping to make are to the type system, such as introducing linear types, which will allow for more type errors to be caught at the initial compilation stage, as opposed to at circuit generation time.

References

1. Aaronson, S., Gottesman, D.: Improved simulation of stabilizer circuits. Physical Review A 70(5), 052328 (2004), arXiv:quant-ph/0406196
2. Altenkirch, T., Green, A.S.: The Quantum IO Monad. In: Gay, S., Mackie, I. (eds.) Semantic Techniques in Quantum Computation, pp. 173–205. Cambridge University Press (2009)
3. Ambainis, A., Childs, A.M., Reichardt, B.W., Spalek, R., Zhang, S.: Any AND-OR formula of size n can be evaluated in time $n^{\frac{1}{2}+o(1)}$ on a quantum computer. SIAM J. Comput. 39, 2513–2530 (2010)
4. Bjesse, P., Claessen, K., Sheeran, M., Singh, S.: Lava: hardware design in Haskell. In: Proceedings of the Third ACM SIGPLAN International Conference on Functional Programming, ICFP 1998, pp. 174–184. ACM, New York (1998), doi:10.1145/289423.289440

5. Childs, A.M., Cleve, R., Deotto, E., Farhi, E., Gutmann, S., Spielman, D.A.: Exponential algorithmic speedup by a quantum walk. In: Proceedings of the 35th Annual ACM Symposium on Theory of Computing, pp. 59–68 (2003)
6. Claessen, K.: Embedded Languages for Describing and Verifying Hardware. Ph.D. thesis, Chalmers University of Technology and Göteborg University (2001)
7. Draper, T.G.: Addition on a Quantum Computer (August 2000), arXiv:quant-ph/0008033
8. Gay, S.J.: Quantum programming languages: Survey and bibliography. Mathematical Structures in Computer Science 16(4) (2006), http://www.dcs.gla.ac.uk/~simon/publications/QPLsurvey.pdf
9. Giles, B.: Programming with a Quantum Stack. Master's thesis, Department of Computer Science, University of Calgary (April 2007), http://pages.cpsc.ucalgary.ca/~gilesb/research/lqpl.html
10. Green, A.S., Lumsdaine, P.L., Ross, N.J., Selinger, P., Valiron, B.: Quipper: A scalable quantum programming language. To appear in PLDI 2013 (2013), arXiv:1304.3390
11. Hallgren, S.: Polynomial-time quantum algorithms for Pell's equation and the principal ideal problem. J. ACM 54(1), 4:1–4:19 (2007), doi:10.1145/1206035.1206039
12. Harrow, A.W., Hassidim, A., Lloyd, S.: Quantum algorithm for linear systems of equations. Phys. Rev. Lett. 103(15), 150502 (2009)
13. IARPA Quantum Computer Science Program: Broad Agency Announcement IARPA-BAA-10-02 (April 2010), https://www.fbo.gov/notices/637e87ac1274d030ce2ab69339ccf93c
14. Magniez, F., Santha, M., Szegedy, M.: Quantum algorithms for the triangle problem (November 2003), arXiv:quant-ph/0310134
15. Nielsen, M.A., Chuang, I.L.: Quantum Computation and Quantum Information. Cambridge University Press (2002)
16. Ömer, B.: A Procedural Formalism for Quantum Computing. Master's thesis, Dept. of Theoretical Physics, Tech. Univ. Vienna (July 1998), http://tph.tuwien.ac.at/~oemer/qcl.html
17. Regev, O.: Quantum computation and lattice problems. SIAM J. Comput. 33(3), 738–760 (2004)
18. Whitfield, J.D., Biamonte, J., Aspuru-Guzik, A.: Simulation of electronic structure hamiltonians using quantum computers. Molecular Physics 109(5), 735–750 (2011)

On the "Q" in QMDDs:
Efficient Representation of Quantum Functionality in the QMDD Data-Structure

Philipp Niemann[1], Robert Wille[1,2], and Rolf Drechsler[1,2]

[1] Institute of Computer Science, University of Bremen, 28359 Bremen, Germany
[2] Cyber-Physical Systems, DFKI GmbH, 28359 Bremen, Germany
{pniemann,rwille,drechsle}@informatik.uni-bremen.de

Abstract. The Quantum Multiple-valued Decision Diagram (QMDD) data-structure has been introduced as a means for an efficient representation and manipulation of transformation matrices realized by quantum or reversible logic circuits. A particular challenge is the handling of arbitrary complex numbers as they frequently occur in quantum functionality. These numbers are represented through edge weights which, however, represent a severe obstacle with respect to canonicity, modifiability, and applicability of QMDDs. Previously introduced approaches did not provide a satisfactory solution to these obstacles. In this paper, we propose an improved factorization scheme for complex numbers that ensures a canonical representation while, at the same time, allows for local changes. We demonstrate how the proposed solution can be exploited to improve the data-structure itself (e.g. through variable reordering enabled by the advanced modifiability) and how applications such as equivalence checking benefit from that.

1 Introduction

Exploiting quantum mechanical phenomena such as superposition and entanglement, quantum computation [1] offers the promise of efficient computing for problems that are of exponential difficulty for classical computing paradigms. For this purpose, information is stored in terms of qubits, i.e. a superposition of the Boolean states 0 and 1. This enables one to solve many important problems (e.g. database search, factorization, graph problems) significantly faster than with classical approaches (see e.g. [2,3,4]). The states of the qubits are modified by quantum operations which can be represented by unitary matrices that may include complex numbers.

Hence, an efficient and compact data-structure for the representation and manipulation of the respective quantum functionality is important for many design tasks in this area. Accordingly, a variety of decision diagram types have been introduced such as the *X-decomposition Quantum Decision Diagram* (XQDD) [5], the *Quantum Information Decision Diagram* (QuIDD) [6], and the *Quantum Multiple-valued Decision Diagram* (QMDD) [7]. In this work, we focus on QMDDs which

G.W. Dueck and D.M. Miller (Eds.): RC 2013, LNCS 7948, pp. 125–140, 2013.

already have successfully been used in applications such as equivalence checking [8], property checking [9], or synthesis [10]. However, in these applications the focus was often on the representation of different quantum realizations for reversible Boolean functions. Although pure quantum functionality has also been represented using QMDDs, some crucial aspects have not been addressed yet.

In particular, the handling of arbitrary complex numbers – a core characteristic of quantum functionality – is unsatisfactory. So far, these numbers are represented through edge weights corresponding to common scalar factors to be applied to all entries of a certain sub-matrix. But, as entries in sub-matrices can be factorized in numerous fashions, several representations of a particular quantum circuit are possible. This has a large influence with respect to canonicity, modifiability, or applicability of QMDDs (this is discussed later in detail in Section 3).

In this work, we investigate this problem of factorization and, eventually, propose a solution allowing for an efficient and modifiable representation of general quantum functionality in the QMDD data-structure. To this end, we review existing factorization efforts by normalization of edge weights and identify their drawbacks. In addition, we prove that QMDD representations of a fixed matrix have the same invariant structure of vertices and connecting edges for a wide range of normalization schemes. However, weights of corresponding edges may differ by some non-zero factor for different schemes. These observations lead to an extension to the QMDD data-structure by so called vertex weights that, independently from the considered quantum functionality, allow for a canonical representation as well as an efficient manipulation. By this, central problems of previous QMDD realizations are solved.

The remainder of this paper is structured as follows. In order to keep the paper self-contained, Section 2 briefly reviews the basics on the QMDD data-structure. Afterwards, the problem with respect to the representation of quantum functionality is discussed and investigated in Section 3. The solution derived from these observations, i.e. the use of vertex weights, is proposed in Section 4. The use of the proposed solution for adjacent variable interchange is demonstrated in Section 5 and evaluated in Section 6. Section 7 concludes the paper.

2 Preliminaries

Quantum systems are composed of *qubits*. Analogously to classical bits, a qubit can be in one of the computational *basis states* $|0\rangle$ and $|1\rangle$, but also in a so called *superposition* $\alpha|0\rangle+\beta|1\rangle$ for complex-valued α, β with $|\alpha|^2+|\beta|^2 = 1$. The number of basis states of a qubit is called its *radix*. Usually, we use radix two but also qubits with more than two basis states (qudits) have been considered [11].

Quantum circuits are commonly represented by their complex-valued, unitary *transformation matrix*. A special case are permutation matrices which represent reversible circuits. The transformation matrix of an n-qubit circuit has dimension $r^n \times r^n$ where r is the radix. These matrices grow exponentially in size, thus standard representations as tables of complex numbers are restricted to circuits with a small number of qubits.

To represent and manipulate larger circuits, we need more elaborate representations that take advantage of the specific properties of transformation matrices:

- Quantum gates often only operate on a small subset of qubits of a quantum system. The transformation matrix for the whole system, which is the Kronecker product of the smaller gate matrix and identity matrices, contains the same pattern (gate matrix) several times. Thus, *similar structures* occur which offers the opportunity for compression.
- Transformation matrices, especially gate matrices, are often sparsely populated, i.e. they contain many zero entries. Therefore, *blocks of zero* can be marked and treated separately.

Taking this into account, we observe that an $r^n \times r^n$ matrix can be partitioned into r^2 sub-matrices of dimension $r^{n-1} \times r^{n-1}$ as

$$M = \begin{bmatrix} M_0 & M_1 & \cdots & M_{r-1} \\ M_r & M_{r+1} & \cdots & M_{2r-1} \\ \vdots & \vdots & \ddots & \vdots \\ M_{(r-1)r} & M_{(r-1)r+1} & \cdots & M_{r^2-1} \end{bmatrix}.$$

This partitioning can be repeated until we reach the level of single matrix entries. Now, the fundamental idea is to create a vertex for each of these matrices with unidirectional edges pointing to the vertices of the respective sub-matrices. More precisely:

Definition 1. *A* Quantum Multiple-valued Decision Diagram (QMDD) *is a directed acyclic graph with the following properties:*

- *There is a single* terminal vertex *representing the complex number 1 without any outgoing edge.*
- Non-terminal vertices *are labelled by an r^2-valued selection variable and have r^2 outgoing edges designated $e_0, e_1, \ldots, e_{r^2-1}$.*
- *There is a single* root vertex *which has a single incoming edge (the* root edge*) that itself has no source vertex.*
- *Every edge (including the root edge) has an associated complex-valued weight and edges with a weight of 0 (0-edges) point to the terminal vertex.*
- *The selection variables are ordered, assume with no loss of generality $x_0 \prec x_1 \prec \cdots \prec x_{n-1}$. On each path from the root vertex to the terminal vertex the variables appear in this order while each variable appears at most once.*
- *There are no* redundant vertices, *i.e. no non-terminal vertex has r^2 identical outgoing edges (destinations and weights).*
- Non-terminal vertices *are* unique, *i.e. no two non-terminal vertices labelled by the same selection variable have the same set of outgoing edges (destinations and weights).*
- Non-terminal vertices *are* normalized *(see details in the following section).*

Each assignment to the selection variables corresponds to choosing the respective sub-matrices in the partitioning process and, therefore, to some matrix entry.

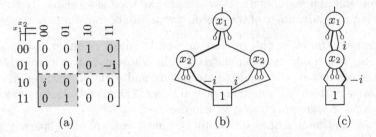

Fig. 1. Matrix and QMDD representations of a 2-qubit quantum circuit

Thus, for any entry of the $r^n \times r^n$ matrix the QMDD can be evaluated in at most n steps by multiplying the weights on the path from the root vertex to the terminal vertex that is determined by the respective assignment.

Example 1. Fig. 1 shows QMDD representations of a 2-qubit quantum circuit. Outgoing edges point to the vertices representing the top left, top right, bottom left, and bottom right sub-matrix from left to right. For example, the highlighted matrix entry $-i$ in Fig. 1a corresponds to the paths highlighted in bold in Fig. 1b and Fig. 1c. Its value can be determined by multiplying the edge weights on these paths.

For simplicity we omit edge weights equal to 1 in illustrations of QMDDs and indicate 0-edges, i.e. edges that point to the terminal vertex with weight 0, by stubs.

3   Normalization of Edge Weights in QMDDs

The main difference between QMDDs and decision diagrams for conventional logic are the complex-valued *edge weights*. They represent common scalar factors to be applied to all entries in a sub-matrix represented by the vertex to which the respective edge is pointing to. Hence, the precise value of a particular matrix entry is determined by multiplying the weights of all edges in the corresponding path from the root vertex to the terminal.

Using weighted edges allows for the representation of structurally equivalent sub-matrices whose entries differ only by a scalar factor with a single vertex. For example, the matrix in Fig. 1a includes two structurally equivalent sub-matrices (highlighted in gray) which differ by a common scalar factor only. But instead of representing each sub-matrix separately (as illustrated in Fig. 1b), weighted edges allow for a representation with a shared vertex (as illustrated in Fig. 1c).

However, as entries in the respective matrices can be factorized in numerous fashions, *normalization* of edge weights plays a significant role. More precisely:

- The representation of structurally equal matrices by the same vertex is only possible if a decomposition into a scalar factor and a normal form is available. In order to determine that, factorization has to be conducted using a normalization scheme.

- Data-structures like QMDDs benefit from providing a possibly canonical representation to be exploited e.g. in equivalence checking [8]. In QMDDs, canonicity is achieved with respect to an applied variable ordering but also depends on how the edge weights (scalar factors) have been determined.
- In many applications, e.g. synthesis, the determination of the smallest or largest magnitude (or even greatest common factors) of matrix entries is of interest. Here, normalization can be exploited as it allows for an *upwards propagation* of the desired values.

Unfortunately, ensuring and maintaining a normalized representation is subject to severe obstacles. In the past, proper normalization rules and corresponding schemes have been proposed. However, they either do not ensure a canonical representation or suffer from the fact that local modifications in the QMDD structure (caused e.g. through re-ordering of vertices as commonly applied in optimization approaches like sifting) possibly destroy the normalized representation.

In this section, we review existing and propose new normalization rules and illustrate the obstacles with them. Afterwards, we discuss the application of these vertex-based rules within generic normalization schemes for entire QMDDs. We focus on canonicity as the primary requirement. Here, we prove that QMDD representations of the same matrix that follow (possibly different) normalization schemes always have the same invariant structure of vertices and edges, and only differ in the weights of corresponding edges by some non-zero factor. These observations lead to an extension to the QMDD data-structure by so called *vertex weights* that maintain the normalized structure after local modifications by only using local re-normalizations.

3.1 Normalization Rules

With the introduction of the QMDD data-structure in [7], various rules for the normalization of edge weights have been proposed. In the following, we define *normalization rules* as follows:

Definition 2. *A* normalization rule *defines a property that the weights of the outgoing edges of a QMDD vertex must exhibit in order to call the vertex normalized. Normalizing a vertex means that we divide the weights of all outgoing edges by a* normalization factor *such that this leads to a normalized vertex.*

The first normalization rule that was used for QMDDs is defined as follows:

Normalization Rule 1. *A QMDD vertex is* normalized *if the first edge with a non-zero edge weight has weight $+1$, i.e. for some k $(0 \leq k \leq r^2 - 1)$ the edge e_k has weight $+1$ and all edges e_i have weight 0 for $i = 0, \ldots, k - 1$.*

Example 2. The application of Rule 1 is illustrated in Fig. 2. Since normalization factors (here: $-i$) can easily be propagated to incoming edges when building a QMDD bottom-up, the common way to ensure normalized vertices according to this rule is to apply the normalization rule as the QMDD is built.

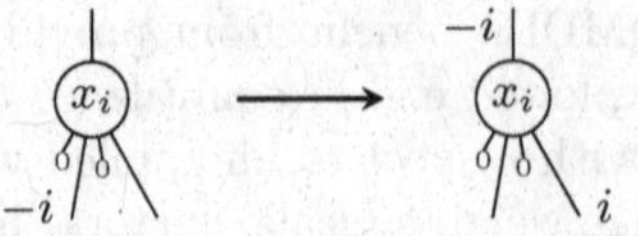

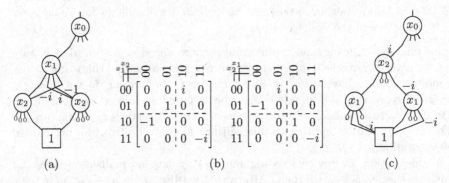

Fig. 2. Normalizing a vertex using Normalization Rule 1

Fig. 3. Matrix and QMDD representations for interchanged variables

Normalization Rule 1 enables a canonical representation [7] and, hence, is very useful for applications like equivalence checking (see e.g. [8]). However, once a QMDD has been built following this scheme, local modifications on the data-structure often require a re-normalization of the entire QMDD.

Example 3. Consider the QMDD shown in Fig. 3a which has been built following Normalization Rule 1. Afterwards, e.g. as part of a re-ordering process, the variables x_1 and x_2 shall be interchanged. According to the corresponding matrices (see Fig. 3b), this leads to a QMDD structure as shown in Fig. 3c, i.e. the weight of the leftmost edge of the x_0-vertex changes from 1 to i. Thus, this vertex is not normalized anymore. In the worst case, changes like this propagate through the entire QMDD structure. As a result, variable interchanges are no longer local operations and, hence, significantly complicate established optimization approaches such as variable re-ordering by adjacent variable interchange as used in sifting [12].

In order to address this problem, an alternative normalization rule has been proposed in [12].

Normalization Rule 2. *A QMDD vertex is normalized if its edges are of the form that the largest[1] weight on any outgoing edge is 1.*

This normalization indeed enables local operations since local maxima, i.e. matrix elements with the largest magnitude appearing in the respective sub-matrix, are propagated upwards to the root edge weight. Since these maxima do not change during a local variable reordering, the resulting structure of the QMDD

---

[1] We refer to [13] for a more detailed consideration on the magnitude-based order of complex numbers that is meant here.

is not affected by this and normalization is preserved. In contrast, this scheme destroys the canonicity of the representation as illustrated in the next example.

Example 4. Consider again the QMDDs shown in Fig. 1. Inspection shows that both are properly normalized according to Rule 2. However, although both QMDDs represent the same functionality and follow the same variable ordering and normalization scheme, their structure is not equivalent. That is, the proposed normalization does not lead to unique representations.

As another alternative, we propose the following normalization rule:

Normalization Rule 3. *A QMDD vertex is normalized if the edges are of the form that (1) no edge has a magnitude larger than 1 and (2) the first edge exhibiting this largest magnitude has exactly weight +1.*

Example 5. In most cases, Rule 3 coincides with Rule 2. E.g., in Fig. 1 the only vertex that is normalized according to Rule 2, but does not obey to Rule 3 is the x_2-vertex on the right of Fig. 1b, where we have edge weight i "before" +1.

Rule 3 again enables a canonical representation of QMDDs as it provides a unique tie breaking mechanism in case of several edge weights having the same (largest) magnitude. But as for Rule 1, swapping adjacent variables is not a local operation in general. This can be seen from Example 3 where the QMDDs are the same when Rule 3 is used instead of Rule 1.

The benefit of Rule 3 is that it still ensures canonicity when using the smallest non-zero magnitude. Moreover, it then realizes an upward propagation of smallest absolute values and, hence, enables a fast determination of how "far" a matrix is "away" from being a Boolean permutation matrix by just looking at the root edge weight.

3.2   Normalization Schemes

As discussed above, several normalization rules for QMDDs exist. Now, we consider their generic application in the normalization process for an entire QMDD. For each vertex in a QMDD, these rules basically compute a normalization factor which has to be applied to the represented (sub-)matrix. More precisely:

Definition 3. *Let* $\mathrm{Mat}(\mathbb{C}) := \{M \in \mathbb{C}^{m \times n} \mid m, n \in \mathbb{N}\}$ *be the set of complex-valued matrices. A map* $\mathrm{N} : \mathrm{Mat}(\mathbb{C}) \to \mathbb{C}$ *is called a* normalization scheme *if it satisfies*

$$\mathrm{N}(\alpha M) = \alpha \, \mathrm{N}(M) \text{ for all } M \in \mathrm{Mat}(\mathbb{C}), \alpha \in \mathbb{C} \tag{1}$$

$$\mathrm{N}(M) = 0 \Leftrightarrow \text{ all entries in } M \text{ are zero.} \tag{2}$$

Using the normalization scheme N*, a QMDD vertex representing a matrix* M *will be* normalized *by dividing all outgoing edge weights by its normalization factor* $\mathrm{N}(M)$ *and will afterwards represent the matrix* $M'_{\mathrm{N}} := \frac{M}{\mathrm{N}(M)}$*.*

Remark 1. Note that property (1) guarantees that structurally equal matrices (which only differ by a scalar factor $\alpha \neq 0$) are compressed to a shared vertex, i.e.

$$(\alpha M)'_{\mathrm{N}} = \frac{\alpha M}{\mathrm{N}(\alpha M)} = \frac{\alpha M}{\alpha \mathrm{N}(M)} = \frac{M}{\mathrm{N}(M)} = M'_{\mathrm{N}},$$

while (2) is just another way of saying that all 0-edges must point to the terminal vertex. Thus, normalization schemes lead to unique QMDD representations. Conversely, any normalization *rule* that ensures canonicity, e.g. Rules 1 and 3, can be extended to a normalization scheme. Note that a vertex is normalized if, and only if, it represents a matrix with normalization factor 1, i.e.

$$\mathrm{N}(M'_{\mathrm{N}}) = \mathrm{N}\left(\frac{M}{\mathrm{N}(M)}\right) = \frac{1}{\mathrm{N}(M)}\mathrm{N}(M) = 1.$$

A generic normalization scheme as defined in Definition 3 is not limited to rules that take into account only local information about edge weights. It may rather rely on arbitrary knowledge about the represented matrix. Thus, one could assume that significantly different QMDD structures result for the same matrix. However, as the following theorem shows, QMDDs representing the same matrix and following (possibly different) normalization schemes indeed exhibit an isomorphic structure of vertices and edges.

Theorem 1. *Consider a QMDD that uniquely represents a complex-valued matrix using a normalization scheme. Any QMDD that represents the same matrix using a different normalization scheme has the same structure of vertices and edges, while the weights of corresponding edges may differ by some non-zero factor.*

Proof (Sketch). Assume there are matrices that lead to different QMDD structures for different normalization schemes. From these we can choose a matrix of minimal size. Clearly, this matrix cannot be a single complex number, so without loss of generality we may consider the regular structure of r^2 sub-matrices. Since these are smaller and the matrix was chosen minimal, their QMDD structure must be the same for any normalization scheme. Now, when creating the top vertex of a QMDD, edges to these sub-structures are used and applying different normalization schemes may result in different (non-zero) edge weights, but does not change the structure of the vertex. This is a contradiction to our assumption and proves the theorem. □

This is an important result. While it was already known that QMDD representations are canonical for certain normalization rules, Theorem 1 now tells that even regardless of the normalization scheme, the QMDD structure is an *invariant* of a matrix. This can be exploited in order to provide a normalization approach that not only guarantees this invariant canonical QMDD structure (as Rule 1 and Rule 3), but additionally also allows for certain local operations (as possible in Rule 2). For this purpose, the QMDD data-structure needs to be slightly extended as described next.

4   Introducing Vertex Weights

So far, we discussed (1) that local changes of edge weights might require to rework a large part of the QMDD in order to restore the normalization (as illustrated in Example 3) and (2) that regardless of the normalization scheme the structure of a QMDD is invariant and can already be established using simple normalization rules such as Rule 1 or Rule 3. Now, these observations are exploited in order to propose a slightly revised QMDD data-structure which is capable of both, representing matrices in a canonical fashion and enabling local operations.

The basic idea is to store weight changes (as they result from local modifications) within the vertices instead of propagating them to incoming edges. Therefore, we suggest to extend the QMDD definition as follows:

Definition 4. *Each non-terminal QMDD vertex is enriched with a complex-valued* vertex weight (v-weight) $\tau \neq 0$. *A vertex weight* $\tau \neq 1$ *is called* effective.

Remark 2. Vertex weights represent scalar factors to be applied to all entries in the sub-matrix represented by the respective vertex. Hence, to determine the value of a particular matrix entry they have to be included when computing the product of the edge weights on the respective path. Besides this *v-weight interpretation*, also the *standard interpretation* can be used to evaluate QMDDs, i.e., ignoring vertex weights. Thus, a QMDD vertex can represent two different matrices depending on which interpretation we use.

Having this extended structure, local operations become possible as illustrated in the following example.

Example 6. Consider a standard QMDD (without effective vertex weights) that is normalized according to a normalization scheme which operates on the standard interpretation of a vertex and ignores vertex weights (denoted by N_{std} in the following). At the beginning, v-weight and standard interpretation match since all vertex weights are ineffective (Fig. 4a). Then, local modifications are applied (Fig. 4b). This can be a variable interchange, but anything that preserves structural equivalence is allowed. More precisely, we require that afterwards the same matrices are structurally equal as before. We will see later that variable interchanges indeed have this property. For now, we note that destroying structural equivalence will definitely require modifications on referencing vertices. Hence, in current implementations which do not store referencing (incoming) edges of a vertex this property is a necessary condition for local operations. As a by-product, this requirement ensures that we do not get vertices representing the same matrix in standard interpretation, but contain different weights.

Finally, the respective vertices are normalized according to N_{std}. But instead of propagating the normalization factor to all referencing edges, now this is stored locally in the vertex weight (see Fig. 4c).

The crucial point is that the resulting QMDD structure is isomorphic to the canonical invariant structure of the equivalent standard representation, i.e. without effective vertex weights. To justify that, note that a QMDD vertex with an

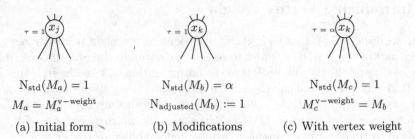

Fig. 4. Using vertex weights to restore normalization (N_{std}). $M_{\{a,b,c\}}$ or $M^{v-weight}$ denotes the matrix represented by the particular vertex in standard or v-weight interpretation, respectively.

effective weight (Fig. 4c) can be transformed to a vertex that is equivalent in v-weight interpretation but has a weight of 1. For this purpose, we simply apply the effective weight to all outgoing edges of the considered vertex. This basically undoes the normalization and leads back to the vertices as in Fig. 4b. The resulting QMDD – now without effective vertex weights – has the same structure as before but is no longer normalized according to N_{std}. However, it can be viewed as normalized according to a normalization scheme $N_{adjusted}$ with "adjusted" normalization factors, i.e. $N_{adjusted}(\tilde{M}_v) = 1$ for all vertices v where $\tilde{M}_v$ denotes the standard interpretation of the vertex after the transformation (see Fig. 4b). Hence, this QMDD representation of the matrix has the canonical structure which is consequently also present in the QMDD with effective vertex weights.

Overall, the proposed extension maintains canonical representations even after local modifications as they are used by optimization techniques such as sifting.

At the same time, a transformation back to trivial vertex weights is always possible. The only problem here is that we might need to replace some vertices with almost identical copies, but without an effective weight (see e.g. the x_2-vertices in Fig. 5).

This can be overcome by building an intermediate QMDD that is not functionally equivalent in v-weight interpretation, but represents the correct matrix in standard interpretation, i.e. when ignoring vertex weights. This intermediate QMDD can be obtained as follows:

Algorithm: "Build intermediate QMDD" for an edge e pointing to vertex v with weight w:

1. If v is the terminal vertex, return e unchanged.
2. Perform "Build intermediate QMDD" on all outgoing edges of v.
3. Create a vertex r (with $\tau_r = 1$) from the edges resulting from Step 2, normalize it and store the normalization factor π.
4. If r is identical to an already existing vertex (up to the vertex weight), the result is an edge pointing to that vertex with edge weight $w \cdot \pi \cdot \tau_v$.
   Else, the result is an edge pointing to r with the same edge weight.

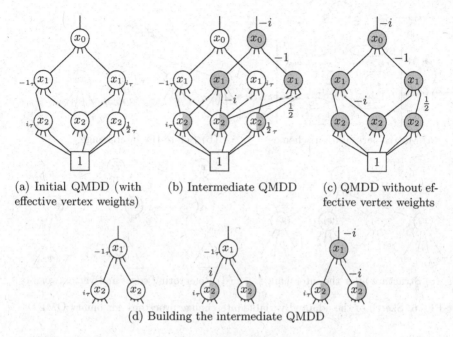

(a) Initial QMDD (with effective vertex weights)   (b) Intermediate QMDD   (c) QMDD without effective vertex weights

(d) Building the intermediate QMDD

Fig. 5. Computing equivalent QMDDs without effective vertex weights

Remark 3. Note that this algorithm can also be used to switch between different normalization rules if we start with a QMDD in one normalization and use the other normalization in step 3 of the algorithm.

We illustrate the algorithm by the following example:

Example 7. The QMDD in Fig. 5a has a few effective vertex weights indicated by $(\cdot)_\tau$. In order to transform it to the equivalent representation without effective vertex weights, we compute the intermediate QMDD (highlighted in gray in Fig. 5b) which shares the x_2-vertices with the still valid initial QMDD representation. Figure 5d shows for the left x_1-vertex how our algorithm first pulls vertex weights from the child vertices to the respective outgoing edges before the new vertex is normalized and the normalization factor (i) and vertex weight (-1) are applied to the referencing edge.

The final QMDD (Fig. 5c) is obtained from the intermediate QMDD (Fig. 5b) by setting all vertex weights to 1.

5   Using Vertex Weights for Variable Interchange

As discussed above, normalization can be a severe obstacle when performing modifications on QMDDs such as adjacent variable interchanges. However, using the concept of vertex weights, this problem is solved, i.e. a local modification such as a variable interchange can be performed without ramifications to other

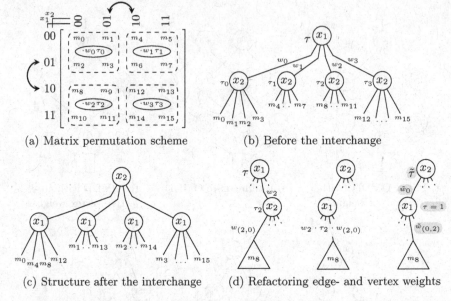

(a) Matrix permutation scheme   (b) Before the interchange

(c) Structure after the interchange   (d) Refactoring edge- and vertex weights

Fig. 6. Sketch of the adapted variable interchange procedure for binary QMDDs

parts of the QMDD structure. The particular way of employing vertex weights is demonstrated in this section.

We use an interchange scheme which is similarly applied in other decision diagram types, e.g. *Binary Decision Diagrams* (BDDs) [14]: Consider a BDD where two adjacent variables x_1 and x_2 shall be interchanged. Then, each x_1-vertex is replaced by an x_2-vertex which shall represent the *same* Boolean function in order to make the swap a local operation. This is done by interchanging the labels of the vertices and permuting the sub-trees representing the respective cofactors [14]. Analogously, for QMDDs each x_1-vertex is replaced by an x_2-vertex which shall represent the same functionality. By doing so, an interchange of variables x_1 and x_2 for a given matrix leads to a permutation of sub-matrices as illustrated in Fig. 6a, i.e. the swapping of certain columns and rows. This accordingly needs to be conducted in the QMDD structure [12,13] in which each of the affected sub-matrices is represented by a vertex as well as weighted edges and vertices.

That is, to interchange two adjacent variables x_1 and x_2 in a QMDD (where x_1 precedes x_2 in the variable order), we process all vertices that are labelled x_1. We skip all such vertices that do not point to any x_2-vertex. For each of the remaining x_1-vertices V with outgoing edges e_i^V $(i = 0, \ldots, r^2 - 1)$, from which at least one edge points to a v_2-vertex, we perform the following three steps:

1. Create an $r^2 \times r^2$ square matrix $T = (t_{ij})$ and set t_{ij} to be the jth outgoing edge of the x_2-vertex pointed to by e_i^V and multiply the weight of t_{ij} with the weight of e_i^V and the (vertex) weight of the v_2-vertex. If the destination of e_i^V is not labelled with x_2, set $t_{ij} = e_i^V$ instead.

2. From each column j of T create a vertex labelled x_1 with outgoing edges $e_i = t_{ij}$ and let e_j^V point to this vertex. Relabel V to x_2.
3. Apply the normalization scheme and store the normalization factor of V by multiplying it to the current vertex weight τ_V.

Remark 4. We could also deal with an effective vertex weight at x_1-level by applying it to all edges in T, but since normalization would propagate this common factor back to its origin, we rather keep it and adapt it appropriately after relabelling.

This procedure is illustrated by the following example:

Example 8. Consider Fig. 6 showing a part of a binary QMDD $(r = 2)$ in which both variables x_1 and x_2 should be interchanged. First, a matrix containing all sub-trees representing the sub-matrices m_0 until m_{15} is created according to Step 1 (see Fig. 6b). Then, these sub-trees are re-arranged in Step 2 eventually leading to the structure shown in Fig. 6c. Finally, the respective vertices are normalized in Step 3. This is illustrated in Fig. 6d for the sub-tree m_8. First, this sub-tree is relocated (according to the previous steps). Then, the product of the corresponding edge and vertex weights is concentrated at the bottom level. The final factorization of this product (highlighted in gray) is achieved by applying normalization to the new structure.

The interchange procedure operates in the same fashion on each sub-matrix of the particular partitioning level that corresponds to the interchanged variables. Thus, it preserves structural equivalence. This allows for the use of effective vertex weights during the variable reordering process and – as discussed in the previous section – thereby allows for the determination of essential information about the QMDD structure without having to perform renormalization after each variable interchange. Hence, a large variety of objective functions (which we try to minimize by variable reordering) will give the same result for the intermediate variable orders as if we had transformed the QMDD to its normalized equivalent without effective vertex weights. We need to perform this potentially expensive transformation at most once, after we have arrived at the final variable order and only if there are effective vertex weights left. For this purpose we can use the algorithm presented in the previous section.

6 Application and Evaluation

The extension of the data-structure as described above has been implemented in C on top of the original QMDD package presented in [7]. In this section, we discuss and evaluate the application of the proposed vertex weights. For this purpose, we consider the task of equivalence checking of quantum circuit functionality. Equivalence checking is an important design task and aims e.g. for checking whether two circuits (the initial realization as well as an optimized version) realize the same functionality. This constitutes a representative application as characteristics like canonicity (for fast equivalence checking) as well as modifiability of the data-structure (allowing for a compact representation) are crucial here.

QMDDs have already been used for checking the equivalence of different quantum realizations of reversible Boolean functions [8]. However, we focus on functionality of general quantum computation like phase shifting, superposition, and entanglement [1] which requires various quantum values to be adequately represented in the QMDD. In this context an extended definition of equivalence is applied:

Definition 5. *Unitary transforms M_1 and M_2 of a quantum system are called equal up to global phase if $M_1 = e^{i\theta} M_2$ for some real number θ, where $e^{i\theta}$ is called the* global phase factor.

Remark 5. Classical equivalence is a special case for $e^{i\theta} = 1$. The reason for using this extended definition is that for global phase equivalent transforms it can not be physically distinguished which of the transforms has been applied to a quantum system since the outcomes have the same measurement statistics [1].

Verifying for global phase equivalence can easily be performed if canonical representations of the two functions are available. Canonicity ensures that global phase equivalent transforms have the same representation up to the weights of the root edges that differ by the global phase factor. Thus, it is sufficient to check whether (1) the root edges of the two QMDDs point to the same vertex and (2) the weights of these edges have the same magnitude. This can be performed in constant time using proper *unique tables*. First, we consider the applicability of the previously available QMDD-based approaches relying on the normalization rules as discussed in Section 3.1:

- QMDDs following the Normalization Rule 1 would allow for a fast check for equivalence as canonicity is ensured. However, the QMDDs would be restricted to the given initial variable order. Optimizations through variable re-ordering (e.g. using sifting which heavily relies on variable interchanges) could destroy the canonical, normalized structure as described in Example 3 or require to rework large parts of the data-structure many times. This lack of modifiability prevents this approach from deriving an efficient representation – a serious obstacle particularly for a task like equivalence checking where a major issue is to maintain a manageable diagram size while building the circuit representation.
- Normalization Rule 2 is not applicable as it does not guarantee canonicity of the representation as demonstrated before in Example 4. Here, an equivalence check would require a complete traversal of the entire data-structure and, hence, becomes computationally expensive. Moreover, the lack of canonicity can make it hard to find a good variable order for a compact representation. Once a promising variable order was found it might not be possible to reproduce the particular diagram (size) and we might end up with a significantly different representation.

Table 1. Size reduction of QMDDs through variable re-ordering

Benchmark	Initial		Sifting		Exact	
	Size	Time (s)	Size	Time (s)	Size	Time (s)
Grover-7	187	0.01	36	<0.01	35	0.37
Grover-9	722	0.02	52	0.01	51	29.14
Grover-11	2817	0.15	67	0.02	66	3709
5-qubit-code-9	90	0.01	57	0.01	43	24.73
7-qubit-code-7	44	<0.01	26	<0.01	26	0.35
9-qubit-codeFigN1-9	40	<0.01	22	0.01	22	24.47
9-qubit-codeFigN2-17	1172	0.01	60	0.04	(84)	>7200
QFT-3	22	<0.01	9	<0.01	9	<0.01
QFT-4	86	<0.01	24	<0.01	24	0.01
QFT-5	342	<0.01	40	<0.01	40	0.01
QFT-6	1366	<0.01	103	<0.01	103	0.1
QFT-7	5462	0.02	167	0.02	167	1.2

In contrast, the proposed extended data-structure supports both, a canonical representation as well as an advanced modifiability. While the canonicity allows for a fast check for equivalence as described above, the modifiability ensures a compact representation of the respective functionality. This is also demonstrated by experimental results summarized in Table 1. Here, the respective QMDD sizes (i.e. the number of vertices; denoted by *Size*) for a selection of benchmark functions is presented if either (1) the initial variable ordering is applied, (2) if the data-structure has been improved through a heuristic approach (sifting technique), and (3) if an exact approach is applied that establishes the optimal variable ordering. As benchmarks, we applied circuits realizing Grover algorithms (*Grover-N*), error correction functionality (*k-qubit-code-N*, taken from [15]), and quantum Fourier transforms (*QFT-N*) where N denotes the number of qubits. Note that the quantum Fourier transforms actually do not show shared vertex compression in the standard variable order and, thus, exhibit the largest possible number of QMDD vertices ($\frac{4^N-1}{3}$ non-terminal vertices) for the respective matrix size. The run-time (in CPU seconds) is additionally provided in the columns denoted by *Time*. All experiments have been conducted on a 2.8 GHz Intel Core i7 machine with 8 GB of main memory running Linux.

It can be seen that the size of the QMDD significantly depends on the applied variable ordering. Reductions of up to a factor of 42 (for the Grover-11 circuit) can be observed. This clearly emphasizes the necessity of a canonical, but also easily modifiable data-structure. While this has not been achieved for general quantum functionality with the previously introduced approaches, the proposed solution relying on vertex weights satisfies these needs.

7   Conclusions

In this paper, we proposed an extension to the QMDD data-structure by so called vertex weights. They provide a method supplemental to edge weights to represent common factors of sub-matrices composed of complex numbers. Vertex weights ensure a canonical representation and allow for an advanced modifiability and applicability of QMDDs – even for complex quantum functionality. An evaluation demonstrated how this can be exploited to improve the data-structure itself (e.g. through variable re-ordering enabled by the advanced modifiability) and how applications such as equivalence checking benefit from that.

Acknowledgments. We would like to sincerely thank D. Michael Miller for many helpful suggestions and discussions as well as for providing us with an implementation of the QMDD package introduced in [7]. This work was supported in part by the German Academic Exchange Service (DAAD).

References

1. Nielsen, M., Chuang, I.: Quantum Computation and Quantum Information. Cambridge Univ. Press (2000)
2. Grover, L.K.: A fast quantum mechanical algorithm for database search. In: Theory of Computing, pp. 212–219 (1996)
3. Shor, P.W.: Algorithms for quantum computation: discrete logarithms and factoring. Foundations of Computer Science, 124–134 (1994)
4. Dürr, C., Heiligman, M., Høyer, P., Mhalla, M.: Quantum query complexity of some graph problems. SIAM J. Comput. 35(6), 1310–1328 (2006)
5. Wang, S.A., Lu, C.Y., Tsai, I.M., Kuo, S.Y.: An XQDD-based verification method for quantum circuits. IEICE Transactions 91-A(2), 584–594 (2008)
6. Viamontes, G.F., Markov, I.L., Hayes, J.P.: Quantum Circuit Simulation. Springer, Heidelberg (2009)
7. Miller, D.M., Thornton, M.A.: QMDD: A decision diagram structure for reversible and quantum circuits. In: Int'l Symp. on Multi-Valued Logic, p. 6 (2006)
8. Wille, R., Große, D., Miller, D.M., Drechsler, R.: Equivalence checking of reversible circuits. In: Int'l Symp. on Multi-Valued Logic, pp. 324–330 (2009)
9. Seiter, J., Soeken, M., Wille, R., Drechsler, R.: Property checking of quantum circuits using quantum multiple-valued decision diagrams. In: Glück, R., Yokoyama, T. (eds.) RC 2012. LNCS, vol. 7581, pp. 183–196. Springer, Heidelberg (2013)
10. Soeken, M., Wille, R., Hilken, C., Przigoda, N., Drechsler, R.: Synthesis of Reversible Circuits with Minimal Lines for Large Functions. In: Asia and South Pacific Design Automation Conference (January 2012)
11. Bullock, S.S., O'Leary, D.P., Brennen, G.K.: Asymptotically optimal quantum circuits for d-level systems. Phys. Rev. Lett. 94, 230502 (2005)
12. Miller, D.M., Feinstein, D.Y., Thornton, M.A.: Qmdd minimization using sifting for variable reordering. Journal of Multiple-valued Logic and Soft Computing, 537–552 (2007)
13. Miller, D.M., Thornton, M.A.: Multiple-Valued Logic: Concepts and Representations. Morgan and Claypool (2008)
14. Bryant, R.E.: Graph-based algorithms for Boolean function manipulation. IEEE Trans. on Comp. 35(8), 677–691 (1986)
15. Mermin, N.D.: Quantum computer science: an introduction, vol. 1. Cambridge University Press (2007)

Modelling of Bonding with Processes and Events

Iain Phillips[1], Irek Ulidowski[2], and Shoji Yuen[3]

[1] Department of Computing, Imperial College London, England
iccp@doc.ic.ac.uk
[2] Department of Computer Science, University of Leicester, England
iu3@mcs.le.ac.uk
[3] Graduate School of Information Science, Nagoya University, Japan
yuen@is.nagoya-u.ac.jp

Abstract. We introduce two forms of modelling of systems that consist of objects that are combined together by the means of bonds. In reaction systems for bonding we define how bonds are created and dissolved via reduction-style semantics. The usefulness of reaction systems is illustrated with examples taken from software engineering and biochemistry. We also introduce reversible event structures and define the notion of configuration. We then discuss how to give semantics of reaction systems for bonding in terms of reversible event structures.

1   Introduction

Undoing of computation in concurrent and distributed systems has many technical and conceptual challenges. There are several forms of undoing computation that have been studied over the last ten years. Backtracking and reversing of computation that preserves causal order were considered, for example, in [5, 3, 10, 11, 7, 2]. Reversing out of causal order, however, which is a very common mode of operation in biochemical systems, has not been studied widely. The first attempt was made in [12] where an extension of the reversible process calculus CCSK with the execution control operator was proposed. A different form of controlling reversibility based on the rollback construct of the higher-order π calculus was given in [6].

Let us recall what backtracking and reversing is, both in causal order and out of causal order [12]. Consider a computation where the event a causes the event b, written $a < b$, and the event c occurs independently of a and b. The three traces of this computation that preserve causality are abc, acb and cab: note that a always precedes b. There are several conceptually different ways of undoing these events. *Backtracking* is undoing in precisely the inverse order in which they happened. So, undo b undo c undo a, written as $\underline{b}\,\underline{c}\,\underline{a}$, is a backtrack of acb. *Reversing* is more general: here events can be undone in any order as long as causality is preserved, meaning that causes cannot be undone before effects. For example, $\underline{c}\,\underline{b}\,\underline{a}$ is a reversal of acb for a, b and c as defined above. However, there are processes, especially common in cell biochemistry, where events are undone, *out of causal order*. The creation and breaking of molecular bonds between the proteins involved in the ERK signalling pathway or the creation of polymers by

G.W. Dueck and D.M. Miller (Eds.): RC 2013, LNCS 7948, pp. 141–154, 2013.
© Springer-Verlag Berlin Heidelberg 2013

scaffolding proteins, described in Sections 2 and 3, are good examples. Simplifying, let us assume that the creation of molecular bonds is represented by events a, b, c where, as above, $a < b$ and c is independent of a and b. In the ERK pathway, the molecular bonds are broken in the following order: $\underline{a}$, $\underline{b}$ and $\underline{c}$, which apparently reverses the cause a before the effect b.

In the paper we propose two alternative methods (to [12]) for defining forwards and reverse computation. We draw some inspiration from the fields of graph and term rewriting, and define reaction systems for creating and dissolving bonds between objects, and explain how computation, both forwards and in reverse, can be modelled as a process of bonding and unbonding. We show with examples that reaction systems for bonding can represent naturally reversing out of order, and that they have an expressive power comparable to CCSK with the execution control operator [12].

Event structures were proposed by Winskel in [16] as a denotational model of concurrent computation. Systems are represented as sets of events which are constrained by relations of *consistency* and *enabling*. Event structures allow us to discuss directly relationships between events such as concurrency, causality and conflict. Our contribution is a definition of *reversible event structures*. To the best of our knowledge this is the first form of event structure where computation can proceed both forwards and in reverse, both in and out of causal order. We also describe, given a reaction system and an initial process, how to construct a reversible event structure that captures the behaviour of the initial process.

The benefits of reaction systems for bonding and reversible event structures are demonstrated with several examples taken from software engineering and cell biochemistry. We consider the modelling of long-running transactions, creation of a polymer by scaffolding proteins, and a signal-passing mechanism employed by a section of the ERK signalling pathway. All our examples show how crucial out-of-order reversing is in the world of artificial and natural systems.

2   Reaction Systems for Bonding

We develop reaction systems for representing objects that can bond with each other, thus creating more complex objects, and where bonds can be dissolved within a composite object. The building blocks of the calculus are the *base objects*, or simply called *bases*. A base object has a *sort*, for example A, and an *arity* which is the maximal number of bonds the base object can have with other base objects. Consider two bases of sort A and arity 1 and a base of sort B and arity 2. We shall write a collection of these three objects simply using their sort names as A, A, B, or as A_1, A_2, B if we wish to distinguish between objects of the same sort (here A). A creation of a *single* bond between A and B is defined by the relation $\rightarrow$, for example

$$A, B \rightarrow A \cdot B$$

where '$\cdot$' in $A \cdot B$ denotes the bond between the A and B, and $A \cdot B$ is a (composite) object consisting of bases A and B. A single bond can be dissolved and this is given by the relation $\rightsquigarrow$, for example

$$A \cdot B \rightsquigarrow A, B$$

A system of objects, also called a *process*, is a collection of objects written with the comma operator ',', for example A, A, B. Many of our examples are inspired by biochemistry, and so we shall call objects *molecules* and a system of objects a *solution*. The order in which objects are written in a system is irrelevant, and can be changed. A molecule can move around in a solution, thus changing relative position with respect to other molecules. This is defined by structural equivalence $X, Y \equiv Y, X$, where X, Y are objects or molecules. Systems, processes or solutions, S and T can be combined by taking their multiset union, written as S, T. Clearly, $S, T \equiv T, S$.

Given $A, B \rightarrow A \cdot B$, we would like to deduce that a system containing A and B can evolve to a system that contains $A \cdot B$. This is done by having two global rules inspired by the laws for the chemical abstract machine [1]:

$$\frac{S \rightarrow S'}{S, T \rightarrow S', T} \quad (c1) \qquad \frac{S \rightsquigarrow S'}{S, T \rightsquigarrow S', T} \quad (c2)$$

We call this substitutivity in the ',' context. We shall also have rules for structural equivalence:

$$\frac{S \equiv S' \quad S' \rightarrow T' \quad T' \equiv T}{S \rightarrow T} \quad (s1) \qquad \frac{S \equiv S' \quad S' \rightsquigarrow T' \quad T' \equiv T}{S \rightsquigarrow T} \quad (s2)$$

We do not have substitutivity in the '$\cdot$' context. If $A \cdot B \rightsquigarrow A, B$, we do not always wish to have $C \cdot A \cdot B \rightsquigarrow C \cdot A, B$, for example, when C inhibits the dissolution of $A \cdot B$. Our reaction systems are unlike term or graph rewrite systems for this reason.

Two bases D of arity 2 can have two bonds between each other; this is written as $\overline{D \cdot D}$ or, equivalently, $\underline{D \cdot D}$. A ring of three copies of D is $\overline{D \cdot D \cdot D}$ or $\underline{D \cdot D \cdot D}$. Let $x \cdot A$ denote an object consisting of a base A and an object x where there is precisely one bond between A and some base in x. We can generalise this notation (using over- or under-bracket notation) to denote that there are k bonds between A and other base molecules in x, assuming that the arity of A is $n \geq k$ and x has capacity for at least k fresh bonds. Since all examples in this paper and in [12] use molecules with arity at most 3 the notation $x \cdot A$, $\overline{x \cdot A}$, $\underline{x \cdot A}$ is sufficient.

Next, we set out rules for structural equivalence for bonding $\equiv$. Objects can be seen as undirected graphs, where the bases of an object are the nodes and the bonds between the bases of the object are the edges, and the arity of a base is an upper bound on the degree of the corresponding node. Structural equivalence of two objects implies that the underlying graphs are isomorphic, and we note that isomorphism of graphs with bounded degree is decidable in polynomial time [8]. For illustration, we give a set of rules for $\equiv$ for objects with bases of arity at most two. Let y represent a possibly empty arbitrary string of bonded bases $A_1 \cdots A_n$ ($n \geq 0$), and let y^{-1} represent y in reverse order, i.e. $A_n \cdots A_1$.

$$\overline{A \cdot y} \equiv \overline{y^{-1} \cdot A} \qquad \overline{A \cdot y \cdot B} \equiv \overline{B \cdot y^{-1} \cdot A}$$

$$\overline{A \cdot y \cdot B \cdot C} \equiv \overline{C \cdot A \cdot y \cdot B} \qquad \overline{A, y \cdot B} \equiv A \cdot B \cdot y^{-1}$$

$$\overline{A \cdot y \cdot B} \equiv \underline{A \cdot y \cdot B}$$

Our first example is a reaction system that models how a catalyst molecule helps otherwise inactive molecules to bond.

Example 2.1. Consider molecules of sort A and B and arity 2 and 1 respectively that cannot bond easily unless they are "assisted" by a catalyst molecule of sort C and arity 1. In a solution that contains copies of A, B and C, molecules C and A bond initially by the rule

$$C, A \to C \cdot A$$

Then, molecules $C \cdot A$ combine with copies of B

$$C \cdot A, B \to C \cdot A \cdot B$$

Finally, having helped A and B to react, the bond between C and A is broken thus releasing C into a solution to help other A, B pairs

$$C \cdot A \cdot B \rightsquigarrow C, A \cdot B$$

Consider a solution $S = A, B, A, B, C$. It computes as follows:

$$S \equiv^* C, A, B, A, B \to C \cdot A, B, A, B \to C \cdot A \cdot B, A, B \rightsquigarrow C, A \cdot B, A, B$$

Next, the molecules rearrange themselves into $A \cdot B, C, A, B$ and the computation continues as follows:

$$A \cdot B, C, A, B \to A \cdot B, C \cdot A, B \to A \cdot B, C \cdot A \cdot B \rightsquigarrow A \cdot B, C, A \cdot B$$

producing two molecules $A \cdot B$ and, of course, the original C. This solution could have produced the same outcome by following a different route: C could have reacted with the second pair of A and B first by positioning itself initially in the middle of the solution.

Definition 2.2. A *reaction system for bonding* is a tuple $\mathrm{P} = (\Sigma, \to, \rightsquigarrow)$ where the signature Σ contains the bonding operator '$\cdot$', the solution operator ',' and the definitions of base objects in the form of sort, arity pairs. Objects are either base objects or collections of bonded bases such that the arities of the bases are not exceeded and each base is connected to another base via a sequence of bonds. A process (or a system or solution) is either an object or a collection of objects composed with the solution operator. Reduction relations $\to$ and $\rightsquigarrow$ are binary relations over processes. A *computation* starts with an initial process (solution), which is a multi-set of bases taken from Σ, and is a sequence of transitions derived from $\to$ and $\rightsquigarrow$ and the rules (c1-c2) and (s1-s2).

In the setting of reaction systems for bonding, we specify which bonds are created and dissolved, and in which order, by the reduction style relations $\rightarrow$ and $\rightsquigarrow$. This is in contrast to the majority of previously considered reversible calculi where the syntax of processes (prefixing, keys, parallel composition and restriction) and global operational semantics determine the forwards and reverse computation.

The next example is a reaction system for the modelling of long-running transactions with a compensation. Previously, transactions were also considered in the setting of reversible process calculi in [4, 12].

Example 2.3. We define the signature first. A transaction is a sequence of $n \geq 3$ steps A_i for $1 \leq i < n$ of sort A and arity 3. It starts with the initial step I, arity 2, which never fails. I is followed by the steps A_i, where A_1 bonds with I and then each consecutive A_{i+1} bonds to A_i, indicating a successful completion of A_i. Finally, a success step S of arity 1 occurs which is represented by a bond between A_n and S. A transaction can fail at any stage after I. This is represented by a fail object F of arity 2 bonding with the last A_i, which represents the failure of A_i. When this happens all steps A_k for $1 \leq k \leq i$ are undone, and then the compensation step C of arity 1 takes place.

The forwards and reverse reduction relations determine which bonds are created and which are dissolved. Firstly, the chain of A_is is created

$$
\begin{aligned}
I, A_1 &\rightarrow I \cdot A_1 \\
I \cdot A_1, A_2 &\rightarrow I \cdot A_1 \cdot A_2 \\
x \cdot A_i \cdot A_{i+1}, A_{i+2} &\rightarrow x \cdot A_i \cdot A_{i+1} \cdot A_{i+2} \quad 1 \leq i < n-2 \\
x \cdot A_n, S &\rightarrow x \cdot A_n \cdot S
\end{aligned}
$$

Fail can occur at any stage of building the chain of A_is, where $1 \leq i < n$:

$$
\begin{aligned}
I \cdot A_1, F &\rightarrow I \cdot A_1 \cdot F &&\rightarrow \overline{I \cdot A_1 \cdot F} \\
x \cdot A_i \cdot A_{i+1}, F &\rightarrow x \cdot A_i \cdot A_{i+1} \cdot F &&\rightarrow x \cdot \overline{A_i \cdot A_{i+1} \cdot F}
\end{aligned}
$$

Following a fail transaction steps are undone

$$
\begin{aligned}
\overline{I \cdot A_1 \cdot F} &\rightsquigarrow \overline{I, \, A_1 \cdot F} &&\rightsquigarrow I \cdot F, \, A_1 \\
x \cdot \overline{A_i \cdot A_{i+1} \cdot F} &\rightsquigarrow x \cdot \overline{A_i, \, A_{i+1} \cdot F} &&\rightsquigarrow x \cdot A_i \cdot F, \, A_{i+1}
\end{aligned}
$$

Note that $\overline{I, \, A_1 \cdot F} \equiv I \cdot F \cdot A_1$ cannot bond with A_2, and correspondingly $x \cdot A_i \cdot F \cdot A_{i+1}$ cannot bond with A_{i+2}. This is due to the form of the first four rules for $\rightarrow$.

Finally, compensation takes place

$$
C, \, I \cdot F \rightarrow C \cdot I \cdot F \rightsquigarrow C \cdot I, \, F
$$

The initial process $I, A_1, \ldots, A_n, S, C, F$ can reach one of the two terminated processes: the transaction has completed successfully $I \cdot A_1 \cdot \ldots \cdot A_n \cdot S, C, F$, or the transaction has failed and the compensation has taken place $I \cdot C, A_1, \ldots, A_n, S, F$.

Example 2.4. This reaction system describes how a polymer is constructed by a scaffolding protein. We have scaffolding proteins S of arity 2 and and polymer molecules Q of arity 3. Firstly, two molecules of sort S combine into a scaffolding and then attract copies of Q

$$S, S \rightarrow S \cdot S \qquad S \cdot S, Q \rightarrow S \cdot S \cdot Q \qquad x \cdot S \cdot S, Q \rightarrow x \cdot S \cdot S \cdot Q$$

Once two copies of Q are bonded to the scaffolding they bond together

$$Q \cdot S \cdot S \cdot Q \quad \rightarrow \overline{Q \cdot S \cdot S \cdot Q} \equiv \overline{Q \cdot Q \cdot S \cdot S}$$

$$x \cdot Q \cdot S \cdot S \cdot Q \rightarrow x \cdot \overline{Q \cdot S \cdot S \cdot Q} \equiv x \cdot \overline{Q \cdot Q \cdot S \cdot S}$$

Note that for the last structural equivalence we need a further rule, where y, z can be empty, in addition to those we gave earlier for arities at most two

$$y \cdot \overline{A \cdot B \cdot z \cdot C} \equiv y \cdot \overline{A \cdot C \cdot z^{-1} \cdot B}$$

Now the bond between the last S and Q breaks

$$\overline{Q \cdot Q \cdot S \cdot S} \quad \rightsquigarrow Q \cdot Q \cdot S \cdot S$$

$$x \cdot \overline{Q \cdot Q \cdot S \cdot S} \rightsquigarrow x \cdot Q \cdot Q \cdot S \cdot S$$

The S at the end is now available to bond to an unattached Q (using the rule $x \cdot S \cdot S, Q \rightarrow x \cdot S \cdot S \cdot Q$ given above), and the process can continue while unattached Qs remain.

An initial solution consisting of two copies of S and four copies of Q becomes eventually the solution $Q \cdot Q \cdot Q \cdot Q \cdot S \cdot S$. If we add two further rules below for breaking bonds between molecules bonded to S, the solution computes further to $Q \cdot Q \cdot Q \cdot Q, S, S$.

$$x \cdot S \cdot S \rightsquigarrow x, \ S \cdot S$$

$$S \cdot S \quad \rightsquigarrow S, \ S$$

The addition of $S \cdot S \rightsquigarrow S, S$ makes the computation potentially non-terminating: $S, S \rightarrow S \cdot S \rightsquigarrow S, S \ldots$.

The last two examples show that reactive systems are capable of expressing both causal reversing and out-of-causal-order reversing and, in this respect, reactive systems are comparable to CCSK with the execution control operator [12] and extend what RCCS [3] and higher order roll-π [6] can express.

3   Reversible Event Structures

In this section we recall what event structures are, define the reversible form of event structures including a new notion of configuration in the reversible setting, and discuss how simple reaction systems from Section 2 can be given meaning in terms of reversible event structures.

3.1   Event Structures

Event structures were defined by Winskel [16] following earlier work by Nielsen, Plotkin and Winskel [9]. They were further developed, for example, in [14, 13, 17] and in [15].

Definition 3.1 ([16, Def. 1.1.1]). *Event structures* are triples $\mathcal{E} = (E, \mathsf{Con}, \vdash)$ where E is a set of events with typical elements e, e', $\mathsf{Con} \subseteq \mathcal{P}_{\mathrm{fin}}(E)$ is the *consistency* relation which is non-empty and satisfies the property $Y \subseteq X \in \mathsf{Con}$ implies $Y \in \mathsf{Con}$ (downwards closure), and $\vdash \subseteq \mathsf{Con} \times E$ is the *enabling* relation which satisfies the *weakening* condition $X \vdash e$ and $X \subseteq Y \in \mathsf{Con}$ implies $Y \vdash e$ for all $e \in E$.

We omit brackets for singleton sets in expressions $X \vdash e$ where convenient.

Informally, events are things that happen, for example a creation of a bond between bases A and B, a communication of a value between a sender and a receiver, a part of a long-running transaction. Configurations are the sets of events that have occurred (in accordance with Con and $\vdash$):

Definition 3.2 ([16, Def. 1.1.2]). Let $\mathcal{E} = (E, \mathsf{Con}, \vdash)$ be an event structure. The set $S(\mathcal{E})$ of *configurations* of $\mathcal{E}$ consists of $X \subseteq E$ which are

- *consistent*: every finite subset of X is in Con;
- *secured*: for all $e \in X$ there is a sequence of events $e_0, \dots, e_n \in X$ such that $e_n = e$ and for all $i < n$, $\{e_0, \dots, e_{i-1}\} \vdash e_i$.

Example 3.3. Consider the events a, b with all subsets of $\{a, b\}$ in Con, and the enabling relation $\emptyset \vdash a$, $a \vdash b$. We notice that $\{a\}$ is a configuration because $\{a\} \in \mathsf{Con}$ and a is enabled without any preconditions: $\emptyset \vdash a$. Once a takes place, b can happen because $\{a, b\} \in \mathsf{Con}$ and b is enabled by the already performed a: $a \vdash b$. We can say here that a *causes* b and b cannot take place before a happens first.

Some events are in *conflict*: they cannot happen in the same computation. Consider the events a, b as above and the event c which is conflict with a. This is represented by $\{a, c\} \notin \mathsf{Con}$ and, by the downwards closure property, $\{a, b, c\} \notin \mathsf{Con}$. The enabling relation is $\emptyset \vdash a$, $a \vdash b$ and $\emptyset \vdash c$. The configurations are $\emptyset$, $\{a\}, \{a, b\}$ and $\{c\}$ representing that either a or c can happen initially, but once one has taken place the other cannot happen.

Example 3.4. Some events are *independent* of each other, or concurrent. Consider the events a, b and d, with no events in conflict. The enabling relation is $\emptyset \vdash a$, $a \vdash b$ and $\emptyset \vdash d$. Since a and d are not in conflict $\emptyset \vdash a$, $\emptyset \vdash d$ imply that a, d can happen independently of one another, in any order. Moreover, b and d are independent and can happen in any order provided that b always follows a. The configurations are $\emptyset$, $\{a\}, \{a, b\}, \{d\}, \{a, d\}, \{a, b, d\}$.

The next definition is equivalent to Definition 3.2; it will be easier to generalise to the reversible setting. It is partly inspired by the step-wise securings of [13, Definition 3.5].

Definition 3.5. Let $\mathcal{E} = (E, \mathsf{Con}, \vdash)$ be an event structure. A set $X \subseteq E$ is a *configuration* of $\mathcal{E}$ if there is an infinite sequence $X_0, \ldots$ with $X = \bigcup_{n=0}^{\infty} X_n$, $X_0 = \emptyset$, $X_n \subseteq X_{n+1}$ and X_n consistent (all $n \in \mathbb{N}$), where for every $n \in \mathbb{N}$, and every $e \in X_{n+1} \setminus X_n$, there is a rule $X' \vdash e$ with $X' \subseteq_{\mathsf{fin}} X_n$.

Proposition 3.6. *Let $\mathcal{E} = (E, \mathsf{Con}, \vdash)$ be an event structure and let $X \subseteq E$. Then X is a configuration according to Definition 3.2 iff X is a configuration according to Definition 3.5.*

There is a natural notion of *computation* for configurations. A transition relation can now be defined to represent how a new event can happen in a configuration giving rise to a bigger configuration. Given configurations X, Y we have $X \to Y$ if $Y = X \cup \{e\}$ (with $e \notin X$) and $X' \vdash e$, for some e and $X' \subseteq_{\mathsf{fin}} X$. A computation of the event structure E is a computation (sequence of transitions) starting from $\emptyset_{\mathcal{E}}$, the empty configuration of $\mathcal{E}$. As an illustration, $\emptyset \to \{d\} \to \{a, d\} \to \{a, b, d\}$ is a part of a computation of the event structure in Example 3.4. We also have $\emptyset \to \{a\} \to \{a, d\} \to \{a, b, d\}$ and $\emptyset \to \{a\} \to \{a, b\} \to \{a, b, d\}$. See Figure 1.

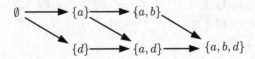

Fig. 1. Configurations and transitions in Example 3.4

We now return to Example 2.1. The bonds in $C \cdot A$ and $A \cdot B$ are the events, and we denote them as ca and ab. The enabling relation is $\emptyset \vdash ca$, $ca \vdash ab$. If we consider the order in which the bonds are created we deduce that ca causes ab. If these bonds were to be dissolved in a causality preserving manner, then ab ought to be reversed first, and only then ca. But breaking the bonds in this manner would not lead to any real change or progress: we would end up where we started. If the bonds are undone out of causal order, then there may be progress. In this example, if ca is dissolved and ab is left untouched, we have the molecule $A \cdot B$ at the end. This would have not been possible if we reversed in causal order. The main question of this paper thus arises: how do we represent undoing of events in any order in the setting of event structures?

3.2   Reversible Event Structures

Let E be a set of events. We define the corresponding set of *undone* events (strictly speaking, events that are to be undone) to be $\underline{E} = \{\underline{e} : e \in E\}$, where $\underline{E}$ is disjoint from E. For $e \in E$, let e^* be either e or $\underline{e}$; we sometimes use the notation $X + e^*$ to mean either $X \cup \{e\}$ or $X \setminus \{e\}$ respectively.

Definition 3.7. A *reversible event structure* (RES for short) is a triple $\mathcal{E} = (E, \mathsf{Con}, \vdash)$ where E and Con are as before and $\vdash \subseteq \mathsf{Con} \times \mathcal{P}(E) \times (E \cup \underline{E})$ is the *enabling* relation satisfying:

1. if $X \otimes Y \vdash e^*$ then $(X \cup \{e\}) \cap Y = \emptyset$;
2. if $X \otimes Y \vdash \underline{e}$ then $e \in X$;
3. *weakening*: if $X \otimes Y \vdash e^*$ and $X \subseteq X' \in \mathsf{Con}$ then $X' \otimes Y \vdash e^*$, provided $X' \cap Y = \emptyset$.

We shall write $X \otimes \emptyset \vdash e^*$ as $X \vdash e^*$ for short. Also we omit brackets for singleton sets in expressions $X \otimes Y \vdash e^*$ where convenient.

The new enabling relation $\vdash$ extends the enabling relation from Definition 3.1 in two directions. Firstly, it permits reversing of events as e^* in $X \otimes Y \vdash e^*$ can be an undone event. Secondly, it allows us to specify which events prevent e^* (here those in Y) in addition to the events that enable e^* (those in X). For example, $\{a, b\} \otimes \{c, d\} \vdash \underline{a}$ says that a can be undone in a configuration which contains a and b and does not contain c and d.

Example 3.8. Consider an RES with a single event e and the enabling rule $\emptyset \vdash e$. As in the previous subsection the sets $\emptyset$ and $\{e\}$ are configurations. Next we add another rule $e \vdash \underline{e}$. This allows us to regress from $\{e\}$ to $\emptyset$. Now the sets $\emptyset$ and $\{e\}$ are reachable from $\emptyset$ in any number of steps; they are configurations according to Definition 3.10 below. There is, however, an infinite computation sequence $\emptyset, \{e\}, \emptyset, \{e\}, \ldots$.

The example illustrates that in the reversible setting sets of events can grow and and shrink as computation progresses. Also, it may happen that sets of events grow non-monotonically as, for example, in $a_0, b, a_1, \underline{b}, a_2, b, a_3, \underline{b}, a_4, \ldots$. So we shall need to consider limits of infinite sequences of subsets of E in order to define configurations. Recall that a subset $S \subseteq \mathbb{N}$ is *cofinite* if $\mathbb{N} \setminus S$ is finite.

Definition 3.9. Let $X_0, \ldots$ be an infinite sequence of subsets of E. We say that $X = \lim_{n \to \infty} X_n$ if for every $e \in E$:

1. $\{n \in \mathbb{N} : e \in X_n\}$ is either finite or cofinite;
2. $e \in X$ iff $\{n : e \in X_n\}$ is cofinite.

Note that a sequence of sets does not necessarily have a limit. The sequence $\emptyset, \{e\}, \emptyset, \{e\}, \ldots$ has no limit, since e belongs to infinitely many sets and does not belong to infinitely many sets. However if $X_n \subseteq X_{n+1}$ (all $n \in \mathbb{N}$) then $\lim_{n \to \infty} X_n$ exists and is $\bigcup_{n=0}^{\infty} X_n$. Also note that a finite sequence $X_0, \ldots, X_n$ can be extended to an infinite sequence by letting $X_m = X_n$ for all $m > n$; the extended sequence has the limit X_n. In Example 3.8 the sequence $\emptyset, \{e\}$ can be extended to an infinite sequence $\emptyset, \{e\}, \{e\}, \ldots$ and has the limit $\{e\}$.

Next we define configurations for RESs. Our aim is that they generalise configurations in Definition 3.5. We use the notational convention that $\underline{e} \in A \setminus B$ means $e \in B \setminus A$.

Definition 3.10. Let $\mathcal{E} = (E, \mathsf{Con}, \vdash)$ be an RES. A set $X \subseteq E$ is a *configuration* of $\mathcal{E}$ if there is an infinite sequence $X_0, \ldots$ with $X = \lim_{n \to \infty} X_n$, $X_0 = \emptyset$ and $X_n \cup X_{n+1}$ consistent (all $n \in \mathbb{N}$), where for every $n \in \mathbb{N}$, and every $e^* \in X_{n+1} \setminus X_n$, there is a rule $X' \otimes Y' \vdash e^*$ such that:

1. $X' \subseteq_{\text{fin}} X_n$ and $X' + e^* \subseteq X_{n+1}$;
2. $Y' \cap (X_n \cup X_{n+1}) = \emptyset$.

We require $X_n \cup X_{n+1}$ to be consistent, as configurations can only be extended in a consistent fashion. However, there is no requirement that $X_i \cup X_j$ is consistent if $j > i + 1$; events in X_i which are inconsistent with X_j can be reversed in constructing $X_{i+1}, \ldots, X_{j-1}$. Also, note that the X_is in the above definition can grow smaller as well as bigger as computation progresses. Moreover, a finite sequence $X_0, \ldots, X_n = X$ that satisfies the conditions of Definition 3.10 is sufficient for X to be a configuration. The sequence $\emptyset, \{e\}$ in Example 3.8 can be extended to an infinite sequence and, since the conditions of Definition 3.10 are satisfied, its limit $\{e\}$ is a configuration.

The next result shows that RESs are a generalisation of event structures.

Proposition 3.11. *Suppose* $\mathcal{E} = (E, \mathsf{Con}, \vdash)$ *is an event structure. Then* $\mathcal{E}' = (E, \mathsf{Con}, \vdash')$ *is a reversible event structure, where we define* $X \otimes \emptyset \vdash' e$ *iff* $X \vdash e$ *(and there are no reverse enablings* $X \otimes Y \vdash' \underline{e}$*). Moreover,* X *is a configuration of* $\mathcal{E}$ *according to Definition 3.5 iff* X *is a configuration of* $\mathcal{E}'$ *according to Definition 3.10.*

Our generalised enabling rules are powerful enough that we no longer need the consistency relation.

Proposition 3.12. *Let* $\mathcal{E} = (E, \mathsf{Con}, \vdash)$ *be an RES. Define* $\mathsf{Con}' = \mathcal{P}_{\text{fin}}(E)$ *and define* $\vdash'$ *by* $X \otimes [Y \cup (E \setminus Z)] \vdash' e^*$ *whenever* X, Y, Z *are such that* $X \otimes Y \vdash e^*$, Z *is consistent with respect to* Con *and* $X + e^* \subseteq Z$. *Then* $\mathcal{E}' = (E, \mathsf{Con}', \vdash')$ *is an RES, and* X *is a configuration of* $\mathcal{E}$ *iff* X *is a configuration of* $\mathcal{E}'$.

In the light of the previous result, we could dispense with Con altogether in the setting of RESs. However we allow Con as sometimes it may be natural or convenient to identify certain configurations as being consistent or inconsistent, before defining enabling rules in detail.

Example 3.13. Let $E = \{a, b, c\}$, $\mathsf{Con} = \{\{a, c\}, \{b, c\}\}$ plus deducible subsets, and $\emptyset \vdash a$, $\emptyset \vdash b$, $a \vdash c$, $b \vdash c$. Then $\mathcal{E} = (E, \mathsf{Con}, \vdash)$ is a (reversible) event structure where either a or b causes c, and $\{a, b\}$ is inconsistent. We can use the procedure of Proposition 3.12 to convert $\mathcal{E}$ into $\mathcal{E}' = (E, \mathsf{Con}', \vdash')$ where $\mathsf{Con}' = \mathcal{P}_{\text{fin}}(E)$ and $\emptyset \otimes b \vdash' a$, $\emptyset \otimes \{b, c\} \vdash' a$, $\emptyset \otimes a \vdash' b$, $\emptyset \otimes \{a, c\} \vdash' b$, $a \otimes b \vdash' c$, $b \otimes a \vdash' c$.

Configurations are $\emptyset, \{a\}, \{b\}, \{a, c\}, \{b, c\}$ for both $\mathcal{E}$ and $\mathcal{E}'$. However in $\mathcal{E}'$ there are two extra consistent sets, namely $\{a, b\}$ and $\{a, b, c\}$.

Note that the converted RES can be optimised by removing $\emptyset \otimes \{b, c\} \vdash' a$ and $\emptyset \otimes \{a, c\} \vdash' b$, since they are implied by $\emptyset \otimes b \vdash' a$ and $\emptyset \otimes a \vdash' b$, respectively.

Definition 3.14. Given configurations X, Y of a reversible event structure $\mathcal{E}$ we let

- $X \rightarrow Y$ if $Y = X \cup \{e\}$ and $X' \otimes Z \vdash e$ for some e, X', Z with $e \notin X$, $X' \subseteq_{\text{fin}} X$ and $Z \cap (X \cup \{e\}) = \emptyset$;

– $X \rightsquigarrow Y$ if $Y = X \setminus \{e\}$ and $X' \otimes Z \vdash \underline{e}$ for some e, X', Z with $X' \subseteq_{\mathrm{fin}} X$ and $Z \cap X = \emptyset$.

As before, a computation of $\mathcal{E}$ is a computation starting from $\emptyset_{\mathcal{E}}$.

Example 3.15. Consider events a and b in Example 3.4. We have that a causes b so if we wish to achieve causal-order reversing we need to add the following to the definition of $\vdash$: $b \vdash \underline{b}$ and $a \otimes b \vdash \underline{a}$. The configuration $\{a, b\}$ can reverse to a by undoing b as allowed by $b \vdash \underline{b}$. But it cannot regress to $\{b\}$ because $a \otimes b \vdash \underline{a}$ can only be applied in a configuration that contains a and does not contain b. See Figure 2(i).

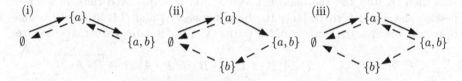

Fig. 2. Configurations and transitions in Example 3.15

If reversing out of order is required, we instead add to the definition of $\vdash$ in Example 3.4 the following: $a \vdash \underline{a}$ and $b \otimes a \vdash \underline{b}$. This means that a can be reversed in any configuration that contains a (with or without b), and b can be reversed only when a is not present. Since a causes b, this means that b can be reversed only when a is reversed. See Figure 2(ii), where reverse transitions are indicated by dashed lines. Finally, if we would like instead that a and b are reversed in any order, then we would extend the enabling relation simply with $b \vdash \underline{b}$ and $a \vdash \underline{a}$. See Figure 2(iii).

We now give an example where we get an infinite configuration as a limit of a non-monotonically increasing sequence.

Example 3.16. Let $\mathcal{E} = (E, \mathsf{Con}, \vdash)$ where $E = \{a_i : i \in \mathbb{N}\} \cup \{b_j : j \in \mathbb{N}\}$ and $\mathsf{Con} = \{a_i, b_0, \dots, b_j\}$ (any $i, j \in \mathbb{N}$) plus deducible subsets, with

$$\emptyset \vdash a_0 \quad a_i \vdash b_i \quad \{a_i, b_i\} \vdash \underline{a_i} \quad b_i \vdash a_{i+1} \quad (\text{all } i \in \mathbb{N})$$

The only possible computation sequence is $a_0, b_0, \underline{a_0}, a_1, b_1, \dots$, with which we can associate a sequence $X_0 = \emptyset$, $X_1 = \{a_0\}, \dots$ This has limit the infinite set $\{b_j : j \in \mathbb{N}\}$, which is therefore a configuration of $\mathcal{E}$; note that each a_i appears finitely often in the sequence X_n, while each b_j appears cofinitely often.

3.3   Modelling of Bonding with Events

We now discuss how reaction systems from Section 2 can be given meaning in terms of reversible event structures. Recall that an object of a reaction system can be seen as an undirected graph, where the bases of the object are the nodes and the bonds between the bases are the edges. We shall represent the bonds, and thus the edges of the associated graph, as events. Given bases X, Y of a reaction system each bond $X \cdot Y$ will be denoted by the event xy.

We begin with a simple reaction system in Example 2.1. The events are ca and ab (representing the bonds $C \cdot A$ and $A \cdot B$) and $\mathsf{Con} = \mathcal{P}(\{ca, ab\})$. The bonds are created by $\emptyset \vdash ca$, $ca \vdash ab$, and are broken by $\{ca, ab\} \vdash \overline{ca}$. Note that we do not require here the full generality of the new enabling relation.

The next example is inspired by the ERK signalling pathway [12].

Example 3.17. We describe bonding and unbonding that takes place along a section of the ERK signalling pathway. The molecule A receives a signal P at the top of the pathway by bonding to it. The molecule $P \cdot A$ travels then towards the middle of the pathway where it combines with B. A bond between P and B is then created and the bond between P and A is dissolved thus, in a sense, passing the signal P to B. Once the bond between A and B is broken B is able to pass P towards the bottom of the pathway. The forwards reduction rules are

$$P, A \to P \cdot A \qquad P \cdot A, B \to P \cdot A \cdot B \qquad P \cdot A \cdot B \to \overline{P \cdot A \cdot B}$$

and the reverse rules for dissolving the bonds are

$$\overline{P \cdot A \cdot B} \rightsquigarrow \overline{P, A \cdot B} \ (\equiv A \cdot B \cdot P) \qquad A \cdot B \cdot P \rightsquigarrow A, B \cdot P \qquad B \cdot P \rightsquigarrow B, P$$

The events are xy for every $X \cdot Y$ and Con is defined as $\mathcal{P}(\{pa, ab, bp\})$. We derive the following enabling rules from the forwards reduction rules

$$\emptyset \vdash pa \qquad pa \vdash ab \qquad \{pa, ab\} \vdash bp$$

and we obtain the following enabling rules from the reverse reduction rules

$$\{pa, ab, bp\} \vdash \underline{pa} \qquad \{ab, bp\} \oslash pa \vdash \underline{ab} \qquad bp \oslash \{pa, ab\} \vdash \underline{bp}$$

Note the form of the last three rules and how the operator $\oslash$ is used in the last two rules to enforce the order of undoing of pa, ab and bp.

The configurations are $\emptyset$, $\{pa\}$, $\{pa, ab\}$, $\{pa, ab, bp\}$, $\{ab, bp\}$, $\{bp\}$, and the creation and dissolving of the bonds happens in the following order: pa, ab, bp, $\underline{pa}$, $\underline{ab}$, $\underline{bp}$. We deduce that pa causes ab which causes bp, and we note that the bonds are reversed out of causal order.

We now return to the reaction system in Example 2.3.

Example 3.18. The events are xy for every bond $X \cdot Y$ among the bases X, Y in Example 2.3. We take Con to be the powerset of the set of all events. Step A_i of the transaction either succeeds by bonding to the next step or it fails by bonding to F for $1 \leq i \leq n$. So we need to express this in the enabling relation by stating that if $a_i a_{i+1}$ takes place then (a) $a_{i+1} a_{i+2}$ can happen if $a_{i+1} f$ did not take place, and (b) $a_{i+1} f$ can happen if $a_{i+1} a_{i+2}$ did not take place for $i < n-1$. This negative information is represented using $\oslash$ in the following two sets of enabling rules. Transaction steps occur as follows:

$$\emptyset \otimes if \qquad\qquad \vdash ia_1$$
$$ia_1 \otimes a_1 f \qquad\quad \vdash a_1 a_2$$
$$a_i a_{i+1} \otimes a_{i+1} f \vdash a_{i+1} a_{i+2} \quad 1 \leq i \leq n-2$$
$$a_{n-1} a_n \otimes a_n f \ \vdash a_n s$$

Fail can bond with the transaction steps as follows:

$$ia_1 \otimes a_1 a_2 \qquad\qquad \vdash a_1 f$$
$$a_1 f \qquad\qquad\qquad \vdash if$$
$$a_i a_{i+1} \otimes a_{i+1} a_{i+2} \qquad \vdash a_{i+1} f \quad 1 \leq i \leq n-2$$
$$a_{n-1} a_n \otimes a_n s \qquad\qquad \vdash a_n f$$
$$a_{i+1} f \otimes \{a_{i+1} a_{i+2}, a_{i+2} f\} \vdash a_i f \quad 1 \leq i \leq n-2$$
$$a_n f \qquad\qquad\qquad\quad \vdash a_{n-1} f$$

Next, bonds of the transaction steps are undone so we need to use the full strength of the enabling relation, where $1 \leq i < n$

$$\{ia_1, a_1 f, if\} \qquad\qquad \vdash \underline{ia_1}$$
$$\{a_1 f, if\} \otimes ia_1 \qquad\quad \vdash \underline{a_1 f}$$
$$\{a_i a_{i+1}, a_{i+1} f, a_i f\} \quad \vdash \underline{a_i a_{i+1}}$$
$$\{a_{i+1} f, a_i f\} \otimes a_i a_{i+1} \vdash \underline{a_{i+1} f}$$

Consider $\{a_i a_{i+1}, a_{i+1} f, a_i f\}$. Here F is bonded with A_i and A_{i+1}. We require that the bond $A_i \cdot A_{i+1}$ breaks first, and then $A_{i+1} \cdot F$ breaks. We achieve this by requiring that all events $a_i a_{i+1}, a_{i+1} f, a_i f$ are present in order to undo $a_i a_{i+1}$, and we undo $a_{i+1} f$ when $a_{i+1} f, a_i f$ are present and $a_i a_{i+1}$ is not. Correspondingly for $\{ia_1, a_1 f, if\}$.

Finally, compensation takes place

$$if \otimes \{ia_1, a_1 f\} \vdash ci \qquad \{if, ci\} \vdash \underline{if}$$

We can reach from $\emptyset$ two terminated configurations (where no forwards or reverse transitions are possible), namely $\{ia_1, \ldots, a_i a_{i+1}, \ldots, a_n s\}$ which denotes the successful completion of the transaction, or $\{ci\}$ which is the compensation following the failure.

4   Conclusion

We have introduced simple reaction systems for bonding and illustrated their usefulness with examples taken from software engineering and biochemistry, including long running transactions with compensation, polymer creation by scaffolding proteins, and a signal passing mechanism used by the ERK pathway. We have proposed reversible event structures, which has not been done before, defined the notion of configuration, and discussed how to give semantics to reaction systems for bonding in terms of reversible event structures.

It remains for future work to clarify the expressive power of reversible event structures and in particular whether they can model reversible process calculi.

Acknowledgements. We thank the referees of Reversible Computation 2013 for their comments and suggestions. The second author acknowledges partial support from the JSPS Invitation Fellowship grant S13054.

References

[1] Berry, G., Boudol, G.: The chemical abstract machine. Theoretical Computer Science 96(1), 217–248 (1992)

[2] Cardelli, L., Laneve, C.: Reversible structures. In: Proceedings of CMSB 2011, pp. 131–140. ACM (2011)

[3] Danos, V., Krivine, J.: Reversible communicating systems. In: Gardner, P., Yoshida, N. (eds.) CONCUR 2004. LNCS, vol. 3170, pp. 292–307. Springer, Heidelberg (2004)

[4] Danos, V., Krivine, J.: Transactions in RCCS. In: Abadi, M., de Alfaro, L. (eds.) CONCUR 2005. LNCS, vol. 3653, pp. 398–412. Springer, Heidelberg (2005)

[5] Danos, V., Krivine, J.: Formal molecular biology done in CCS-R. In: Proceedings of BioConcur 2003. ENTCS, vol. 180, pp. 31–49 (2007)

[6] Lanese, I., Mezzina, C.A., Schmitt, A., Stefani, J.-B.: Controlling reversibility in higher-order pi. In: Katoen, J.-P., König, B. (eds.) CONCUR 2011. LNCS, vol. 6901, pp. 297–311. Springer, Heidelberg (2011)

[7] Lanese, I., Mezzina, C.A., Stefani, J.-B.: Reversing higher-order pi. In: Gastin, P., Laroussinie, F. (eds.) CONCUR 2010. LNCS, vol. 6269, pp. 478–493. Springer, Heidelberg (2010)

[8] Luks, E.M.: Isomorphism of graphs of bounded valence can be tested in polynomial time. Journal of Computer and System Sciences 25(1), 42–65 (1982)

[9] Nielsen, M., Plotkin, G.D., Winskel, G.: Petri nets, event structures and domains, part I. Theoretical Computer Science 13, 85–108 (1981)

[10] Phillips, I.C.C., Ulidowski, I.: Reversibility and models for concurrency. In Proceedings of SOS 2007. ENTCS, vol. 192, pp. 93–108 (2007)

[11] Phillips, I.C.C., Ulidowski, I.: Reversing algebraic process calculi. Journal of Logic and Algebraic Programming 73, 70–96 (2007)

[12] Phillips, I.C.C., Ulidowski, I., Yuen, S.: A reversible process calculus and the modelling of the ERK signalling pathway. In: Glück, R., Yokoyama, T. (eds.) RC 2012. LNCS, vol. 7581, pp. 218–232. Springer, Heidelberg (2013)

[13] van Glabbeek, R.J., Plotkin, G.D.: Configuration structures, event structures and Petri nets. Theoretical Computer Science 410(41), 4111–4159 (2009)

[14] van Glabbeek, R.J., Plotkin, G.D.: Event structures for resolvable conflict. In: Fiala, J., Koubek, V., Kratochvíl, J. (eds.) MFCS 2004. LNCS, vol. 3153, pp. 550–561. Springer, Heidelberg (2004)

[15] Varacca, D., Yoshida, N.: Typed event structures and the linear π-calculus. Theoretical Computer Science 411(19), 1949–1973 (2010)

[16] Winskel, G.: Event structures. In: Brauer, W., Reisig, W., Rozenberg, G. (eds.) APN 1986. LNCS, vol. 255, pp. 325–392. Springer, Heidelberg (1987)

[17] Winskel, G.: Events, causality and symmetry. Computer Journal 54(1), 42–57 (2011)

Universal Gates in Other Universes

Jonathan A. Poritz

Department of Mathematics and Physics
Colorado State University – Pueblo
2200 Bonforte Blvd.
Pueblo, CO 81001
USA
jonathan.poritz@gmail.com
http://www.poritz.net/jonathan

Abstract. I describe a new formalization for computation which is similar to traditional circuit models but which depends upon the choice of a family of [semi]groups – essentially, a choice of the structure group of the universe of the computation. Choosing the symmetric groups results in the reversible version of classical computation; the unitary groups give quantum computation. Other groups can result in models which are stronger or weaker than the traditional models, or are hybrids of classical and quantum computation.

One particular example, built out of the semigroup of doubly stochastic matrices, yields classical but probabilistic computation, helping explain why probabilistic computation can be so fast. Another example is a smaller and entirely Real version of the quantum one which uses a (real) rotation matrix in place of the (complex, unitary) Hadamard gate to create algorithms which are exponentially faster than classical ones.

I also articulate a conjecture which would help explain the different powers of these different types of computation, and point to many new avenues of investigation permitted by this model.

Keywords: reversible computation, quantum computation, structure group, universal families of gates, unitary groups, symmetric groups, circuit models of computation, probabilistic computation, exponential speed-up.

1 Introduction

The foundations of quantum mechanics place unitary groups, and the Hilbert spaces on which they act, in a surprisingly central location. The complex linear algebraic structure, Hermitian form, and group of transformations that preserve this structure are certainly unexpected when compared to classical mechanics, where phase spaces are symplectic manifolds and the passage of time is a symplectomorphism.

When quantum computation arrived on the scene, it posited wires with quantum states in a Hilbert space interacting in gates which were unitary transformations in the tensor product of the Hilbert spaces of the input wires. This was

G.W. Dueck and D.M. Miller (Eds.): RC 2013, LNCS 7948, pp. 155–167, 2013.

again a striking contrast with classical circuit models of computation with values from a finite alphabet on the wires, the alphabet being $\mathbb{Z}_2$ in the simplest case or some other finite alphabet when the circuit is viewed as embodying a Turing machine.

In this paper, I describe a new model of circuits with very general gates which allows a uniform description of several important issues in computation. In particular, the gates are to lie in a structure group – really, a system of groups – as specified below, with the wires carrying elements in a vector spaces on which representations of the structure groups act.

The first examples I consider are when the structure groups are permutation groups, which encompasses classical (reversible) computation. What is then very interesting is that I can use even a semigroup, and when the semigroup is the Birkhoff polytope of doubly stochastic matrices, the model implements classical probabilistic/non-deterministic computation. There are the first hints here, to my knowledge, of why probabilistic computation can be faster than deterministic.

After this, I proceed to the unitary structure group, which gives just standard quantum computation. However, the simple algebraic structure of the representation of the unitary group which allows destructive interference to create exponential speed-up over classical approaches can also be realized in a purely real situation which I then describe. In particular, using the special orthogonal structure group and a gate in $SO(2)$ which has a very similar form to the Hadamard gate of quantum computation, I provide an explicit example of such an exponential speed-up.

As Blum, Cucker, Shub and Smale [5] brought techniques of ring theory and algebraic geometry to a computation model which generalized classical computation, and Coecke and many co-workers [7] brought category theory and graphical calculi, the goal of the current work is to bring techniques of [Lie] group theory and (eventually) functional analysis to a different generalization.

1.1 Notation

Here are some basic notations and assumptions I use in this entire paper:

- $\mathbb{F}$ is a fixed field.
- Hilbert spaces are always assumed to be defined over $\mathbb{F}$. When $\mathbb{F} = \mathbb{R}$, we shall use the term *Hilbert space* to refer to a complete (real) inner product space; When $\mathbb{F} = \mathbb{C}$, inner products are always Hermitian.
- No matter the base field $\mathbb{F}$, we shall use the adjective *unitary* to mean a transformation which preserves the inner product. For example, where we say *unitary representation* below, if $\mathbb{F} = \mathbb{R}$ this is what is usually called an *orthogonal representation*.
- Linear transformations are always assumed to be bounded, when defined on an infinite dimensional Hilbert space.
- For a Hilbert space V, $\mathrm{Aut}(V)$ denotes the (bounded) linear self-maps – in particular, even if V has an inner product, $\mathrm{Aut}(V)$ does not contain only isometries – and likewise for maps between different Hilbert spaces.

– Σ will be a fixed finite alphabet, often used when we need to do symbolic computation on strings; it usually suffices to use $\Sigma = \{0,1\}$.

2   The Computational Model

In this section, I present the new generalized computational model ... but first, some foundations. The goal is to replace classical logical gates acting on bits or the unitary group acting on qubits with a general [semi]group action on a vector space. Therefore, *wires* in circuits (or *cells* in a Turing machine tape) will have values in this vector space.

2.1   Generalizing Gates and Wires

The operations in our computations come from the following:

Definition 1. *Let V a vector space and for each $k \in \mathbb{N}$ let G_k be a group (resp., semigroup) and $\rho_k : G_k \to \mathrm{End}(V^{\otimes k})$ a homomorphism. We shall call the collection $\mathcal{G} = \{G_k, \rho_k \mid k \in \mathbb{N}\}$ a* **system of groups** *(resp.,* **semigroups***) acting on [the tensor powers of] V.*

Here are the most basic examples:

Example 1. Fix $d \in \mathbb{N}$ and let $V = \mathbb{F}^d$. Then there is the usual representation of the symmetric group S_d on V as permutation matrices (permuting the standard basis vectors), and of S_{d^k} on $V^{\otimes k}$ in the same way.

Using $G_k = S_{d^k}$ and this standard representation results in the **system** $\mathcal{S}ym$ **of symmetric groups acting on [the tensor powers of]** $V = \mathbb{F}^d$.

Example 2. Again fix $d \in \mathbb{N}$ and let $V = \mathbb{F}^d$. A very general system of groups acting on V is **the system $\mathcal{G}l$ of general linear groups acting on V** given by the full general linear group $GL(d^k, \mathbb{F})$ acting on $V^{\otimes k}$ under the usual representation.

There is an interesting example which mixes these first two, built out of the following.

Definition 2. *An $n \times n$ matrix over $\mathbb{R}$ is called* **doubly stochastic** *if all the column- and row-sums equal 1. The set of such matrices is denoted $\mathbf{B}_n$ and called the* **Birkhoff polytope***.*

The Birkhoff-von Neumann Theorem states that the convex hull of the permutation matrices, viewed as sitting in $\mathbb{R}^{n^2}$, is exactly the Birkhoff polytope $\mathbf{B}_n$ (see, *e.g.*, the original [4] or a more modern [14]). A simple calculation shows that $\mathbf{B}_n$ is a semigroup but not a group: it contains the identity and all products, but not inverses.

Example 3. The **Birkhoff-von Neumann system of semigroups** $\mathcal{B}v\mathcal{N}$ **acting on $V = \mathbb{R}^2$** is the system which has the semigroup $\mathbf{B}_{2^d}$ acting on $V^{\otimes d}$ by the standard representation.

Going instead in the direction of complexity, we have

Example 4. Fix $d \in \mathbb{N}$ and now let $V = \mathbb{C}^d$. The group of unitary matrices $U(d)$ acts on V and the group $U(d^k)$ acts on $V^{\otimes k}$ by the natural representation. This collection of groups and representations will be called the **system $\mathcal{U}$ of unitary groups acting on [the tensor powers of]** $V = \mathbb{C}^d$ or, if we restrict to matrices of determinant one, the **system $\mathcal{SU}$ of special unitary groups**.

In exactly the same way, if $\mathbb{F} = \mathbb{R}$, we get the **system $\mathcal{SO}$ of special orthogonal groups acting on [the tensor powers of]** $V = \mathbb{R}^d$.

Let us first fix a notation with tensor products and corresponding suggestive terminology which will be useful when we want to promote an endomorphism of a tensor power of a vector space to one of a higher tensor power of that space.

Definition 3. *Suppose V is a vector space over $\mathbb{F}$ and $j, k, l \in \mathbb{N}$ satisfy $j - 1 + l \le k$. If $T \in \mathrm{End}(V^{\otimes l})$, we use T on the l factors of $V^{\otimes k}$ starting with the jth to define an endomorphism $T^{\wedge j} = \mathrm{Id}^{\otimes(j-1)} \otimes T \otimes \mathrm{Id}^{\otimes(k-j+1-l)}$ of $V^{\otimes k}$ which we shall call the T-gate starting at j operating on $V^{\otimes k}$.*

[Here the associativity of the tensor product is crucial.]

Once we have a system of [semi]groups acting on the tensor powers of a vector space, we can let a set of its elements act on n-tuples of "wires" in an appropriate sense.

Definition 4. *Given a system $\mathcal{G} = \{G_k, \rho_k\}$ of groups acting on the vector space V and $n, m \in \mathbb{N}$, a **circuit** $\mathcal{C}$ **with structure group** $\mathcal{G}$ **on** n **wires using** m **gates** is a sequence $((g_1, j_1, d_1), \dots, (g_m, j_m, d_m))$ of triples of the form (g, j, d) where $g \in G_d$ and $j, d \in \mathbb{N}$ satisfy $j - 1 + d \le n$.*

Such a circuit induces a map, for which we shall also use the same symbol,

$$\mathcal{C} : V^{\otimes n} \to V^{\otimes n} : v \mapsto \rho_{d_m}(g_m)^{\wedge j_m} \cdot \dots \cdot \rho_{d_1}(g_1)^{\wedge j_1}(v)$$

*called the **computation with $\mathcal{C}$ on vectors** (or **raw computation with $\mathcal{C}$**); this element $\rho_{d_m}(g_m)^{\wedge j_m} \cdot \dots \cdot \rho_{d_1}(g_1)^{\wedge j_1} \in \mathrm{End}(V^{\otimes k})$ will be called the **program implemented by the circuit $\mathcal{C}$**.*

Note 1. These circuits use wires in a slightly different way from some other authors (see, *e.g.,* [6]), where sometimes gates are permitted to operate on any input wires, in any order, selected from all the available wires. The difference is that in the approach of this paper, some permutation gates would have to be used first to bring these wires together, and $\mathcal{G}$ would have to be large enough to contain these permutations as well.

We need some additional information before we can use the above circuits to do symbolic computation. In particular, we need a way to get information out of a circuit.

Definition 5. *Given a Hilbert space V and a finite alphabet Σ, an* **observable decomposition** *of V* **with values in** *Σ is a collection of mutually orthogonal, closed subspaces $\mathcal{O} = \{V_\sigma \mid \sigma \in \Sigma\}$ indexed by Σ which is complete in the sense that its sum is all of V, so $V = \bigoplus_{\sigma \in \Sigma} V_\sigma$. This decomposition allows us to define a probabilistic function (again overloading the notation) $\mathcal{O} : S^1(V) \to \Sigma$ by saying that $\mathcal{O}(v) = \sigma$ with probability $\|P_\sigma(v)\|^2$, where $S^1(V)$ is the unit sphere in V and $P_\sigma : V \twoheadrightarrow V_\sigma$ is the orthogonal projection.*

Such an $\mathcal{O}$ induces also a decomposition of $V^{\otimes n}$ and hence a similar probabilistic function $\mathcal{O} : S^1(V^{\otimes n}) \to \Sigma^n$.

Definition 6. *Fix a circuit $\mathcal{C}$ with structure group $\mathcal{G}$ on n wires having values in the Hilbert space V. Given a function $\epsilon : \Sigma \to S^1(V)$ (called the* **encoding function***) and an observable decomposition $\mathcal{O}$ of V, we define a probabilistic function*

$$\mathcal{C} : \Sigma^n \to \Sigma^n : (\sigma_1, \ldots, \sigma_n) \mapsto \mathcal{O}(\mathcal{C}(\epsilon(\sigma_1) \otimes \cdots \otimes \epsilon(\sigma_n)))$$

called the **symbolic** *(or* **cooked***) computation with $\mathcal{C}$.*

Example 5. For any base field $\mathbb{F}$, let $d \in \mathbb{N}$ and $V = \mathbb{F}^d$. We will use the physicists' notation for the standard orthonormal basis of V, being $\{|0\rangle, \ldots, |d-1\rangle\}$. Then the **standard d-ary encoding** is the encoding function on the alphabet $\Sigma = \mathbb{Z}_d$ defined by $\epsilon_d : a \mapsto |a\rangle$. In this situation, vectors in V are often called **qudits**. When $d = 2$, the encoding is termed **binary** and the vectors **qubits**.

Corresponding to the standard basis, there is an observable decomposition of V with values in Σ defined by the subspaces $\{\mathbb{F} \cdot |0\rangle, \ldots, \mathbb{F} \cdot |d-1\rangle\}$ which is called **measurement in the d-ary computational basis**, written $\mathcal{O}_{|d\rangle}$.

2.2 Notions of Universality

There are a number of ways in which the word "universal" could be used in this computational model. One way is external to the computational processes we are using here, in that it asks if our cooked computations can yield some large known universe of computations, such as perhaps computing all Boolean functions. This will be investigated below in §3.2.

Another sense for universality is bases on the practical consideration that if we are to construct computational circuits in the real world, we want to have a limited number of specific gates which we can figure out how to construct, but which in combination will be able to do a large universe of useful work. Since in practice it is hard to anticipate what circuits we will eventually figure out do useful computation, we usually seek a small number of gates which in combination will create *any* gate from the structure group in question, operating on any number of wires.

There are in fact two versions of this notion of sufficiently powerful sets of gates which are useful.

Definition 7. *Let V be a vector space on which a system $\mathcal{G} = \{G_k, \rho_k\}$ of groups acts. A collection of sets of gates in specific dimensions $\mathcal{H} = \{H_k \mid k \in K\}$, where $K \subseteq \mathbb{N}$ is some index set and $H_k \subseteq G_k \;\forall k \in K$, generates a set of circuits built just as in Def. 4 except that only group elements from one of the H_k are allowed, only operating on k wires, where $k \in K$.*

*We say the collection $\mathcal{H}$ is **exactly universal** for $\mathcal{G}$ if the program implemented by any circuit with structure group $\mathcal{G}$ is also implemented by a circuit generated as above with gates only from $\mathcal{H}$.*

*$\mathcal{H}$ is instead said to be **approximately universal** for $\mathcal{G}$ if the programs of circuits with structure group $\mathcal{G}$ on n wires can be approximated to any desired accuracy in the operator norm on $\mathrm{End}(V^{\otimes n})$ by the programs of circuits generated as above with gates only from $\mathcal{H}$.*

3   Relation to Classical Circuits

3.1   Deterministic Classical

The first thing to notice about our computational model is that it includes all of classical, deterministic computation.

For this, use the standard binary encoding ϵ_2, the system $\mathcal{S}ym$ of symmetric groups acting on $\mathbb{F}^2$ ($\mathbb{F}$ being either $\mathbb{R}$ or $\mathbb{C}$) and finish with measurement $\mathcal{O}_{|2\rangle}$ in the binary computational basis. As has been well known for some time (see for example [3], [17], or [11] for early work, or many explanations of quantum computing, such as [2] or [15], for more modern descriptions) all functions computed by a traditional Boolean circuit can be realized as computations of reversible circuits with ancilla (extra wires).

Reversible gates are permutations of their input spaces, which amounts to the standard basis vectors in $(\mathbb{F}^2)^{\otimes d}$ for a d-bit gate, and such gates are all available in the full symmetric system $\mathcal{S}ym$. Further, observation in the computational basis simply decodes this association of the objects being permuted and the standard basis elements of $(\mathbb{F}^2)^{\otimes d}$.

3.2   Universality in Deterministic Classical

The classical results mentioned above give a kind of universality for the circuit based on permutations, *external* in the sense of §2.2: with ancilla and techniques such as Bennett's famous "trick", any of these external objects – Boolean functions – can be computed by our $\mathcal{S}ym$-structured circuits.

Note that it was traditional even before the connection with reversible computation to say that the NAND gate is universal in the context of Boolean circuits. This simply meant that the other basic gates of Boolean circuits could be built up out of NAND. Then within the realm of reversible computation often uses the Toffoli gate as its basic universal and reversible gate, in the same sense (now with ancilla).

Taking into account the crossing of wires implicit in traditional circuit models (as mentioned above in Note 1), we can rephrase this result as

Theorem 1. *The two gates*

$$SWAP = \begin{pmatrix} 1 & 0 & 0 & 0 \\ 0 & 0 & 1 & 0 \\ 0 & 1 & 0 & 0 \\ 0 & 0 & 0 & 1 \end{pmatrix} \quad and \quad TOF = \begin{pmatrix} 1 & 0 & 0 & 0 & 0 & 0 & 0 & 0 \\ 0 & 1 & 0 & 0 & 0 & 0 & 0 & 0 \\ 0 & 0 & 1 & 0 & 0 & 0 & 0 & 0 \\ 0 & 0 & 0 & 1 & 0 & 0 & 0 & 0 \\ 0 & 0 & 0 & 0 & 1 & 0 & 0 & 0 \\ 0 & 0 & 0 & 0 & 0 & 1 & 0 & 0 \\ 0 & 0 & 0 & 0 & 0 & 0 & 0 & 1 \\ 0 & 0 & 0 & 0 & 0 & 0 & 1 & 0 \end{pmatrix}$$

generate a set of set of circuits acting on the tensor powers of $V = \mathbb{R}^2$ large enough to compute all Boolean functions, using ancilla and the Bennett trick.

Notice that this notion of universality is not the one described in §2.2 for small sets generating all of an ambient structure group. There are many obvious families which work in this particular case, however, particularly easily because the groups are finite. A favorite of mathematicians, for example, would be to take some traditional set of generators for each S_{2^k}, such as all the transpositions, or a large cycle and a single appropriate transposition. Which generating set is most convenient depends upon the physical realization one wants to attempt: nearest-neighbor interactions may be the easiest to realize, plus some single larger operation (such is in linear ion traps). Any proposed generating set can then be tested to see if it generates, in the sense of §2.2 the structure group Sym (or some subset necessary for a particular family of computations).

3.3   Nondeterministic Classical

There is a tension between nondeterminism and reversibility which I have not seen spelled out explicitly elsewhere, but which is fairly clear using the computational approach of this paper. The issue is that a circuit with access to nondeterminism – which is usually imagined as a gate with no inputs but an output that is uniformly distributed on $\{0,1\}$ – really cannot be reversed. That random bit came from nowhere, and even if we imagine the gate as having an input wire in addition to the output, we have no way of knowing what the input was simply by knowing the output.

In our model, this amounts to a wire on which the gate that produces a random bit is realized as the matrix (remember we are using $V = \mathbb{R}^2$ or $\mathbb{C}^2$)

$$RAND_{1/2} = \begin{pmatrix} 1/2 & 1/2 \\ 1/2 & 1/2 \end{pmatrix} .$$

Notice that this $RAND_{1/2}$ is an equally weighted convex combination of the identity $\mathrm{Id}_2 = \begin{pmatrix} 1 & 0 \\ 0 & 1 \end{pmatrix}$ and the gate $NOT = \begin{pmatrix} 0 & 1 \\ 1 & 0 \end{pmatrix}$ and implements a tradition fair coin.

Biased coins can also be incorporated into this model. For $\alpha \in [0,1]$, let

$$RAND_{\alpha} = \begin{pmatrix} \alpha & 1-\alpha \\ 1-\alpha & \alpha \end{pmatrix} = \alpha\,\mathrm{Id}_2 + (1-\alpha)\,NOT .$$

If for some physical reason in our computational hardware, we only have access to a biased $RAND_{\alpha}$ but want the fair $RAND_{1/2}$, there are well known ways to make a fair coin out of a biased one. These methods perhaps began with the *von Neumann extractor* [18] but have been improved over the years in several ways, see [12] and [16], for example. All of these methods require several flips of the biased coin (hopefully independently) and some (Boolean) computation, which may therefore require additional ancilla.

On the other hand, once we have a circuit which implements $RAND_{1/2}$, if we wish in some computation to use a $RAND_\alpha$ for some other $\alpha \in [0,1]$, we can proceed as follows. First, choose some $e \in \mathbb{N}$, from which we shall allow an error bound of size 2^{-e}. Run e copies of the gate $RAND_{1/2}$ in parallel and apply (the reversible version of) a Boolean circuit which compares the resulting bits to the first e binary digits of α to the right of the binary point and outputs a 1 if the random number is less than that portion of α, or 0 otherwise. This output bit, once ancilla are discarded, amounts to a $RAND_\alpha$.

Suppose we wish to add the single random-bit gate $RAND_\alpha$ on the jth wire at the beginning of a computation performed by a circuit over the structure group $\mathcal{S}ym$ with program $P = \rho_{d_m}(g_m)^{\wedge j_m} \cdot \cdots \cdot \rho_{d_1}(g_1)^{\wedge j_1}$ (in the sense of Def. 4). Since tensoring with other matrices commutes with taking linear combinations, the resulting program will be the linear combination

$$\alpha \, \mathrm{Id}_2^{\wedge j} \cdot P + (1-\alpha)\, NOT^{\wedge j} \cdot P \ = \alpha P + (1-\alpha)\, NOT^{\wedge j} \cdot P$$

Adding further nondeterministic gates to the circuit – additional randomness in the form of $RAND_\alpha$ gates – results in circuits with raw computations coming from convex combinations of permutation matrices with additional NOT's at arbitrary locations. The coefficients in these convex combinations resulting from using several fair coins or any number of the $RAND_\alpha$'s produced by the simple scheme described above will always be dyadic rationals.

Nevertheless, it makes sense (by continuity, if for no other reason) to allow all convex combinations of permutations in non-deterministic circuits. As mentioned before, the Birkhoff-von Neumann Theorem then tells us that this amounts to using gates in the semigroup $\mathbf{B}_n$. In summary:

Theorem 2. *The symbolic computations performed by circuits with structure semigroup $\mathcal{B}v\mathcal{N}$ [using ancilla] are exactly the computations performed by classical probabilistic Boolean circuits.*

This theorem points to a kind of answer to the old question of why classical probabilistic computation produces algorithms which seem faster than deterministic: probabilistic computations are basic on the structure [semi]group $\mathcal{B}v\mathcal{N}$ which maybe have an algebraic defect (no inverses) but is a very large superset of the permutation structure group $\mathcal{S}ym$ which underlies deterministic computation. Furthermore, the doubly stochastic matrices in $\mathbf{B}_n$ have a quality of creating a mixture, or probabilistic superposition, of many computational paths simultaneously. That this only leads to some improvement and not the the exponential speed-up of quantum computation seems to be due to the fact that we cannot cancel the unwanted computational paths in the same way as the famous quantum computational algorithms. In §6 below, a conjecture is formulated which makes this crucial distinction precise.

4   Relation to Quantum Circuits

If we want to generalize classical computation in a way that allows both probabilistic and reversible computation, we can change our structure group from the symmetric $\mathcal{S}$ to something which includes mixtures like the gate providing a random bit and yet remains a group. The way this happened in the history of computer science was by going to the unitary structure group $\mathcal{U}$ and full-fledged quantum computation. With this group, we have access to the Hadamard gate

$$H = \frac{1}{\sqrt{2}} \begin{pmatrix} 1 & 1 \\ 1 & -1 \end{pmatrix}$$

which is a nice generalization of the random-bit gate $RAND_{1/2}$ above, with only a well placed negative entry to make it invertible (and different over-all scale).

The computation model in this paper is clearly designed primarily to be an extension of that standard version of quantum computation, so using the structure group $\mathcal{U}$ simply implements that standard. The one thing I do here which is not always done in the basic quantum set-up is that I do all measurement at the end. However, the *principle of deferred measurement* (to use the name coined, I believe, by [15]) says that we may always do this, at least if we are not interested in the raw computation of a circuit, its effect on qubits, but want only to work with the symbolic computation. Thus

Theorem 3. *The symbolic computations produced by circuits in the sense of this paper with structure group $\mathcal{U}$, binary encoding, and measurement $O_{|2\rangle}$ in the computational basis are exactly the symbolic computations produced by the standard model of quantum computation.*

4.1   Universal Quantum Gates

The machinery set up in this paper allows a different approach to proving universality of sets of quantum gates: one must show how to build up exactly or approximately the elements of $U(2^d)$ out of the chosen set of gates by multiplication of tensor products of the smaller gates from the set. This can be applied to the specific choices of universal families from [1], [10], or [6], for example. I defer those calculations to another work, in order to pursue further generalizations of the quantum model here.

I note here only a couple of facts which are known about universal families of quantum gates: it is known that almost any 2-bit gate, together will the whole set of 1-qubit gates, is an exactly universal family for quantum computation; also several finite subsets of the 1-qubit gates, again together with a 2-qubit gate, are known to be approximately universal. See references mentioned immediately above, as well as [13] and many other references in [15].

5   Universes with Other Structure Groups

The promise of the computational model presented in this paper is that it generalizes both classical and quantum computation, and leaves open the possibilities to explore computation performed by circuits using other structure groups.

Since the unitary group carries the basic physics of the quantum universe in which we live, and the permutation group carries the basic physics of idealized classical computation (à la billiard ball computers or ideal Turing machines in a Newtonian universe), one way to think of this new possibility is as examining computation in other universes, with their own structure groups.

5.1   An Un-real but Real Universe

Here is just one example. The first quantum algorithm to show exponential speed-up was the algorithm to solve Deutsch's Problem [8], which uses the linear structure of the tensor product and the particular action of the Hadamard transformation. But the Hadamard matrix shown above looks very much like another matrix from elementary linear algebra: the real, special orthogonal 2×2 matrix

$$R_{\pi/4} = \frac{1}{\sqrt{2}} \begin{pmatrix} 1 & -1 \\ 1 & 1 \end{pmatrix}$$

which implements rotation by $\pi/4$ counterclockwise in $\mathbb{R}^2$. So let us use the structure group $\mathcal{SO}$ with the vector space $V = \mathbb{R}^2$ to build an entirely Real circuit that solves this problem in much the same was as the structure group $\mathcal{U}$ solves it in our universe governed by complex quantum mechanics.

Following the model exposition in [15], we suppose that we have a function $f : \{0,1\} \to \{0,1\}$ which may or may not be constant. We imagine have an oracle U_f in our Real world which can compute the $\mathcal{SO}$ version of f, as $U_f : |x\rangle |y\rangle \mapsto |x\rangle |f(x) \oplus y\rangle$.

We start with the initial state $|01\rangle = |0\rangle \otimes |1\rangle$ and apply $R_{\pi/4} \otimes R_{\pi/4}$, yielding

$$\left(R_{\pi/4}\right)^{\otimes 2}(|01\rangle) = \frac{1}{2}\left(|0\rangle + |1\rangle\right)\left(-|0\rangle + |1\rangle\right)$$

which we submit to the oracle U_f, yielding

$$\frac{1}{2}\left[|0\rangle \left(-|f(0) \oplus 0\rangle + |f(0) \oplus 1\rangle\right) + |1\rangle \left(-|f(1) \oplus 0\rangle + |f(1) \oplus 1\rangle\right)\right]$$

which simplifies a bit as

$$(-1)^{f(0)}\frac{1}{2}\left(|0\rangle + (-1)^{f(0) \oplus f(1)}|1\rangle\right)\left(-|0\rangle + |1\rangle\right).$$

Finally, we apply $R_{\pi/4}^{\wedge 1} = R_{\pi/4} \otimes \mathrm{Id}_2$ ["$R_{\pi/4}$ on the first qubit"] to get

$$|f(0) \oplus f(1) \oplus 1\rangle \frac{1}{\sqrt{2}}\left(-|0\rangle + |1\rangle\right)$$

so the first bit of the measurement $\mathcal{O}_{|2\rangle}$ tells us the if $f(0) \oplus f(1)$ is 0 or 1, hence if f is constant or not.

The above is merely a toy model, but its use of the Real analogue $R_{\pi/4}$ of the quantum Hadamard demonstrates that the full Deutsch-Jozsa algorithm [9], based as it is on repeated use of the Hadamard gate and its tensor powers, will go straight through in the Real world of $\mathcal{SO}$ circuits.

Pulling back a little from the science-fictional conceit above that physical implementation of this approach would involve a visit to another universe, we can imagine now solving these kinds of problems – with exponential speed-up over classical computation – by finding a system with $SO(2)$ symmetry (a round ring, or rotationally (in $\mathbb{R}^2$) symmetric object or field, or ...?) of which multiple copies can be coupled, in the manner of the tensor products underlying our circuit model. Such a system would implement the Real computation described above, so would permit all of the usual exponential speed-up from quantum computation, regardless of whether the hardware used quantum mechanics at all – the only necessary ingredient being the algebraic structure described above.

6 Future Directions, Including a Conjecture and a Proposal

The computational model of this paper allows a search for other structure groups which may

1. be associated with physically realizable systems, and
2. be used to perform calculations at significant speedup over classical algorithms

There are two directions which I think are particularly promising for this approach. One is to vary the structure group (which variation so far has not be much the subject of investigation) in order to determine which groups and representations admit quantum speedup. On that matter, it seems to me that useful information is extracted, out of the exponentially large tensor product spaces in which states of the many wires of our circuits lie, only when there can be destructive interference.

Conjecture 1. I conjecture that structure groups $\mathcal{G} = \{G_k, \rho_k\}$ can only exhibit exponential speedup over classical algorithms if there are matrix coefficients of with different signs.

The converse probably needs some additional hypotheses, however.

In this context, it is worth thinking about the hierarchy of computational power we have seen in this paper, and how delicate it is:

- Straight permutations give circuits over $\mathcal{S}ym$ which yield classical deterministic computation.
- Other finite groups presumably do not give any speed-up – all finite groups arise as subgroups of permutation groups.
- Taking convex combinations of permutations yields $\mathcal{B}v\mathcal{N}$ circuits, and probabilistic classical computation – which is intriguingly faster than deterministic. This structure semigroup is no longer finite (it is uncountable), but it is compact and non-Abelian, and its standard representation has only positive matrix coefficients.

- We have seen above an example (the Real world of circuits over $\mathcal{SO}$) with exponential speed-up over classical computation. The structure group here is an actual group: compact and Abelian, and has a representation on a real vector space, but also with negative matrix coefficients.
- The (complex) unitary structure group of quantum mechanics also has its famous algorithms with exponential speed-up over classical ones. $U(n)$ is compact and non-Abelian, with non-positive matrix coefficients in its standard representation. Yet **finite** [universal] **families of gates** can implement these fast algorithms.

That finite structure groups are classical (slow) and finite families of unitary gates are quantum (fast) is quite surprising, as is the example of quantum-like algorithms in a two-dimensional Real set-up.

Finally, having opened up the possibility of circuits with different structure groups, we can seek out much larger groups where there may be radically different behavior. I therefore propose that some of these much large groups, but perhaps groups which are symmetries of real, known, physical systems, be investigated. Of particular interest would be

1. non-compact, non-Abelian Lie groups – these usually have their interesting representations on infinite dimensional vector spaces, but such function spaces and group actions do occur in quantum mechanics; and
2. really large groups, such as ones which are not even locally compact (as sometimes arise in quantum field theory, among other areas), for example the group of isometries of a separable Hilbert space, or the group of diffeomorphisms of some manifold.

Acknowledgements. I would like to thank Normal Herzberg for a very important comment at a crucial point in this work.

References

1. Barenco, A.: A universal two-bit gate for quantum computation. Proceedings of the Royal Society of London. Series A: Mathematical and Physical Sciences 449(1937), 679–683 (1995)
2. Barenco, A., Bennett, C.H., Cleve, R., DiVincenzo, D.P., Margolus, N., Shor, P., Sleator, T., Smolin, J.A., Weinfurter, H.: Elementary gates for quantum computation. Physical Review A 52(5), 3457 (1995)
3. Bennett, C.H.: Logical reversibility of computation. IBM Journal of Research and Development 17(6), 525–532 (1973)
4. Birkhoff, G.: Tres observaciones sobre el algebra lineal. Univ. Nac. Tucumán Rev. Ser. A 5, 147–151 (1946)
5. Blum, L., Cucker, F., Shub, M., Smale, S.: Complexity and real computation. Springer (1998)
6. Brylinski, J.L., Brylinski, R.: Universal quantum gates. Mathematics of Quantum Computation, 101–116 (2002)
7. Coecke, B.: New structures for physics, vol. 813. Springer (2010)

8. Deutsch, D.: Quantum theory, the church-turing principle and the universal quantum computer. Proceedings of the Royal Society of London. A. Mathematical and Physical Sciences, vol. 400(1818), pp. 97–117 (1985)
9. Deutsch, D., Jozsa, R., Deutsch, D., Jozsa, R.: Rapid solution of problems by quantum computation. Proceedings of the Royal Society of London, vol. 439(1907), pp. 553–558 (1992)
10. DiVincenzo, D.P.: Two-bit gates are universal for quantum computation. Physical Review A 51(2), 1015 (1995)
11. Fredkin, E., Toffoli, T.: Conservative logic. International Journal of Theoretical Physics 21(3), 219–253 (1982)
12. Juels, A., Jakobsson, M., Shriver, E., Hillyer, B.K.: How to turn loaded dice into fair coins. IEEE Transactions on Information Theory 46(3), 911–921 (2000)
13. Lloyd, S.: Almost any quantum logic gate is universal. Physical Review Letters 75(2), 346–349 (1995)
14. Minc, H.: Nonnegative matrices. Wiley-Interscience Series in Discrete Mathematics and Optimization. John Wiley & Sons, New York (1988)
15. Nielsen, M.A., Chuang, I.L.: Quantum computation and quantum information. Cambridge University Press (2010)
16. Shaltiel, R.: Recent developments in explicit constructions of extractors. Current Trends in Theoretical Computer Science: Algorithms and Complexity 1, 189 (2004)
17. Toffoli, T.: Reversible computing. In: de Bakker, J.W., van Leeuwen, J. (eds.) ICALP 1980. LNCS, vol. 85, Springer, Heidelberg (1980)
18. Von Neumann, J.: Various techniques used in connection with random digits. Applied Math. Series 12, 36–38 (1951)

Time-Symmetric Machines

Martin Kutrib[1] and Thomas Worsch[2]

[1] Institut für Informatik, Universität Giessen
Arndtstr. 2, 35392 Giessen, Germany
kutrib@informatik.uni-giessen.de
[2] Karlsruhe Institute of Technology
worsch@kit.edu

Abstract. Reversible computational models with discrete internal states are said to be time-symmetric, if they can go back and forth in time by applying the same transition function. The direction in time is adjusted by a weak transformation of the phase-space, that is, an involution. So, these machines themselves cannot distinguish whether they run forward or backward in time. From this viewpoint, finite state machines and pushdown machines are studied in detail. In essence, it turns out that there are reversible machines which are not time-symmetric, but equivalent time-symmetric machines can effectively be constructed. The notion of time-symmetry is discussed, several examples are given, and further results concerning unary inputs and descriptional complexity issues are shown.

1   Introduction

Computational models with discrete internal states can to some extent be seen as prototypes of computing devices that, in principle, can be constructed in the real world. So, computational models being able to obey physical laws are of natural interest. The physical observation that a loss of information results in heat dissipation [22] strongly suggests to study computations in which no information is lost. A first study of this kind has been done in [6] for Turing machines where the notion of *reversible* Turing machines is introduced. The main result obtained there is that every Turing machine can be simulated by a reversible one in a constructive way. See [5,27] for improved constructions. On the opposite end of the automata hierarchy, reversibility in simpler devices has been studied in [3,29] for deterministic finite automata, in [18] for pushdown automata, and in [4,20,25,26] for multi-head finite automata. Reversible deterministic finite automata are also studied in the context of quantum computing [12,13], whereas construction problems are investigated in [9,10,23]. Reversible versions of parallel models have been studied as well. For cellular automata, it is shown in [2] that global reversibility is decidable for one-dimensional cellular automata, whereas the problem is undecidable for higher dimensions [14]. Reversible cellular automata in connection with language theory are studied in [16,17]. The paper [24] summarizes results on reversible cellular automata, logic gates, logic circuits, and logic elements

G.W. Dueck and D.M. Miller (Eds.): RC 2013, LNCS 7948, pp. 168–181, 2013.

with memory. A motivation for studying reversible computing from the vantage point of physics can be found in [7]. Other reversible computational devices and other perspectives on reversible computing can be found in [28,30,31].

In [21] a further aspect of reversibility in real systems is discussed. In [8] it is motivated that, for example, in Newtonian mechanics, relativity, or quantum mechanics one can go back in time by applying the same dynamics, provided that the sense of time direction is changed by a specific transformation of the phase-space. For Newtonian mechanics, the transformation leaves masses and positions unchanged but reverses the sign of the momenta. This aspect is called *time-symmetry*. In this connection, computational models with discrete internal states have been studied in [8] for the first time. In this seminal paper reversible cellular automata were considered.

Here we investigate time-symmetry for several reversible computational models with discrete internal states that evolve in discrete time. The "direction of time" is adjusted by a weak transformation of the phase-space, that is, an involution. So, these machines themselves cannot distinguish whether they run forward or backward in time.

The rest of this paper is organized as follows. In the next section we recall some basic definitions and discuss the notion of time-symmetry from a general viewpoint on computational models with discrete internal states. In Section 3 deterministic finite-state machines are considered. The notion of time-symmetry is clarified and discussed in more detail. In particular, it turns out that there are reversible machines which are not time symmetric, but equivalent time-symmetric machines can effectively by constructed. In general, this construction requires to increase the size of the machines to twice as many states. It is shown that this bound is tight for infinitely many machines. Moreover, we obtain that every reversible finite-state machine on unary input is necessarily time symmetric. Section 4 is devoted to the study of time-symmetry for pushdown machines. The handling of the additional resource makes the definitions of reversibility and time-symmetry more involved. An example reveals that there are non-regular languages accepted by time-symmetric pushdown automata. Furthermore, the situation for finite automata is complemented and contrasted by proving that there are reversible unary pushdown automata that are not time symmetric, and that from every reversible pushdown automaton one can effectively construct an equivalent time-symmetric one.

2 Preliminaries and Definitions

Let Σ^* denote the *set of all words* over the finite alphabet Σ. The *empty word* is denoted by λ, and $\Sigma^+ = \Sigma^* \setminus \{\lambda\}$. For convenience, we use Σ_λ for $\Sigma \cup \{\lambda\}$. The *reversal of a word* w is denoted by w^R and for the *length of* w we write $|w|$. Set *inclusion* is denoted by $\subseteq$, and *strict set inclusion* by $\subset$. Let A, B, C be arbitrary sets, and $f : B \to C$, $g : A \to B$ two mappings. For their *composition* we write $f \circ g : A \to C$. A mapping $\tau : A \to A$ is said to be an *involution* if $\tau \circ \tau = \text{id}$, where id denotes the identity mapping.

In the following we consider computing machines with a finite number of discrete internal states. The machines may be equipped with further resources, and evolve in discrete time, where each computation step is driven by a so-called transition function δ. The transition function is used to compute the successor configuration of a given configuration. It depends on the current internal state and maybe on the status of further resources the machine is equipped with. It deterministically gives the successor state and maybe changes the status of the resources.

A first study of reversibility of such devices has been done in [6] for Turing machines. Deterministic Turing machines are called *reversible* when they are also backward deterministic. That is, any configuration occurring in any computation must have at most one predecessor which, in addition, is computable by a deterministic Turing machine, say, with transition function $\delta^{\leftarrow}$. Generalizing this convention, we assume that for any reversible computing machine with discrete internal states and transition function δ the reverse transition function is denoted by $\delta^{\leftarrow}$.

We denote the (global) one-step relation $\vdash$ from one configuration to the next on by $\vdash$. So, for a machine M to be reversible there has to be a machine $M^{\leftarrow}$ with global one-step relation $\vdash^{\leftarrow}$ such that $c \vdash c'$ if and only if $c' \vdash^{\leftarrow} c$. Since we only consider deterministic machines in this paper, it follows that $\vdash$ and $\vdash^{\leftarrow}$ are injective. As a very special case it might be that $M = M^{\leftarrow}$ is its own inverse, so that the machine always switches back and forth between a configuration and its successor. However, the time-symmetric machines considered in this paper are more involved. The basic requirement is that each modification of a configuration can be undone by the machine itself, but in order to do so it may be necessary to change the internal state before and after the step back. Loosely speaking, a time-symmetric machine M itself does not know whether it runs forward or backward in time, it just applies its transition function. The direction in time is changed by a weak transformation of the phase-space, where weak means that the transformation is an involution. More precisely, we say that a machine M with state set S is *time symmetric* if there exists an involution τ on the phase-space so that $\tau \circ \delta \circ \tau = \delta^{\leftarrow}$, which means the following. Given a configuration c of the machine, an application of the involution τ transforms it, then δ is used to compute a new configuration, which is again transformed by a second application of τ. The result is the predecessor configuration of c. Precise definitions are given for the specific machines where considered.

3   Time-Symmetry in Finite-State Machines

We first look at the simplest type of device in question, deterministic finite automata (DFA) which can accept the regular languages. A *deterministic finite automaton* is a system $M = \langle S, \Sigma, \delta, s_0, F \rangle$, where S is the finite set of *internal states*, Σ is the finite set of *input symbols*, $s_0 \in S$ is the *initial state*, $F \subseteq S$ is the set of *accepting states*, and $\delta : S \times \Sigma \to S$ is the *transition function*. Note, that here the transition function is not required to be total. The *language accepted* by the finite automaton M is defined as $L(M) = \{w \in \Sigma^* \mid \delta(s_0, w) \in F\}$, where the transition function is recursively extended to $\delta : S \times \Sigma^* \to S$.

A DFA is called *reversible* if and only if for each input symbol $x \in \Sigma$ the (possibly partial) function $\delta_x : S \to S : s \mapsto \delta(s, x)$ is injective. We write $\delta^{\leftarrow}$ for the function $S \times \Sigma \to S$ satisfying $\delta^{\leftarrow}(s, a) = \delta_a^{-1}(s)$. A reversible DFA is *time symmetric* if and only if there is an involution $\tau : S \to S$ such that $\delta_x^{-1} = \tau \circ \delta_x \circ \tau$ holds for all $x \in \Sigma$. At first sight this seems to be a strong condition, since the same τ has to work for all δ_x. Theorems 1 and 2 will shed more light on this.

Reversible DFA have been investigated in [3,29], where it turned out that there are finite automata that cannot be made reversible. That is, there are regular languages which cannot be accepted by any reversible DFA (see Figure 1). So, a question arises immediately: Are there regular languages accepted by reversible DFA which cannot be accepted by time-symmetric DFA?

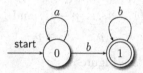

Fig. 1. Example of an irreversible DFA accepting the language a^*b^+ (a double circled state is accepting). There is no reversible DFA accepting this language.

Before we turn to answer these questions, we clarify the notion time-symmetry. Consider the p-state DFA $M = \langle \{0, 1, \ldots, p-1\}, \{a\}, \delta, 0, \{0\} \rangle$, where $\delta(i, a) = (i + 1) \bmod p$, for $0 \leq i \leq p - 1$ (see Figure 2). The language accepted by M is $\{a^{j \cdot p} \mid j \geq 0\}$. The automaton M is reversible since with $\delta^{\leftarrow}(i, a) = (i + p - 1) \bmod p$, we have $\delta^{\leftarrow}(\delta(i, a), a) = i$.

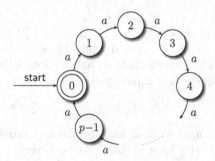

Fig. 2. Example of a unary reversible DFA accepting the language $\{a^{j \cdot p} \mid j \geq 0\}$

In order to obtain time-symmetry one has to go back in time by applying the same transition function. But an involution $\tau : S \to S$ of the phase-space is allowed which satisfies $\delta_x^{-1} = \tau \circ \delta_x \circ \tau$. Looking at two successive steps, we obtain $\delta_x^{-1} \circ \delta_y^{-1} = \tau \circ \delta_x \circ \tau \circ \tau \circ \delta_y \circ \tau = \tau \circ \delta_x \circ \delta_y \circ \tau$. Obviously this generalizes to arbitrary numbers of steps. In some sense τ reverses the direction in time permanently (that is, until τ is applied again).

It turns out that the DFA M *is* time symmetric. As witness involution one can take $\tau(i) = p - i - 1$. We have

$$\tau(\delta_a(\tau(i))) = \tau(\delta_a(p - i - 1)) = \tau(p - i) = i - 1 = \delta_a^{-1}(i) = \delta^{\leftarrow}(i, a),$$

for all i (all arithmetic being done mod p). Now the question arises whether all reversible DFA are already time-symmetric. The next theorem answers this question in the negative.

Theorem 1. *There are reversible DFA which are not time symmetric.*

Proof. Let $p \geq 6$. We use the DFA $M = \langle \{0, 1, \ldots, p - 1\}, \{a, b\}, \delta, 0, \{0\} \rangle$, with

$$\delta(i, a) = (i + 1) \bmod p, \text{ for } i \in \{0, 1, \ldots, p - 1\},$$
$$\delta(i, b) = i, \text{ for } i \in \{1, 3, 4, \ldots, p - 3\}, \text{ and}$$
$$\delta(0, b) = 2, \ \delta(2, b) = 0, \ \delta(p - 2, b) = p - 1, \ \delta(p - 1, b) = p - 2$$

as witness for the assertion (see Figure 3).

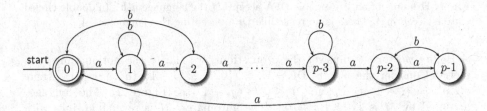

Fig. 3. Example of a reversible DFA that is not time symmetric

Assume there is an involution $\tau : \{0, 1, \ldots, p-1\} \to \{0, 1, \ldots, p-1\}$ such that $\tau \circ \delta_x \circ \tau = \delta_x^{-1}$, for all $x \in \Sigma$. We consider possible states for $\tau(0)$ and will show that every choice leads to a contradiction. As mentioned above $\delta_x^{-1} = \tau \circ \delta_x \circ \tau$ can be extended to sequences of input symbols, that is,

$$\delta_{x_1}^{-1} \circ \cdots \circ \delta_{x_k}^{-1} = \tau \circ \delta_{x_1} \circ \cdots \circ \delta_{x_k} \circ \tau.$$

As a consequence if an input word w leads from some state i back to i, then the same word w also leads $\tau(i)$ back to itself (and vice versa).

If $\tau(0) = q$ with $q \in \{1, 3, 4, \ldots, p - 3\}$, then

$$\tau(\delta_b(\tau(0))) = \tau(\delta_b(q)) = \tau(q) = 0 \neq 2 = \delta_b^{-1}(0)$$

implies a contradiction.

Analogously, the input word aab leads from state 0 back to itself, but this is not the case for states 2, $p - 2$ and $p - 1$; therefore $\tau(0)$ has to be different from them.

The only remaining possibility is $\tau(0) = 0$. By

$$\tau(\delta_b(\tau(\tau(2)))) = \tau(0) = 0 = \delta_b^{-1}(\tau(2))$$

the equation $\tau(2) = 2$ follows. But by $\tau(\delta_a(\tau(0))) = \tau(1) = \delta_a^{-1}(0) = p - 1$ and, thus, by $\tau(\delta_a(\tau(p-1))) = \tau(2) = \delta_a^{-1}(p-1) = p-2$ we obtain $\tau(2) = p-2$, which is a contradiction to $\tau(2) = 2$. So, $\tau(0)$ cannot be equal to 0 which concludes the proof, since we have shown that state 0 cannot be mapped to any other state, either. □

By Theorem 1 there are reversible DFA which are not time symmetric. However, the relation between reversible and time-symmetric DFA is different from the relation between arbitrary and reversible DFA.

Theorem 2. *Let $p \geq 1$ and M be a p-state reversible DFA. Then there exists an equivalent $2p$-state time-symmetric DFA M'.*

Proof. Let $M = \langle S, \Sigma, \delta, s_0, F \rangle$ be a reversible DFA. The idea is to put a copy of M and a copy of its inverse side by side. To this end, we construct a DFA $M' = \langle S', \Sigma, \delta', s_0', F' \rangle$ by setting $S' = S \times \{\rightarrow, \leftarrow\}$, $F' = F \times \{\rightarrow, \leftarrow\}$, and $s_0' = (s_0, \rightarrow)$. For all $s \in S$ and $a \in \Sigma$, the transition function is defined by $\delta'((s, \rightarrow), a) = (\delta(s, a), \rightarrow)$ and $\delta'((s, \leftarrow), a) = (\delta^{\leftarrow}(s, a), \leftarrow)$.

Clearly, the DFA M' works like M while in states from $S \times \{\rightarrow\}$, and it works like the inverse of M while in states from $S \times \{\leftarrow\}$. In order to conclude the proof of the theorem we notice that $L(M') = L(M)$, since M' starts in $(s_0, \rightarrow)$ and there is no transition leading from a state in $S \times \{\rightarrow\}$ to a state in $S \times \{\leftarrow\}$, and that M' is reversible, since M and its inverse are reversible.

Now, for all $s \in S$, let the involution τ be defined by $\tau((s, \rightarrow)) = (s, \leftarrow)$ and $\tau((s, \leftarrow)) = (s, \rightarrow)$. We consider an arbitrary state $(s, \rightarrow)$ and an input symbol $a \in \Sigma$. Then

$$\tau(\delta_a'(\tau((s, \rightarrow)))) = \tau(\delta_a'((s, \leftarrow))) =$$
$$\tau((\delta_a^{-1}(s), \leftarrow)) = (\delta_a^{-1}(s), \rightarrow) = \delta_a'^{-1}((s, \rightarrow))$$

and analogously for the case of a state $(s, \leftarrow)$ shows $\tau \circ \delta_a' \circ \tau = \delta_a'^{-1}$.   □

The previous theorem reveals that the families of languages accepted by reversible and time-symmetric DFA coincide. However, the state complexity may increase by at most a factor two. The next result shows that this upper bound is tight, that is, there are languages accepted by p-state reversible DFA such that the minimal equivalent time-symmetric DFA requires $2p$ states.

Theorem 3. *Let $p \geq 6$. There is a p-state reversible DFA so that every equivalent time-symmetric DFA has at least $2p$ states.*

Proof. The reversible but not time-symmetric p-state DFA M depicted in Figure 3 is used as a witness for the assertion. We consider the language $L(M)$.

Let $M' = \langle S', \Sigma, \delta', s_0', F' \rangle$ be any time-symmetric DFA equivalent to M, that is, $L(M) = L(M')$.

Since $L(M') \cap a^* = \{ a^{j \cdot p} \mid j \geq 0 \}$, on long inputs of the form a^* automaton M' runs into a cycle. But M' is reversible and, thus, the only possibility to run through cycles on unary input is from the very beginning. Therefore, the initial state belongs to the cycle. Moreover the cycle length must be a multiple of p. Otherwise unary words not belonging to $L(M)$ would be accepted. If the cycle length is at least $2p$, the assertion follows immediately. So, we assume the cycle length to be p. More precisely, we consider the states $C = \{0, 1, \ldots, p-1\} \subseteq S'$, where $i = \delta'(s_0', a^i)$, for $0 \leq i \leq p - 1$. In addition, we know $\delta'(s_0', a^p) = s_0'$.

Let us assume $|S'| < 2p$. Then $|S' \setminus C| < p$ since $|C| = p$. Moreover, any involution on $|S'|$ is bijective. So, any involution on $|S'|$ has to map at least one of the p states from C to a state from C, say state i is mapped to state j. By $\tau(\delta_a(\tau(i))) = \tau((j + 1) \bmod p) = \delta_a^{-1}(i) = (i + p - 1) \bmod p$, the involution τ necessarily maps the successor of j to the predecessor of i. Continuing inductively with these two states, we obtain that the successor of the successor of j is mapped to the predecessor of the predecessor of i. The induction stops when the two states mapped to each other are their own successor and predecessor, or are one and the same state. For example, let $p = 7$, $i = 6$, and $j = 1$. Then $\tau(5) = 2$ and $\tau(4) = 3$ follows. For $p = 7$, $i = 5$, and $j = 1$, we obtain $\tau(4) = 2$ and $\tau(3) = 3$.

Similarly, by $\tau(\delta_a(\tau(j))) = \tau((i + 1) \bmod p) = \delta_a^{-1}(j) = (j + p - 1) \bmod p$, we derive that the involution τ necessarily maps the successor of i to the predecessor of j, and so on. Completing the example, $\tau(6) = 1$ and $\tau(7) = 0$ follows for the first case, and $\tau(6) = 0$ and $\tau(7) = 7$ for the second case.

Altogether, all states from the set C are mapped to states from C.

Now we turn to the structure of M' and denote the set of states which are not part of the a-cycle as $C' = S' \setminus C$. Since M' is reversible, there are no a-transitions from C' to the cycle C. Since M' is deterministic, there are no a-transitions from C to C'.

If there is a b-transition from C to C', then there must be an a-transition back from C' to C. Otherwise subsequent cycle runs on input suffixes from a^* have solely to appear within the states from C', but $|C'| < p$. Since this a-transition back to C cannot exist, there is no b-transition from C to C'.

So, since the initial state belongs to C, all states from C' are unreachable by transitions. Since furthermore τ maps all states from the set C to states from C, which in turn implies that all states from C' are mapped to states from C', we can safely omit all states from C' without altering the language accepted by M' and without violating the time-symmetry of M'. The resulting equivalent time-symmetric DFA M'' has exactly as many states as M. However, since M is easily verified to be minimal, and minimal DFA are unique (up to isomorphic renaming of states), there is no other p-state DFA equivalent to M. So, M'' must be equal to M which in turn is not time symmetric. $\square$

Finally, we come back to the question whether every reversible DFA is time symmetric. This general question has been answered negatively by Theorem 1. However, we can answer it in the affirmative for unary alphabets.

Theorem 4. *Each reversible* unary *DFA is time symmetric.*

Proof. We distinguish whether the language $L(M)$ is finite or infinite. If it is infinite, then M eventually runs through cycles. Since M is reversible, the only possibility to run through cycles on unary input is from the very beginning and, thus, M as a whole is one cycle. Now we can continue similar as in the proof of Theorem 3, where an involution τ witnessing the time-symmetry of M is constructed. There it turned out that, starting with two arbitrary states i and j, one can set $\tau(i) = j$ and gets the complete involution as a consequence of the choice of i and j (cf. Example 5).

Now let $L(M)$ be finite. In this case, the structure of M is just a finite chain of, say p, states $\{0, 1, \ldots, p-1\}$, which are connected by the transitions $\delta(i, a) = i+1$, for $0 \le i \le p - 2$. We define the involution τ by $\tau(0) = p - 1$, $\tau(1) = p - 2, \ldots$ In particular, it follows $\tau(\delta_a(\tau(0))) = \tau(\delta_a(p-1))$ is undefined as required, since $\delta_a^{-1}(0) = \delta^{\leftarrow}(0, a)$ is undefined. For $1 \le i \le p - 1$, the equation $\tau(\delta_a(\tau(i))) = \tau(p - i) = i - 1 = \delta_a^{-1}(i)$ shows that, in fact, τ witnesses the time-symmetry of M. $\qquad\square$

Example 5. We reconsider the reversible unary DFA in Figure 2. Arbitrarily, we choose $i = 1$ and $j = 4$. Then by the construction in the proof of Theorem 3, the involution $\tau(1) = 4$, $\tau(2) = 3$, $\tau(0) = 5$, $\tau(p - 1) = 6, \ldots$ follows. It is immediately verified that τ witnesses the fact that M is time symmetric. $\qquad\square$

Corollary 6. *Let M be a reversible unary DFA with at least three states accepting an infinite language. Then the involution witnessing the time-symmetry of M is not unique.*

4 Time-Symmetry in Pushdown Machines

Now we turn to a type of machine in question having an additional resource. In particular we consider the resource *pushdown store* or *stack* and obtain the so-called pushdown automata, whose deterministic variants have important applications in parser theory. They capture the deterministic context-free languages that can still be parsed in linear time using the well-known parsing algorithms for $LR(1)$ grammars (see, for example, [1]). The handling of the additional resource makes the definitions of reversibility and time-symmetry more involved. A *deterministic pushdown automaton* (DPDA) is a system $M = \langle S, \Sigma, \Gamma, \delta, s_0, \bot, F \rangle$, where S is the finite set of *internal states*, Σ is the finite set of *input symbols*, Γ is the finite set of *pushdown symbols*, $s_0 \in S$ is the *initial state*, $\bot \in \Gamma$ is a distinguished pushdown symbol, called the *bottom-of-stack symbol*, which initially appears on the stack, $F \subseteq S$ is the set of *accepting states*, and the *transition function* δ maps $S \times \Sigma_\lambda \times \Gamma$ to $S \times \Gamma^*$. As for DFA we allow δ to be a partial function. The input word is provided on an input tape, which can be scanned by the DPDA "from left to right" using a reading head. A DPDA may, but need not, read the next input symbol in a step. There must never be a choice of using an input symbol or of using λ input. So, it is required that for all s in S and Z in Γ: if $\delta(s, \lambda, Z)$ is defined, then $\delta(s, a, Z)$ is undefined for all a in Σ.

Let $\delta(q, a_\lambda, Z) = (p, \beta)$, for some $p, q \in S$, $a_\lambda \in \Sigma_\lambda$, $Z \in \Gamma$, and $\beta \in \Gamma^*$. For the explanation of its meaning we first have a look at configurations. A *configuration* of a DPDA is a quadruple (v, s, w, γ), where s is the current state, v is the part of the input to the left of the input head, and w the part of the input to the right of the input head, and γ the current content of the pushdown store, the leftmost symbol of γ being the top symbol. On input w the initial configuration is defined to be $(\lambda, s_0, w, \perp)$. For $s \in S$, $a_\lambda \in \Sigma_\lambda$, $v, w \in \Sigma^*$, $\gamma \in \Gamma^*$, and $Z \in \Gamma$, let $(v, q, a_\lambda w, Z\gamma)$ be a configuration. Then its *successor configuration* is $(va_\lambda, p, w, \beta\gamma)$, where $\delta(q, a_\lambda, Z) = (p, \beta)$. We write $(v, q, a_\lambda w, Z\gamma) \vdash (va_\lambda, p, w, \beta\gamma)$ in this case.

Thus the size of the stack can only decrease (by exactly 1) if $\beta = \lambda$; this is usually called a pop operation. If $|\beta| = 1$ the top of stack symbol is exchanged, leaving the size of the stack unchanged. If $|\beta| > 1$ the size of the stack increases (by $|\beta| - 1$; we call this a push operation.

While the usual presentation of DPDA uses the transition function δ, in the present context it is advantageous to consider its induced *extended transition function* $\hat{\delta} : S \times \Sigma_\lambda \times \Gamma^* \to S \times \Gamma^*$ as follows. For any $\gamma \in \Gamma^*$ set $\hat{\delta}(q, a_\lambda, Z\gamma) = (p, \beta\gamma)$ if and only if $\delta(q, a_\lambda, Z) = (p, \beta)$.

The reflexive transitive closure of $\vdash$ is denoted by $\vdash^*$. The *language accepted* by M with accepting states is

$$L(M) = \{\, w \in \Sigma^* \mid (\lambda, s_0, w, \perp) \vdash^* (w, q, \lambda, \gamma), \text{ for some } q \in F \text{ and } \gamma \in \Gamma^* \,\}.$$

Now we turn to reversible pushdown automata which have been introduced in [19], where a weaker form of reversibility has been studied. There, reversibility is considered only for configurations that are reachable from some valid initial configuration. To remain in context, here we require reversibility for all configurations. To this end, the pushdown automata have to be backward deterministic. That is, any configuration must have at most one predecessor which, in addition, is computable by a DPDA. A DPDA is called *reversible* if and only if for each input symbol $x \in \Sigma_\lambda$ the (possibly partial) function $\delta_x : S \times \Gamma \to S \times \Gamma^*$: $(s, Z) \mapsto \delta(s, x, Z)$ is injective. As before, we write $\delta^\leftarrow$ for the *reverse transition function* $\delta^\leftarrow : S \times \Sigma_\lambda \times \Gamma \to S \times \Gamma^*$ satisfying $\delta^\leftarrow(s, x, Z) = \delta_x^{-1}(s, Z)$, and we write $\hat{\delta}_x$ for the extension of δ_x.

In [19], basically it is observed that the following structure of transitions enables reversibility.

Fact 7. Let M be a DPDA and $M^\leftarrow$ its inverse. In one operation $M^\leftarrow$ can decrease the height of its stack by at most one. Therefore, M may increase the height of its stack only by at most one, too. Furthermore, when $M^\leftarrow$ pops a symbol this operation simply reveals the next-to-top symbol. Therefore when M increases the height of its stack, it must do so by leaving the previous top-of-stack symbol intact: If $\delta(s, a_\lambda, Z) = (t, \beta)$ and $|\beta| > 1$ then $\beta = YZ$ for some symbol $Y \in \Gamma$. Thus for a reversible DPDA M there are only the following possibilities:

push: $\delta(s, a_\lambda, Z) = (t, YZ) \implies \delta^\leftarrow(t, a_\lambda, Y) = (s, \lambda)$
change top: $\delta(s, a_\lambda, Z) = (t, Y) \implies \delta^\leftarrow(t, a_\lambda, Y) = (s, Z)$
pop: $\delta(s, a_\lambda, Z) = (t, \lambda) \implies$ for all $X \in \Gamma$: $\delta^\leftarrow(t, a_\lambda, X) = (s, ZX)$

A reversible DPDA is *time symmetric* if and only if there is an involution $\tau : S \times \Gamma^* \to S \times \Gamma^*$ so that, $\hat{\delta}_x^{-1} = \tau \circ \hat{\delta}_x \circ \tau$ holds for all $x \in \Sigma_\lambda$. To clarify our notion we continue with an example.

Example 8. The linear context-free language

$$\{\, wcv \mid w \in \{a,b\}^*, w^R = vu, 0 \le |u| \le |w| \,\}$$

is accepted by the time-symmetric DPDA

$$M = \langle \{s_0, s_1\}, \{a, b, c\}, \{a, b, \bot\}, \delta, s_0, \bot, \{s_1\} \rangle,$$

where the transition functions δ and $\delta^\leftarrow$ are as follows.

Transition function δ	Reverse transition function $\delta^\leftarrow$
(1) $\delta(s_0, a, \bot) = (s_0, a\bot)$	(1) $\delta^\leftarrow(s_0, a, a) = (s_0, \lambda)$
(2) $\delta(s_0, b, \bot) = (s_0, b\bot)$	(2) $\delta^\leftarrow(s_0, b, b) = (s_0, \lambda)$
(3) $\delta(s_0, a, a) = (s_0, aa)$	
(4) $\delta(s_0, a, b) = (s_0, ab)$	(3) $\delta^\leftarrow(s_1, c, \bot) = (s_0, \bot)$
(5) $\delta(s_0, b, a) = (s_0, ba)$	(4) $\delta^\leftarrow(s_1, c, a) = (s_0, a)$
(6) $\delta(s_0, b, b) = (s_0, bb)$	(5) $\delta^\leftarrow(s_1, c, b) = (s_0, b)$
(7) $\delta(s_0, c, \bot) = (s_1, \bot)$	(6) $\delta^\leftarrow(s_1, a, a) = (s_1, aa)$
(8) $\delta(s_0, c, a) = (s_1, a)$	(7) $\delta^\leftarrow(s_1, a, b) = (s_1, ab)$
(9) $\delta(s_0, c, b) = (s_1, b)$	(8) $\delta^\leftarrow(s_1, b, a) = (s_1, ba)$
	(9) $\delta^\leftarrow(s_1, b, b) = (s_1, bb)$
(10) $\delta(s_1, a, a) = (s_1, \lambda)$	(10) $\delta^\leftarrow(s_1, a, \bot) = (s_1, a\bot)$
(11) $\delta(s_1, b, b) = (s_1, \lambda)$	(11) $\delta^\leftarrow(s_1, b, \bot) = (s_1, b\bot)$

The transitions (1) through (6) of δ are used by M to store the input prefix w. When a c appears in the input, transitions (7) through (9) are used to change to state s_1 while the pushdown store remains unchanged. By transitions (10) and (11) the input suffix is matched with the stored prefix.

For the backward computation the transitions of $\delta^\leftarrow$ are constructed according to Fact 7.

So, M is reversible. In order to show that it is time symmetric, we define the involution $\tau(s_0, \gamma) = (s_1, \gamma)$ for any $\gamma \in \Gamma^*$. The condition $\hat{\delta}_x \circ \tau = \tau \circ \hat{\delta}_x^{-1}$ implies time-symmetry. It is easily verified, for example, by truth table since τ only changes the state. Exemplarily, we mention that

$$(\hat{\delta}_b \circ \tau)(s_0, b\gamma) = (s_1, \gamma) = (\tau \circ \hat{\delta}_b^{-1})(s_0, b\gamma)$$

and that $(\hat{\delta}_c \circ \tau)(s_0, \gamma)$ as well as $\hat{\delta}_c^{-1}(s_0, b\gamma)$ are undefined. Therefore, the principle of time-symmetry is matched. Again exemplarily, let

$$(v, s_1, aw, ab\gamma) \vdash (va, s_1, w, b\gamma)$$

be a computation step. Applying τ on the configuration $(va, s_1, w, b\gamma)$ gives $(va, s_0, w, b\gamma)$, on which δ is applied while the a following the prefix v is provided as input. This yields $(v, s_0, aw, ab\gamma)$. Applying τ again results in the configuration $(v, s_1, aw, ab\gamma)$ which is the predecessor of $(va, s_1, w, b\gamma)$. □

Corollary 9. *There is a non-regular language which is accepted by a time-symmetric DPDA.*

The next theorem contrasts the situation for DFA.

Theorem 10. *There are reversible unary DPDA which are not time symmetric.*

Proof. Let $n \geq 1$ be a constant. Then the unary language $\{a^i \mid i \geq n\}$ is accepted by the reversible DPDA $M = \langle\{s_0, s_1, \ldots, s_n\}, \{a\}, \{a, \bot\}, \delta, s_0, \bot, \{s_n\}\rangle$, where $\delta(s_i, a, \bot) = (s_{i+1}, \bot)$, for $0 \leq i \leq n-1$, and $\delta(s_n, a, \bot) = (s_n, a\bot)$, $\delta(s_n, a, a) = (s_n, aa)$.

So, on any sufficiently long input M runs into a cycle with state s_n. However, since in every step in the cycle a symbol is pushed, in reverse computations a DPDA can detect that it has to leave the cycle: when the pushdown store gets empty. The reverse transition function can thus be defined as $\delta^{\leftarrow}(s_n, a, a) = (s_n, \lambda)$ and $\delta^{\leftarrow}(s_i, a, \bot) = (s_{i-1}, \bot)$, for $1 \leq i \leq n$.

In order to give evidence that M is not time symmetric we consider state s_n. In any forward step starting in state s_n a symbol is pushed. In particular, this means that a backward step has to pop a symbol. However, there are no states appearing in a transition from δ that pop a symbol. Therefore, there is no state to which s_n could be mapped by an involution witnessing the time-symmetry.   □

As for DFA any reversible DPDA can be simulated by a time-symmetric DPDA with at most twice as many states.

Theorem 11. *Let $p \geq 1$ and M be a p-state reversible DPDA. Then there exists an equivalent $2p$-state time-symmetric DPDA M'.*

Proof. We argue similar as for finite automata. Therefore, given some reversible DPDA $M = \langle S, \Sigma, \Gamma\delta, s_0, \bot, F\rangle$ we construct an equivalent and time-symmetric DPDA $M' = \langle S', \Sigma, \Gamma\delta', s_0, \bot, F'\rangle$ by setting $S' = S \times \{\rightarrow, \leftarrow\}$, $s_0' = (s_0, \rightarrow)$, and $F' = F \times \{\rightarrow\}$. For all $s \in S$, $a_\lambda \in \Sigma_\lambda$, and $Y, Z \in \Gamma$, the transition function is defined as follows.
If $\delta(s, a_\lambda, Z) = (t, YZ)$ (and hence $\delta^{\leftarrow}(t, a_\lambda, Y) = (s, \lambda)$) then

$$\delta'((s, \rightarrow), a_\lambda, Z) = ((t, \rightarrow), YZ) \quad \text{(push) and}$$
$$\delta'((t, \leftarrow), a_\lambda, Y) = ((s, \leftarrow), \lambda) \quad \text{(pop).}$$

If $\delta(s, a_\lambda, Z) = (t, Y)$ then

$$\delta'((s, \rightarrow), a_\lambda, Z) = ((t, \rightarrow), Y) \quad \text{(change top) and}$$
$$\delta'((t, \leftarrow), a_\lambda, Y) = ((s, \leftarrow), Z) \quad \text{(change top).}$$

If $\delta(s, a, Z) = (t, \lambda)$ then

$$\delta'((s, \rightarrow), a_\lambda, Z) = ((t, \rightarrow), \lambda) \quad \text{(pop) and}$$
$$\text{for all } X \in \Gamma: \delta'((t, \leftarrow), a_\lambda, X) = ((s, \leftarrow), ZX) \quad \text{(push).}$$

Clearly, the DPDA M' works like M while in states from $S \times \{\rightarrow\}$ and it works like the inverse $M^{\leftarrow}$ while in states from $S \times \{\leftarrow\}$. Furthermore, we notice that

$L(M') = L(M)$ since M' starts in $(s_0, \rightarrow)$ and there is no transition leading from a state in $S \times \{\rightarrow\}$ to a state in $S \times \{\leftarrow\}$, and that M' is reversible, since M and its inverse are reversible.

Now, for all $s \in S$, let the involution τ be defined by $\tau((s, \rightarrow), \gamma) = ((s, \leftarrow), \gamma)$ and $\tau((s, \leftarrow), \gamma) = ((s, \rightarrow), \gamma)$, for any $\gamma \in \Gamma^*$. Then it is easily verified that M' is time symmetric. $\qquad\qquad\qquad\qquad\qquad\qquad\qquad\qquad\qquad\qquad\qquad\qquad\qquad\sqcap$

Though it is well known that every unary context-free language is regular [11], the families of reversible and time-symmetric unary languages are different.

Theorem 12. *(1) The family of languages accepted by time-symmetric (unary) DFA is properly included in the family of languages accepted by time-symmetric (unary) DPDA.*

(2) The family of languages accepted by reversible (unary) DFA is properly included in the family of languages accepted by reversible (unary) DPDA.

Proof. The inclusions are straightforward. Their propernesses follow by the unary language of the proof of Theorem 10, which cannot be accepted by any reversible DFA. However, the language is accepted by some time-symmetric DPDA by Theorem 11. $\qquad\qquad\qquad\qquad\qquad\qquad\qquad\qquad\qquad\qquad\qquad\qquad\qquad\square$

5   Conclusion

Let $k \geq 1$ be a natural number. A two-way k-head finite automaton is a finite automaton having a single read-only input tape whose inscription is the input word in between two endmarkers. The k heads of the automaton can move freely on the tape but not beyond the endmarkers. If the heads are not allowed to move to the left, the k-head automaton is said to be one-way. Reversible multi-head automata have been studied in [4,20,25,26].

Without going into deep details, we just mention that the idea to put a reversible k-head finite automaton and its inverse "side by side" shows that for any reversible p-state k-head finite automaton one can effectively construct an equivalent time-symmetric one with $2p$ states. Furthermore, it is evident that this technique also works for reversible Turing machines.

However, whether the increase in size caused by doubling the number of states is always necessary is an interesting question for further investigations.

The authors gratefully acknowledge corrections and suggestions by the referees which lead to an improved presentation.

References

1. Aho, A.V., Ullman, J.D.: The theory of parsing, translation, and compiling Parsing vol. I. Prentice-Hall Inc. (1972)
2. Amoroso, S., Patt, Y.N.: Decision procedures for surjectivity and injectivity of parallel maps for tesselation structures. J. Comput. System Sci. 6, 448–464 (1972)
3. Angluin, D.: Inference of reversible languages. J. ACM 29, 741–765 (1982)

4. Axelsen, H.B.: Reversible multi-head finite automata characterize reversible logarithmic space. In: Dediu, A.-H., Martín-Vide, C. (eds.) LATA 2012. LNCS, vol. 7183, pp. 95–105. Springer, Heidelberg (2012)

5. Axelsen, H.B., Glück, R.: A simple and efficient universal reversible Turing machine. In: Language and Automata Theory and Applications (LATA 2011). LNCS, vol. 6638, pp. 117–128. Springer (2011)

6. Bennet, C.H.: Logical reversibility of computation. IBM J. Res. Dev. 17, 525–532 (1973)

7. Frank, M.P.: Introduction to reversible computing: motivation, progress, and challenges. In: Computing Frontiers 2005, pp. 385–390. ACM (2005)

8. Gajardo, A., Kari, J., Moreira, A.: On time-symmetry in cellular automata. J. Comput. System Sci. 78, 1115–1126 (2012)

9. García, P., Vázquez de Parga, M., Cano, A., López, D.: On locally reversible languages. Theoret. Comput. Sci. 410, 4961–4974 (2009)

10. García, P., Vázquez de Parga, M., López, D.: On the efficient construction of quasi-reversible automata for reversible languages. Inform. Process. Lett. 107, 13–17 (2008)

11. Ginsburg, S., Rice, H.G.: Two families of languages related to ALGOL. J. ACM 9, 350–371 (1962)

12. Gruska, J.: Quantum Computing. McGraw-Hill (1999)

13. Gudder, S., Ball, R.: Properties of quantum languages. Int. J. Theoret. Phys. 41, 569–591 (2002)

14. Kari, J.: Reversibility and surjectivity problems of cellular automata. J. Comput. System Sci. 48, 149–182 (1994)

15. Kari, J.: Theory of cellular automata: a survey. Theoret. Comput. Sci. 334, 3–33 (2005)

16. Kutrib, M., Malcher, A.: Fast reversible language recognition using cellular automata. Inform. Comput. 206, 1142–1151 (2008)

17. Kutrib, M., Malcher, A.: Real-time reversible iterative arrays. Theoret. Comput. Sci. 411, 812–822 (2010)

18. Kutrib, M., Malcher, A.: Reversible pushdown automata. In: Dediu, A.-H., Fernau, H., Martín-Vide, C. (eds.) LATA 2010. LNCS, vol. 6031, pp. 368–379. Springer, Heidelberg (2010)

19. Kutrib, M., Malcher, A.: Reversible pushdown automata. J. Comput. System Sci. 78, 1814–1827 (2012)

20. Kutrib, M., Malcher, A.: One-way reversible multi-head finite automata. In: Glück, R., Yokoyama, T. (eds.) RC 2012. LNCS, vol. 7581, pp. 14–28. Springer, Heidelberg (2013)

21. Lamb, J.S., Roberts, J.A.: Time-reversal symmetry in dynamical systems: A survey. Phys. D 112, 1–39 (1998)

22. Landauer, R.: Irreversibility and heat generation in the computing process. IBM J. Res. Dev. 5, 183–191 (1961)

23. Lombardy, S.: On the construction of reversible automata for reversible languages. In: Widmayer, P., Triguero, F., Morales, R., Hennessy, M., Eidenbenz, S., Conejo, R. (eds.) ICALP 2002. LNCS, vol. 2380, pp. 170–182. Springer, Heidelberg (2002)

24. Morita, K.: Reversible computing and cellular automata – A survey. Theoret. Comput. Sci. 395, 101–131 (2008)

25. Morita, K.: Two-way reversible multi-head finite automata. Fund. Inform. 110, 241–254 (2011)

26. Morita, K.: A deterministic two-way multi-head finite automaton can be converted into a reversible one with the same number of heads. In: Glück, R., Yokoyama, T. (eds.) RC 2012. LNCS, vol. 7581, pp. 29–43. Springer, Heidelberg (2013)

27. Morita, K., Shirasaki, A., Gono, Y.: A 1-tape 2-symbol reversible Turing machine. Trans. IEICE E72, 223–228 (1989)

28. Phillips, I.C.C., Ulidowski, I.: Reversing algebraic process calculi. J. Log. Algebr. Program. 73, 70–96 (2007)

29. Pin, J.E.: On reversible automata. In: Simon, I. (ed.) LATIN 1992. LNCS, vol. 583, pp. 401–416. Springer, Heidelberg (1992)

30. Yokoyama, T.: Reversible computation and reversible programming languages. Electron. Notes Theor. Comput. Sci. 253, 71–81 (2010)

31. Yokoyama, T., Axelsen, H.B., Glück, R.: Reversible flowchart languages and the structured reversible program theorem. In: Aceto, L., Damgård, I., Goldberg, L.A., Halldórsson, M.M., Ingólfsdóttir, A., Walukiewicz, I. (eds.) ICALP 2008, Part II. LNCS, vol. 5126, pp. 258–270. Springer, Heidelberg (2008)

Reversible Circuit Synthesis of Symmetric Functions Using a Simple Regular Structure

Arighna Deb[1], Debesh K. Das[1], Hafizur Rahaman[2],
Bhargab B. Bhattacharya[3], Robert Wille[4], and Rolf Drechsler[4]

[1] Computer Science and Engineering, Jadavpur University, Kolkata, India
arighna87@rediffmail.com, debeshd@hotmail.com
[2] Information Technology, Bengal Engg. and Sci. University, Howrah, India
rahaman_h@hotmail.com
[3] Nanotechnology Research Triangle, Indian Statistical Institute, Kolkata, India
bhargab@isical.ac.in
[4] Institute of Computer Science, University of Bremen, Bremen, Germany
Cyber-Physical Systems, DFKI GmbH, Bremen, Germany
rwille@informatik.uni-bremen.de, drechsler@uni-bremen.de

Abstract. In this paper, we introduce a new method to realize symmetric functions with reversible circuits. In contrast to earlier methods, our solution deploys a simple and regular cascade structure composed of low-cost gates which enables significant reductions with respect to quantum costs. However, the number of garbage outputs increases slightly. To overcome this, we next propose an optimized design by reusing the garbage outputs. The resulting design thus offers a powerful approach towards reversible synthesis of symmetric Boolean functions.

Keywords: Quantum computation, Reversible logic, Symmetric functions.

1   Introduction

Reversible computing has become one of the major research areas in the recent times. Reversible logic has found applications in quantum computing [1,2], low power design [3,4], optical computing [5], DNA computing [6], as well as in nanotechnology [7]. These promising applications mandate new solutions for design automation of the emerging classes of circuits and systems.

Among the various research problems related to the field of reversible circuit design, logic synthesis has received significant attention. A number of reversible synthesis methods has been proposed for this purpose [8–16]. Usually, they aim for reducing the quantum costs, i.e. the number of elementary operations to be conducted in a quantum device, as well as the number of garbage outputs, i.e. output connections that are sometimes required to ensure reversibility but are not utilized to represent the desired function.

In this paper, we address the problem of synthesizing symmetric Boolean functions using reversible logic. These special types of functions have many applications to cryptology and to the design of secured systems, control and communications circuits. Accordingly, synthesis methods for such functions have been

G.W. Dueck and D.M. Miller (Eds.): RC 2013, LNCS 7948, pp. 182–195, 2013.

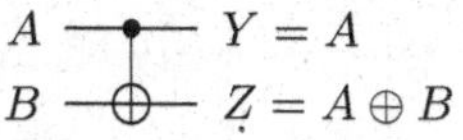

$$A \longrightarrow Y = A$$
$$B \longrightarrow Z = A \oplus B$$

Fig. 1. Feynman (CNOT) Gate

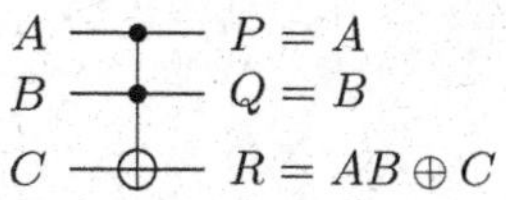

$$A \longrightarrow P = A$$
$$B \longrightarrow Q = B$$
$$C \longrightarrow R = AB \oplus C$$

Fig. 2. Toffoli Gate

studied extensively [17–21]. Realizations of symmetric functions by reversible logic gates have been described in [9,22,23]. Picton used Fredkin gates to realize digital summation threshold logic (DSTL) devices [23]. An efficient realization of arbitrary symmetric functions using a Reversible Programmable Gate Array (RPGA) has been proposed in [9,22].

We propose a new approach for designing symmetric functions using an array of Peres gates. Our solution uses simpler reversible gates compared to previously introduced designs [9,13] and is inspired by a regular structure proposed in [19]. This yields a significant reduction in the quantum cost. However, the number of garbage outputs increases slightly. This is eventually addressed by proposing an optimization of the regular structure that enables reuse of garbage outputs and hence, leading to a reduction of them. The benefits of the proposed design is demonstrated by comparing ours with the solutions obtained by previously proposed techniques [9,13].

The rest of the paper is organized as follows. In Section 2, we provide the basics of reversible functions, reversible gates, and symmetric functions. Section 3 introduces the proposed regular structure as well as its optimization. Based on that, Section 4 describes how general symmetric functions can be realized with this structure. Finally, the resulting design is compared to previous work in Section 5 and the paper is concluded in Section 6.

2   Preliminaries

2.1   Reversible Logic Functions

A function f is said to be reversible if and only if $f : \mathbb{B}^n \to \mathbb{B}^n$ over variables $X = (x_1, x_2, \cdots, x_n)$ maps each input to a unique output and if f has the same number of input and output variables. It implies that there are 2^n input rows and 2^n output rows in the truth table of f and the output rows are the permutation of the input rows. We use the notation $(n \times n)$ to represent an n-input reversible function f.

2.2   Reversible Logic Gates

A reversible circuit is a fan-out free cascade of reversible gates. The common reversible gates include the Feynman gate, the Fredkin gate, the Toffoli gate, and the Peres gate.

Feynman Gate:- A (2×2) Feynman gate (FG), also known as controlled-NOT gate or simply CNOT gate, is shown in Fig. 1. It has two inputs, known as the

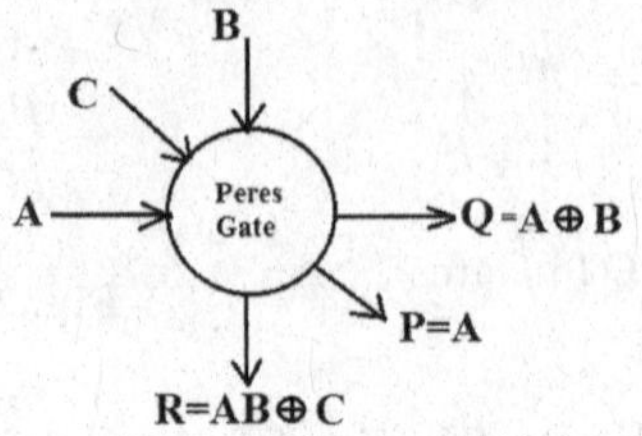

Fig. 3. Peres Gate

control input (A) and the target input (B), respectively. The logical relationship between inputs and outputs can be written as: $Y = A$, $Z = A \oplus B$.

Toffoli Gate:- A multiple control Toffoli gate (TG) t_m has the form $t_m(C, t)$, where $C = \{x_{i_1}, x_{i_2}, \cdots, x_{i_m}\} \subset X$ is the set of control lines and $t = \{x_j\}$ with $C \cap t = \emptyset$ is the target line. The value of t is inverted if and only if all control lines are set to 1. For $m = 0$ and $m = 1$, the gates are called NOT and CNOT, respectively. Fig. 2 illustrates the Toffoli gate with three inputs (A, B, C) and three outputs (P, Q, R), where (A,B) are control inputs that are unaffected by the action of the Toffoli gate. The third input is a target input (C) that is inverted if both, A and B, are 1 and otherwise remains unchanged. Thus, we get $P = A$, $Q = B$, $R = C \oplus AB$.

Peres Gate:- Fig. 3 shows a 3×3 Peres gate (PG). This gate performs the following operation: $P = A$, $Q = A \oplus B$, $R = C \oplus AB$, where the outputs are denoted as (P,Q,R) and inputs are denoted as (A,B,C).

Besides that, the following definitions related to reversible circuits are important in this work.

Control input and target input:- A reversible gate consists of two sets of inputs: control set and target set. If at least one control line is set to 0, then nothing happens to the target lines. If instead all control lines are set to 1, then the gate function is applied to the target line.

Constant input:- A constant input of a reversible function is a fixed input value (either 0 or 1).

Garbage outputs:- They refer to the outputs that are not assigned a certain function value. Garbage outputs are very much essential without which reversibility cannot be achieved for irreversible functions. For example, an AND operation of the two inputs A and B can only be achieved using the structure in Fig. 2 with C=0. In this example, the unused outputs P and Q are garbage outputs.

Quantum Cost (QC):- For its operation, a reversible gate offers a quantum cost given by the number of elementary quantum operations, which are performed by elementary quantum gates called as controlled-NOT (CNOT) gate, controlled-V gate, controlled-V+ gate, etc.; each having quantum cost of unity. The quantum costs of different reversible gates are shown in Table 1.

Table 1. Quantum cost

Reversible Gate	Quantum Cost
CNOT gate	1
TOF(a,b;c)	5
TOF(a,b,c;d)	14
PERES gate	4
Fredkin gate	5

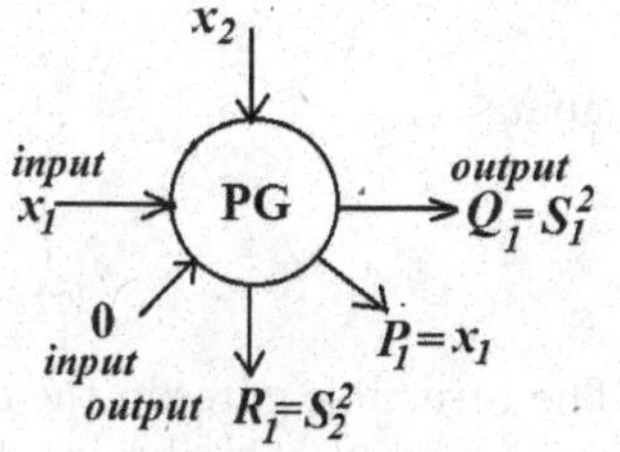

Fig. 4. Design for 2-inputs

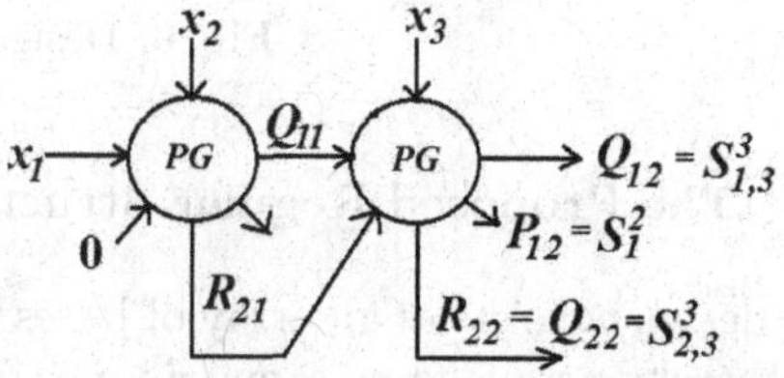

Fig. 5. Design for 3-inputs

2.3   Symmetric Functions

A switching function over n variables is a function $f(x_1, x_2, \cdots, x_n) : Q^n \to Q$, where Q denotes the set that consists of two values $\{0, 1\}$. A switching function $f(x_1, x_2, \cdots, x_n)$ is totally symmetric if it is unchanged by any permutation of its variables $(x_1, x_2, \cdots, x_n)$.

For a symmetric function, it is sufficient to specify the number of inputs that are to be set to logic 1 for the function to be 1. An n-variable symmetric function is represented as $S^n(A)$, where A is a set of integers $(a_i, \cdots, a_j, \cdots, a_k)$ and $\forall a_i, a_j, 1 \leq a_i, a_j \leq n, a_i \neq a_j$. This is denoted by $S^n_{a_i, \cdots, a_j, \cdots, a_k}$. For n variables, $2^{n+1} - 2$ different symmetric functions (excluding constant functions 0 and 1) can be constructed. If the set A contains only consecutive integers $(a_l, a_{l+1}, \cdots, a_q)$ with $a_l < a_q$, the symmetric function is called consecutive symmetric function and denoted by $S^n_{a_l - a_q}$. A totally symmetric function $S^n(A)$ can be expressed as a union of maximal consecutive symmetric functions, such that $S^n(A) = S^n(A_1) + S^n(A_2) + \cdots + S^n(A_m)$, with m being the minimum and such that $\forall i, j, 1 \leq i, j \leq m, A_i \cap A_j = \emptyset$, whenever $i \neq j$.

Example 1. $S^{15}_{4,5,6,7,12,13,14,15}$ can be written as the summation of two consecutive symmetric functions S^{15}_{4-7} and S^{15}_{12-15}.

3   Synthesis of Symmetric Boolean Functions

In this section, we present our approach to the synthesis of symmetric Boolean functions as reversible circuits. First, we introduce the proposed regular structure followed by possible optimization. This builds the basis of a generic synthesis scheme for general symmetric functions, which is outlined in the next section.

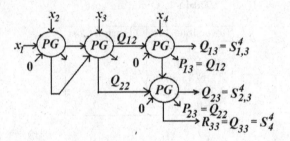

Fig. 6. Design for 4-inputs

3.1   The Proposed Regular Structure

Our design consists of an array of Peres gates. The reversible gates in the design are thereby arranged as a matrix, i.e. in the form of rows and columns. In the following, this is illustrated for certain values of n, i.e., for different input sizes.

Consider the design for $n = 2$ inputs, i.e. for x_1 and x_2. The design is composed of a single (3×3) Peres gate. Throughout the design, the input line C of the Peres gate is assigned a value 0. Hence, a structure as depicted in Fig. 4 results. When C is set to 0, the Peres gate produces the following outputs: $P_1 = x_1$, $Q_1 = x_1 \oplus x_2$, and $R_1 = x_1 x_2$. Thus, this design produces two symmetric Boolean functions, namely $Q_1 = S_1^2$ and $R_1 = S_2^2$. The output P_1 is a garbage output.

Consider the design for $n = 3$ inputs, i.e., for x_1, x_2, and x_3. In this case, the design deploys two (3×3) Peres gates. There are two rows and two columns. In the first row, we have two Peres gates, whereas the second row does not contain any gate. The design is shown in Fig. 5. In this case, the output Q_{11} from the first Peres gate is given as one of the inputs to the second Peres gate in the first row. The other two inputs of the second Peres gate are x_3 and R_{21} (output of the 1st Peres gate). Therefore, the outputs that are obtained from the 2nd Peres gate are: $P_{12} = Q_{11}, Q_{12} = Q_{11} \oplus x_3, R_{22} = Q_{11} x_3 \oplus R_{21}$. Here, also P_{12} is the garbage output. The output R_{22} appears in the second row as Q_{22}. This structure already realizes two other symmetric functions, namely $Q_{12} = S_{1,3}^3$ and $Q_{22} = S_{2,3}^3$.

Consider the design for $n = 4$ inputs, i.e., for x_1, x_2, x_3, and x_4. Then, the top row contains three Peres gates, whereas the second row contains a single Peres gate. Fig. 6 shows this design. At the first row, the output Q_{12} of the 2nd Peres gate is given as input to the 3rd Peres gate along with inputs x_4 and 0. This produces outputs $P_{13} = Q_{12}, Q_{13} = (Q_{12} \oplus x_4)$, and $R_{23} = Q_{12} x_4$. The output R_{23} from the top row and the output Q_{22} from the previous column appear as inputs to the Peres gate at the second row, which generates $Q_{23} = Q_{22} \oplus R_{23}$. This equals to $S_{1,3}^4$. The third row has the output $R_{33} = Q_{33} = Q_{22} R_{23}$ realizing S_4^4.

It may be observed that, for $n = 2$ $(n = 3)$, there are two output lines producing S_1^2 and S_2^2 $(S_{1,3}^3, S_{2,3}^3)$. For $n = 4$, there are three output lines producing $S_{1,3}^4$, $S_{2,3}^4, S_4^4$. Hence, a regular structure results where each output line corresponding to a row in the design produces a certain symmetric Boolean function.

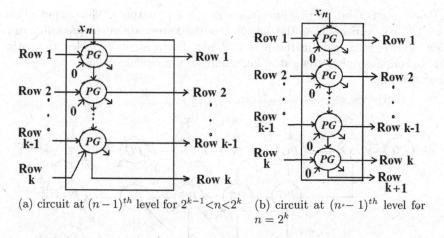

(a) circuit at $(n-1)^{th}$ level for $2^{k-1}<n<2^k$ (b) circuit at $(n-1)^{th}$ level for $n = 2^k$

Fig. 7. The circuit structure at $(n-1)^{th}$ level

This can be generalized as follows: Consider the structure to be designed for n inputs, i.e. for $x_1, \ldots, x_n$. Here, we can think of different columns, where columns may be termed as levels and respectively introduce a new input x_i. Hence, the inputs x_1 and x_2 are considered in the 1st level, the input x_3 in the 2nd level, the input x_4 in the 3rd level, and so on. Notice that the network for $n = 4$, subsumes the complete structure for $n = 3$. If we have the circuit for any $n = i$, then the circuit for $n = i+1$ can be obtained by appending one more level. Thus, there are $(n-1)$ columns or levels in the array. Therefore, for a circuit structure of n input lines, there are k rows and $(n-1)$ columns with $k = \lfloor \log_2 n \rfloor + 1$. The circuit structure to be appended after the $(n-2)^{th}$ level is shown in Fig. 7(a) for $2^{k-1}<n<2^k$ and in Fig. 7(b) for $n = 2^k$. Let the inputs to the $(n-1)^{th}$ level be represented as $Y_{n-1}^1, Y_{n-1}^2, \cdots, Y_{n-1}^k$. Then, the outputs after the $(n-1)^{th}$ level can be recursively determined using following relation:

$$Y_n^i = Y_{n-1}^i \oplus y_n^i \text{ for } 1 \leq i \leq k \tag{1}$$

where

$$Y_0^i = 0 \tag{2}$$

$$y_n^i = x_n \text{ for } i = 1$$
$$= Y_{n-1}^{i-1} y_n^{i-1} \text{ for } i>1 \tag{3}$$

It can be observed that a new row is added to the design for every $n = 2^k$ input variables, where $(k = 2, 3, 4, ...)$. Thus, for any n, the number of rows is $\lfloor \log_2 n \rfloor + 1$. For $2^{k-1}<n<2^k$, the kth row does not contain any gate. The output R from the Peres gate of the $(k-1)^{th}$ row is given as the target line to the Peres gate in the same row and next column. This results in a cascade of Peres gates with quantum costs of $2m + 2$ [24], where m is the number of Peres gate in the cascade. For $n = 2^k$, the kth row contains CNOT gates except the last one where a Peres gate is used. In this case, there are $(k + 1)$ outputs. The output in the $(k+1)^{th}$ row appears from the output R of the Peres gate of the preceding row. Hence, there is no gate in the $(k + 1)^{th}$ row. For n-input variables, the entire design contains only Peres gates. For example, the circuit structure for $n = 8$ is shown in Fig. 8.

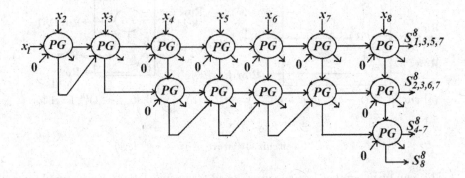

Fig. 8. Circuit for 8-inputs

Following the structure outlined above, $k = (\lfloor \log_2 n \rfloor + 1)$ symmetric functions are produced. The $i^{th}(1 \leq i \leq k)$ output line represents thereby the symmetric function $S^n_{a_{i_1}, a_{i_2}, \cdots, a_{i_q}}$, where each a_{i_j} is an integer whose binary representation has a 1 in the ith bit. Apart from these symmetric functions produced at k output lines, the Boolean functions realized by the garbage outputs are also symmetric with a fewer number of literals. For $n = 8$, the corresponding inputs, outputs, and garbage outputs at the different levels of the network are listed in Table 2.

Table 2. Inputs and outputs at each level

Levels	Inputs	Outputs	Garbage Outputs
1	x_1, x_2	S^2_1, S^2_2	x_1
2	x_3	$S^3_{1,3}, S^3_{2,3}$	S^2_1, S^2_2
3	x_4	$S^4_{1,3}, S^4_{2,3}, S^4_4$	$S^3_{1,3}, S^3_{2,3}$
4	x_5	$S^5_{1,3,5}, S^5_{2,3}, S^5_{4,5}$	$S^4_{1,3}, S^4_{2,3}, S^4_4$
5	x_6	$S^6_{1,3,5}, S^6_{2,3,6}, S^6_{4-6}$	$S^5_{1,3,5}, S^5_{2,3}, S^5_{4,5}$
6	x_7	$S^7_{1,3,5,7}, S^7_{2,3,6,7}, S^7_{4-7}$	$S^6_{1,3,5}, S^6_{2,3,6}, S^6_{4-6}$
7	x_8	$S^8_{1,3,5,7}, S^8_{2,3,6,7}, S^8_{4-7}, S^8_8$	$S^7_{1,3,5,7}, S^7_{2,3,6,7}, S^7_{4-7}$

For an n-input function, the total number of Peres gates is therefore given by

$$N_{PG} = (n\lceil \log_2 n \rceil - n - 2^{\lceil \log_2 n \rceil} + \lfloor \log_2 n \rfloor + 2) \qquad (4)$$

The design requires $n\lceil \log_2 n \rceil - 2n - 2^{\lceil \log_2 n \rceil} + 2\lfloor \log_2 n \rfloor + 3$ constant inputs (fixed to 0). It may be observed that the total number of garbage in the design is equal to the sum of the total number of Peres gates. Therefore, the design produces

$$N_{garbage} = N_{PG} \tag{5}$$

garbage lines for any n.

3.2   Further Optimization of the Proposed Structure

The proposed regular structure generates a large number of garbage lines. The design can further be improved in this respect. Notice that once the garbage lines are used as control lines, they no longer play any role in the circuit. Therefore, the structure can be improved by reusing the garbage lines as target or control lines in the rest of the circuit.

The resulting reversible circuit for $n = 4$ inputs is redrawn in Fig. 9 (the original realization is depicted in Fig 6). The circuit remains the same for up to $n = 3$ inputs, i.e., the 1st row produces the output $Q_{12} = S_{1,3}^3$ and the 2nd row produces the output $R_{22} = S_{2,3}^3$. For $n = 4$, now a (3×3) Toffoli gate with two control lines Q_{12} and x_4 is added to the design. This produces the output $T_{23} = Q_{12}x_4 = S_{1,3}^3 x_4$. Since the design adds a new row to the structure at $n = 4$, the 2nd row will have a Peres gate producing outputs at the 2nd and the 3rd rows. This Peres gate takes R_{22} and T_{23} as control inputs and produces $R_{33} = R_{22}T_{23} = S_4^4$ at the 3rd row with the target input line set to 0. It also produces the output $Q_{23} = T_{23} \oplus R_{22} = S_{2,3}^4$ at the 2nd row. Now, a Peres gate is introduced in the 1st row, which works on the same set of control and target lines. This means that the Toffoli gate with two control lines present in the Peres gate is an exact replica of the (3×3) Toffoli gate added previously in the 1st row. This makes the garbage output T_{23} to become zero. Later, this line can be reused again in the circuit.

In general, for $2^{k-1} \le n < 2^k$ ($k \neq 1, 2$), the optimized design inserts a single Toffoli gate before every Peres gate present in the $(k-1)^{th}$ row. Initially, a Toffoli gate in the $(k-1)^{th}$ row and the jth ($1 \le j \le n-1$) column produces an output which appears as one of the inputs to the Peres gate in the kth row and the jth column. Once this output line is used, and if it is not required any more, it becomes a garbage output. The presence of a Peres gate in the $(k-1)^{th}$ row results in a structure of Toffoli gates followed by another Toffoli gate and a CNOT gate (since Peres gate is equivalent to a Toffoli gate followed by CNOT gate) in the same row. The two back-to-back Toffoli gates work on the same set of control lines and target line. Since the Peres gate preceded by the Toffoli gate in the same row works on the same set of control and target lines, this makes the garbage output to become zero. Therefore, this line can now be reused as a target line to other gates in the next level in the structure as shown in Fig. 10 for $n = 5$ inputs. Note that any row where a Peres gate and a Toffoli gate share the same target line and one of the control lines, a so called Peres-Toffoli double gate can be applied. The quantum cost of such a gate is 7 [24].

This optimization technique results in $(2\lfloor \log_2 n \rfloor - 1)$ constant input lines for an n-input design, which is less than that of the original structure. On the

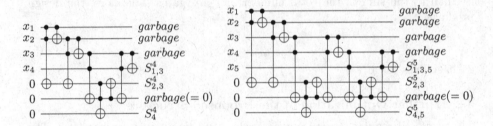

Fig. 9. Optimized design for 4-inputs   **Fig. 10.** Optimized design for 5-inputs

contrary, the optimized design requires some additional Toffoli gates along with the Peres gates of the main structure. The total number of Toffoli gates in the design is given by

$$N_{toffoli} = n\lfloor \log_2 n \rfloor - n - 2^{\lfloor \log_2 n \rfloor + 1} + \lfloor \log_2 n \rfloor + 3 \tag{6}$$

while the total number of Peres gates remains the same as in the original design.

The total number of garbage lines required for the optimized design is given as

$$N_{reduced-garbage} = n + \lfloor \log_2 n \rfloor - 2. \tag{7}$$

Comparing this with the result shown in Equation (4), we observe that the number of garbage lines in the optimized structure is less than that of the original structure.

4   Reversible Synthesis of General Symmetric Functions

For any n inputs, the proposed structure produces $\lfloor \log_2 n \rfloor + 1$ number of symmetric functions. Two symmetric functions S_A^n and S_B^n are true for any weight w of input vectors, $w = (1, 2, \cdots n)$, if $A \cap B = \{w : w \in A \text{ and } w \in B\}$, where A and B are a set of integers containing the Hamming weights of the input vectors. The aim here is to separate these common weights between any two symmetric functions and represent all the symmetric functions in terms of individual weight of its input vector. To do this, the output lines of the regular structure are fed to a network consisting of a number of blocks called *extraction-elimination (EE)* modules.

4.1   Extraction-Elimination (EE) Module

As the name implies, this module performs two operations: the first one is an "extraction", which extracts the common weight of an input vector from two symmetric functions for which the functions are true. The second one is an "elimination", which eliminates the common weight from those two symmetric

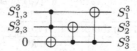

Fig. 11. *Extraction-Elimination* module: $S_{1,3}^3, S_{2,3}^3$ are inputs along with target line set to 0 and S_1^3, S_2^3, S_3^3 are outputs

functions. This module produces three symmetric functions of single weight. The extraction operation is implemented using a Toffoli gate whose target line is set to 0. The two elimination operations (one for each symmetric function) are performed using two CNOT gates. The quantum cost of this module is 7. The complete module is shown in Fig. 11. It is a garbage-free circuit where each output line is essential.

4.2 Realization of General Symmetric Functions

The *EE module* is used to decompose $k = \lfloor \log_2 n \rfloor + 1$ symmetric functions of multiple weights realized by the regular structure described in Section 3 into n symmetric functions of single weight of its input vector, where $k < n$. This is done using the following procedure:

1) First, the regular structure as described in Section 3 is constructed for n inputs. The structure produces $k = \lfloor \log_2 n \rfloor + 1$ outputs, each of which is a symmetric function of n inputs. For any given regular structure, we represent integers 1 to n with its binary equivalent, i.e., for any n, the bit positions are $(2^{\lfloor \log_2 n \rfloor} \cdots 2^3 2^2 2^1 2^0)$, where $2^{\lfloor \log_2 n \rfloor}$ is the most significant bit of the number n. Each bit position of the decimal number n indicates an output line of the regular structure. Hence, there are $\lfloor \log_2 n \rfloor + 1$ outputs in the regular structure. The total number of 1's present in any bit position 2^m, where $m = 0, 1, 2, \cdots \lfloor \log_2 n \rfloor$ indicates the corresponding output line of the regular structure realizing a symmetric function. If a 1 is present at the bit position 2^m, which is an *MSB*, then the regular structure has at most $m + 1$ output lines. It is noticed that the integers 1 to n denote the weights of the input vector for which the functions are true. Once all the integers are represented in their equivalent binary forms, the process of identification follows.

2) During this process, we identify all the 2^m bit positions that are 1 for binary equivalents of all the consecutive integers 1 to n. This helps in indicating all the corresponding output lines realizing symmetric functions, i.e., they are true for that integer (weight of the input vector). Two cases related to the identification of bit positions are considered. The first case implies if any one of the 2^m bit positions is 1 and rest of the bit positions are 0. Then, the symmetric function in the corresponding output line is true only for that integer (weight of the input vector). In the second case, if more than one bit positions are 1, then the corresponding output lines realizing the functions, are true. Whenever the second case is encountered, the output lines of the regular structure are identified

Table 3. Binary representations of five consecutive numbers

Decimal number	its binary equivalent
1	0001
2	0010
3	0011
4	0100
5	0101

from the bit positions of the binary number equal to 1. Now an *EE* module is applied to the two lines indicated by the two bit positions. This results in the extraction of the corresponding integer value. The extracted integer is copied at the target line of a (3×3) Toffoli gate by setting the line to 0. This integer is a weight of the input vector for which the functions in those two lines are set to 1. Following the extraction operation, the elimination operations are performed on these two lines by two CNOT gates, one for each line. This results in three symmetric functions with no common input weight. This process continues until all the integers are considered.

Following this procedure, we require $(n - \lfloor \log_2 n \rfloor - 1)$ number of *EE* modules for an n-input structure to convert $\lfloor \log_2 n \rfloor + 1$ symmetric functions of multiple weights to n symmetric functions of single weight.

Example 2. Consider the regular structure for $n = 5$ inputs. There are three output lines producing outputs $f_1 = S_{1,3,5}^5$, $f_2 = S_{2,3}^5$ and $f_3 = S_{4,5}^5$ on line $1, 2$, and 3 respectively. The possible weights of the input vector and their binary equivalents are shown in Table 3. From the table, it can be observed that the first binary number has a single 1 at its bit position 1. This represents weight 1 for which f_1 will be true. Similarly, the second binary number has a single 1 at its bit position 2, thus representing weight 2 for which f_2 is true. In the third binary number, we have two 1's - one in bit position 1 and another in bit position 2, indicating weight 3 for which the functions in line 1 (f_1) and line 2 (f_2) are true. Therefore, we append an *EE* module to line 1 and 2 which produces three outputs- $S_{1,5}^5$ at line 1, S_2^5 at line 2, and S_3^5 at line 4. In the fourth binary number, there is a single 1 at bit position 3 meaning that the output line 3 is true for weight 4. In the last binary number, we observe that there are two 1's in bit positions 1 and 3. Thus, line 1 and line 3 are now applied to the *EE* module which produces outputs S_1^5 at line 1, S_4^5 at line 3, and S_5^5 at line 5. Therefore,

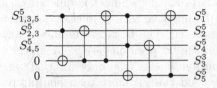

Fig. 12. *EE* modules appended at the end of the regular structure for 5 inputs

using two *EE* modules five symmetric functions of single weight are produced as shown in Fig. 12.

5 Comparison to Previous Work

We have compared the cost metrics of the proposed regular and the optimized structure with those reported in previous work [9, 13]. The comparison is made on the basis of quantum cost and the number of garbage lines. The results are reported in Table 4. We observe that the realizations of benchmark functions obtained by the first technique have less quantum costs as compared to those reported in previous work [9, 13]. The number of garbage bits in this design is larger in comparison to those from [13], but fewer than those of [9]. However, these garbage outputs also implement symmetric functions with a fewer number of literals and, thus, can be utilized to synthesize other symmetric functions. Furthermore, by slightly increasing the quantum costs, the number of garbage lines can further be reduced using the proposed optimization technique.

Table 4. Comparison of quantum cost

Function			Quantum cost				Garbage			
Name	In	Out	[9]	[13]	Sect. 3.1	Sect. 3.2	[9]	[13]	Sect. 3.1	Sect. 3.2
$rd53$	5	3	145	36	20	28	15	5	6	5
$rd73$	7	3	303	64	32	46	30	7	10	7
$rd84$	8	4	403	98	44	66	39	11	13	9
$9sym$	9	1	505	94	59	88	37	11	19	14

6 Conclusion

In this paper, we have proposed a synthesis scheme for realizing symmetric Boolean functions with reversible logic. Compared to earlier synthesis methods, our solution relies on a simple and regular cascade structure. The garbage outputs of our design can also be used to realize symmetric Boolean functions with a fewer number of literals. We have evaluated the proposed design on some well known benchmark symmetric functions. Our simulation results reveal that the proposed design significantly reduces the quantum cost, but may require additional ancillary lines thereby increasing the number of garbage outputs. To reduce these garbage lines further, we have also proposed a modified structure in which these garbage lines can be properly reused while implementing the output functions. Both of these design approaches admit a hierarchical structure and can thus be built in an iterative fashion. This regular structure thus obtained can be fed to a network of extraction-elimination *(EE)* modules to synthesize symmetric functions of single weights from those having multiple weights. The *EE* network is an entirely garbage-free network.

Acknowledgement. This work was partly supported by CSIR grant (ref.-22(0590)/12/$EMR - II$) and UGC MRP grant (ref.-41 $- 620/2012(SR)$).

References

1. Knill, E., Laflamme, R., Milburn, G.J.: A scheme for efficient quantum computation with linear optics. Nature, 46–52 (2001)
2. Nielsen, M., Chuang, I.: Quantum Computation and Quantum Information. Cambridge Univ. Press (2000)
3. Wille, R., Drechsler, R., Oswald, C., Garcia-Ortiz, A.: Automatic design of low-power encoders using reversible circuit synthesis. In: DATE, pp. 1036–1041 (2012)
4. Desoete, B., Vos, A.D.: A reversible carry-look-ahead adder using control gates. INTEGRATION, the VLSI Jour. 33(1-2), 89–104 (2002)
5. Cuykendall, R., Andersen, D.R.: Reversible optical computing circuits. Optical Letters 12(7), 542–544 (1987)
6. Thapliyal, H., Srinivas, M.B.: The need of DNA computing: reversible designs of adders and multipliers using fredkin gate. In: Proc. SPIE, Optomechatronic Micro/Nano Devices and Components (2005)
7. Merkle, R.C.: Reversible electronic logic using switches. Nanotechnology 4, 21–40 (1993)
8. Agarwal, A., Jha, N.K.: Synthesis of reversible logic. In: DATE, pp. 21384–21385 (2004)
9. Perkowski, M., Kerntopf, P., Buller, A., Chrzanowska-Jeske, M., Mishchenko, A., Song, X., Al-Rabadi, A., Jozwiak, L., Coppola, A., Massey, B.: Regularity and symmetry as a base for efficient realization of reversible logic circuits. In: IWLS, pp. 245–252 (2001)
10. Mishchenko, A., Perkowski, M.: Logic synthesis of reversible wave cascades. In: IWLS, pp. 197–202 (2002)
11. Gupta, P., Agrawal, A., Jha, N.: An algorithm for synthesis of reversible logic circuits. IEEE TCAD 25(11), 2317–2330 (2006)
12. Shende, V.V., Prasad, A.K., Markov, I.L., Hayes, J.P.: Synthesis of reversible logic circuits. IEEE TCAD 22(6), 723–729 (2003)
13. Maslov, D.: Efficient reversible and quantum implementations of symmetric Boolean functions. IEEE Proc. of the Circuits, Devices and Systems 153(5), 467–472 (2006)
14. Große, D., Wille, R., Dueck, G.W., Drechsler, R.: Exact multiple control Toffoli network synthesis with SAT techniques. IEEE TCAD 28(5), 703–715 (2009)
15. Miller, D.M., Maslov, D., Dueck, G.W.: A transformation based algorithm for reversible logic synthesis. In: Design Automation Conf., pp. 318–323 (2003)
16. Wille, R., Drechsler, R.: BDD-based synthesis of reversible logic for large functions. In: Design Automation Conf., pp. 270–275 (2009)
17. Rovetta, C., Mouffron, M.: De Bruijan sequences and complexity of symmetric functions. Cryptography and Communications Journal 3(4), 207–225 (2011)
18. Yanushekvich, S.N., Butler, J.T., Dueck, G.W., Shmerko, V.P.: Experiments on FPRM expressions for partially symmetric logic functions. In: IEEE International Symposium on Multiple Valued Logic, pp. 141–146 (2000)
19. Lauradoux, C., Videau, M.: Matriochka symmetric Boolean functions. In: IEEE ISIT, pp. 1631–1635 (2008)

20. Keren, O., Levin, I., Stankovic, S.R.: Use of gray decoding for implementation of symmetric functions. In: International Conference on VLSI, pp. 25–30 (2007)
21. Rahaman, H., Das, D.K., Bhattacharya, B.B.: Implementing symmetric functions with hierarchical modules for stuck-at and path-delay fault testability. Journal of Electronic Testing: Theory and Applications 22(2), 125–142 (2006)
22. Perkowski, M., Kerntopf, P., Buller, A., Chrzanowska-Jeske, M., Mishchenko, A., Song, X., Al-Rabadi, A., Jozwiak, L., Coppola, A., Massey, B.: Regular realization of symmetric functions using reversible logic. In: EUROMICRO Symp. on Digital Systems Design, pp. 245–252 (2001)
23. Picton, P.: Modified Fredkin gates in logic design. Microelectronics Journal 25, 437–441 (1994)
24. Moraga, C., Hadjam, F.Z.: On double gates for reversible computing circuits. In: Proc. Intl. Workshop on Boolean Problems (2012)

White Dots *do* Matter: Rewriting Reversible Logic Circuits

Mathias Soeken[1] and Michael Kirkedal Thomsen[2],[*]

[1] Group of Computer Architecture, University of Bremen
`msoeken@informatik.uni-bremen.de`
[2] DIKU, Department of Computer Science, University of Copenhagen
`shapper@diku.dk`

Abstract. The increased effort in recent years towards methods for computer aided design of reversible logic circuits has also lead to research in algorithms for optimising the resulting circuits; both with higher-level data structures and directly on the reversible circuits. To obtain structural patterns that can be replaced by a cheaper realisation, many direct algorithms apply so-called *moving rules*; a simple form of rewrite rules that can only swap gate order.

In this paper we first describe the few basic rules that are needed to perform rewriting directly on reversible logic circuits made from general Toffoli circuits. We also show how to use these rules to derive more complex formulas. The major difference compared to existing approaches is the use of *negative controls* (white dots), which significantly increases the algebraic strength. We show how existing optimisation approaches can be adapted as problems based on our rewrite rules.

Finally, we outline a path to generalising the rewrite rules by showing their forms for *reversible control-gates*. This can be used to expand our method to other gates such as the controlled-swap gate or quantum gates.

Keywords: Reversible logic, term rewriting, circuit optimisation, circuit equivalence.

1   Introduction

When Landauer presented his seminal paper [9] he exemplified some of his ideas with a simple reversible logic gate; a gate that is equivalent to the controlled-controlled-not gate or Toffoli gate. Fredkin and Toffoli [7,17] later formalized the computational model for reversible logic and reversible logic circuits have since been associated with low-power computing circuits.

An important aspect of reversible logic design is to be able to find an implementation of a desired functionality. This problem has been researched at many different levels: from hand-made (arithmetic) circuits (*e.g.* [3,5,16,19]), over different variants of synthesis algorithms (*e.g.* [11–13]), to specification languages that can ease the implementation phase (*e.g.* [14,15,20]). But another, just as

---

[*] Alphabetically sorted author list.

G.W. Dueck and D.M. Miller (Eds.): RC 2013, LNCS 7948, pp. 196–208, 2013.

important, aspect is to have a good or (even better) optimal implementation of the reversible circuit. Of course, some synthesis methods seek optimality, but for larger functions this is hard to achieve. This has lead to the development of algorithms for optimising reversible circuits, where some of these work directly on reversible logic circuits: these include *moving rules* [10] (there referred to as *passing rule*), for locally swapping gates without changing their functionality, and *template matching* [11], that over several gates can recognise sub-circuits which are functionally equivalent to smaller circuits.

In this work the goal is *not* to design a new and better optimisation algorithm. Instead, we desire a better understanding of the reversible circuit constructions. We do this by exploring which basic rules are necessary to perform transformations directly on reversible logic circuits. At first, we limit ourselves to general (mixed-polarity multiple-controlled) Toffoli gates. In this small, but widely used, subset of reversible gates, it is still possible to show many of the interesting features that this approach gives. In particular the use of *negative controls* (white dots) significantly increase the algebraic strength; this is shown by the power of the very simple rules. Furthermore, we also show how to use these rules to derive more complex formulas that can then be used to derive more rules.

A particular use of these rules (or algebraic laws) is in the implementation of a term rewriting system, *cf.* [4]. One use of rewriting is for optimisation, which gives a connection to template matching and moving rules. We will show this connection by deriving some template transformations and simple moving rules. Another use of rewriting is to do equivalence checking. Here an example will show how a circuit cascaded with the inverse of another can be rewritten into the identity circuit. We will only shortly discuss (but not present) a term rewriting system based on our rules. Implementing term rewriting systems is not a simple task and, among other, avoiding divergence poses a problem. The rewriting strategy based on the general decomposition of reversible circuits into V-shaped target lines [18].

Finally, it is possible to generalise the basic rules to cover other reversible logic gates than the general Toffoli gates, *e.g.* a controlled-swap (Fredkin) gate or quantum gates. We will exemplify this by defining a general control-gate and show some of the rules for these.

Some, but not all of our rules, have been used in previously presented papers, often without explicitly considering them rules. The most related work is [2], in which rules are used in order to optimise reversible circuits. However, they have either used very simple rules or rules that require the simulation of the functionality which is afterwards optimised based on Karnaugh maps and the approach is therefore not efficient for large functions. In contrast, the rules presented in this paper can all be applied structurally, hence, the size of the circuit does not matter. Also in [8] a rule-based approach is presented, but their rules only apply for a small subset of the reversible circuits (they call them *quantum Boolean circuits*), where only one single line is semantically updated: reversible many-to-one functions. In comparison our approach applies to all reversible circuits.

2   Reversible Logic and Circuits

In this paper we use the formalism of Toffoli and Fredkin [7, 17] to describe *reversible logic circuits* with diagram-notation based on Feynman [6]. In general, a *reversible gate* is defined as a bijective function from n to n Boolean values. There exist many such gates and in this work we restrict ourselves to mixed-polarity multiple-controlled Toffoli gates.

Definition 1. *Given a set of variables* $X = \{x_1, \ldots, x_n\}$, *a mixed-polarity multiple-controlled Toffoli gate (referred to as* Toffoli gate *in the following) is defined as a tuple* (C, x_t) *of control lines* C *and target line* x_t *such that*

$$C \subset \{x, \bar{x} \mid x \in X\} \quad and \quad \{x, \bar{x}\} \not\subset C \text{ for all } x \in X$$

and

$$\{x_t, \bar{x}_t\} \cap C = \emptyset .$$

Control lines x *and* $\bar{x}$ *are referred to as* positive *and* negative, *respectively. From the control lines the* control function *of the gate* $f : \mathbb{B}^{n-1} \to \mathbb{B}$ *is defined as*

$$f : (x_1, \ldots, x_{t-1}, x_{t+1}, \ldots, x_n) \mapsto \bigwedge_{c \in C} c .$$

The gate represents the Boolean function $g : \mathbb{B}^n \to \mathbb{B}^n$ *with*

$$g : (x_1, \ldots, x_n) \mapsto (x_1, \ldots, x_{t-1}, x_t \oplus f(\boldsymbol{x}), x_{t+1}, \ldots, x_n)$$

with $\boldsymbol{x} = x_1, \ldots, x_{t-1}, x_{t+1}, \ldots, x_n$.

In other words, we restrict to reversible gates with a single updated target line, x_t, and multiple control lines that are inputs to a control function f. Here f is defined as the conjunction of its inputs, where each input can be identity, negated, or not used at all. The target line is updated with the result of the exclusive-or product of x_t and the result of f. Although f cannot be any Boolean function, it is possible to define any Boolean function as an *exclusive-sum of products* (ESOP) of control functions, which will result in a *reversible circuit* with several cascaded gates that have the target line in common.

A *reversible circuit* is a cascade of reversible gates and the function defined by the reversible circuit is defined as the composition of all functions defined by the gates. It has been shown that every reversible function can be represented by a reversible circuit consisting of Toffoli gates [17].

Notation. Our notation is based on the widely-used diagrams that were introduced by Feynman [6]. The notation is illustrated in Fig. 1 by means of an example for the reversible circuit $(\{x_1, \bar{x}_2\}, x_3), (\{x_3\}, x_1), (\{\bar{x}_1\}, x_2), (\emptyset, x_3)$. The target line is marked with $\oplus$, positive and negative control lines with $\bullet$ and $\circ$, respectively. To accommodate a more general use, we will denote Toffoli gates as:

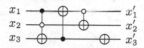

Fig. 1. Reversible circuit

Lines marked with '/' indicate that this line may consist of several bits. Note here that the control function f is not (necessarily) a reversible function (following from Def. 1), but the entire gate is still reversible as it is constructed as *reversible update* [21].

3 Rewriting Toffoli Circuits

In this section we will show how to rewrite Toffoli circuits and define the basic rewrite rules that are needed. We will show how to use these rules to derive some well-known formulas, which can then be used to rewrite the Toffoli circuits in fewer steps. When performing rewrites one has infinitely many possible ways to apply the rules. It is, therefore, often helpful to have guiding strategies and we will also outline some of them here.

3.1 Rewrite Rules

We now introduce the rewrite rules. Most rules are very simple, but this is also the intention. They should contain exactly enough for us to later derive more advanced rules and this is what we will do in Sect. 3.2.

First, however, note that gate composition is associative. By this we mean that in a cascade of gates the order in which we look at the gates does not matter; *e.g.* in Fig. 1 we are free to either look at the two first gates and perform some rewriting on these, or start with the middle or last two gates. Just as we assume the existence of identity gates between all other gates.

Gate Modifying Rules. The first rule is for introducing and eliminating Not-gates and states that we can always rewrite the empty line (the identity function) to two Not-gates. This is true because the Not-gate is self-inverse.

$$\text{------} = \text{-⊕-⊕-} \tag{R1}$$

Although simple, the rule is very useful as we will see in a moment.

But before this, we will introduce the first rules with negative controls. The rule (there are two rules to be exact) simply states that we can "move" a Not-gate over a control if we negate this control.

$$\tag{R2}$$

Notice that only one of the rules is elementary and the other one can be derived from it:

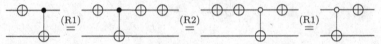

With these simple rule we, for the first time, see the power of having negative controls. Without negative controls a similar rule would not exist, which will result in a less powerful rewriting system.

Control Aware Rules. We can always extend a gate by copying it and adding once a positive and once a negative control line to it. Conversely, if two adjacent gates are equal except for one control line in which the polarity differs, the gates can be merged and the control on that line can be removed.

$$(R3)$$

Furthermore, two arbitrary adjacent gates, which can also have different target lines, can be interchanged whenever they have a common control line with different polarities. Then, at most one of the gates can be applied.

$$(R4)$$

Notice, that the diagram notation only depicts one special case of the rule. To capture this rule in the diagrams we would need a more general notation, which will only be introduces in the generalisation (*cf.* Sect. 5).

Grouping Rules. Whenever two gates share the same control line with the same polarity, these two gates can be grouped together where the group is controlled by that control line, *e.g.*

$$(R5)$$

Also this rule is more general than to what is depicted in the diagram notation.

The next rule is for introducing and eliminating groups of wires. A group of wires is either zero or more gates that are controlled by the same wire; it is analogous to parenthesis in Boolean logic and can be used to work on smaller parts of the circuits. These two rules state that either a positive or negative control on a group that only contains the identity gate is equal to the identity.

$$(R6)$$

and

Similar to Rule R2, one rule can be derived from the other one:

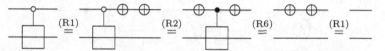

These two rules can be generalised to arbitrary control functions, *i.e.*

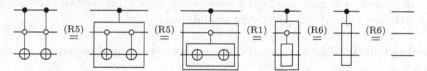

The proof is by structural induction, but we will not show it here.

Deriving More General Rules. Based on the rules described above, we are now introducing more general rules that apply to arbitrary Toffoli gates. Based on Rules R1, R5, and R6 we can derive what is famously known as *deletion rule*, *i.e.* two adjacent equal Toffoli gates can be removed:

$$\text{(D1)}$$

As f is defined as conjunction of is inputs (Def. 1), the proof is by structural induction with Rule R1 being the base case and Rule R5 applied in the inductive step. The proof illustrated by the following example:

With Not-gates the control line of an arbitrary Toffoli line can be negated:

$$\text{(D2)}$$

This can also be proved using structural induction and the proof is sketched by means of the following example.

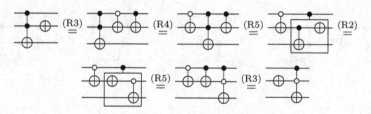

Similarly we can also generalize Rule R3 for arbitrary Toffoli gates:

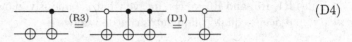

(D3)

3.2 Derived Formulas

We now have seen how to use the basic rules to derive more general forms of these rules. Now, we will use the rules to derive new formulas; some of which are well-known from Boolean logic. We will use these formulas later in the paper, but at the same time it also gives more examples of using the rewrite rules. In an EXOR expression, the polarity of the operands can be swapped, *i.e.* $\bar{x} \oplus y = x \oplus \bar{y}$. This formula can also be expressed using the above introduced rewrite rules.

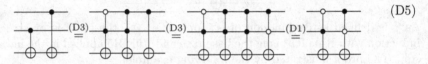

(D4)

Also the following rewrite rule turns out to be quite helpful.

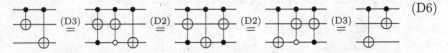

(D5)

As can be seen, new rules can be composed solely from other derived rules which shows the strength of the underlying formalism.

Moving Rules. Also the classical moving rule can be derived from other rewrite rules:

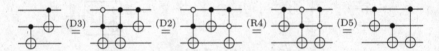

(D6)

The general moving rule can be applied to any two adjacent gates (C_i, t_i) and (C_{i+1}, t_{i+1}) if and only if $\{t_i, \bar{t}_i\} \cap C_{i+1} = \emptyset$ and $\{t_{i+1}, \bar{t}_{i+1}\} \cap C_i = \emptyset$, *i.e.* controls cannot be on wires where the other gate has a target.

But the rewrite rules are more powerful than the moving rule and allow us to interchange gates such as for which moving rules are not sufficient:

We can generalize this rule to

$$
\begin{array}{c}
x_1 \quad\quad (f_1) \quad x_1 \quad\quad x_1 \quad (f_1) \quad\quad (f_1) \quad x_1 \\
x_2 (f_2) \quad\quad x_2 \; = \; x_2 \quad\quad (f_2)(f_2) \quad x_2 \\
t_2 \quad\quad\oplus\quad t_2' \quad\quad t_2 \quad\oplus \quad\quad t_2' \\
t_1 \quad\quad\quad\quad t_1' \quad\quad t_1 \quad\quad\oplus\quad\oplus\quad t_1'
\end{array}
\qquad (\text{D7})
$$

This can also be proven using Boolean logic. On the left-hand side we have $t_1' = t_1 \oplus (t_2 \wedge f_2(x_2))$ and $t_2' = t_2 \oplus f_1(x_1)$. Clearly, on the right-hand side we also have $t_2' = t_2 \oplus f_1(x_1)$. For t_1' we have

$$
\begin{aligned}
t_1' &= t_1 \oplus ((t_2 \oplus f_1(x_1)) \wedge f_2(x_2)) \oplus (f_1(x_1) \wedge f_2(x_2)) \\
&= t_1 \oplus (t_2 \wedge f_2(x_2)) \oplus (f_1(x_1) \wedge f_2(x_2)) \oplus (f_1(x_1) \wedge f_2(x_2)) \\
&= t_1 \oplus (t_2 \wedge f_2(x_2))
\end{aligned}
$$

Limitations. The proposed rewrite rules cover almost all combinations in which two adjacent gates can occur. However, there is one combination that cannot be rewritten on its own. Interchanged gates with one control line such as

do not match any of the rules introduced above. However, they can often be rewritten if they occur as a sub-circuit in a larger circuit, which is *e.g.* shown later in Sect. 4 when rewriting the template with the id 5.1.

3.3 Rewriting Strategies

In order to implement an algorithm that makes use of the rewrite rules, a good rewriting strategy is inevitable as otherwise convergence is not necessarily guaranteed. As one rewriting strategy we suggest to bring the circuit into a V-shape. Gates in V-shaped circuits are arranged in a way that the target line for each gate moves down from the top to the bottom and afterwards moves up again. Adjacent gates can have their target on the same line. That each reversible function can be represented as V-shaped circuit has *e.g.* been shown in [12]. In their paper, Algorithm B describes a synthesis algorithm that can be applied to all reversible functions and naturally results in V-shaped circuits.

4 Examples

Given our new rewrite rules, it is possible to rewrite templates to the empty circuit. As an example we consider the following template which has been proposed in [11].

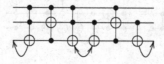

The arrows indicate all rewrite possibilities if only the classical moving rule can be applied, as it has been done in previous work. With the classical moving rule, the middle gates can be interchanged but also the first gate can be swapped with the last gate since the circuit represents the identity. However, it can easily be seen that the moving rules are not sufficient in order to remove gates from the circuit. In particular it is not possible to move the fifth gate next to the second, which is indeed possible using the proposed rewrite rules. For this purpose, we first apply Rule D3 to the fourth gate resulting in

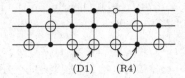

Note that the third and the fourth gate can be removed since they represent the identity and the fifth and sixth gate can be swapped since they have disjoint controls. Applying both rules allows to place the Toffoli gates with target on the second line next to each other:

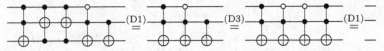

Following the previous example, we can apply rewrite rules in order to perform structural equivalence checking. Taking two circuits representing the functions G_1 and G_2, we can construct a new circuit that represents $G = G_1 \circ G_2^{-1}$ by appending the reverse of G_2 to G_1. If both circuits represent the same function, then G must represent the identity function and therefore it must be possible to rewrite G to the empty circuit.

We will illustrate this approach by means of an example in which we consider the circuits:

$$G_1 = \qquad\qquad G_2 = \qquad\qquad$$

In order to rewrite $G_2 \circ G_1^{-1}$ to the empty circuit the following rewrite rules can be applied:

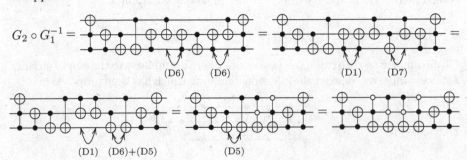

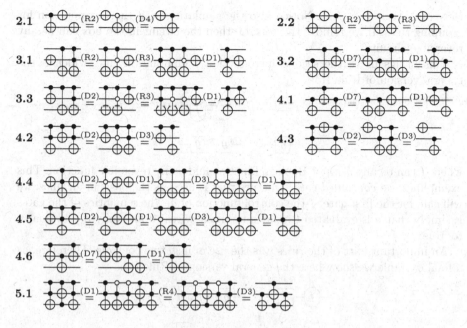

Fig. 2. Rewriting templates

Notice, that as a strategy we are bringing the combined circuit to the V-shape and finally apply the deletion rule starting from the inner gates towards the outer gates.

Figure 2 shows examples in which all Toffoli templates from [11] have been considered. The templates have been listed with a left-hand side and right-hand side circuit instead of giving the identity circuit explicitly. We applied our rewrite rules in order to write the left-hand side to the right-hand side. The identifiers have been taken from the original paper.

5   General Rewriting of Reversible Gates

All previous rules and derivations have, in essence, been specialised to a subset of the reversible logic gates, namely the general Toffoli gates. However, depending on the implementation technology (CMOS, quantum technology, *etc.*) other reversible gates are also of interest. In this section we will, therefore, show the first steps towards a general set of rules.

First, we need gate introduction / elimination rules similar to Rule R1:

$$\text{------} = -\boxed{f}-\boxed{f^{-1}}-$$

where f can be any reversible logic function defined over any number of lines[1]. That this rule is true is obvious and if f is a self-inverse function (such as the

---

[1] As all lines can represent more than one bit-wire, we have, for aesthetic reasons, omitted the slash (/) on the lines.

Not-gate), then $f = f^{-1}$. Notice also the similarity with the box-notation for grouping rules. If we remove the control, then the circuit in the box can be any reversible circuit.

This brings us to the second introduction / elimination rule, which is the general version of Rule R3:

where f can be any n-input Boolean function and g any reversible function. This exemplifies the *controlled-gate* structure that is used as the basis in all rules; we will call, for the first gate, f the control function of g. The semantics of the gates is simply that g is evaluated (updates its input wires) if and only if f evaluates to True.

An important part of the rules was the use of negative controls. Therefore, as a final example we show here the general version of Rule R2:

where the number of inputs to the control function f must equal the number of bit-wires that the reversible function h maps over.

This section has only shown a bit of the rules that is needed to describe the general system. Future work will provide the formalisation to general rules and show how other known reversible gates (*e.g.* the controlled-swap / Fredkin gate) relate to this.

6   Conclusion

In this paper, we have presented a rewrite system for reversible logic. We have illustrated our approach by means of Toffoli circuits but also illustrated how it can be generalised to be applied to all kind of reversible circuits. We have categorised the rules into basic ones and rules that can be derived from them. It turns out that the set of basic rules remains compact.

Since the rewrite rules can be applied to almost all possible gate combinations, an expensive matching step as it is required in similar methods such as template matching can be omitted. Instead, the rewrite rules require appropriate rewrite strategies in order to be applied efficiently, which we want to consider in future work, *e.g.* with rewrite strategies based on Boolean satisfiability (*cf.* with the template matching approach presented in [1]). Also to show completeness, in the sense that these rules can rewrite a circuit to all its equivalent circuits, is left for future work. Though not constructive, such a proof will also show that it is possible to rewrite a circuit into its minimal representation according to some metric.

Furthermore, we want to generalise the rewrite rules to arbitrary reversible circuits. Also the consideration of multiple-valued logic circuits, *e.g.* quantum circuits based on the NCV library, is an interesting target for future work.

Acknowledgement. The authors thank the *Danish Council for Strategic Research* for partially supporting this work through the *MicroPower* research project (http://topps.diku.dk/micropower).

References

1. Abdessaied, N., Soeken, M., Wille, R., Drechsler, R.: Exact template matching using Boolean satisfiability. In: Int'l. Symp. on Multiple-Valued Logic, ISMVL (2013)
2. Arabzadeh, M., Saeedi, M., Zamani, M.S.: Rule-based optimization of reversible circuits. In: Asia and South-Pacific Design Automation Conference, ASP-DAC, pp. 849–854 (2010)
3. Axelsen, H.B., Thomsen, M.K.: Garbage-free reversible integer multiplication with constants of the form $2^k \pm 2^l \pm 1$. In: Glück, R., Yokoyama, T. (eds.) RC 2012. LNCS, vol. 7581, pp. 171–182. Springer, Heidelberg (2013)
4. Baader, F., Nipkow, T.: Term rewriting and all that. Cambridge University Press, New York (1998)
5. Cuccaro, S.A., Draper, T.G., Kutin, S.A., Moulton, D.P.: A new quantum ripple-carry addition circuit arXiv:quant-ph/0410184v1 (2005)
6. Feynman, R.P.: Quantum mechanical computers. Optics News 11, 11–20 (1985)
7. Fredkin, E., Toffoli, T.: Conservative logic. International Journal of Theoretical Physics 21(3-4), 219–253 (1982)
8. Iwama, K., Kambayashi, Y., Yamashita, S.: Transformation rules for designing cnot-based quantum circuits. In: Design Automation Conference, DAC 2002, pp. 419–424. ACM (2002)
9. Landauer, R.: Irreversibility and heat generation in the computing process. IBM Journal of Research and Development 5(3), 183–191 (1961)
10. Maslov, D., Miller, D.M., Dueck, G.W.: Fredkin/Toffoli templates for reversible logic synthesis. In: Int'l Conf. on Computer Aided Design, ICCAD, pp. 256–261 (2003)
11. Miller, D.M., Maslov, D., Dueck, G.W.: A transformation based algorithm for reversible logic synthesis. In: Design Automation Conference, DAC, pp. 318–323 (2003)
12. Regergem, Y.V., Vos, A.D.: Young subgroups for reversible computers. Advances in Mathematics of Communications 2(2), 183–200 (2008)
13. Soeken, M., Wille, R., Hilken, C., Przigoda, N., Drechsler, R.: Synthesis of reversible circuits with minimal lines for large functions. In: Asia and South-Pacific Design Automation Conference, ASP-DAC, pp. 85–92 (2012)
14. Thomsen, M.K.: Describing and optimising reversible logic using a functional language. In: Gill, A., Hage, J. (eds.) IFL 2011. LNCS, vol. 7257, pp. 148–163. Springer, Heidelberg (2012)
15. Thomsen, M.K.: A functional language for describing reversible logic. In: Specification & Design Languages, FDL, pp. 135–142. IEEE (2012)

16. Thomsen, M.K., Glück, R., Axelsen, H.B.: Reversible arithmetic logic unit for quantum arithmetic. Journal of Physics A: Mathematical and Theoretical 43(38), 382002 (2010)
17. Toffoli, T.: Reversible computing. In: de Bakker, J.W., van Leeuwen, J. (eds.) ICALP 1980. LNCS, vol. 85, pp. 632–644. Springer (1980)
18. Van Rentergem, Y., De Vos, A., Storme, L.: Implementing an arbitrary reversible logic gate. Journal of Physics A: Mathematical and General (38), 3555–3577 (2005)
19. Vedral, V., Barenco, A., Ekert, A.: Quantum networks for elementary arithmetic operations. Physical Review A 54(1), 147–153 (1996)
20. Wille, R., Offermann, S., Drechsler, R.: SyReC: A programming language for synthesis of reversible circuits. In: Specification & Design Languages, FDL, pp. 1–6. IET (2010)
21. Yokoyama, T., Axelsen, H.B., Glück, R.: Principles of a reversible programming language. In: Conference on Computing Frontiers, CF, pp. 43–54. ACM Press (2008)

Exploiting Negative Control Lines
in the Optimization of Reversible Circuits

Kamalika Datta[1], Gaurav Rathi[2], Robert Wille[3,4]
Indranil Sengupta[2], Hafizur Rahaman[1], and Rolf Drechsler[3,4]

[1] Department of Information Technology, Bengal Engineering & Science University,
Shibpur, Howrah 711103, India
kdatta.iitkgp@gmail.com, rahaman_h@it.becs.ac.in
[2] Department of Computer Science & Engineering, Indian Institute of Technology,
Kharagpur 721301, India
gaurav.rathi01@gmail.com, isg@iitkgp.ac.in
[3] Institute of Computer Science, University of Bremen, 28359 Bremen, Germany
{rwille,drechsle}@informatik.uni-bremen.de
[4] Cyber-Physical Systems, DFKI GmbH, 28359 Bremen, Germany

Abstract. The development of approaches for synthesis and optimization of reversible circuits received significant attention in the past. This
is partly due to the increasing emphasis on low power design method-
ologies, and partly motivated by recent works in quantum computation.
While most of them relied on a gate library composed of multiple-control
Toffoli (MCT) gates with positive control lines, some initial works also
exist which additionally incorporate negative control lines. This usually
leads to smaller circuits with respect to the number of gates as well as the
corresponding quantum costs. However, despite these benefits, negative
control lines have hardly been considered in post-synthesis optimization
of reversible circuits so far. In this paper, we address this issue. We are
presenting an optimization scheme inspired by template matching which
explicitly makes use of negative control lines. Experimental evaluations
demonstrate that exploiting negative control lines in fact lead to a reduction in the number of gates and the quantum costs by up to 60%
and 25%, respectively.

Keywords: Reversible Circuits, Optimization, Negative control gates,
Template Matching.

1 Introduction

Despite the sustained advancements in semiconductor technology over the last
few decades, conventional circuit technologies are approaching severe physical
boundaries particularly caused by the exponential miniaturization. Besides that,
engineers are facing consequent demands for the development of ultra-low-power
designs. Motivated by this, there has been several attempts by researchers to look
for alternative circuit technologies. In the recent past, reversible logic circuits

G.W. Dueck and D.M. Miller (Eds.): RC 2013, LNCS 7948, pp. 209–220, 2013.

received significant attention as a viable and futuristic technology to address these issues.

For low-power design, reversible logic offers interesting advantages since almost zero power dissipation will only be possible if computation is reversible [1, 2]. Also in the domain of low-power on-chip interconnect encoding promising solutions can be achieved when exploiting reversible computations [3]. Besides that, research on reversible circuits has been further strengthened by recent accomplishments in the domain of quantum computation [4], since the basic quantum operations are reversible in nature.

Consequently, the development of approaches for synthesis and optimization of reversible circuits received significant attention in the past (see e.g. [5–8]). The problem is thereby significantly different from that of conventional logic circuits – in particular, since established concepts such as fan-out and feedback are not directly allowed in reversible circuits [4]. Because of the complexity of the problem, most of the approaches generate sub-optimal netlists of reversible gates. Hence, there is an ample scope for post-synthesis optimization.

Approaches addressing this issue have already been introduced. More precisely, techniques such as template matching [9] or window optimization [10] have been presented. But they relied on a gate library composed of multiple-control Toffoli (MCT) gates with positive control lines. Instead, additionally considering negative control lines often leads to reductions in the number of gates and quantum cost. However, while the functional power of negative control lines has already been exploited in synthesis, this has hardly been considered in post-synthesis optimization of reversible circuits so far.

In this paper, we address this issue. We are presenting an optimization scheme inspired by template matching which explicitly makes use of negative control lines. That is, so-called templates (generalized to rules) are introduced that allow for a substitution of a cascade of (positively controlled) Toffoli gates with a single but functional equivalent (negatively controlled) Toffoli gate. Rules for both, positive and negative controlled Toffoli gates, have thereby been proposed. Experimental evaluations demonstrate that exploiting negative control lines in fact leads to a reduction in the number of gates and the quantum costs by up to 60% and 25%, respectively.

The rest of the paper is organized as follows. Section 2 gives a brief introduction to reversible circuits followed by the general motivation of the work in Section 3. The proposed optimization approach is discussed in Section 4. Section 5 presents and discusses the obtained results followed by conclusions in Section 6.

2   Reversible Functions and Circuits

A Boolean function $f : \mathbb{B}^n \to \mathbb{B}^n$ is *reversible* if it is bijective, i.e. if each input pattern is uniquely mapped to a corresponding output pattern. The *synthesis problem* is defined as the task of determining a reversible circuit for a given function f.

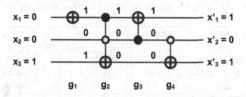

Fig. 1. Reversible Circuit

Reversible circuits differ from conventional circuits, since e.g. fanout and feedback are not directly allowed [4]. Usually, they are built as a cascade of reversible gates, like the Toffoli gate [11] or the Fredkin gate [12]. In this paper, we focus on circuits composed of multiple-control Toffoli (MCT) gates.

Definition 1. *Let $X = \{x_1, \ldots, x_n\}$ be a set of variables or lines. Then, a reversible circuit is described as a cascade $g_1 \ldots g_d$. A multiple control Toffoli (MCT) gate $g_i = (C_i, t_i)$, $i \in \{1, \ldots, d\}$, is a tuple of a set $C_i \subset \{x^\varrho \mid x \in X, \varrho \in \{-, +\}\}$ of (positive and negative) control lines and a target line $t_i \in X$ with $\{t_i^-, t_i^+\} \cap C_i = \emptyset$. The target line t_i of a Toffoli gate is inverted if and only if all positive (negative) control lines evaluate to one (zero). The values of all remaining lines are passed through the gate unaltered. That is, the Toffoli gate maps $(x_1, \ldots, x_{t_i}, \ldots, x_r)$ to $(x_1, \ldots, \bigwedge_{x \in C_i} \dot{x} \oplus x_{t_i}, \ldots, x_r)$ with $\dot{x} = x$ for any x^+ and $\dot{x} = \overline{x}$ for any x^-.*

Example 1. Fig. 1 shows a reversible circuit with three lines and composed of four gates. The target lines are denoted by $\oplus$, while a • represents a positive control line and a ∘ represents a negative control line. For example, assigning the input pattern 001 to the circuit results in the output pattern 101. Due to the reversibility, this computation can be performed in both directions.

In order to evaluate the *costs* of a reversible circuit, the following two metrics are applied:

- The *gate count* (GC) denotes the number of MCT gates in the final netlist.
- The *quantum costs* (QC) denote the effort needed to transform a reversible circuit to a quantum circuit based on the principles proposed in [13]. For positively controlled Toffoli gates, we apply thereby the metric as used in *RevKit* [14]. If negative control lines occur, the same cost metric is applied except for the case where the Toffoli gate is entirely composed of negative controls. In this special case, the costs are increased by one for this particular gate [15].

3   Motivation and General Idea

Synthesis and optimization of reversible circuits received significant attention in the past. For this purpose, various approaches have been introduced (see e.g. [5–8]). The majority of them relied thereby on a gate library exclusively composed

Table 1. All 3-input negative and positive gate realizations

Toffoli Gate Netlist	GC	QC	Equivalent Netlist Netlist	GC	QC	Toffoli Gate Netlist	GC	QC	Equivalent Netlist Netlist	GC	QC
(circuit)	1	6	(circuit)	4	8	(circuit)	1	5	(circuit)	2	6
(circuit)	1	6	(circuit)	4	8	(circuit)	1	2	(circuit)	2	2
(circuit)	1	6	(circuit)	4	8	(circuit)	1	2	(circuit)	2	2
(circuit)	1	5	(circuit)	2	6	(circuit)	1	2	(circuit)	2	2
(circuit)	1	5	(circuit)	2	6	(circuit)	1	2	(circuit)	2	2
(circuit)	1	5	(circuit)	2	6	(circuit)	1	2	(circuit)	2	2
(circuit)	1	5	(circuit)	2	6	(circuit)	1	2	(circuit)	2	2
(circuit)	1	5	(circuit)	2	6						

of MCT gates with positive control lines only. However, if negative control lines are additionally considered, significant reductions with respect to the number of gates as well as the resulting quantum costs can be achieved.

As an example, consider Table 1 showing the pictorial representation of all the possible 3-input Toffoli gates with negative-control lines together with the corresponding *minimal* realizations composed of (positively controlled) Toffoli gates only[1]. Columns denoted by GC and QC provide the number of gates and quantum costs, respectively. The table clearly shows that a consideration of negative control lines allows for a significantly more compact realization of reversible functionality with respect to both, number of gates and quantum costs.

However, despite these benefits, the exploitation of negative control lines for circuit optimization has hardly been considered yet. Although synthesis and optimization approaches which create circuits composed of negatively controlled Toffoli gates already exist (e.g. ESOP-based synthesis [16–18] or QMDD-based synthesis [19]), they often just exploited the structure of the respective function representation. More precisely, in ESOP-based synthesis, negative control lines are just applied as they allow for a straight-forward realization of negative literals. In QMDD-based synthesis, negative control lines have been utilized in order to address negatively controlled paths in the data-structure.

---

[1] Note that the minimal realizations have been obtained using the exact synthesis methods proposed in [7].

Just recently, first approaches have been presented that directly considered negative control lines in order to obtain more efficient circuit realizations. For example, in [20] an exact synthesis approach was proposed that enabled the determination of minimal realizations for small functions. In [21], a group theory-based synthesis approach has been proposed that uses both, negative and positive control lines for synthesis. The results show that, compared to previous approaches, significant reductions in gate count and quantum costs can be achieved directly at the synthesis level.

In this work, we propose an alternative approach that addresses the post-synthesis stage. That is, an optimization approach is presented that explicitly aims for a reduction in the number of gates and the quantum costs of reversible circuits by exploiting the functional power of negative control lines. The general idea for our rules is motivated by Table 1. A careful analysis of the depicted cascades unveils that certainly structured cascades of positively controlled Toffoli gates often subsume into a single negatively controlled Toffoli gate. For example, a cascade of Toffoli gates with all possible combinations of positive control connections can be subsumed into a single Toffoli gate with negative control lines only (see first row in Table 1). Similar observations can be made for the remaining cases in Table 1. By analyzing these patterns, we have formulated *generalized* rules which can be applied in order to reduce the number of gates and the quantum costs for given circuit realizations. In the next section, these rules as well as the resulting optimization approach are described in detail.

4   Proposed Optimization Approach

In this section, we present an approach for optimizing a given MCT gate netlist using certain rules consisting of both positive and negative control lines. As mentioned above, the design of the rules is motivated by an analysis of all possible 3-input negative control gates and the corresponding minimum realizations with positive control gates (see again Table 1). In the following, first the derived rules are presented before the resulting optimization algorithm is sketched and briefly discussed.

4.1   Proposed Templates and Rules

Table 2 presents the proposed rules in terms of the templates together with the equivalent minimal netlists that can be used to replace them. Rules can be applied to cascades of Toffoli gates composed of a different number of lines as denoted in Column n, with certain target line connections as denoted in Column *Targ.L.*, and a total size of gates as denoted on Column GC (for gate count). Besides that, the additional requirements as denoted in Column *Requirement* must hold. If all these conditions are satisfied, the considered cascade can be replaced by a more efficient alternative as described in Column *Replace Template by*. Examples illustrating the application of these rules are provided in Table 3.

More precisely, the templates corresponding to rules R1 and R2 can be applied to any cascade composed of 2^{k-1} k-input gates, where all possible combinations of (positive/negative) control line patterns are present. Rules R3 and R4 can be considered as extensions to rules R1 and R2, respectively, where the gate with all control dots has reverse dot polarity as compared to the other gates in the template. For cases in which not an exact but a partial match of the rules R1, R2, R3 or R4 can be determined, rule R5 can be applied (as long as this leads to a reduction in the quantum cost). Rule R6 is a simple rule where two CNOT gates of opposite control polarities are combined into a single NOT gate. Rule R7 can be applied to reduce NOT gates in any MCT gate netlist.

The rules are general and, except for R6, can be applied to cascades of MCT gates with an arbitrary number k number of lines.

Table 2. The generalized templates and their rules for application

	n	Targ.L.	GC	REQUIREMENT	REPLACE TEMPLATE BY
		TEMPLATE SPECIFICATION			
R1	k	All on line x	2^{k-1}	Positive control dots appear in all 2^{k-1} possible ways, in lines other than x	One k-input MCT gate, with target on line x, and negative controls on all other lines
R2	k	All on line x	2^{k-1}	Negative control dots appear in all 2^{k-1} possible ways, in lines other than x	One k-input MCT gate, with target on line x, and positive controls on all other lines
R3	k	All on line x	2^{k-1}	One gate with all negative control dots, and other gates having all other possible combinations of positive control dots, in lines other than x	One k-input MCT gate, with target on line x, and positive controls on all other lines
R4	k	All on line x	2^{k-1}	One gate with all positive control dots, and other gates having all other possible combinations of negative control dots, in lines other than x	One k-input MCT gate, with target on line x, and negative controls on all other lines
R5	k	All on line x	$r < 2^{k-1}$	Unique combinations of the control dots appear in the gates (*as per rules R1, R2, R3, R4*)	One k-input MCT gate with all positive (or negative) controls, and the remaining $(2^{k-1} - r)$ MCT gates with the missing unique patterns of control dots
R6	2	All on line x	2	One CNOT gate with negative control dot and one CNOT gate with positive control dot	One NOT gate on line x
R7	k	No restriction	No restriction	Two NOT gates on a line y, with no target placed on line y in any of the gates in between	Remove the NOT gates and complement the polarities of all control dots on line y between the two NOT gates

Table 3. Example application of the rules

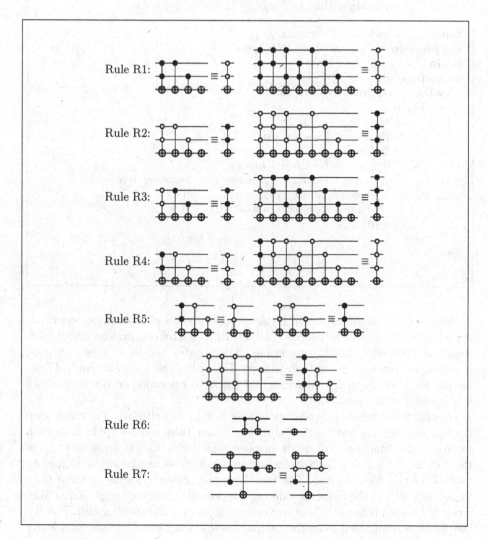

4.2   Algorithm

Using the rules introduced above, the proposed optimization approach traverses the given reversible circuit and checks for any possible application of rules R1-R7. This procedure is iterated until no further reduction is possible. This is because, the application of a rule may change a netlist in such a way that a subsequent application of rules is possible in a next iteration. For instance, if the initial netlist consists of positive control MCT gates only, then just rules R1, R5 or R7 can be applied during the first iteration. However, some negative control gates may get added to the netlist during the process, so that also the other rules may become applicable in the subsequent iterations.

Algorithm 1. *Template Matching Algorithm*

Input: Cascade of MCT gates $G = \{g_1, g_2, \ldots, g_p\}$
Output: Optimized cascade of MCT gates
begin
   $ngates = p$;
   while (there is change in G) **do**
      begin
         $index = 1$;
         while ($index \leq ngates$) **do**
            begin
               $G_{seg} = find\_seg(G, index)$;
               $apply\_rule(G_{seg})$;   // Using gate swapping, if required
               $index = index + |G_{seg}|$;
               $ngates = compact\_netlist(G)$;
            end
      end
end

Besides that, the order in which the respective gates of a template occur in a circuit does not matter as long as the lines with control connections are disjoint from the lines with target connections. Then, gates can be swapped without changing the function of the (sub-)circuit. This is because values on control lines are not modified by such a structure and the XOR operation on the target lines is commutative in general.

Overall, this leads to a procedure as sketched in Algorithm 1. The outer loop iterates through the gate netlist until no further rules can be applied. In each iteration, the function *find_seg* is invoked which identifies a segment G_{seg} in the gate netlist starting from *index* within which gates can be swapped (i.e. no control dots on the outputs). The function *apply_rule* checks the segment G_{seg} for applicability of the rules, considering the possible gate swappings, and applies a rule if a match is found. The iteration continues over the entire netlist. Finally, the netlist is compacted using the *compact_netlist* function. The time complexity of every iteration is linear in the number of gates.

The application of the algorithm is illustrated by the following example:

Example 2. Consider the reversible circuit depicted in the top-left corner of Fig. 2. In a first step, the NOT gates at the two top lines can obviously been removed. They only affect the positive control lines of the sixth and seventh gate which can simply be replaced by corresponding negative lines according to R7. Afterwards, the first three gates can be replaced by a smaller cascade according to R5, while R2 allows for the reduction of the last two gates. Finally, R2 allows for another reduction eventually leading to the circuit as shown in the bottom-right corner of Fig. 2. By this, the number of gates is reduced from 9 to 2 while the quantum costs are reduced from 17 to 11.

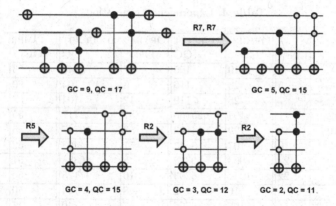

Fig. 2. Application of the proposed optimization

Due to the generic fashion of the rules, the approach described above can be applied to arbitrary circuits, i.e. realizations obtained by various synthesis approaches. However, our evaluations showed that the proposed methodology is particularly suited for circuits derived by ESOP-based synthesis [16–18]. Here, the targets lines are usually assumed to be placed on certain output lines, while control lines are usually placed on the separate input lines. By this, patterns as the ones from R1-R7 occur frequently.

5   Experimental Evaluation

This section provides experimental results for the proposed approach. To this end, the method and the rules described above have been implemented in C on top of *RevKit* [14] and applied to benchmarks circuits from the *RevLib* reversible logic website [22]. All experiments have been conducted on a Pentium dual-core desktop system with 4 GB of main memory running Ubuntu version 11.10.

Table 4 provides the results. The first columns denote thereby the name of the respective benchmark circuits (denoted by CIRCUIT) together with its number of lines (denoted by LINES). Afterwards, the gate count (denoted by GC) and the quantum costs (denoted by QC) of the original circuit as well as the optimized circuits are provided. Finally, the last columns show the percentage improvement with respect to the gate count and the quantum costs. *All* results have been determined in less than one CPU second. Because of this, a detailed listing of the run-time for the respective benchmarks is omitted.

The results clearly show the effect of the proposed rules to the size of the corresponding circuits. Improvements of almost up to two-third can be achieved. Even for large circuits composed of more than 1,000 gates a reduction of half the number of gates can be observed (see e.g. *alu4_201* or *tial_265*). Considering that these results have been generated in almost no run-time, this represents a worthwhile achievement. Similar template matching algorithms such as the one proposed in [9] usually require significantly more computation time and lead to a smaller reduction.

Table 4. Experimental evaluation

		Original circuit		Optimized circuit		Impr. (%)	
Circuit	Lines	GC	QC	GC	QC	GC	QC
sf_274	5	19	155	7	143	63	8
rd32_273	5	20	116	8	104	60	10
rd53_131	7	28	119	12	104	57	13
sym10_262	11	194	25866	87	22717	55	12
9symml_195	10	129	14193	58	12747	55	10
max46_240	10	107	5444	51	4498	52	17
alu4_201	22	1063	55388	523	46388	51	16
tial_265	22	1041	56203	516	47125	50	16
sf_276	5	16	152	8	144	50	5
life_238	10	107	6766	57	5740	47	15
f51m_233	22	663	37400	358	33316	46	11
sf_275	5	11	51	6	42	45	18
example2_231	16	157	5654	87	4767	45	16
mux_246	22	35	1078	20	804	43	25
ham15_298	45	153	309	100	290	35	6
mlp4_245	16	131	3753	93	3531	29	6
cm150a_210	22	53	1096	38	822	28	25
in0_235	26	338	20031	245	18988	28	5
dc2_222	15	75	1886	55	1777	27	6
f2_232	8	19	255	14	238	26	7
rd73_252	10	80	1143	60	1066	25	7

All results have been determined in less than one CPU second.

Moreover, also the resulting quantum costs of the circuits can considerably been reduced. Here, improvements of up to 25% (e.g. for *mux_246*) are reported – in many cases we see reductions of 10-20%. Note that alternative synthesis approaches such as the one proposed in [20] indeed reduced the number of gates using negative control lines, but were not able to reflect this improvement to the quantum costs. In fact, quantum costs increased in the results shown in [20]. Using the approach proposed in this paper, we achieve substantial improvements with respect to both, number of gates and quantum costs. Besides that, determining better mappings of Toffoli circuits including negative control lines is subject to ongoing research (see e.g. [23, 24]). Thus, we expect better mappings and accordingly better quantum costs here.

6   Conclusions

In this work, we presented a post-synthesis optimization approach for reversible circuits which explicitly exploits the functional power of negative control lines. For this purpose, we analyzed that certain structured cascades of positively controlled Toffoli gates often subsume into a single negatively controlled Toffoli gate. Based on these observations, generalized rules have been derived which are applied in order to reduce the size of the given circuits. An experimental evaluation confirmed that the proposed approach leads to substantial reductions in both, the number of gates as well as the quantum costs. As a future work better gate reordering and template matching mechanism can be implemented to provide further reduction in gate count and quantum cost.

References

1. Landauer, R.: Irreversibility and heat generation in computing process. Journal of IBM Research and Development 5, 183–191 (1961)
2. Bennett, C.H.: Logical reversibility of computation. Journal of IBM Research and Development 17, 525–532 (1973)
3. Wille, R., Drechsler, R., Oswald, C., Garcia-Ortiz, A.: Automatic design of low-power encoders using reversible circuit synthesis. In: Design Automation Test in Europe, pp. 208–212 (2012)
4. Nielsen, M., Chuang, I.: Quantum Computation and Quantum Information. Cambridge University Press (2000)
5. Maslov, D., Dueck, G.W., Miller, D.M.: Techniques for the synthesis of reversible Tofolli networks. ACM Trans. on Design Automation of Electronic Systems 12(4), 42.1–42.28 (2007)
6. Wille, R., Drechsler, R.: BDD-based synthesis of reversible logic for large functions. In: Design Automation Conference, pp. 270–275 (2009)
7. Grosse, D., Wille, R., Dueck, G.W., Drechsler, R.: Exact multiple control Toffoli network synthesis with SAT techniques. IEEE Trans. on CAD of Integrated Circuits and Systems 28(5), 703–715 (2009)
8. Datta, K., Rathi, G., Sengupta, I., Rahaman, H.: Synthesis of reversible circuits using heuristic search method. In: Intl. Conference on VLSI Design, pp. 328–333 (2012)
9. Maslov, D., Dueck, G.W., Miller, D.M.: Toffoli network synthesis with templates. IEEE Trans. on CAD of Integrated Circuits and Systems 24(6), 807–817 (2005)
10. Soeken, M., Wille, R., Dueck, G.W., Drechsler, R.: Window optimization of reversible and quantum circuits. In: Symposium on Design and Diagnostics of Electronic Circuits and Systems, pp. 341–345 (2010)
11. Toffoli, T.: Reversible computing. In: de Bakker, J., van Leeuwen, J. (eds.) Automata, Languages and Programming. LNCS, vol. 85, pp. 632–644. Springer, Heidelberg (1980)
12. Fredkin, E., Toffoli, T.: Conservative logic. Inernational Journal of Theoretical Physics 21, 219–253 (1982)
13. Barenco, A., Bennett, H.H., Cleve, R., DiVinchenzo, D.P., Margolus, N., Shor, P., Sleator, T., Smolin, J.A., Weinfurter, H.: Elementary gates for quantum computation. Physical Review A (Atomic, Molecular, and Optical Physics) 52(5), 3457–3467 (1995)
14. Soeken, M., Frehse, S., Wille, R., Drechsler, R.: RevKit: An open source toolkit for the design of reversible circuits. In: De Vos, A., Wille, R. (eds.) RC 2011. LNCS, vol. 7165, pp. 64–76. Springer, Heidelberg (2012)
15. Michael Miller, D., Sasanian, Z.: Recent developments on mapping reversible circuits to quantum gate libraries. In: Int'l Symposium on Electronic System Design, ISED (December 2012)

16. Fazel, K., Thornton, M.A., Rice, J.E.: ESOP-based Toffoli gate cascade generation. In: Pacific Rim Conference on Communications, Computers and Signal Processing, pp. 206–209 (2007)

17. Sanaee, Y., Dueck, G.W.: ESOP-based Toffoli network generation with transformations. In: Intl. Symposium on Multiple-Valued Logic, pp. 276–281 (2010)

18. Drechsler, R., Finder, A., Wille, R.: Improving ESOP-based synthesis of reversible logic using evolutionary algorithms. In: Di Chio, C., et al. (eds.) EvoApplications 2011, Part II. LNCS, vol. 6625, pp. 151–161. Springer, Heidelberg (2011)

19. Soeken, M., Wille, R., Hilken, C., Przigoda, N., Drechsler, R.: Synthesis of reversible circuits with minimal lines for large functions. In: Asia and South Pacific Design Automation Conference, pp. 85–92 (2012)

20. Wille, R., Soeken, M., Przigoda, N., Drechsler, R.: Exact synthesis of Toffoli gate circuits with negative control lines. In: Intl. Symposium on Multi-valued Logic (ISMVL), pp. 69–74 (2012)

21. Datta, K., Sengupta, I., Rahaman, H.: Group theory based reversible logic synthesis. In: International Conference on Computers and Devices for Communication, CODEC (December 2012)

22. Wille, R., Grosse, D., Teuber, L., Dueck, G.W., Drechsler, R.: Revlib: An online resource for reversible functions and reversible circuits. In: Intl Symp. on Multi-Valued Logic, pp. 220–225 (2008)

23. Moraga, C.: Hybrid Reed Muller – de Morgan expressions for reversible computing circuits. In: Workshop on Reversible Computing (RC), pp. 155–162 (July 2011)

24. Sasanian, Z., Wille, R., Miller, M.: Realizing reversible circuits using a new class of quantum gates. In: Design Automation Conference 2012, pp. 36–41 (2012)

Reducing the Depth of Quantum Circuits Using Additional Circuit Lines

Nabila Abdessaied[1], Robert Wille[1,2], Mathias Soeken[1,2], and Rolf Drechsler[1,2]

[1] Institute of Computer Science, University of Bremen
Group of Computer Architecture, D-28359 Bremen, Germany
[2] Cyber-Physical Systems, DFKI GmbH
D-28359 Bremen, Germany
{nabila,rwille,msoeken,drechsle}@informatik.uni-bremen.de

Abstract. The synthesis of Boolean functions, as they are found in many quantum algorithms, is usually conducted in two steps. First, the function is realized in terms of a reversible circuit followed by a mapping into a corresponding quantum realization. During this process, the number of lines and the quantum costs of the resulting circuits have mainly been considered as optimization objectives thus far. However, beyond that also the depth of a quantum circuit is vital. Although first synthesis approaches that consider depth have recently been introduced, the majority of design methods did not consider this metric.

In this paper, we introduce an optimization approach aiming for the reduction of depth in the process of mapping a reversible circuit into a quantum circuit. For this purpose, we present an improved (local) mapping of single gates as well as a (global) optimization scheme considering the whole circuit. In both cases, we incorporate the idea of exploiting additional circuit lines which are used in order to split a chain of serial gates. Our optimization techniques enable a concurrent application of gates which significantly reduces the depth of the circuit. Experiments show that reductions of approx. 40% on average can be achieved when following this scheme.

1 Introduction

Quantum computation has become an active research field due to its promising results for important tasks such as factorization or database search. Motivated by this, researchers have developed several synthesis approaches [1–5]. Many quantum algorithms are often described by means of a structured quantum circuit in which only the representation of Boolean components differs. Hence, for the synthesis of these components into quantum circuits, usually a two-step approach is applied: First, the desired Boolean functionality is realized as a reversible circuit only consisting of reversible gates which is afterwards mapped to an equivalent realization based on quantum gates. For this purpose, mapping schemes as introduced e.g. in [6, 15] are applied.

In this flow, minimizing the number of lines and the quantum costs have been considered as the major optimization objectives thus far. However, beyond that

G.W. Dueck and D.M. Miller (Eds.): RC 2013, LNCS 7948, pp. 221–233, 2013.

also the depth of the circuit is vital. Depth optimization techniques consider the concurrent application of single gates in order to reduce the overall execution time of the circuit realization.

While first approaches for synthesis with respect to depth have recently been introduced (see e.g. [7–11]), the vast majority of design methods does not consider this metric. As an example in [7, 11], a cycle representation was chosen and input cycles where partitioned into three subsets. Each subset is synthesized independently on a different set of ancillae in parallel. This method requires $2n$ additional lines and focuses only on reducing the depth of reversible circuit rather than the quantum circuit. This is crucial since the execution times for two reversible gates can differ significantly when taking the respective quantum circuit mapping into account. As a consequence, even a depth-optimal reversible circuit likely leads to a quantum circuit with non-optimal depth. Another post-synthesis approach has been presented in [8]. However, their approach makes use of a special class of templates. Finally, the work presented in [10] describes an exhaustive algorithm aiming to find a minimal depth quantum circuit using a special gate library. However, due to its exponential time complexity, it is only applicable to circuits with a small number of qubits.

In this paper, we present an idea on how depth of quantum circuits can be reduced by adding an additional line to the circuit. Based on this idea, two depth optimization approaches are presented. The first method aims to reduce the depth by applying the reduction gate-per-gate, whereas the second method focuses on the whole circuit. An experimental evaluation of both approaches shows that a significant improvement of depth can be achieved for quantum circuits.

The remainder of this paper is structured as follows. The next section briefly introduces reversible and quantum circuits. Depth metrics and the general idea are presented in Sect. 3. Afterwards, both proposed approaches are described and evaluated in Sect. 4 and Sect. 5, respectively. Finally, Sect. 6 concludes the paper.

2 Background

To keep the remainder of this paper self-contained, this section briefly introduces the basics on reversible circuits, quantum circuits, and the corresponding mapping from reversible to quantum circuits.

2.1 Reversible Circuits

Boolean reversible functions are those functions $f : \mathbb{B}^n \to \mathbb{B}^n$ that are bijective, i.e. there exists an 1-to-1 mapping from the inputs to the outputs and vice versa. Reversible functions can be realized by reversible circuits that consist of at least n lines. Reversible circuits are cascades of reversible gates that belong to a gate library. One gate library that is often used consists of multiple control Toffoli gates [12].

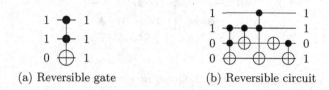

(a) Reversible gate   (b) Reversible circuit

Fig. 1. Reversible circuitry

Definition 1. *Given a set of variables* $\mathcal{V} = \{x_1, \ldots, x_n\}$, *a multiple control Toffoli gate* $T(C, t)$ *has control lines* $C = \{x_{j_1}, x_{j_2}, \ldots, x_{j_l}\} \subset \mathcal{V}$ *and a target line* $t \in \mathcal{V} \setminus C$. *The gate maps* $t \mapsto t \oplus (x_{j_1} \wedge x_{j_2} \wedge \cdots \wedge x_{j_l})$ *and leaves all other lines unaltered. In the special cases* $|C| = 0$ *and* $|C| = |\{c\}| = 1$, *the gates are referred to as* NOT *and* CNOT *gate and denoted* $N(t)$ *and* $C(c, t)$, *respectively.*

In [13], it has been shown that any reversible function $f : \mathbb{B}^n \to \mathbb{B}^n$ can be realized by a reversible circuit with n lines when using Toffoli gates.

Example 1. Figure 1(a) shows a Toffoli gate with two control lines. The control lines are denoted by ●, while the target line is denoted by ⊕. The annotated values demonstrate the computation of the gate for a given input assignment. Figure 1(b) shows different Toffoli gates in a cascade forming a reversible circuit.

2.2 Quantum Boolean Circuits

Instead of bits, quantum circuits manipulate qubits which can represent the classical Boolean values but also the superposition of them. More precisely, a *qubit* $|\varphi\rangle$ is a vector $\binom{a}{b}$ where $a, b \in \mathbb{C}$ such that $|a|^2 + |b|^2 = 1$. If $a = 1$, then $|\varphi\rangle$ represents the classical 0, denoted $|0\rangle$, and if $b = 1$, then $|\varphi\rangle$ represents the classical 1, denoted $|1\rangle$.

In general, a quantum gate acting on n qubits represents a $2^n \times 2^n$ unitary matrix [14], where a matrix U is unitary if $U^\dagger U = UU^\dagger = I$ and $U^\dagger$ is the adjoint matrix $U^\dagger = U^{*^T}$. Using this gate definition, many quantum mechanical effects such as superposition and entanglement can be formulated. However, in the scope of this paper we are considering circuits that realize pure Boolean functionality but still need to be realized using quantum gates in order to embed them into quantum algorithms such as Deutsch-Josza, Grover, or Shor. Toffoli gates represent a unitary matrix and are hence suitable for realizing quantum Boolean circuits. However, with respect to the actual physical implementation, it is of interest to obtain circuits that make use of gates from a library with only a few elements [6]. For the present paper, we are making use of a common gate library consisting of four quantum gates that only change one qubit at a time and is defined as follows.

Definition 2. *A quantum gate* $U(C, t)$ *applies the unitary* 2×2 *matrix to the qubit that corresponds to the* target line t, *if and only if all control lines* C *are*

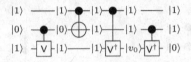

Fig. 2. Quantum circuitry

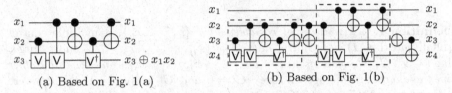

(a) Based on Fig. 1(a)   (b) Based on Fig. 1(b)

Fig. 3. Mapping reversible circuits to quantum circuits

assigned 1. *We consider a gate library* $X(\{\}, t)$, $X(\{c\}, t)$, $V(\{c\}, t)$, *and* $V^\dagger(\{c\}, t)$ *with* $X = \begin{pmatrix} 0 & 1 \\ 1 & 0 \end{pmatrix}$, $VV = X$, *and* $V^\dagger$ *being the adjoint of* V.

Note that $X(\{\}, t) = N(t)$ and $X(\{c\}, t) = C(c, t)$. The gate library is often referred to as NCV library.

Example 2. Figure 2 depicts a quantum circuit consisting of four gates, where $|v_0\rangle = V^\dagger |1\rangle = V|0\rangle$.

2.3 Mapping Reversible Circuits to Quantum Circuits

Since any quantum operation can be represented by a unitary matrix [14], each quantum circuit is inherently reversible. As discussed above, when reversible circuits should be represented as a quantum circuit, the Toffoli gates are too general and, thus, not suitable for a realization. As a consequence, reversible circuits are mapped to quantum circuits that only consists of gates of a particular gate library, e.g. the NCV library. For this purpose, each gate of the reversible circuit is *mapped* into a cascade of functionally equivalent quantum gates.

Example 3. Consider a Toffoli gate with two control lines as shown in Fig. 1(a). A functionally equivalent realization in terms of quantum gates is depicted in Fig. 3(a). This cascade can be applied to fully map the reversible circuit shown in Fig. 1(b) into an equivalent quantum circuit. For this purpose, all corresponding Toffoli gates are respectively substituted with a corresponding quantum gate cascade. The 2nd, 4th, and 5th gate remain unchanged as they already represent quantum gates. The resulting fully equivalent quantum circuit is shown in Fig. 3(b).

Similar mappings exist for Toffoli gates with more than two control lines. But with increasing number of control lines, the resulting quantum circuits become more expensive, i.e. require more quantum gates. The currently best known mappings of single Toffoli gates into quantum cascades have been introduced in [15]. In this work, we are following the mappings introduced there. As single quantum gates are assumed to have unit costs, the number of gates of the resulting cascades usually is referred to as *quantum costs*.

3   Reducing the Depth of Quantum Circuits

In this work, we are proposing optimization approaches aiming for a reduction of the depth in quantum circuits using additional circuit lines. This section first motivates the consideration of depth in quantum circuits, whereas the general idea of the proposed approaches is outlined afterwards.

3.1   Consideration of Depth in Quantum Circuits

Thus far, the major optimization objectives for synthesis have been the number of lines and the quantum costs of the resulting circuits as reviewed above. However, beyond that also the *depth* of a quantum circuit is vital. This metric recognizes whether gates can concurrently be applied which likely leads to a reduction in the execution time of a circuit.

Definition 3. *Let $U_i(C_i, t_i)$ and $U_{i+1}(C_{i+1}, t_{j+1})$ be two consecutive quantum gates. These gates can be applied* concurrently *if*

$$|C_i \cup C_{i+1} \cup \{t_i, t_{i+1}\}| = |C_i| + |C_{i+1}| + 2.$$

In other words, if the lines used by each gate (both control and target line) are disjoint. Let G be a quantum circuit with k elementary quantum gates, then G can be partitioned into $m \leq k$ subcircuits whose gates can be pairwise applied concurrently. We refer to the minimal m as the depth *of the circuit.*

Algorithm D (*Determine Circuit Depth*). Given a quantum circuit $G = U_1(C_1, t_1) \ldots U_k(C_k, t_k)$ over n variables $x_1, \ldots, x_n$. This algorithm determines the depth m of the circuit according to Definition 3 by applying a greedy search to gates that can be executed in parallel. For the computation, we are making use of the integers $b_1, \ldots, b_n$.

D1. [Initialize.] Set $m \leftarrow 1$, $i \leftarrow 1$, and $b_j \leftarrow 0$ for $1 \leq j \leq n$.

D2. [Terminate?] If $i > k$, terminate.

D3. [Apply gate.] For each $x_j \in C_i \cup \{t_i\}$, set $b_j \leftarrow b_j + 1$.

D4. [Gates do not overlap?] If there exists no $j \in \{1, \ldots, n\}$ such that $b_j = 2$, set $i \leftarrow i + 1$ and goto Step D2.

D5. [Gates overlap.] For each $j \in \{1, \ldots, n\}$, set $b_j \leftarrow 1$, if $x_j \in C_i \cup \{t_i\}$, otherwise set $b_j \leftarrow 0$; set $m \leftarrow m + 1$, $i \leftarrow i + 1$, and goto Step D2.   ∎

Example 4. Figure 4 illustrates the depth for the reversible circuit shown in Fig. 1(b).

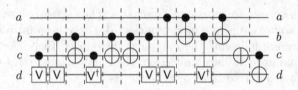

Fig. 4. Quantum depth for the reversible circuit shown in Fig. 1(b)

Although the *coherence time*, i.e. the time a qubit can keep its quantum state, and the *gate operation time*, i.e. the time a gate needs to perform its operation, may vary from one technology to another (see e.g. Table III of [16]), keeping the overall execution time as small as possible is essential in all these cases. Consequently, the depth metric can be applied in a generic manner, as it provides a proper model which can be considered already at the synthesis stage in the absence of precise technological constraints. Despite the fact that quantum algorithms already exploit algorithmic parallelism to increase the processing speed, synthesis approaches should aim for producing circuits with at least as possible circuit depth.

Motivated by this, we are considering the question how the depth of a quantum circuit can be reduced in the remainder of this paper. For this purpose, we are making use of additional circuit lines as motivated in the following.

3.2 Exploiting Additional Circuit Lines

Keeping the number of circuit lines as small as possible is well accepted in the synthesis of quantum circuits. This is mainly motivated by the fact that each circuit line has to be represented by a qubit, which is a very limited resource. Nevertheless, evaluations also showed that a (slight) extension of a circuit with additional lines may have significant benefits. For example in [6, 15], it has been demonstrated that a larger amount of circuit lines allow for a much cheaper mapping of reversible circuits to quantum circuits in terms of gate count. In [3], evaluations showed that using twice the number of circuit lines reduces the quantum costs by up to two orders of magnitude. Eventually, this led to a post-synthesis optimization approach [17] which enables reductions in quantum costs of up to 69% only by adding a single additional line to the circuit.

In this work, we show that similar concepts also help in reducing the depth of quantum circuits. We are following the established synthesis flow reviewed in Sect. 2.3, i.e. first a reversible circuit is realized which afterwards is mapped to a quantum circuit. However, by incorporating additional lines during this process, a depth-aware optimization becomes possible. The additional circuit lines are introduced as *helper lines*.

Definition 4. *Let G be a reversible or quantum circuit. A* helper line *is an additional line whose input is set to a constant* 0 *and is used in a way throughout the circuit such that the output of the line is also* 0.

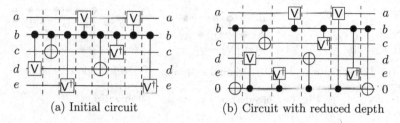

(a) Initial circuit   (b) Circuit with reduced depth

Fig. 5. Depth reduction by using additional helper lines

Following the concept from [17], helper lines can now be applied in order to "buffer" values of circuit lines so that they can be re-used later by other gates. Whenever the current value of a helper line h is 0, another signal line x can be copied to h by appending a *copy gate* $C(\{x\}, h)$ to the circuit. The helper line can be restored with the same gate if no other gate has used h as target line in between.

In [17], this buffering has been exploited to remove common control lines connections between Toffoli gates in order to reduce the quantum cost. However, the same concept can similarly be applied to reduce the depth of quantum circuits as illustrated by the following example.

Example 5. Figure 5(a) shows a circuit in which no gates can be performed in parallel since they all share the same control line b. In Fig. 5(b) a helper line has been added to copy the value of b. By doing this, the gates can be rearranged which reduces the depth from 8 to 6.

Clearly, Example 5 presents a rather artificial circuit. However, based on this general idea we are proposing different optimization approaches whose evaluations show that indeed a significant reduction of depth in quantum circuits can be achieved.

4   Optimization Approaches

Motivated by the general idea outlined above, two optimization approaches are proposed in this section which aim for reducing the depth by exploiting additional circuit lines. The first approach follows a local scheme, i.e. considers each Toffoli gate independently, where the second approach considers the whole circuit instead. Finally, techniques are presented to further reduce the depth and the quantum costs which can be applied to the resulting quantum cascades.

4.1   Consideration of Single Toffoli Gates

The availability of a helper line as introduced in the previous section allows for an improvement of the mapping scheme reviewed in Sect. 2.3. Recall that, when

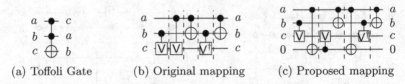

(a) Toffoli Gate   (b) Original mapping   (c) Proposed mapping

Fig. 6. Consideration of single Toffoli gates

following the default mapping scheme, each Toffoli gate is mapped to a quantum realization of depth 5 as shown in Fig. 6(b). However, as the second and the third gate share the same control line, an additional helper line allows for a concurrent execution of both gates as shown in Fig. 6(c). Since additionally the copy gates can be inserted without increasing the depth, a depth reduction for the quantum circuit realization for each Toffoli gate from 5 to 4 can be obtained.

Example 6. Consider again the reversible circuit from Fig. 1(b). Using the established mapping scheme from Sect. 2.3, a quantum circuit with depth 12 results (as shown in Fig. 3(b); none of the gates except for the single NOT gate can be executed concurrently). In contrast, applying the additional helper line as proposed in Fig. 6, the circuit depicted in Fig. 7(a) results. This reduces the depth from 12 to 9.

Note that this procedure can also be applied to Toffoli gates with more than two control lines. In fact, state-of-the-art mapping schemes (such as described in [15]) decompose these gates into cascades of two-controlled Toffoli gates. For them, the depth-optimized mapping to quantum gates as proposed in Fig. 6 can be applied. Moreover, the same scheme can be applied to other reversible gates such as the Peres gate as well.

This scheme is not beneficial in all cases. In fact, if concurrent Toffoli gates are mapped to a quantum circuit, the original mapping leads to better results. This is illustrated by means of Fig. 8. Applying the original mapping scheme to the two Toffoli gates shown in Fig. 8(a) leads to the quantum cascade as shown in Fig. 8(b). As both Toffoli gates are applied concurrently, also the resulting quantum gate cascades can be applied concurrently, i.e. a depth of 5 results. Applying the proposed scheme from Fig. 6 would worsen the result. In fact, the helper line together with the required copy gates would increase the depth to 7 as shown in Fig. 8(c).

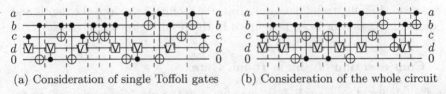

(a) Consideration of single Toffoli gates   (b) Consideration of the whole circuit

Fig. 7. Application of the proposed approaches to the circuit from Fig. 1(b)

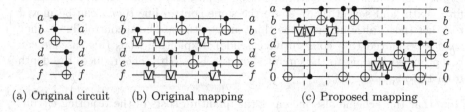

(a) Original circuit   (b) Original mapping   (c) Proposed mapping

Fig. 8. Application of the local scheme to concurrent Toffoli gates

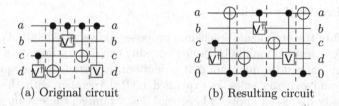

(a) Original circuit   (b) Resulting circuit

Fig. 9. Consideration of the whole circuit

Consequently, this scheme is only applied in cases where an actual depth improvement can be achieved. However, experiments summarized in Sect. 5 clearly confirm that substantial improvements with respect to the depth can still be achieved. As a drawback, this obviously comes with the price of increased quantum costs in the resulting cascade. But also here, experiments show the resulting increase to be moderate.

4.2   Consideration of the Whole Circuit

While so far the helper line has been exploited in a local context, also a global consideration turns out to be beneficial. The idea is to identify subcircuits of gates sharing the same control line and use the helper line in order to partition the gates. Then, each consecutive pair of gates in such a cascade can concurrently be executed by using the original control line for the first gate and the copied value at the helper line for the second gate.

Example 7. Figure 9(a) shows a quantum circuit composed of gates that share the same control lines. Using the helper line, an equivalent realization as shown in Fig. 9(b) can be derived. This reduces the depth from 5 to 4.

This scheme can additionally be improved by applying the *moving rule* for quantum circuits. In fact, two adjacent gates $U(C_1, t_1)$ and $U(C_2, t_2)$ can be interchanged if $t_2 \notin C_1$ and $t_1 \notin C_2 \cap \{t_1\} = \emptyset$. As a result, gates can be moved through the circuit which might lead to larger subcircuits of gates sharing the same control line. In this case, a more substantial reduction can be achieved.

Example 8. Consider again the quantum circuit shown in Fig. 4. The second, fifth, sixth, and seventh gate share the same control line *b and* can be moved together (note, although also the third and tenth gate have control line *b*, they cannot be moved to a consecutive cascade). Exploiting that, this cascade can be optimized leading to the circuit shown in Fig. 7(b). This reduces the depth from 12 to 9.

Note that this scheme also increases the quantum costs of the resulting circuit. However, since for each identified subcircuit only two copy gates have to be added, the increase is almost negligible.

4.3   Further Optimizations

Independent of the optimization schemes proposed above, the depth of quantum gate cascades can additionally be improved using existing optimization schemes that originally aimed for quantum cost reduction. In particular, the application of merging and deletion rules as explained in [18] together with the moving rule as already discussed above is beneficial. For example, the circuit shown in Fig. 7(b) (obtained using existing mapping schemes) obviously can be improved by removing the fifth and the sixth gate which cancel each other. This reduces the quantum costs but also improves the depth of the circuit. Accordingly, such simple optimizations are also applied in our approach. For the experimental evaluation summarized in Sect. 5, the methods exploiting additional helper lines are applied to circuits already optimized using moving, merging, and deletion rule.

5   Experimental Results

In order to confirm the efficiency of the proposed idea, the approaches described above have been implemented and experimentally evaluated. For this purpose, the open source toolkit *RevKit* [19] has been applied and benchmarks have been taken from the *RevLib* [20] database. All experiments have been conducted on an Intel Core i5 Processor with 4 GB of main memory. In this section, we summarize and discuss the obtained results.

Table 1 provides the obtained numbers. For all benchmarks listed in the first column, the number of lines (*Lines*), the quantum costs (*Costs*), and the depth (*Depth*) of the respective circuit realizations as well as the run-time (*Time*) needed to generate them are provided. We distinguish between the following circuits:

- INITIAL CIRCUITS (IC) represent the circuits as taken from *RevLib* and mapped to quantum circuits as described in Sect. 2.3, i.e. without any depth optimization whatsoever.
- OPTIMIZED CIRCUITS (OC) represent the circuits that have additionally been optimized using the straightforward techniques reviewed in Sect. 4.3.

Table 1. Experimental evaluation

Benchmark	Initial Circuits				Optimized Circuits (Sect. 4.3, +0 line)				Local (Sect. 4.1, +1 line)					Global (Sect. 4.2, +1 line)				
	Lines	Cost	Depth	Time	Cost	Depth	Time	Imprc	Cost	Depth	Time	Imprc	Improc	Cost	Depth	Time	Imprc	Improc
ex5p_296	206	1843	1584	0,00	1578	1352	46,95	15%	1775	303	181,48	81%	78%	1578	226	139,92	86%	83%
hwb9_304	170	2275	1916	0,01	1853	1624	77,71	15%	2144	424	410,64	78%	74%	1853	305	313,58	84%	81%
c2_181	35	368	280	0,00	344	262	0,04	6%	378	71	0,73	75%	73%	344	71	0,66	75%	73%
hwb8_303	112	1461	1226	0,01	1202	1049	20,88	14%	1410	294	116,59	76%	72%	1202	212	89,21	83%	80%
hwb7_302	73	909	769	0,01	754	658	4,09	14%	898	222	34,28	71%	66%	754	167	28,44	78%	75%
bw_291	87	943	788	0,01	782	681	5,26	14%	932	230	29,11	71%	66%	782	189	21,47	76%	72%
hwb6_301	46	507	426	0,00	432	376	0,67	12%	507	136	5,79	68%	64%	432	109	4,42	74%	71%
add64_184	193	768	642	0,00	642	516	0,23	20%	770	197	10,06	69%	62%	642	198	5,99	69%	62%
add32_183	97	384	322	0,00	322	260	0,06	19%	386	101	1,35	69%	61%	322	102	0,85	68%	61%
add16_174	49	192	162	0,00	162	132	0,02	19%	194	53	0,19	67%	60%	162	54	0,14	67%	59%
ham15_298	45	309	279	0,00	242	209	0,51	25%	282	84	1,35	70%	60%	242	77	1,22	72%	63%
add8_172	25	96	82	0,00	82	68	0,00	17%	98	29	0,03	65%	57%	82	30	0,03	63%	56%
hwb5_300	28	276	237	0,00	237	208	0,11	12%	289	92	1,15	61%	56%	237	83	0,95	65%	60%
mod5adder_306	32	292	252	0,00	249	219	0,17	13%	292	97	1,80	62%	56%	249	77	1,55	69%	65%
rd73_312	25	217	186	0,00	180	158	0,08	15%	206	71	0,80	62%	55%	182	63	0,73	66%	60%
rd84_313	34	304	258	0,00	247	218	0,30	16%	295	99	2,65	62%	55%	247	71	1,79	72%	67%
e64-bdd_295	195	907	748	0,01	779	620	3,00	17%	973	322	58,58	57%	48%	779	323	57,99	57%	48%
cnt3-5_179	16	65	56	0,00	62	53	0,00	5%	71	28	0,03	50%	47%	62	34	0,04	39%	36%
ham7_299	21	141	124	0,00	111	96	0,03	23%	144	56	0,14	55%	42%	111	49	0,12	60%	49%
mod5d2_70	5	16	14	0,00	15	13	0,00	7%	18	10	0,00	29%	23%	15	9	0,00	36%	31%
urf2_277	8	7521	6750	0,04	7172	6390	10,19	5%	7885	4998	347,74	26%	22%	7244	4832	330,03	28%	24%
4mod5-v0_18	5	25	24	0,00	16	14	0,00	42%	22	11	0,00	54%	21%	16	9	0,00	63%	36%
aryy6_256	17	5593	5491	0,03	4873	4810	20,36	12%	5197	3963	517,14	28%	18%	4949	3877	647,55	29%	19%
alu3_200	18	3387	3322	0,01	2970	2926	8,19	12%	3170	2413	262,46	27%	18%	2982	2363	319,25	29%	19%
Average Improvement								15%				60%	52%				63%	56%

Both, the initial circuits and optimized circuits, allow for a comparison to the circuits obtained by the proposed techniques, namely:

- Circuits that have been obtained by using the optimization scheme that considers single Toffoli gates (LOCAL) as described in Sect. 4.1.
- Circuits that have been obtained by using the optimization scheme that considers the whole circuit (GLOBAL) as described in Sect. 4.2.

The percentage depth-improvement of the circuits obtained by the proposed techniques with respect to the initial circuit and the optimized circuits are provided in the columns denoted by $Impr_{IC}$ and $Impr_{OC}$, respectively.

First of all, it can be observed that already the naive approaches reviewed in Sect. 4.3 lead to significant improvements (15% on average and up to 42% in the best case for *4mod5-v0_18*). However, exploiting additional circuit lines enables further improvements which are factors beyond that. In the best case (*ex5p_296*), depth can be reduced from 1352 to 303 (using the local approach from Sect. 4.1) or 226 (using the global approach from Sect. 4.2). But also for the other benchmarks substantial reductions can be observed, even compared to the already optimized circuits.

As discussed above, these improvements in the depth may come at the price of higher quantum costs. As our evaluations show, this particularly holds for the local consideration of single Toffoli gates (see columns denoted LOCAL). Here, quantum costs increase by 18% on average compared to the already optimized circuit. However, for the global scheme, no such disadvantages can be observed. In fact, quantum costs remain unchanged here (see columns denoted GLOBAL).

Overall, even compared to already optimized circuits, improvements of more than 50% on average can be achieved. If the global scheme is applied, these achievements are possible without the need to accept an increase in the quantum costs. This is made possible by the addition of a single circuit line. Although this eventually results in the consideration of another qubit to be physically realized, the possible benefits with respect to timing and particularly decoherence time might be worth the overhead.

6   Conclusion

In this paper, depth optimization by adding a helper line to quantum circuits has been introduced and evaluated. Two approaches, namely gate based and circuit based, have been considered. Experimental results for the two methods have shown significant depth reductions which reaches over 50% for quantum circuits. Although these methods increase quantum cost, applying further improvements to the quantum circuits have fixed the problem.

References

1. Fazel, K., Thornton, M., Rice, J.: ESOP-based toffoli gate cascade generation. In: Pacific Rim Conference on Communications, Computers and Signal Processing, PacRim 2007, pp. 206–209 (2007)

2. Miller, D.M., Maslov, D., Dueck, G.W.: A transformation based algorithm for reversible logic synthesis. In: Design Automation Conf., pp. 318–323 (2003)

3. Wille, R., Drechsler, R.: BDD-based synthesis of reversible logic for large functions. In: Design Automation Conf., pp. 270–275 (2009)

4. Soeken, M., Wille, R., Otterstedt, C., Drechsler, R.: A synthesis flow for sequential reversible circuits. In: Int'l Symposium on Multiple-Valued Logic, pp. 299–304 (2012)

5. Soeken, M., Wille, R., Hilken, C., Przigoda, N., Drechsler, R.: Synthesis of reversible circuits with minimal lines for large functions. In: ASP Design Automation Conf., pp. 85–92 (2012)

6. Barenco, A., Bennett, C.H., Cleve, R., DiVinchenzo, D., Margolus, N., Shor, P., Sleator, T., Smolin, J., Weinfurter, H.: Elementary gates for quantum computation. The American Physical Society 52, 3457–3467 (1995)

7. Arabzadeh, M., Saheb Zamani, M., Sedighi, M., Saeedi, M.: Depth-optimized reversible circuit synthesis. Quantum Information Processing, 1–23 (2012)

8. Maslov, D., Dueck, G., Miller, D., Negrevergne, C.: Quantum circuit simplification and level compaction. Transactions on Computer-Aided Design of Integrated Circuits and Systems 27(3), 436–444 (2008)

9. Bocharov, A., Svore, K.M.: A depth-optimal canonical form for single-qubit quantum circuits arXiv preprint arXiv:1206.3223 (2012)

10. Amy, M., Maslov, D., Mosca, M., Roetteler, M.: A meet-in-the-middle algorithm for fast synthesis of depth-optimal quantum circuits arXiv preprint arXiv:1206.0758 (2012)

11. Arabzadeh, M., Zamani, M., Sedighi, M., Saeedi, M.: Logical-depth-oriented reversible logic synthesis. In: Int'l Workshop on Logic and Synthesis (2011)

12. Toffoli, T.: Reversible computing. In: de Bakker, J., van Leeuwen, J. (eds.) Automata, Languages and Programming. LNCS, vol. 85, pp. 632–644. Springer, Heidelberg (1980)

13. Shende, V.V., Prasad, A.K., Markov, I.L., Hayes, J.P.: Synthesis of reversible logic circuits. Transactions on Computer-Aided Design of Integrated Circuits and Systems 22(6), 710–722 (2003)

14. Nielsen, M., Chuang, I.: Quantum Computation and Quantum Information. Cambridge Univ. Press (2000)

15. Miller, D.M., Wille, R., Sasanian, Z.: Elementary quantum gate realizations for multiple-control Toffolli gates. In: Int'l Symp. on Multi-Valued Logic, pp. 217–222 (May 2011)

16. Meter, R.V., Oskin, M.: Architectural implications of quantum computing technologies. J. Emerg. Technol. Comput. Syst. 2(1), 31–63 (2006)

17. Miller, D.M., Wille, R., Drechsler, R.: Reducing reversible circuit cost by adding lines. In: Int'l Symp. on Multi-Valued Logic, pp. 217–222 (2010)

18. Zahra, S.: Technology Mapping and Optimization for Reversible and Quantum. PhD thesis, University of Victoria (2012)

19. Soeken, M., Frehse, S., Wille, R., Drechsler, R.: Revkit: an open source toolkit for the design of reversible circuits. In: De Vos, A., Wille, R. (eds.) RC 2011. LNCS, vol. 7165, pp. 64–76. Springer, Heidelberg (2012), RevKit is available at http://www.revkit.org

20. Wille, R., Große, D., Teuber, L., Dueck, G.W., Drechsler, R.: RevLib: an online resource for reversible functions and reversible circuits. In: Int'l Symp. on Multi-Valued Logic, pp. 220–225 (2008), RevLib is available at http://www.revlib.org

Quantum Process Calculus
for Linear Optical Quantum Computing

Sonja Franke-Arnold[1], Simon J. Gay[2], and Ittoop V. Puthoor[1,2,*]

[1] School of Physics and Astronomy and
[2] School of Computing Science,
University of Glasgow, UK

Abstract. We extend quantum process calculus in order to describe linear optical elements. In all previous work on quantum process calculus a qubit was considered as the information encoded within a 2 dimensional Hilbert space describing the internal states of a localised particle, most often realised as polarisation information of a single photon. We extend quantum process calculus by allowing multiple particles as information carriers, described by Fock states. We also consider the transfer of information from one particular qubit realisation (polarisation) to another (path encoding), and describe post-selection. This allows us for the first time to describe linear optical quantum computing (LOQC) in terms of quantum process calculus. We illustrate this approach by presenting a model of an LOQC CNOT gate.

Keywords: Formal methods, quantum computing, linear optics, semantics, quantum process calculus.

1 Introduction

Quantum information processing (QIP) is a well established field of research which offers high potential in computation, communication and quantum key distribution [1]. It provides reasonable improvements in the efficiency of performing certain computations. Secure quantum communication systems using quantum key distribution (QKD) are now commercially available [2,3]. Optical implementations offer to date the most advanced system for QIP, and photons naturally allow to integrate quantum computation and quantum communication. Photons can easily be generated, manipulated and detected and they also possess large coherence times which makes them suitable for computation and communications. Linear optical quantum computing (LOQC) is one potential way for implementing small-scale quantum computing [4]. The computation is based on *spatial encoding* where a quantum bit is represented by two optical or spatial modes containing a single photon. Precise manipulation of the quantum information inscribed in the internal (polarisation) and external (path) states

---

* Supported by a Lord Kelvin / Adam Smith Scholarship from the University of Glasgow.

G.W. Dueck and D.M. Miller (Eds.): RC 2013, LNCS 7948, pp. 234–246, 2013.

of a photon are routinely achieved using linear optical elements [5]. Recently it has been shown that quantum optical circuits can be miniaturized using optical fibre and integrated waveguide circuits [6]. In order to ensure that the QIP systems are reliable, there is now the requirement to develop techniques and tools for formal modelling and analysis of quantum communication and cryptographic systems.

The field of *formal methods* has been a successful approach in the analysis of classical systems. *Formal methods* provide us with the necessary theories and tools to develop and verify systems in a systematic manner. The success of this field for classical computation provided the main motivation to develop quantum formal methods. One line of research in quantum formal methods, based on process calculus, referred to as *quantum process calculus*, is used to describe and analyse the behaviour of systems that arise from the combination of quantum and classical computation and communication.

Our own approach is based on a particular quantum process calculus called Communicating Quantum Processes (CQP), developed by Gay and Nagarajan [7]. Modelling in CQP provides us an abstract view of the quantum system. Our aim is to model realistic (non-ideal) systems and the associated experimental processes. CQP assumes that a qubit is a *localised* unit of information. This view works well with QKD but not with LOQC as it cannot describe *spatial encoding*. In this paper we extend CQP in order to model LOQC. We illustrate this by defining various linear optical elements such as beam splitters and phase shifters in CQP and by modelling an LOQC CNOT gate. *Post-selection* plays an important role in LOQC, where one considers only a subset of all experimental runs that fulfil predefined criteria, e.g. given by the desired number of detected photons in particular channels. Therefore the computation succeeds with a certain probability, and with the complementary probability it is aborted with no result. We describe post-selection in CQP by modelling a linear optic CNOT gate.

The rest of the paper is organised as follows. In Section 2 we recall the basic concepts of quantum optics which are needed to understand LOQC. We review the language of CQP in Section 3 and illustrate it by defining the linear optical elements in CQP. With the help of our definitions, we present a model of the LOQC CNOT gate in Section 4 and describe the post-selection process. Section 5 provides a brief summary of the extension of the syntax and semantics of CQP that are required to describe LOQC. We provide the labelled transition rules and illustrate a few of them with some examples. Finally, Section 6 concludes with an indication of directions for future work.

Related Work: All the quantum process calculi which have been established so far considered qubits as a unit of information that could be sent or received through channels. Lalire and Jorrand developed a quantum process calculus called QPAlg [8] and Feng *et al.* [9] developed qCCS, a quantum extension of the classical value-passing CCS [10]. The present paper extends CQP, for the first time, to describe details of an experimental realisation of quantum computing.

2   Preliminaries

The fundamental unit of QIP is a *quantum bit* or a *qubit*. A *qubit* is a physical system which is the quantum analogue of a classical bit. It is associated with a complex *Hilbert space* $\mathbb{H}$, called its *state space*, which is a 2-dimensional vector space over the complex numbers, $\mathbb{C}$ with a basis denoted by $\{|0\rangle_q, |1\rangle_q\}$ that is called the *standard* basis. The state space of a qubit therefore consists of all *superpositions* of the basis states: $|\psi\rangle = \alpha|0\rangle_q + \beta|1\rangle_q$ where $\alpha, \beta \in \mathbb{C}$ are complex amplitudes such that $|\alpha|^2 + |\beta|^2 = 1$. The states can be represented by column vectors:

$$\begin{pmatrix} \alpha \\ \beta \end{pmatrix} = \alpha \begin{pmatrix} 1 \\ 0 \end{pmatrix} + \beta \begin{pmatrix} 0 \\ 1 \end{pmatrix} = \alpha|0\rangle_q + \beta|1\rangle_q$$

When the two basis states represent the polarisation state of a photon ($|0\rangle_q = |H\rangle$ and $|1\rangle_q = |V\rangle$), we refer to the qubit as a polarisation qubit where H and V are horizontal and vertical polarisations of the photon respectively. An individual photon can encode a single qubit. We introduce the notation $\alpha|H\rangle + \beta|V\rangle = \alpha|10\rangle_{HV} + \beta|01\rangle_{HV}$, where the entries in the ket states represent the number of photons in the state basis indicated by the subscripts. This will allow us to generalise the notation to more than one photon. Two photons in the states $\alpha_i|H\rangle + \beta_i|V\rangle$ (where i is 1,2 respectively for each photon) can then be encoded in the shorthand $\alpha_1\alpha_2|20\rangle_{HV} + \beta_1\beta_2|02\rangle_{HV} + (\alpha_1\beta_2 + \alpha_2\beta_1)|11\rangle_{HV}$, if they are indistinguishable in all other parameters. In LOQC [4], we consider qubits which are encoded in different optical paths 'a' and 'b' rather than different polarisation states. This is referred to as *dual rail logic*. Again, we denote the quantum states in the number state basis, giving the number of photons travelling along the different paths. The basis states in dual rail logic are then $|0\rangle_q \rightarrow |1\rangle_a|0\rangle_b$, and similarly for $|1\rangle_q \rightarrow |0\rangle_a|1\rangle_b$.

In experiments, the conversion of a *polarisation* qubit into a *dual rail* qubit is accomplished by the combination of a polarising beam splitter (PBS) and a phase shifter (PR) as shown in Figure 1(a). The PBS has two input ports and two output ports, where the unused input port is denoted by X. The superposition of $|H\rangle$ and $|V\rangle$ is converted into a superposition of paths a and b. The PBS therefore links polarisation information with path information. A subsequent phase shifter rotates the polarisation of the vertical output by $90°$ so that the components of the dual rail qubit are indistinguishable in their polarisations and can interfere [5]. The combination of a PBS and phase shifter, works as a unitary operation PS which converts a polarisation encoded qubit into a dual rail encoded qubit.

Definition 1 (PS operator) *A* PS *is an operator that transforms a polarisation qubit* $|\psi\rangle \in \mathbb{H}_1$ *to a dual rail qubit* $|\phi\rangle \in \mathbb{H}_2$ *represented by spatial modes* (a, b). *The action of* PS *is defined by*

$$\mathsf{PS}|Y\rangle \equiv \mathsf{PS}|nm\rangle_{HV} = |nm\rangle_{ab}$$

where n *and* $m \in \{0, 1\}$ *and* $n = m \oplus 1$ *and* $Y \in \{H, V\}$.

The evolution of a closed quantum system can be described by *unitary transformations*. In LOQC, optical elements such as phase shifters and beam splitters generate the evolutions. The total photon number is preserved by these transformations. If the state of a qubit is represented by a column vector then a unitary transformation U can be represented by a matrix.

Operations on number states or *Fock states* ($|n\rangle$) are described in terms of the creation and annihilation operators $\hat{a}^\dagger$ and $\hat{a}$, which when acting on a state $|n\rangle$ increase or decrease the photon number (n) by one. Therefore, each Fock state can be built up from creation operators given by $|n\rangle = \frac{(\hat{a}^\dagger)^n}{\sqrt{n!}}|0\rangle$. A unitary transformation in LOQC [11] can be described by its effect on each mode's creation operator. A phase shifter (PR) is given by the unitary transformation $U(PR) : |n\rangle \to e^{in\phi}|n\rangle$ and a non polarising beam splitter (BS) is defined by the transformation matrix

$$U(BS) = \begin{pmatrix} \cos\theta & e^{i\phi}\sin\theta \\ e^{-i\phi}\sin\theta & -\cos\theta \end{pmatrix}.$$

The reflectivity of BS is given by $\eta = \cos^2\theta$, where $\cos\theta$ and $\sin\theta$ are the probability amplitudes and ϕ is the relative phase. Here we consider $\phi = 0$, which is the case for BSs in integrated circuits. If we consider the state $|mn\rangle_{ab}$ incident on a beam splitter with m photons along path a and n photons along path b, the transformation is:

$$\begin{aligned}|mn\rangle_{ab} = \frac{(\hat{a}_a^\dagger)^m}{\sqrt{m!}}\frac{(\hat{a}_b^\dagger)^n}{\sqrt{n!}}|00\rangle_{ab} \to \\ \frac{1}{\sqrt{m!n!}}(\hat{a}_a^\dagger\cos\theta + \hat{a}_b^\dagger\sin\theta)^m(\hat{a}_a^\dagger\sin\theta - \hat{a}_b^\dagger\cos\theta)^n|00\rangle_{ab}.\end{aligned} \tag{1}$$

Figure 1(b) provides a description of the LOQC CNOT gate [5]. The BSs used in this CNOT gate have reflectivities of $\frac{1}{2}$ or $\frac{1}{3}$. The theory and operation of the gate is provided in [12] and we summarise it here. Consider the general input state

$$|\phi\rangle = (\alpha|HH\rangle + \beta|HV\rangle + \gamma|VH\rangle + \delta|VV\rangle)|00\rangle, \tag{2}$$

where the ordering in the kets is $|c_0 c_1 t_0 t_1\rangle|x_0 x_1\rangle$. Here c_0, c_1 are the number states for the control qubit, t_0, t_1 are for the target qubit and x_0, x_1 are the vacuum states and we use the shorthand $|1010\rangle = |HH\rangle$, etc., where appropriate. Using the operators as discussed in Eq. 1 and applying it to the input state, Eq. 2 we get the number of photons in the respective output ports ($C_{1,out}, C_{0,out}, T_{1,out}, T_{0,out}, X_{1,out}$ and $X_{0,out}$) of the CNOT gate as shown in Figure 1.

$$\begin{aligned}|\phi\rangle_{out} = \tfrac{1}{3}\{(\alpha|HH\rangle + \beta|HV\rangle + \gamma|VV\rangle + \delta|VH\rangle)|00\rangle + \sqrt{2}(\alpha+\beta)|0100\rangle|10\rangle + \\ \sqrt{2}(\alpha-\beta)|0000\rangle|11\rangle + (\alpha+\beta)|1100\rangle|00\rangle + (\alpha-\beta)|1000\rangle|01\rangle + \sqrt{2}\alpha|0010\rangle|10\rangle + \\ \sqrt{2}\beta|0001\rangle|10\rangle - \sqrt{2}(\gamma+\delta)|0200\rangle|00\rangle - (\gamma-\delta)|0100\rangle|01\rangle + \sqrt{2}\gamma|0020\rangle|00\rangle \\ + (\gamma-\delta)|0010\rangle|01\rangle + (\gamma+\delta)|0011\rangle|00\rangle + (\gamma-\delta)|0001\rangle|01\rangle + \sqrt{2}\delta|0002\rangle|00\rangle\}.\end{aligned} \tag{3}$$

From these states we post-select only those where one photon is found in the target and one in the control state, giving

$$|\phi\rangle_{ps} = \alpha|HH\rangle + \beta|HV\rangle + \gamma|VV\rangle + \delta|VH\rangle. \tag{4}$$

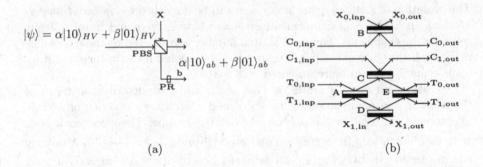

(a)   (b)

Fig. 1. (a) Conversion of a polarisation qubit to a spatially encoded qubit, which is given as input to the LOQC CNOT gate shown in (b). (b) A sign change occurs upon reflection of the optically thicker side (indicated in black) of the BSs. A and E are BSs of reflectivity $\frac{1}{2}$ and the rest (B,C,D) are of reflectivity $\frac{1}{3}$. X indicates that the respective input port of the PBS or BS is not used and the photons coming out of output ports $X_{1,out}$ and $X_{0,out}$ are not considered. $C_{0,inp}, C_{1,inp}$ are the control (C) input ports and $T_{0,inp}, T_{1,inp}$ are the target (T) input ports. The output ports are $C_{0,out}, C_{1,out}, T_{0,out}, T_{1,out}$.

This occurs with a probability of one-ninth and the relationship between Eq. 2 and Eq. 4 is a controlled-NOT transformation.

3   Defining Linear Optical Elements in CQP

CQP [7] is a quantum process calculus, which was developed for formally defining the structure and behaviour of systems that are a combination of both quantum and classical communication and computation. The language is based on the π-calculus [13,14] with primitives for quantum information. The general idea is that a system is considered to be made up of independent components or *processes*. The *processes* can communicate by sending and receiving data along *channels* and these data are qubits or classical values. A distinctive feature of CQP is its static type system [15], the purpose of which is to classify classical and quantum data and also to enforce the no-cloning property of quantum information. The concept of *behavioural equivalence* between processes, which provides a formal description of the idea of observational indistinguishability, has been defined in CQP [16] and applied to the analysis of a quantum error correcting code [17]. We will now define the elements used in the LOQC CNOT gate, in an extension of CQP which will be formally defined in Section 5.

We have seen in Section 2 that the combination of a PBS and PR converts a polarisation qubit to a dual rail qubit as shown in Figure 1. We define the combination as a process *PolSe* which provides the input to the LOQC CNOT gate.

$$PolSe(a{:}^\frown[\mathsf{Qbit}], c{:}^\frown[\mathsf{NS}], d{:}^\frown[\mathsf{NS}]) = a?[q_0{:}\mathsf{Qbit}] . [(s_0{:}\mathsf{NS}, s_1{:}\mathsf{NS}) *= \mathsf{PS}(q_0)]$$
$$. c![s_0] . d![s_1] . \mathbf{0}$$

PolSe is parameterized by three channels, a, c and d. The polarisation qubit (say q_0) is received through channel a whose type is $\hat{\ }[\mathsf{Qbit}]$. The qubit q_0 will be encoded in terms of the number of photons (s_0 and s_1) travelling along channels c and d respectively.

The right hand side of the definition specifies the behaviour of the process *PolSe*. The first term, $a?[q_0:\mathsf{Qbit}]$ specifies that the qubit is received from channel a and given the local name q_0. The following sequence of terms, separated by dots, indicate temporal sequencing. The term $[(s_0:\mathsf{NS}, s_1:\mathsf{NS}) *= \mathsf{PS}(q_0)]$ specifies that the PS operation is applied to qubit q_0 thereby generating s_0 and s_1 of type number states (NS). PS corresponds to the transformation produced by the combination of PBS and PR, introduced by Definition 1. The last two terms ($c![s_0]$ and $d![s_1]$) indicate that the respective values of the number states are sent through the respective output channels. The term $\mathbf{0}$ simply indicates termination.

The CQP definition of the beam splitter BS is

$$BS(e:\hat{\ }[\mathsf{NS}], f:\hat{\ }[\mathsf{NS}], h:\hat{\ }[\mathsf{NS}], i:\hat{\ }[\mathsf{NS}], \eta) = e?[s_2:\mathsf{NS}] \cdot f?[s_3:\mathsf{NS}] \cdot \{s_2, s_3 *= \mathsf{B}_\eta\} \cdot$$
$$h![s_2] \cdot i![s_3] \cdot \mathbf{0}$$

where η is the reflectivity. Process BS has input channels e and f, and output channels h and i, all of type $\hat{\ }[\mathsf{NS}]$. After receiving inputs s_2 and s_3 from e and f, the unitary operation of BS represented by $\{s_2, s_3 *= \mathsf{B}_\eta\}$ is carried out on the input number states as defined by Eq. 1. Here B_η is the unitary operation represented by the matrix $U(BS)$ for $\phi = 0$. The number states are then output on h and i.

Finally, we define the process *Det* which encapsulates measurement of a number state as a detector component. This will be used for the post-selecting measurement of the outputs of the CNOT gate.

$$Det(l:\hat{\ }[\mathsf{NS}], u:\hat{\ }[\mathsf{Val}]) = l?[s_0:\mathsf{NS}] \cdot u![\mathsf{measure}\ s_0] \cdot \mathbf{0}$$

The expression $\mathsf{measure}\ s_0$ probabilistically evaluates to a positive integer which is the number of photons detected.

4   The LOQC CNOT Gate in CQP

The structure of the system is shown in Figure 2. The system receives two polarisation qubits (control and target) as inputs through the channels a and b. The qubits are then converted to number states by the process $PolSe_{CT}$, and these are provided as the input to the CNOT gate represented by process $CNOT$. The output of $CNOT$ is then *post-selected* by the process PSM. We demonstrate this by removing the unsuccessful outcomes of the gate and recording a coincidence count for every successful outcome. The output of the system are the classical values of the CNOT gate output for which a coincidence count is obtained. The whole system is then defined as a parallel composition of $PolSe_{CT} | CNOT | PSM$,

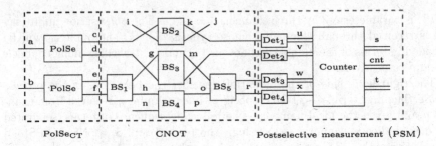

Fig. 2. Model of LOQC CNOT gate: The dashed lines enclose the subsystems which are defined in the text

which is indicated by the vertical bar (|). It means that the processes can proceed simultaneously and interact with each other, and the CQP definition of the system is

$$System(a, b, s, t, cnt) = (\text{new } c, d, e, f, g, h, i, j, k, l, m, n, o, p, u, v, w, x, q, r)$$
$$(PolSe_{CT}(a, b, c, d, e, f) \mid CNOT(c, d, e, f, i, j, n, j, k, l, p, q, r)\mid$$
$$PSM(k, l, q, r, s, t, cnt))$$

where the channels (a,b) are of type $\widehat{\ }[\text{Qbit}]$, channels $(c, \ldots, r)$ are of type $\widehat{\ }[\text{NS}]$, channels $(s, \ldots, x)$ are of type $\widehat{\ }[\text{Val}]$ and the channel cnt is of type $\widehat{\ }[\text{Bit}]$. The scope of the channels is restricted, indicated by new in the definition. We have omitted the types from our definitions, for brevity. Each process is parameterised by the channels on which it interacts with other processes.

$PolSe_{CT}$ represents the conversion of the control and target qubits from polarisation encoding to spatial encoding or number states given by the definition:

$$PolSe_{CT}(a, b, c, d, e, f) = PolSe(a, c, d) \mid PolSe(b, e, f)$$

Recall from Section 3 that $PolSe$ represents the combination of a PBS and PR. The number states are then provided as inputs to the CNOT gate.

The CNOT gate, represented by the process $CNOT$, is a combination of five beam splitters. Each BS is represented by a process BS and is annotated to show the correspondence with Figure 2. The process $CNOT$ consists of all BSs in parallel. BS_2 and BS_3 have their inputs crossed over, corresponding to their orientation in Figure 1(b). Vacuum states y and z (which means absence of a photon) are created by (ns y, z) and communicated to BS_2 and BS_4 respectively through the channels i and n. The CQP definition of $CNOT$ is:

$$CNOT(c, d, e, f, i, n, j, k, l, p, q, r) = (\text{new } g, h, m, o)(\text{ns } y, z)(BS_1(e, f, g, h, \tfrac{1}{2})\mid$$
$$i![y].\mathbf{0} \mid BS_2(i, c, j, k, \tfrac{1}{3}) \mid j?[y:\text{NS}].\mathbf{0} \mid BS_3(d, g, l, m, \tfrac{1}{3}) \mid n![z].\mathbf{0}\mid$$
$$BS_4(h, n, o, p, \tfrac{1}{3}) \mid p?[z:\text{NS}].\mathbf{0} \mid BS_5(m, o, q, r, \tfrac{1}{2}))$$

The parallel composition of processes in $CNOT$ permits interaction between processes. This means that the output on the channels g, h, m and o of the respective processes BS_1, BS_3 and BS_4 synchronises with the input on channels

$T ::= \mathsf{Int} \mid \mathsf{Qbit} \mid \mathsf{NS} \mid \widehat{\,}[\tilde{T}] \mid \mathsf{Op}(1) \mid \mathsf{Op}(2) \mid \cdots$

$v ::= 0 \mid 1 \mid \cdots \mid \mathsf{H} \mid \mathsf{PS} \mid \cdots$

$e ::= v \mid x \mid \mathsf{measure}\ \tilde{e} \mid \tilde{e} \mathbin{*=} e^e \mid e + e$

$P ::= 0 \mid (P|P) \mid P + P \mid e?[\tilde{x} : \tilde{T}].P \mid e![\tilde{e}].P \mid \{e\}.P \mid [e].P \mid (\mathsf{qbit}\ x)P \mid (\mathsf{ns}\ x)P \mid$
$\qquad (\mathsf{new}\ x : \widehat{\,}[T])P$

Fig. 3. Syntax of CQP

g,h,m and o of processes BS_3, BS_4 and BS_5. The outputs (number states) of $CNOT$ are communicated through the channels k, l, q and r, to the process PSM. The unused BS outputs j and p are absorbed by $j?[y : \mathsf{NS}]$ and $p?[z : \mathsf{NS}]$.

$$PSM(k,l,q,r,s,t,cnt) = (\mathsf{new}\ u,v,w,x)(Det_1(k,u) \mid Det_2(l,v) \mid Det_3(q,w) \mid$$
$$Det_4(r,x) \mid Counter(u,,v,w,x,s,t,cnt))$$

PSM performs the *post-selective* measurement. This is achieved with the parallel composition of detectors and a process $Counter$. Detectors Det_1, Det_2, Det_3, Det_4 are annotated to match Figure 2 and measure the number states associated with the control and target qubits. The output of a detector is a classical value which represents the measurement outcome, that is the number of photons detected. The outcomes of the detector processes are given as inputs to the process $Counter$.

$Counter(u,v,w,x,s,t,cnt) = u?[c_0 : \mathsf{Val}] . v?[c_1 : \mathsf{Val}] . w?[t_0 : \mathsf{Val}] . x?[t_1 : \mathsf{Val}] .$
$\quad$ **if** $(c_0 + c_1 = 1$ and $t_0 + t_1 = 1)$ **then** $s![c_1] . t![t_1] . cnt![1] . 0$ **else** $cnt![0] . 0$

$Counter$ is a process which represents the coincidence measurement. Coincidence is observed by detecting two photons, one at channels u or v and the other at w or x. It also provides the correct output of the CNOT gate in terms of classical values through the channels s and t. The output is received only for coincidence. This is determined by the **if ... else** conditions in the definition. When the condition is satisfied, then a count is registered by outputting a value 1 through the channel cnt. If the condition is not satisfied then a value 0 is given as output, which signifies no coincidence and we don't get any values from the channels s and t. Thus, we achieve post-selection in the coincidence basis in our model.

5   Syntax and Semantics of CQP

The intended behaviour of the processes which represent the linear optical elements of the CNOT gate model was described informally in the previous section but in fact the behaviour is precisely specified by the formal semantics of CQP. In this section we will explain the operational semantics of CQP, excluding named process definitions and recursion, which can easily be added. In this paper, our

$$v ::= \ldots \mid q \mid s \mid c$$
$$E ::= [] \mid \text{measure } E, \tilde{e} \mid \text{measure } v, E, \tilde{e} \mid \ldots \mid \text{measure } \tilde{v}, E \mid E + e \mid v + E$$
$$F ::= []?[\tilde{x}].P \mid []![\tilde{e}].P \mid v![[], \tilde{e}].P \mid v![v, [], \tilde{e}].P \mid \cdots \mid v![\tilde{v}, []].P \mid \{[]\}.P$$

Fig. 4. Internal syntax of CQP

focus is to provide the new additions to the previously defined formal syntax and semantics of CQP [16], in order to describe the behaviour of the linear optical CNOT gate.

The syntax of CQP is defined by the grammar as shown in Figure 3. We use the notation $\tilde{e} = e_1, \ldots, e_n$, and write $|\tilde{e}|$ for the length of a tuple. The syntax is similar to the previous version of CQP which consists of types T, values v, expressions e (including quantum measurements and the conditional application of unitary operators $\tilde{e} *= e^e$), and processes P. We have a new type called NS for number state. Values v consist of variables (x, y, z etc), literal values of data types $(0, 1, ..)$, unitary operators such as the Hadamard operator H and PS. Expressions e consist of values, measurements measure $e_1, \ldots, e_n$, applications $e_1, \ldots, e_n *= e$ of unitary operators, and expressions involving data operators such as $e + e'$. Processes include the nil process **0**, parallel composition $P|P$, inputs $e?[\tilde{x} : \tilde{T}].P$, outputs $e![\tilde{e}].P$, actions $\{e\}.P$ (typically a unitary operation or measurement), $[e].P$ (typically for PS operation), typed channel restriction (new $x : \hat{\ }[\tilde{T}])P$, qubit declaration (qbit $x)P$ and number state declaration (ns $x)P$. In order to define the operational semantics we provide the *internal syntax* in Figure 4. Values are supplemented with either qubit names q or number state names s, which are generated at run-time and substituted for the variables used in qbit and ns declarations respectively. Evaluation contexts for expressions ($E[]$) and processes ($F[]$) are used to define the operational semantics [18].

In quantum process calculus such as CQP, the execution of a system is not completely described by the process term (which is the case for classical process calculus) but also depends on the quantum state. Hence the operational semantics are defined using *configurations*, which represent both the quantum state and the process term.

Definition 2 (Configuration) *A configuration is defined as a tuple of the form $(\tilde{x} : \tilde{T}; \sigma; \omega; P)$ where $\tilde{x}$ is a list of names (qubits $\tilde{q}$, number states $\tilde{s}$ or both) associated with their types $\tilde{T}$, σ is a mapping from names ($\tilde{x}$) to the quantum state and ω is a list of names associated with the process P*

We operate with configurations such as

$$(q_1 : \text{Qbit}, s_0 : \text{NS}, s_1 : \text{NS}; [q_1, s_0, s_1 \mapsto (|0\rangle|10\rangle + |1\rangle|01\rangle)]; q_1; c![q_1] . P)$$

We interpret the NS variables as dual-rail representations of qubits, which were in the initial configuration. For example, in this case, s_0 and s_1 represent the original qubit q_0. There is a fixed relationship between the indices of qubits and number state variables: q_i is represented by s_{2i}, s_{2i+1}. There may be additional

$$(\tilde{x} : \tilde{T}; \sigma; \omega; u + v) \longrightarrow_v (\tilde{x} : \tilde{T}; \sigma; \omega; w) \text{if } u \text{ and } v \text{ are integer literals and } w = u + v$$
$$\text{(R-Plus)}$$

$$(\tilde{x} : \tilde{T}; [\tilde{x} \mapsto \sum_{\tilde{s}} \alpha_{\tilde{s}} |\beta\rangle |\gamma\rangle]; \omega; \text{measure } s_r) \longrightarrow_v \qquad \text{(R-Measure-NS)}$$

$$\boxplus_{u>0} p_u \bullet (\tilde{x} : \tilde{T}; [\tilde{x} \mapsto \sum_{\tilde{s}'} \frac{\alpha_{\tilde{s}'}}{p_u} |\beta\rangle |\gamma'\rangle]; \omega; u) \text{ where } p_u = \sum_{\tilde{i}} |\alpha_{\tilde{s}'}|^2,$$

$$\tilde{s} = s_0, \ldots, s_{2n-1}, \tilde{s}' = s_0, \ldots, s_{r-1}, u, s_{r+1}, \ldots, s_{2n-1}, \tilde{i} = s_0, \ldots, s_{r-1}, s_{r+1}, \ldots, s_{2n-1}$$

$$(\tilde{q} : \text{Qbit}, \tilde{s} : \text{NS}; [\tilde{q}, \tilde{s} \mapsto |\beta\rangle |\gamma\rangle]; \omega; s_0, \ldots, s_{2r-1} \mathrel{*\!=} U) \longrightarrow_v \qquad \text{(R-Trans-NS)}$$

$$(\tilde{q} : \text{Qbit}, \tilde{s} : \text{NS}; [\tilde{q}, s_0, \ldots, s_{2n-1} \mapsto |\beta\rangle (U \otimes I_{(n-r)}) |\gamma\rangle]; \omega; \text{unit})$$

$$\frac{(\tilde{x} : \tilde{T}; \sigma; \omega; e) \longrightarrow_v \boxplus_i p_i \bullet (\tilde{x} : \tilde{T}; \sigma_i; \omega_i; e_i)}{(\tilde{x} : \tilde{T}; \sigma; \omega; E[e]) \longrightarrow_e \boxplus_i p_i \bullet (\tilde{x} : \tilde{T}; \sigma_i; \omega_i; E[e_i])} \qquad \text{(R-Context)}$$

Fig. 5. Transition rules for values and expressions

NS variables, introduced by the ns declarations, representing vacuum states. This configuration means that the global quantum state consists of a qubit, q_1, number states s_0 and s_1, in the specified state; that the process term under consideration has access to qubit q_1 but not to the number states; and that the process itself is $c![q_1] . P$.

For the evaluation of expressions we also introduce *expression configurations* $(\tilde{x} : \tilde{T}; \sigma; \omega; e)$, which are similar to configurations, but include an expression in place of the process. The semantics of expressions is defined by the reduction relations $\longrightarrow_v$ (on values) and $\longrightarrow_e$ (on expressions), given in Figure 5. Rules R-Plus, R-Measure-NS and R-Trans-NS deal with the evaluation of terms that result in values, including measurement which produces a probabilistic distribution over the possible measurement outcomes u, and unitary transformations which result in literal unit. R-Trans-NS operate on number states listed first in the state. The important aspect of R-Trans-NS and R-Measure-NS is the effect they have on the quantum state. R-Measure-NS is a rule defined for the measurement of number states. On the right of the rule R-Measure-NS, we have a probabilistic configuration in which the $\boxplus$ ranges over the possible outcomes u of the measurement and the $|\alpha_{\tilde{s}'}|^2$ are the weights of the components of the mixture. The measurement outcomes are classical values which are the number of photons detected.

The semantics of the process calculus is defined by labelled transitions between processes. The transition takes the form $P \xrightarrow{\alpha} P'$ where α is an action that can be classified as either *input*, *output* (representing potential interaction with the environment) or *internal* action (representing a step of internal activity, which may be the result of internal communication). The actions $c?[x], c![x]$ and τ represents input on channel c, output on channel c, and internal action respectively.

$$\boxplus_i p_i \bullet (\tilde{x} : \tilde{T}; \sigma_i; \omega; P_i) \xrightarrow{p_i} (\tilde{x} : \tilde{T}; \sigma_i; \omega; P_i) \qquad \text{(L-Prob)}$$

$$(\tilde{x} : \tilde{T}; \sigma; \omega, \tilde{v}; c![\tilde{v}].P) \xrightarrow{c![\tilde{v}]} (\tilde{x} : \tilde{T}; \sigma; \omega; P) \qquad \text{(L-Out)}$$

$$(\tilde{x} : \tilde{T}; \sigma; \omega; c?[\tilde{y}].Q) \xrightarrow{c?[\tilde{v}]} (\tilde{x} : \tilde{T}; \sigma; \omega, \tilde{v}; Q\{\tilde{v}/\tilde{y}\}) \qquad \text{(L-In)}$$

$$\frac{(\tilde{x} : \tilde{T}; \sigma; \omega, \tilde{v}; P) \xrightarrow{c![\tilde{v}]} (\tilde{x} : \tilde{T}; \sigma; \omega; P') \quad (\tilde{x} : \tilde{T}; \sigma; \omega; Q) \xrightarrow{c?[\tilde{v}]} (\tilde{x} : \tilde{T}; \sigma; \omega; \tilde{y}; Q')}{(\tilde{x} : \tilde{T}; \sigma; \omega, \tilde{v}; P|Q) \xrightarrow{\tau} (\tilde{x} : \tilde{T}; \sigma; \omega, \tilde{v}; P'|Q')} \quad \text{(L-Com)}$$

$$\frac{(\tilde{x} : \tilde{T}; \sigma; \omega; P) \xrightarrow{\alpha} \boxplus_i p_i \bullet (\tilde{x} : \tilde{T}; \sigma_i; \omega; P_i)}{(\tilde{x} : \tilde{T}; \sigma; \omega; P + Q) \xrightarrow{\alpha} \boxplus_i p_i \bullet (\tilde{x} : \tilde{T}; \sigma_i; \omega; P_i)} \quad \text{(L-Sum)}$$

$$\frac{(\tilde{x} : \tilde{T}; \sigma; \omega; P) \xrightarrow{\alpha} \boxplus_i p_i \bullet (\tilde{x} : \tilde{T}; \sigma_i; \omega; P_i)}{(\tilde{x} : \tilde{T}; \sigma; \omega; P|Q) \xrightarrow{\alpha} \boxplus_i p_i \bullet (\tilde{x} : \tilde{T}; \sigma_i; \omega; P_i|Q)} \quad \text{(L-Par)}$$

$$\frac{(\tilde{x} : \tilde{T}; \sigma; \omega; P) \xrightarrow{\alpha} (\tilde{x} : \tilde{T}; \sigma'; \omega; P')}{(\tilde{x} : \tilde{T}; \sigma; \omega; (\mathsf{new}\ c{:}\widehat{\ }[T]).P) \xrightarrow{\alpha} (\tilde{x} : \tilde{T}; \sigma'; \omega; (\mathsf{new}\ c{:}\widehat{\ }[T]).P')} \quad \text{if } \alpha \notin \{c?[.], c![.]\}$$
$$\text{(L-Res)}$$

$$(\tilde{x} : \tilde{T}; \sigma; \omega; \{v\}.P) \xrightarrow{\tau} (\tilde{x} : \tilde{T}; \sigma; \omega; P) \qquad \text{(L-Act)}$$

$$(\tilde{x} : \tilde{T}; [x \mapsto |\phi\rangle]; \omega; (\mathsf{ns}\ s)P) \xrightarrow{\tau} (\tilde{x} : \tilde{T}, s : \mathsf{NS}; [\tilde{x}, s \mapsto |\phi\rangle|0\rangle]; \omega, s; P) \text{ if } s \text{ is fresh}$$
$$\text{(L-Ns)}$$

$$(\tilde{x}, \tilde{y} : \mathsf{Qbit}, q_c : \mathsf{Qbit}, \tilde{z} : \tilde{\mathsf{NS}}; [\tilde{x}, q_c, \tilde{y}, \tilde{z} \mapsto |\phi\rangle]; \omega; [s_{2c}, s_{2c+1} \mathbin{*=} \mathsf{PS}(q_c)].P) \qquad \text{(L-Ps)}$$
$$\xrightarrow{\tau} (\tilde{x}, \tilde{y} : \mathsf{Q\tilde{b}it}, \tilde{z} : \tilde{\mathsf{NS}}, s_{2c} : \mathsf{NS}, s_{2c+1} : \mathsf{NS}; [\tilde{x}, \tilde{y}, \tilde{z}, s_{2c}, s_{2c+1} \mapsto |\psi\rangle]; \omega'; P)$$

$$\frac{(\tilde{x} : \tilde{T}; \sigma; \omega; e) \longrightarrow_e \boxplus_i p_i \bullet (\tilde{x} : \tilde{T}; \sigma_i; \omega; e_i)}{(\tilde{x} : \tilde{T}; \sigma; \omega; F[e]) \xrightarrow{\tau} \boxplus_i p_i \bullet (\tilde{x} : \tilde{T}; \sigma_i; \omega; F[e_i])} \quad \text{(L-Expr)}$$

Fig. 6. Transition Relation Rules

The semantics of CQP consists of labelled transitions between configurations, which are defined in a similar way to classical process calculus. This is given by a set of rules called the *labelled transition rules* which are needed to describe the behaviour of a system. Due to space constraints, we have provided just a few important rules that are shown in Figure 6 and shall explain some of them.

The rule L-Prob is a probabilistic transition in which p_i is the probability of the transition. The rules L-In and L-Out represent the input and output actions respectively, which are the *visible* interactions with the environment. $Q\{\tilde{v}/\tilde{y}\}$ in rule L-In indicates that Q with a list of values $\tilde{v}$ substituted for the list of variables $\tilde{y}$. When the two processes of the input and output actions are put in parallel then each has a partner for its potential interaction, and the input and output can synchronise, resulting in a τ transition which is given by the rule L-Com. The rule L-Act just removes actions. This is a reduction of the action expression to v which would involve effects like measurement or transformation of the quantum state. The rules discussed are similar to the rules in [16] with the modification of introducing the number states into the configuration in order to describe the behaviour of LOQC.

Rule L-PS describes the PS operation, which is the conversion of a polarisation qubit (q_c) to the number states (s_{2c} and s_{2c+1}). Here $\tilde{x}$, $\tilde{y}$ and $\tilde{z}$ means a list of names of the form q_i, q_j and s_k where $k \neq (2i, 2i + 1, 2j,$ and $2j + 1)$. The quantum state of the system before the operation is given as $|\phi\rangle = |\alpha\rangle|0\rangle|\beta\rangle|\gamma\rangle + |\alpha'\rangle|1\rangle|\beta'\rangle|\gamma'\rangle$. The initial configuration shows that $q_c \in \omega$ and $s_{2c}, s_{2c+1} \notin \omega$ where ω is a list of names that is owned by the process P and after the operation we have a new list ω' (where $q_c \notin \omega'$ and $s_{2c}, s_{2c+1} \in \omega'$) and the quantum state of the system is given as $|\psi\rangle = |\alpha\rangle|\beta\rangle|\gamma\rangle|10\rangle + |\alpha'\rangle|\beta'\rangle|\gamma'\rangle|01\rangle$.

Example 1.
$(q_0 : \mathsf{Qbit}, q_2 : \mathsf{Qbit}, s_2 : \mathsf{NS}, s_3 : \mathsf{NS}; [q_0, q_2, s_2, s_3 \mapsto \alpha|00\rangle|10\rangle + \beta|11\rangle|01\rangle];$
$q_0, q_2, s_2, s_3; [s_0, s_1 \mathrel{*}= \mathsf{PS}(q_0)] . P) \xrightarrow{\tau}$
$(q_2 : \mathsf{Qbit}, \tilde{s}' : \mathsf{NS}; [q_2, s_0, s_1, s_2, s_3 \mapsto \alpha|0\rangle|1010\rangle + \beta|1\rangle|0101\rangle]; q_2, s_0, s_1, s_2, s_3; P).$

Example 1 shows the effect of PS operation on qubit q_0. The qubit is converted to the number states s_0, s_1 and $\tilde{s}'$ indicates that it is a list of names comprising s_0, s_1, s_2 and s_3 of type NS.

The original papers on CQP [7,15] defined the semantics in terms of *reductions*, corresponding to τ transitions. The reduction semantics allows us to define the behaviour of a whole system but the labelled transitions and their interpretation are needed to define equivalence between processes, which is an area of future work.

6   Conclusion and Future Work

The main contribution of this paper is the extension of CQP to describe linear optical quantum computing. This is the first work in using quantum process calculus to describe a physical realisation of quantum computing. We have defined the linear optical elements in CQP, and have described a model of an LOQC CNOT gate. Using our model, we have also described post-selection in CQP.

The importance of process calculus is that it provides a systematic methodology for verification of quantum systems. Previous work on CQP defined behavioural equivalence [16]; considering a qubit has to be a *localised* unit of information. Equivalence is a congruence, meaning that equivalent processes remain equivalent in any context, and supporting equational reasoning. Our next step for this line of research is to extend the theory of equivalence in CQP to LOQC. This would not only help us to verify systems but would also give a more physical understanding of the property of equivalence. The fact that CQP can also express classical behaviour means that we have a uniform framework in which to analyze classical and quantum computation and communication. The long-term goal is to develop software for automated analysis of CQP models, following the established work in classical process calculus.

Acknowledgement. We would like to thank Scott N. Walck for valuable comments.

References

1. Nielsen, M.A., Chuang, I.L.: Quantum Computation and Quantum Information. Cambridge University Press (2000)
2. IDQ: http://www.idquantique.com/company/presentation.html
3. MagiQ: http://www.magiqtech.com/magiq/home.html
4. Knill, E., Laflamme, R., Milburn, G.J.: A scheme for efficient quantum computation with linear optics. Nature 409, 46 (2001)
5. O'Brien, J.L., Pryde, G.J., White, A.G., Ralph, T.C., Branning, D.: Demonstration of an all-optical quantum controlled-not gate. Nature 426, 264 (2003)
6. Politi, A., Cryan, M.J., Rarity, J.G., Yu, S., O'Brien, J.L.: Silica-on-silicon waveguide quantum circuits. Science 320, 646 (2008)
7. Gay, S.J., Nagarajan, R.: Communicating Quantum Processes. In: Proceedings of the 32nd Annual ACM Symposium on Principles of Programming Languages, pp. 145–157. ACM (2005)
8. Jorrand, P., Lalire, M.: Toward a quantum process algebra. In: CF 2004: Proceedings of the 1st Conference on Computing Frontiers, pp. 111–119. ACM Press (2004)
9. Feng, Y., Duan, R., Ji, Z., Ying, M.: Probabilistic bisimilarities between quantum processes arXiv:cs.LO/0601014 (2006)
10. Milner, R.: Communication and Concurrency. Prentice-Hall (1989)
11. Myers, C.R., Laflamme, R.: Linear optics quantum computation: an overview arXiv: quant-ph/0512104v1 (2005)
12. Ralph, T.C., Lanford, N.K., Bell, T.B., White, A.G.: Linear optical controlled-not gate in the coincidence basis. Physical Review Letters A 65, 62324–1 (2002)
13. Milner, R.: Communicating and Mobile Systems: the Pi-Calculus. Cambridge University Press (1999)
14. Milner, R., Parrow, J., Walker, D.: A calculus of mobile processes, I. Information and Computation 100(1), 1–40 (1992)
15. Gay, S.J., Nagarajan, R.: Types and Typechecking for Communicating Quantum Processes. Mathematical Structures in Computer Science 16(3), 375–406 (2006)
16. Davidson, T.A.S.: Formal Verification Techniques using Quantum Process Calculus. PhD thesis, University of Warwick (2011)
17. Davidson, T.A.S., Gay, S.J., Nagarajan, R., Puthoor, I.V.: Analysis of a quantum error correcting code using quantum process calculus. EPTCS 95, 67–80 (2011)
18. Wright, A.K., Felleisen, M.: A syntactic approach to type soundness. Information and Computation 115(1), 38–94 (1994)

Logically and Physically Reversible
Natural Computing: A Tutorial

Chris Thachuk*

Department of Computer Science, University of Oxford, Oxford, UK
`chris.thachuk@cs.ox.ac.uk`

Abstract. This year marks the 40th anniversary of Charles Bennett's seminal paper on reversible computing. Bennett's contribution is remembered as one of the first to demonstrate how any deterministic computation can be simulated by a logically reversible Turing machine. Perhaps less remembered is that the same paper suggests the use of nucleic acids to realise physical reversibility. In context, Bennett's foresight predates Leonard Adleman's famous experiments to solve instances of the Hamiltonian path problem using strands of DNA — a landmark date for the field of natural computing — by more than twenty years. The ensuing time has seen active research in both reversible computing and natural computing that has been, for the most part, unrelated. Encouraged by new, experimentally viable DNA computing models, there is a resurgent interest in logically reversible computing by the natural computing community. We survey these recent results, and their underlying ideas, which demonstrate the potential for logically and physically reversible computation using nucleic acids.

Keywords: reversible computing, natural computing.

1 Introduction

By the 1960's, scientists and mathematicians concerned with the study of computing had already begun to ask and answer the question: what can be computed *efficiently*? Many results emerged showing that seemingly difficult problems could be solved by algorithms that had time complexity bounded by a polynomial — a criterion Edmonds advocated as a measure of a (time) efficient algorithm [7]. We can extend this question to ask: what constitutes an *energy* efficient algorithm? More generally, can any computation be performed in an energy efficient manner? By 1961, this question was partially answered when Landauer proved that it was only logically irreversible operations — those which cause information loss — that must expend energy [12]. Unfortunately, deterministic computation is not necessarily logically reversible and typical programming is unlikely to be so. Fortunately, it was later shown that any deterministic computation could be simulated by a logically reversible Turing machine, thus showing that computation does not, in principle, have a fundamental limit with respect to energy expenditure. The result emerged independently by Lecerf [14] in 1963 and later by Bennett [2]

---

* This work is supported by the ERC Advanced Grant VERIWARE and by the Oxford Martin School.

G.W. Dueck and D.M. Miller (Eds.): RC 2013, LNCS 7948, pp. 247–262, 2013.

in 1973; although Lecerf's result was little known and Bennett's is often cited as the seminal paper for logically reversible Turing machines.

While Turing machine models can be used to reason about theoretical improvements, any reaped benefit of energy efficient computation must occur in the physical world. Thus, one must also consider computing with physically reversible systems, whether they be electronic or quantum circuits, billiard-ball computers [8], or an altogether different physical system. In his seminal paper, Bennett suggests using the standard machinery of a cell for the bio-synthesis and bio-degradation of messenger RNA — a nucleic acid similar to DNA — as a means for physically reversible computation, where the synthesis and degradation actions are analogous to reading and writing, respectively, to a Turing machine tape. Interestingly, this idea predates the demonstrated use of nucleic acids for computation by more than twenty years [1], and the field of DNA nanotechnology in general, by nearly a decade [24].

Using just four bases (A,C,G, and T), DNA acts as a storage device by encoding genes and other blueprint sequences that can be inherited by future generations. This purpose of DNA is very much in line with Bennett's original insight. However, DNA is not limited to the role of information carrier. Consider the most common shape associated with DNA — the famous double helix. This structure is formed by two sequences, in opposite orientation,[1] that *hybridize* together by forming bonds between complementary bases (see Fig. 1 (top left)). The A base will bond with a T base and, similarly, C will bond with G. The beginning of DNA nanotechnology is largely attributed to a paper by Seeman [24] in 1982 where he demonstrated the potential for DNA to assume shapes other than the double helical structure. This is accomplished by a careful design of strands and, in particular, by a careful design of *domains*, or subsequences, of those strands so that when they are added into the same solution, they *self-assemble*, via hybridization, into the intended shape (see Fig. 1 (top right)). DNA has since proven itself to be an effective and programmable construction material for engineering arbitrary shapes at the nanoscale [19].

In addition to self-assembly into static structures, DNA hybridization can be leveraged for creating dynamic systems that change over time. This has led to the exploration of using DNA to perform computation. The advantage? A natural interface with biological systems that can be implemented *in vitro* and, potentially, *in vivo*. Many models of computing with DNA have arisen over the years, including the *Adleman-Lipton* model — based on the ideas underlying Adleman's famous experiments to solve instances of the Hamiltonian path problem [1], the *Sticker* model [22] — where short DNA molecules 'stick' and 'unstick' to a long template strand, analogous to a Turing machine tape, and the *Tile self-assembly* model [27] where 'tiles' of DNA containing different types of 'glue' on each side can hybridize together and give rise to periodic shapes such as the Sierpinski triangle [20].

In the remainder of this tutorial, we limit our focus to one natural computing model that overlaps with the goals of reversible computing. In particular, we concentrate on a relatively new DNA computing model using so-called *DNA strand displacement* systems (DSDs) that provide a natural mechanism to perform physically reversible

---

[1] A *strand* of DNA is oriented and has a 5' end and a 3' end. Hybridization can only occur between two complementary sequences of DNA in opposite orientation.

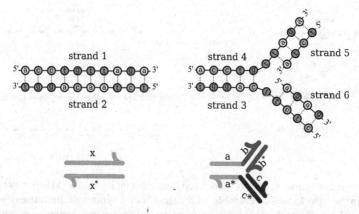

Fig. 1. Single stranded DNA molecules, or *strands*, are polymers over four monomer units called bases. The strands are oriented and have a 5' end and a 3' end. A sequence of DNA, or substrand, is complementary to another if their bases are complementary and in opposite orientation. An A base is complementary to the T base, as the C base is to the G base. When single stranded DNA molecules are added in solution, complementary sequences will hybridize together to form stable double stranded structures. For example, when strand 1 and strand 2 are added in the same solution, a DNA duplex forms (top left). Similarly, when strands 3,4,5 and 6 are added in the same solution, they form a branched structure (top right). When designing strands to self-assemble into different shapes, it is common to abstract their sequences into labeled *domains* which are used to indicate complementary sequences (bottom).

computation steps. We focus on DSD systems as they are simple, widely studied and experimentally practical. These systems leverage the fact that an unbound strand A can still hybridize with a complementary domain on some strand B, even if it is already hybridized to some other strand C. If A does hybridize to B, strand C is said to be *displaced* and can next be used to displace some other strand [28]. DNA strand displacement mechanisms have been experimentally implemented and verified to simulate neural networks [18], Boolean logic circuits [23,5], and even reversible Boolean logic circuits [9], among numerous other applications. As we will see, they are also capable, in principle, of physically and logically reversible Turing-universal computation [16,11].

2   Background

In the natural computing results we study in this tutorial, a distinct notion of logically reversible computation is used that differs from the standard definition. We begin with a discussion of this distinction in terms of configuration graphs, as opposed to restrictions on Turing machine transitions [2], which will be used to simplify our presentation of natural computing examples. This is followed by an overview of the DNA strand displacement model, and stochastic chemical reaction networks.

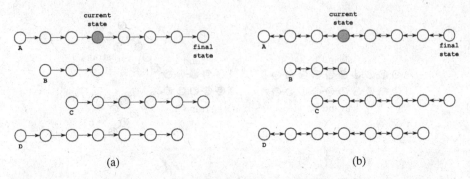

Fig. 2. Example configuration graphs, induced on four different inputs, for (a) logically reversible computation, and (b) logically reversible computation (with symmetric transitions) arising in some chemical reaction networks. Nodes represent possible states in a computation and directed edges denote valid state transitions.

2.1 Logical Reversibility

The reversible computing results we will discuss in this tutorial use a slightly different notion of logical reversibility. As we will see, this distinction is important as the physical reversibility of these systems is actively exploited to achieve space efficient computation. For our purposes here, it suffices to understand the important difference distinguishing this notion from the standard notion of logically reversible computation. The intuition of the difference is captured well by considering the *configuration graph* of a computation which has a node for every possible state on every possible input for the underlying Turing machine being modeled. There is a directed edge from node i to node j if and only if state j is reachable from state i in a single state-transition of the Turing machine.

Shown in Fig. 2a is a configuration graph of a typical logically reversible computation, shown for four different inputs (source nodes A-D). Importantly, a logically reversible computation for a particular input forms a directed path, from its input to its final state, which is unconnected to any state for any other possible input. This means any state along the chain can be deterministically reached from the final state, if the entire chain is reversed. Thus, information is *not* lost. Contrast this with the configuration graph of a logically reversible computation (with symmetric transitions) for the same four inputs shown in Fig. 2b. The only difference is that each non-terminal node along the chain has two possible choices of where to next proceed: its successor state, or its predecessor state. Therefore, each transition, and the overall computation, is *symmetric* [15]. As we will see, the state transitions in the systems we consider model reversible chemical reactions. That is, after each reaction it is possible the reaction is immediately reversed. The computation is still logically reversible in the following sense. One choice is always the previous state of the computation. (Retreating to the previous state is equivalent to the transition never having occurred.) The important point is that at any given node, the computation cannot proceed to more than one other node that is not the previous state.

2.2 DNA Strand Displacement Systems (DSD)

A DNA strand displacement system (DSD) consists of *unbound* strands and double stranded complexes consisting of one or more bound strands to a long *template* strand. For example, in Fig. 3a there is one unbound strand labeled I and one double stranded complex consisting of the strand labeled E bound to the template strand labeled S. Strands in the system are composed of two types of strand domains: short *toehold* domains, and *long* domains. Distinct domains are assumed to have a distinct sequence design. The short length of toehold domains is chosen to ensure strands bound together only by a toehold can spontaneously unbind from one another at the experimental temperature. In contrast, two strands bound by a complementary long domain is considered a stable binding such that that they cannot spontaneously unbind at the experimental temperature.

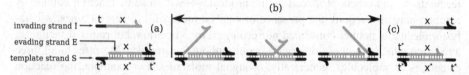

Fig. 3. A successful toehold mediated strand displacement. (a) Toehold t (black subsequence) of the invading strand I binds with its unpaired complement, t^*, on the template strand S. (b) The invading and evading strands share the common long domain x (gray subsequence). They compete, via a random walk process, to bind with the complementary long domain x^* of the template strand until all bases of the invading strand are paired. (c) Toehold of the evading strand E detaches from the template strand S, at which point it has been displaced. Since there remains a free toehold on S, the process is reversible as strand E could displace strand I.

The fundamental operation in a DSD is strand displacement, whereby a toehold domain of an unbound strand, called the invading-strand, binds to an unbound complementary toehold domain of a template strand and, if the adjacent long domain is complementary, it can displace a currently bound signal strand, called the evading strand, of the same length. We illustrate a simple, reversible version of strand displacement in Fig. 3. First, the toehold t of the invading strand, I, binds (forms base-pairs) to the complementary toehold t^* of the template strand, S. Note that any strand with toehold t could initially bind here. However, the process only continues if the adjacent long domain of invading strand I is identical to the long domain of evading strand E. If I and E do share an identical long domain, then in random walk process (often referred to as three-way branch migration), the bases of the long domain of I compete with those belonging to the identical long domain of E to form base pairs with the complementary long domain of the template strand S. Once the long domain of I has bound to its complement domain on the template strand, strand E remains bound by just its short toehold domain. Due to their short length, the toehold bonds can break, thereby releasing signal E. (Of course I may detach from the template before E is released, in which case the displacement does not happen.) The displacement is physically reversible because signal E can next bind to the template strand S to displace strand I

via the same principles. However, the template complex does have an orientation. For example, after I has displaced E in the original displacement, another strand identical to I cannot be used to displace another strand identical to E. This will only be possible, using this same template complex, after some strand E displaces the bound strand I. Alternatively, an I strand can displace and E strand if a another copy of the template complex is present in its original orientation.

2.3   Chemical Reaction Networks (CRN)

Just as a DSD abstracts sequence level details of interacting DNA strands using the concept of domains, stochastic chemical reaction networks (CRN) abstract details about displacements. CRNs provide a concise language for writing molecular programs and affords us the opportunity to express complex ideas more succinctly. A chemical reaction equation details a process whereby certain molecule types can be consumed — the reactants — and others produced — the products — within some reaction volume. A reaction may also require the presence of catalyst molecules of certain types. A catalyst molecule is neither consumed nor produced by a reaction, but rather it facilitates a reaction which could not otherwise occur without its presence. We refer to all three categories of molecules, generically, as signal molecules. For example, the reaction $A + B \overset{C}{\to} D$ consumes a signal of type A and a signal of type B and produces a signal of type D in the presence of the catalyst[2] signal C. This is an example of an irreversible reaction; however, $A + B \overset{C}{\rightleftharpoons} D$ is an example of a reversible reaction meaning that both a signal of type A and of type B can also be produced by consuming a signal of type D in the presence of the catalyst signal C. A CRN is a set of chemical reactions, in addition to a multiset of signals present within the reaction volume, prior to any reaction occurring, called the initial signal multiset. The current signal multiset is the current composition of signals of a given CRN within a reaction volume — in terms of computation, this specifies the state of the system. From a given state, any reaction can be applied if both the required reactants and catalysts are in the current signal multiset. Thus, arbitrary CRNs are not necessarily deterministic. Importantly, it has been shown that any chemical reaction equation can be realized by a physically reversible DNA strand displacement cascade [16,3].

   Let us consider a concrete example of a 3-bit standard binary counter that should begin at count 000, advance to 001, and so on, until reaching the count 111. In our molecular program, we let signal 0_i and signal 1_i denote that bit i has value 0 and 1, respectively, for $1 \le i \le 3$. Thus, our 3-bit counter will have the following initial signal multiset: $\{0_3, 0_2, 0_1\}$. Fig. 4a gives three chemical reaction equations for exchanging signals and thus changing the state, or current signal multiset, of the counter. Initially, only reaction 1 can be applied in the forward direction. This is because all other reactions require at least one of the bits to be set to 1. When reaction 1 occurs, signal 0_1 is consumed and signal 1_1 is produced, putting the counter in state $\{0_3, 0_2, 1_1\}$.

---

[2] Some reactions require the presence of one or more signals, called *catalysts*, which they do not consume. Note how we represent catalysts in our reaction equations. These are not to be confused with rate constants which do not factor into our current discussion. Catalysts do play a significant role and this representation was chosen for its succinctness.

$$
\begin{aligned}
(1)\ & 0_1 & \rightleftharpoons\ & 1_1 \\
(2)\ & 0_2 + 1_1 & \rightleftharpoons\ & 1_2 + 0_1 \\
(3)\ & 0_3 + 1_2 + 1_1 & \rightleftharpoons\ & 1_3 + 0_2 + 0_1
\end{aligned}
$$

(a)

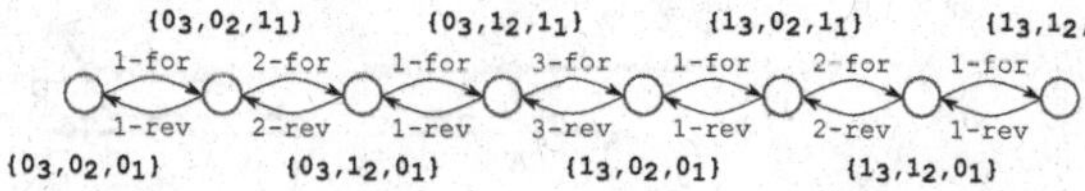

$$
\begin{array}{cccc}
\{0_3,0_2,1_1\} & \{0_3,1_2,1_1\} & \{1_3,0_2,1_1\} & \{1_3,1_2,1_1\}
\end{array}
$$

1-for 2-for   1-for 3-for   1-for 2-for   1-for

1-rev 2-rev   1-rev 3-rev   1-rev 2-rev   1-rev

$$
\begin{array}{cccc}
\{0_3,0_2,0_1\} & \{0_3,1_2,0_1\} & \{1_3,0_2,0_1\} & \{1_3,1_2,0_1\}
\end{array}
$$

(b)

Fig. 4. (a) Chemical reaction equations for a 3-bit standard binary counter. (b) The configuration graph of the computation performed by the 3-bit standard binary counter forms a chain and is logically reversible (with symmetric transitions). The nodes represent the state of the computation and the edges are directed between states reachable by a single reaction.

From this state, two reactions are next possible. Either the previous reaction is reversed (i.e., reaction 1 next occurs in the reverse direction), or reaction 2 can occur in the forward direction, resulting in state $\{0_3, 1_2, 0_1\}$. Similarly, either reaction 2 is reversed, or reaction 1 next occurs once again, bringing the counter to state $\{0_3, 1_2, 1_1\}$. This continues until the counter reaches the final state $\{1_3, 1_2, 1_1\}$. Fig. 4b represents all reachable states of the counter as nodes and has edges between states that are reachable within one reaction step. Notice that this CRN specifies a logically reversible computation (with symmetric transitions). This 3-bit counter can be extended to a 4-bit counter by adding signal 0_4 to the initial signal multiset, and by adding the reversible reaction $0_4 + 1_3 + 1_2 + 1_1 \rightleftharpoons 1_4 + 0_3 + 0_2 + 0_1$. In a similar manner, the CRN can be extended to simulate any n-digit counter.

3 Reversible and Turing-Complete Natural Computing

Are DNA strand displacement systems capable of logically and physically reversible Turing-universal computation? This question was answered in the affirmative by Qian *et al.* [16] whose work stands as one of the most important theoretical contributions to the area. In a first major contribution of that work, the authors offer a design for a reversible DSD reaction cascade that can realise any chemical reaction. An example for the reversible reaction $A + B \rightleftharpoons C + D$ is given in Fig. 5. The signal molecules are represented by the strands in the shaded boxes, consisting of three domains. The other strands and complexes, which facilitate the reaction, are collectively called the reaction *transformer*. Note that for a reversible reaction cascade, the transformer has two orientations — one for each direction of the reaction. In Fig. 5, the forward orientation is shown top-to-bottom, where the DNA strands for the signals A and B are consumed, and those for C and D are produced. The reverse is shown from bottom-to-top. Consider the forward reaction (top-to-bottom) in Fig. 5. Initially, the only available toehold complement on the template strand is adjacent to a domain complementary to a long domain of strand A. Once strand A displaces a bound strand, a new toehold is available for strand B to bind. Next, auxiliary strands are used to displace C and D — the intended products of this reaction. Once the transformer is in this orientation, it cannot be used to consume A and B and produce C and D. It can however perform the reverse reaction next.

In their second major contribution, the authors enriched the DSD computing model by showing how displacement reactions could be used to add and remove strands to

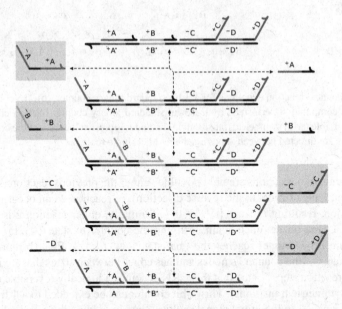

Fig. 5. A strand displacement implementation of the bi-molecular chemical reaction equation $A + B \rightleftharpoons C + D$ using the construction proposed by Qian *et al.* [16]

a growing polymer. Consider the example in Fig. 6, clockwise from state 1 to state 4, showing how a signal denoting the value X can be appended to a growing polymer. Initially, in state 1, the polymer is considered to be an empty list and consists of a single strand, with one toehold and one long domain, that denotes the head of the list. In state 2, the domains denoting the head can interact with a transformer, containing the value X, to form a new extended complex. However, X is only tentatively appended. The process can continue into state 3 if a signal strand, denoting that value X is present, interacts with the new extended complex. Finally, the process in finalized in state 4 when the new extended complex interacts with another transformer resulting in the original exposed domains denoting the head of the list. At this point a new value could be appended to the list, or the previous value X could be removed by performing the reaction sequence in reverse.

Coupled with a clever design of reactions to control state, the authors were able to simulate a (multi) stack machine using only strands of DNA. As the stack machine could be used to simulate Bennett's original reversible Turing machine, and since the reaction cascades of the stack machine simulation are reversible, the authors demonstrated that Turing-universal computation could be realized by a logically and physically reversible DSD sytem enriched with polymers.

One important issue must not be overlooked. As Bennett points out [2], a physical system performing a computation of length t, with no positive drift in the forward direction, will reach the end state in t^2 expected steps. However this should not be considered a computation, as the process can immediately reverse once reaching the output state — the probability of observing the output in this manner is only $\frac{1}{t}$. To overcome

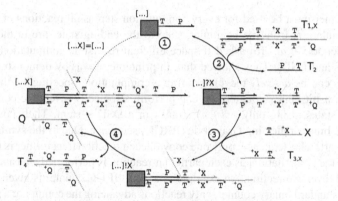

Fig. 6. A reproduction of a figure from Qian *et al.* [16] illustrating (clockwise from the top) how a new signal X can be *pushed* on to a stack by a reaction cascade for polymer extension

this in the stack machine construction, the authors introduce a small bias in favour of forward reactions, thus introducing a positive drift in the computation chain towards the output state. The positive drift is accomplished as follows. DSD reactions are always bi-molecular reactions between two distinct species types (one invading strand and one transformer complex). The propensity of a reaction $A + B \rightarrow \dots$ within a well-mixed solution of size v is $\frac{|A||B|}{v}$, where $|X|$ is the count of molecules of type X. Consider the reaction $X + T_f \rightleftharpoons Y + T_r$ and suppose T_f is the transformer for the forward reaction, and T_r is the transformer for the reverse. The propensity of the forward reaction can be made to be twice as large as the propensity of the reverse by ensuring $|T_F| = 2|T_R|$. Thus, in the stack machine construction, the authors ensure more copies of each reaction transformer is in the forward orientation, rather than the reverse, for the duration of the computation. To next reverse the computation towards the beginning state, additional transformers in the reverse orientation could be added to the system to bias the computation to next reverse.

4   Reversible and Space-Efficient Natural Computing

As with Bennett's original reversible Turing machine, the stack machine construction uses space proportional to the length of the computation. This is because a new copy

(1) $0_1 \rightleftharpoons 1_1$

(2) $0_2 \overset{1_1}{\rightleftharpoons} 1_2$

(3) $0_3 \overset{1_2+0_1}{\rightleftharpoons} 1_3$

(a)

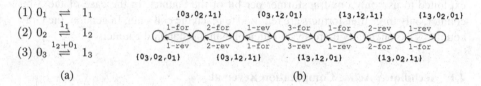

(b)

Fig. 7. (a) Chemical reaction equations for a 3-bit binary reflecting Gray code counter. (b) The configuration graph of the computation performed by the 3-bit binary reflecting Gray code counter forms a chain and is logically reversible (with symmetric transitions).

of a transformer must be used for every computation step as all reactions of the stack machine simulation, from the beginning state to the ending state, are in the forward direction. Condon *et al.* [6] asked if space-efficient reversible computation is possible in CRNs and DSDs. They showed that, in principle, it was by demonstrating how transformers can be *actively* recycled during a computation. Specifically, the authors proposed an n-bit binary counter that can perform a logically reversible computation through 2^n states, using only $poly(n)$ strands in a DSD system. Their counter was based on the binary reflecting Gray code (BRGC) sequence. Due to the symmetric nature of that particular sequence, only one copy of each reaction transformer is necessary to complete the computation, as each particular reaction is performed alternately in the forward and reverse direction. An example of a 3-bit BRGC counter is given in Fig. 7. As with the standard binary counter, only reactions advancing the counter to a successor state, or to the predecessor state is ever possible.

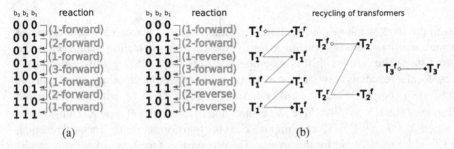

(a)   (b)

Fig. 8. Comparing two different binary counters over 3 bits. (a) To reach the end state, the standard binary counter must perform a sequence of reactions that always occur in the forward direction, thus requiring a new transformer for every reaction as they are not recycled. (b) The binary reflecting Gray code counter only requires one transformer per reaction equation as each reaction occurs alternately in the forward and the reverse direction.

Contrast the sequence of reactions required for the standard counter in Fig. 8a with that of the Gray counter in Fig. 8b. A standard n-bit binary counter, much like the stack machine, performs only forward reactions when progressing in a computation and would therefore require $2^n - 1$ transformers to reach the end state. In the case of the 3-bit counter, seven transformers are required in total for the standard counter to reach the end state. However, the Gray counter has a regular symmetry which can be exploited to use only one transformer per bit of the counter. In the case of the 3-bit counter, only three transformers are required to reach the end state. In general, the Gray counter is exponentially more space-efficient than the standard counter.

4.1   Technique: Active Computation Reversal

Interestingly, the recursive nature of the binary reflecting Gray code sequence leads to a powerful technique for logically reversible computing. To extend the 3-bit BRGC counter to a 4-bit BRGC counter, all that is required is to add the signal 0_4 to the initial

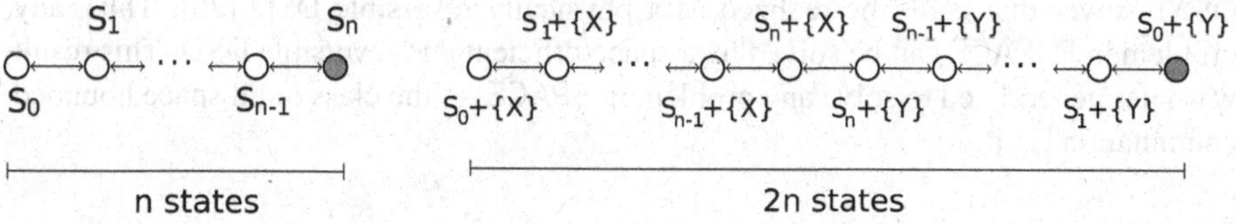

S_1 S_n $S_1+\{X\}$ $S_n+\{X\}$ $S_{n-1}+\{Y\}$ $S_0+\{Y\}$

S_0 S_{n-1} $S_0+\{X\}$ $S_{n-1}+\{X\}$ $S_n+\{Y\}$ $S_1+\{Y\}$

n states

2n states

(a)   (b)

Fig. 9. (a) The computation chain of a logically reversible CRN (with symmetric transitions). (b) The computation chain from (a) doubled by adding one new initial signal, X, and one new reaction, $X \overset{S_n}{\rightleftharpoons} Y$, that requires the signals of the previous final state as catalysts.

signal multiset and to add the new reaction $0_4 \overset{1_3+0_2+0_1}{\rightleftharpoons} 1_4$. The new signal molecule does not affect the reactions for the first 3 bits; furthermore, the new reaction requires as catalysts the signals of the final state of the 3-bit counter. This means the original reaction sequence of the 3-bit counter will proceed prior to the new reaction. Once the 3-bit sequence is complete, the new reaction can occur for the first time to produce 1_4. Other than next reversing this new reaction — stepping back in the computation chain — the only other possibility is to perform the entire reaction sequence of the 3-bit counter in reverse. Note that since the 1_4 signal was not present before, this means the computation is actually stepping forward towards a new end state. By introducing one new signal, and one new reaction, we can effectively double the computation chain length, and ensure active recycling of transformers. The general technique is illustrated in Fig. 9.

When using active recycling of transformers the computation chain must be unbiased as reactions are repeated in alternating orientations — thus we cannot force a positive drift as in the stack machine construction. To ensure the output of the computation can be witnessed with high probability, this same technique can be used to repeatedly extend the overall computation chain. For instance, consider a computation for a decision problem where a special signal is produced to indicate if the input is accepted and another signal is produced to indicate if it is not. This extension technique can be used to double the overall computation chain length, ensuring the output signal can be observed in strictly more than half of the states. As the computation performs an unbiased random walk along the logically reversible computation state space, the steady state probability of observing the output signal is $p > 0.5$. In this manner, for every new reaction added to the CRN to double the chain length, the probability of not observing an output signal is cut in half. Formally, the probability of observing an answer becomes $p'' > 1 - 2^{-(1+c)}$ when $c \geq 0$ number of new reactions are added to extend the computation chain. Thus, we can make the steady state probability of observing a solution signal arbitrarily high.

This same chain extension technique was used by Thachuk & Condon who gave a space-efficient and logically reversible CRN for performing an in-order traversal of a complete binary tree. Coupled with the ideas for verifying a 3-SAT formula (which we explore next), and the new tree traversal procedure, the authors demonstrated how any *quantified* 3-SAT problem instance could be solved, by giving a logically reversible

QSAT solver that could be realized as a physically reversible DSD [26]. Thus, any problem in PSPACE can be solved by a space-efficient and reversible DSD. This result was later generalized to solve any problem in SPACE — the class of all space bounded computation [25].

4.2 Designing a 3-SAT Solver

In this section, we will explore, at a high level, how the logically reversible and space-efficient BRGC counter can be used in conjunction with a 3-SAT verification procedure to solve 3-SAT instances. We will use a very simple strategy. For a formula with n variables, an n-bit counter can enumerate every possible variable assignment, and a verification procedure can be run every time the counter changes. The entire computation can be made to halt either when a satisfying solution is found, or when all states of the counter have been exhausted. Furthermore, the entire computation chain will be logically reversible. We do not discuss the specifics of how the counter and the verification procedure can be coupled, but a set of auxiliary reactions are sufficient to achieve the desired result [25]. We note that one detail which cannot be overlooked in such a coupling is that the entire verification procedure must be reversed in between invocations for different variable assignments. Next, we discuss how a 3-SAT formula can be verified. The procedure illustrates the use of history signals to ensure the overall procedure is logically reversible.

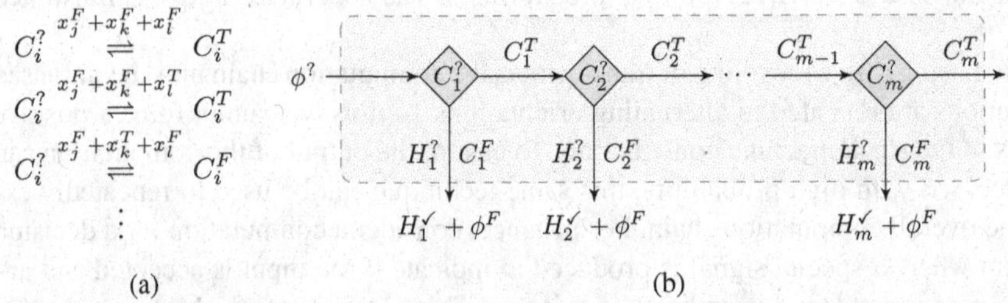

$$C_i^? \overset{x_j^F + x_k^F + x_l^F}{\rightleftharpoons} C_i^T$$
$$C_i^? \overset{x_j^F + x_k^F + x_l^T}{\rightleftharpoons} C_i^T$$
$$C_i^? \overset{x_j^F + x_k^T + x_l^F}{\rightleftharpoons} C_i^F$$
$$\vdots$$

(a)   (b)

Fig. 10. (a) A set of reactions acting as a *truth table* for clause i. (b) Flow control when verifying a formula ϕ having m clauses.

Verifying an Arbitrary Clause. Consider an arbitrary 3-SAT clause over three literals, each for a distinct variable. There are exactly eight possible truth assignments to the three distinct variables. Thus, for each such clause, we create a set of eight reversible reactions to determine if the clause is satisfied. The reactions for verifying the ith clause, containing literals for variables x_j, x_k and x_l are given in Fig. 10a. When the clause signal molecule $C_i^?$ is present, exactly one of the eight reactions can be applied, specified by the current variable assignment. The variable signals act as catalysts and the $C_i^?$ signal is consumed producing either a C_i^T signal if the clause is satisfied, or C_i^F otherwise. In this example, it is supposed that the variable assignment $x_j = F, x_k = T, x_l = F$ does not satisfy the clause, while the first two variable assignments do. Note that for a particular variable assignment, only one reaction will apply in both the forward and reverse direction, ensuring the process is logically reversible.

Verifying the Overall Formula. For the formula to be true, all clauses must be satisfied. However, any combination of unsatisfied clauses will result in ϕ being false. To ensure reversibility, verification of the overall formula must be completed systematically. A diagram illustrating the flow control of the procedure is given in Fig. 10b. The verification is initiated by consuming the signal $\phi^?$ and will complete either by producing the signal ϕ^T, if ϕ is satisfied, or by producing the signal ϕ^F, otherwise. Note that the signals for the variable assignment (which are manipulated by the counter) only act as catalysts in this procedure. Each clause is checked in order. Suppose the formula is not satisfied. Then the first clause i to be unsatisfied will produce the signal C_i^F. This is followed by a reaction that not only produces the ϕ^F signal, but also produces a unique history signal which records the first unsatisfied clause. This history signal ensures that the entire process remains logically reversible. Should the overall formula be satisfied, the ϕ^T signal will be produced. Once ϕ^F or ϕ^T is produced, the verification is complete.

5   Unique Challenges in Natural Computing

Consider the additional challenges of computing with a *soup* of interacting molecules, such as DNA. At once the molecules form the hardware and the software of the system. The state of the computation is denoted only by the presence or absence of certain signals, and this in turn fully dictates which reactions can next occur. Despite this, constructions such as the stack machine and the BRGC counter demonstrate that not only is logically reversible computation possible in these systems, it can also be Turing-universal and space-efficient. However, both constructions share a common assumption: certain signal molecules in the initial set must occur as a single copy. Theoretical results have emerged that suggest these systems will not operate correctly when this single copy assumption is violated [4,6]. To illustrate this point, we again consider the 3-bit BRGC counter. Initially, in a single copy of the construction, the signal molecules $\{0_3, 0_2, 0_1\}$ denote the state $0_3 0_2 0_1$. Consider a two-copy network where the initial multiset of present signal molecules is duplicated, yielding the multiset $\{0_3, 0_3, 0_2, 0_2, 0_1, 0_1\}$. (We also assume a duplicate multiset of transformers is available.) As in the single copy case, assume reaction (1) occurs in the forward direction, followed by reaction (2) in the forward direction. The resulting multiset of signal molecules is $\{0_3, 0_3, 0_2, 1_2, 0_1, 1_1\}$. In the single copy case, we intend that reaction (1) in the reverse direction will occur next; however, given the current multiset of present signal molecules in the two-copy case, reaction (3) in the forward direction could instead occur, resulting in the multiset $\{0_3, 1_3, 0_2, 1_2, 0_1, 1_1\}$. At this point, a copy of every signal molecule is present, and any reaction can occur, in either direction. Furthermore, the single copy case required *at least* seven reactions to produce the final state $1_3 0_2 0_1$, whereas the two-copy case can reach it in three. Crosstalk between the copies has broken the counter. The intuition as to why the single copy assumption is important is that it gives us a means to (temporarily) *erase* information. In a single copy setting, once a molecule of a particular type is consumed, it is no longer present. In a multi-copy setting, once a molecule of a particular type is consumed, there is no guarantee that the other copies are simultaneously consumed.

While the single copy restriction permitted us to study systems pushing the limits of computation for a *chemical soup*, it imposes a significant engineering challenge. All DSD implementations to-date use concentrations of strands of each type. Producing and successfully executing a DSD with a single copy restriction is currently challenging, but feasible. For instance, the first published result on the measurement of a single enzyme molecule was by Boris Rotman, in 1961 [21]. The experimental techniques developed in that first paper are still influential and in use, and new advancements in single molecule studies continue to be made [10].

6   Conclusion

Progress in natural computing, both on the theoretical and experimental side, has been steady. New, experimentally viable computing models, such as DNA strand displacement systems, have inspired promising results to realize logically and physical reversible computing systems using nucleic acids. In this brief tutorial, we have highlighted some of these results and discussed their underlying ideas. These constructions we studied are theoretical, have not been experimentally realized, and are not without unique, practical challenges. An underlying assumption in all constructions surveyed is that certain signal species occur within the reaction volume as a single copy. This contrasts sharply with DNA based computations that have been experimentally realized — copies of each type of strand typically number in the millions or billions. While it may be possible to ensure the single-copy assumption is met, another promising direction is to tether strands to a surface [17,11], such as a DNA origami tile [19].

Finally, we find the current complexity classes for logically reversible computation too general to capture the realities of logically reversible chemical reaction networks (CRNs) and DNA strand displacement systems (DSDs). The class ReversibleSPACE represents all problems that can be solved by a space-bounded logically reversible Turing machine. As with any Turing machine, the space bound is with respect to the length of tape necessary to complete the computation. In CRNs and DSDs, bits of information are represented with the presence and absence of signal molecules. Thus, the length of tape required in the Turing machine computation corresponds well with the maximum quantity of signals required during the CRN computation. However, this does not account for *fuel* (transformers) that a CRN may require to complete its computation. The reaction is the fundamental operation in a CRN just as a state transition is the fundamental operation for a Turing machine. However, with current technology, a reaction in a CRN requires *fuel*, which in turn requires physical space, whereas a Turing machine state transition does not. In essence, a logically reversible Turing machine could perform all state transitions in only one direction, while still using significantly less space than the number of computation steps. This is not currently possible in molecular programming. It has been demonstrated that any space-bounded computation can be realized with a logically reversible CRN that requires only one copy of fuel species (transformers) per reaction equation [25]. It is conceivable this CRN could be simulated with a logically reversible Turing machine. It is also conceivable that such a simulation could be constructed to ensure that each state transition of the Turing machine either strictly alternates being applied in the forward and reverse direction, or adheres to a polynomial bound in the difference between forward and reverse transitions, at every step of the computation. Such a construction would be a logically reversible Turing machine (with symmetric transitions), capable of simulating any space-bounded Turing computation, that is semantically restricted to capture the notion of *fuel*. We let ReversibleSPACE* denote the class of problems solvable by such a Turing machine. It has already been shown by Lange *et al.* [13] that ReversibleSPACE = SPACE. An open question is whether ReversibleSPACE* = SPACE.

Acknowledgments. The author would like to thank the reviewers for their suggestions.

References

1. Adleman, L.M.: Molecular computation of solutions to combinatorial problems. Science 266(5187), 1021–1024 (1994)
2. Bennett, C.H.: Logical reversibility of computation. IBM Journal of Research and Development 17(6), 525–532 (1973)
3. Cardelli, L.: Two-domain DNA strand displacement. Developments in Computational Models 26, 47–61 (2010)
4. Chen, H.-L., Doty, D., Soloveichik, D.: Deterministic function computation with chemical reaction networks. In: Stefanovic, D., Turberfield, A. (eds.) DNA 2012. LNCS, vol. 7433, pp. 25–42. Springer, Heidelberg (2012)
5. Chiniforooshan, E., Doty, D., Kari, L., Seki, S.: Scalable, time-responsive, digital, energy-efficient molecular circuits using DNA strand displacement. In: Sakakibara, Y., Mi, Y. (eds.) DNA 16 2010. LNCS, vol. 6518, pp. 25–36. Springer, Heidelberg (2011)
6. Condon, A., Hu, A.J., Maňuch, J., Thachuk, C.: Less haste, less waste: on recycling and its limits in strand displacement systems. Journal of the Royal Society: Interface Focus 2(4), 512–521 (2012)
7. Edmonds, J.: Paths, trees, and flowers. Canadian Journal of mathematics 17(3), 449–467 (1965)
8. Fredkin, E., Toffoli, T.: Conservative logic. International Journal of Theoretical Physics 21, 219–253 (1982)
9. Genot, A.J., Bath, J., Turberfield, A.J.: Reversible logic circuits made of DNA. Journal of the American Chemical Society 133(50), 20080–20083 (2011)
10. Knight, A.E.: Single enzyme studies: A historical perspective. In: Mashanov, G.I., Batters, C. (eds.) Single Molecule Enzymology. Methods in Molecular Biology, vol. 778, pp. 1–9. Humana Press (2011)
11. Lakin, M.R., Phillips, A.: Modelling, simulating and verifying Turing-powerful strand displacement systems. In: Cardelli, L., Shih, W. (eds.) DNA 17. LNCS, vol. 6937, pp. 130–144. Springer, Heidelberg (2011)
12. Landauer, R.: Irreversibility and heat generation in the computing process. IBM Journal of Research and Development 5(3), 183–191 (1961)
13. Lange, K.J., McKenzie, P., Tapp, A.: Reversible space equals deterministic space. Journal of Computer and System Sciences 60(2), 354–367 (2000)
14. Lecerf, Y.: Machines de Turing réversibles. Récursive insolubilité en $n \in N$ de l'équation $u = \Theta^n$, où Θ est un "isomorphisme de codes". Comptes Rendus 257, 2597–2600 (1963)

15. Lewis, H.R., Papadimitriou, C.H.: Symmetric space-bounded computation. Theoretical Computer Science 19(2), 161–187 (1982)

16. Qian, L., Soloveichik, D., Winfree, E.: Efficient Turing-universal computation with DNA polymers. In: Sakakibara, Y., Mi, Y. (eds.) DNA 16 2010. LNCS, vol. 6518, pp. 123–140. Springer, Heidelberg (2011)

17. Qian, L., Winfree, E.: Scaling up digital circuit computation with DNA strand displacement cascades. Science 332(6034), 1196–1201 (2011)

18. Qian, L., Winfree, E., Bruck, J.: Neural network computation with DNA strand displacement cascades. Nature 475(7356), 368–372 (2011)

19. Rothemund, P.W.K.: Folding DNA to create nanoscale shapes and patterns. Nature 440(7082), 297–302 (2006)

20. Rothemund, P.W.K., Papadakis, N., Winfree, E.: Algorithmic self-assembly of DNA Sierpinski triangles. PLoS Biology 2(12), e424 (2004)

21. Rotman, B.: Measurement of activity of single molecules of β-D-galactosidase. Proceedings of the National Academy of Sciences of the United States of America 47(12), 1981 (1961)

22. Roweis, S., Winfree, E., Burgoyne, R., Chelyapov, N.V., Goodman, M.F., Rothemund, P.W.K., Adleman, L.M.: A sticker-based model for DNA computation. Journal of Computational Biology 5(4), 615–629 (1998)

23. Seelig, G., Soloveichik, D., Zhang, D.Y., Winfree, E.: Enzyme-free nucleic acid logic circuits. Science 314(5805), 1585–1588 (2006)

24. Seeman, N.C.: Nucleic acid junctions and lattices. Journal of Theoretical Biology 99(2), 237–247 (1982)

25. Thachuk, C.: Space and energy efficient molecular programming and space efficient text indexing methods for sequence alignment. PhD thesis, University of British Columbia (2012)

26. Thachuk, C., Condon, A.: Space and energy efficient computation with DNA strand displacement systems. In: Stefanovic, D., Turberfield, A. (eds.) DNA 2012. LNCS, vol. 7433, pp. 135–149. Springer, Heidelberg (2012)

27. Winfree, E.: Algorithmic self-assembly of DNA. PhD thesis, California Institute of Technology (1998)

28. Yurke, B., Turberfield, A.J., Mills, A.P., Simmel, F.C., Neumann, J.L.: A DNA-fuelled molecular machine made of DNA. Nature 406(6796), 605–608 (2000)

Author Index